S0-AGV-153

FOREIGN ECONOMIC POLICY OF THE UNITED STATES

edited by

STUART BRUCHEY
University of Maine

A GARLAND SERIES

PUTTING FOREIGN POLICY TO WORK

The Role of Organized Labor in American Foreign Relations, 1932–1941

JOHN W. ROBERTS

GARLAND PUBLISHING, Inc.
New York & London / 1995

Library of Congress Cataloging-in-Publication Data

Roberts, John W. (John Walter), 1954– .
Putting foreign policy to work : the role of organized labor in American foreign relations, 1932–1941 / John W. Roberts.
p. cm. — (Foreign economic policy of the United States)
Includes bibliographical references and index.
ISBN 0-8153-2006-X (alk. paper)
1. United States-Foreign Relations—1933–1945. 2. United States—Foreign Relations—1929–1933. 3. Trade unions—United States—Political activity. 4. Working class—United States—Political activity. 5. American Federation of Labor—History. 6. Congress of Industrial Organizations (U.S.)—History. I. Title. II. Series.
E806.R7216 1995
337.73—dc20

95-37067

Printed on acid-free, 250-year-life paper
Manufactured in the United States of America

This book is dedicated to my parents

Walter I. Roberts

and

Lucile K. Roberts

TABLE OF CONTENTS

Acknowledgments

First and foremost, I wish to express my thanks to Wayne S. Cole, Professor Emeritus at the University of Maryland History Department, who was my principal adviser for my dissertation and who continued to provide thoughtful advice as I revised my dissertation into this book. I am also grateful to Professors Stuart B. Kaufman, E.B. Smith, Keith W. Olson, and Mancur Olson, of the University of Maryland, for reading and commenting on this work when it was still in the dissertation stage.

I am indebted to many librarians and archivists for assisting me as I conducted my research, most notably: Peter Hoeffer of the George Meany Center, Harold L. Miller of the Wisconsin State Historical Society, Warner Pflug of the Walter P. Reuther Library, Richard Strassberg and Hope Nisly of Cornell University's Labor-Management Documentation Center, and staff members at the National Archives, the Hoover Institution Archives, the Library of Congress, the U.S. Labor Department Library, Seely Mudd Manuscript Library at Princeton University, the Immigration History Research Center at the University of Minnesota, and Catholic University Library.

My thanks also go Kristen Mosbaek of Kristen Mosbaek Communications, Professor Stuart Bruchey of the University of Maine, and Robert McKenzie of Garland Publishing, for their efforts that helped make possible the publication of this book.

—J.W.R.

Putting Foreign Policy to Work

Introduction

CHAPTER 1

Foreign policy is a matter of great importance to labor unions. Treaties, tariffs, military policies, wars, immigration laws—all can have enormous impact upon productivity, wages, labor markets, work rules, union organizing, collective bargaining, and even the very lives of the rank-and-file. Unions therefore study foreign policy proposals seriously, and support or oppose foreign policies based largely on estimates of how those policies would affect union initiatives and union members.

During 1993, for example, organized labor in the United States fought bitterly and unsuccessfully against adoption of the North American Free Trade Agreement, fearing that it would increase unemployment. Its opposition to that treaty coincided with its well-publicized resentment of Japanese imports and its endorsement of stronger immigration restrictions, and it reinforced organized labor's neo-isolationist image. Indeed, organized labor had adopted what might be considered isolationist positions often during the last quarter of the 20th century.[1]

Isolationist sympathies in the labor movement, however, have not always been dominant. During the first 100 years since a stable national labor movement appeared in the United States with the creation of the American Federation of Labor (AFL) in 1886, organized labor shifted back and forth between endorsing isolationist foreign policies and internationalist foreign policies, depending on circumstances of the moment and labor interests. In so doing, it usually reflected national trends outside the labor movement. Moreover, the labor movement often was divided between isolationist and internationalist elements, or simultaneously adopted isolationist positions on some issues and internationalist positions on others. Again, the foreign policy debates and dichotomies within the labor movement paralleled debates and dichotomies in the country as a whole.

One of the most volatile foreign policy debates within the labor movement occurred between 1932 and 1941. That debate produced a dramatic shift in labor's position, from its strong isolationist bent of the 1920s to an aggressive political and economic internationalism that would flourish until the late 1960s, when the war in Vietnam would help bring about a reassessment of labor's foreign policy perspective.

The transformation of organized labor's foreign policy views took shape during an era of international crises and domestic uncertainty, as well as upheaval within the labor movement itself. Between 1932 and 1941, totalitarian governments in Europe and East Asia extinguished democracy in their own countries and threatened their neighbors. In the United States, the struggle to end the Great Depression gave way to the disruptive challenge of converting from a peacetime to a wartime economy. Meanwhile, apparent unity in the House of Labor was shattered when a new amalgamation of labor unions, the Congress of Industrial Organizations (CIO), split off from the AFL. And as the AFL and the CIO battled each other for supremacy within the labor movement, they both had to fend off attacks from outside the labor movement in the form of company unions, industrial espionage, strikebreakers, and restrictive legislation. It was a perilous time for American labor and for the world.

Labor's transition to a more internationalist perspective on world affairs reflected its concern with all of those issues. An internationalist perspective evolved during that period because it appeared better suited to the changing interests of the AFL and the CIO. This transformation, however, was not the first time the labor movement had reversed itself on foreign policy matters.

During the last years of the 19th century and the first years of the 20th century, the AFL maintained a fairly internationalist point of view. The AFL's founding president, Samuel Gompers, advocated overseas commercial expansion. In 1898, the AFL endorsed a national mood for overseas expansion by supporting the Spanish-American War. And in 1910, the AFL joined the international labor movement as a member of the International Secretariat of Trade Union Centers.[2]

Later, the AFL became actively involved in the implementation of President Woodrow Wilson's internationalist foreign policies. When World War I broke out in Europe in 1914, Gompers gave strong backing to Wilson's program of preparing the United States for possible involvement in that conflict and became a harsh critic of Germany. Shortly before the United States entered the war in April 1917, Wilson appointed the AFL president to the Advisory Commission of the Council on National Defense, which did much early planning for the war effort. In 1918, Gompers dispatched an AFL vice president to participate in a State Department delegation that negotiated unsuccessfully to keep Russia in the war against Germany. Also in 1918, the AFL sent missions to Europe to generate support for Wilson's war aims among labor groups in France and Britain. After World War I, Gompers chaired the Commission on International Labor Legislation, which devised the International Labor Office.[3]

Thereafter, the AFL—like the rest of the United States—turned away from Wilsonian internationalism. It withdrew from the international labor movement and essentially ceased its advocacy of overseas commercial expansion. The AFL's isolationist tendencies carried over into the early and middle 1930s, when it resisted the efforts of the Franklin D. Roosevelt administration to expand overseas trade via reciprocal agreements.

Its opposition to more active American involvement in international affairs during that period led the AFL into some paradoxical situations. It condemned the dictatorships that were coming to power in Europe and East Asia, primarily because those dictatorships attacked organized labor; the AFL even instituted boycotts against the totalitarian states and raised funds to assist their victims. But it was also as determined as Americans generally to avoid involvement in overseas hostilities. Accordingly, the AFL opposed governmental action to thwart the dictators, called for strict neutrality laws, and professed to accept revisionist interpretations that profit-seeking business interests had engineered United States entry into World War I and might attempt to embroil the United States in another war for their own selfish ends. Finally, the AFL was ambivalent on the subject of military preparedness, but tended to oppose rearmament if its funding came from budget reductions in domestic programs.

By the later 1930s, however, labor was shifting to a more aggressive foreign policy stance. The military victories of Germany after World War II began in 1939 helped persuade the AFL and its rival, the CIO, that America's own security might be in jeopardy. Gradually, the two national labor centers came to support intervention in the Second World War. By 1941, there was strong consensus in favor of devoting national resources to building a modern war machine and providing massive American aid to the Allied powers fighting the fascists.

The transition was neither smooth nor automatic. Reflecting national trends, the American labor movement at first exhibited substantial divisions on the issue of intervening in World War II. Labor opinions tended to break down along regional and occupational lines, as was typical for the country as a whole. In the Middle West and Far West, anti-interventionist sentiments were stronger among union members than it was in other areas. Labor in the Northeast and South, in common with others in those regions, and workers in industries that could expect immediate benefits from defense spending, were more prone to support intervention. Ideological commitments were also influential: communists in the labor movement—predominately in the CIO—followed Moscow's lead on foreign policy matters, resulting in sudden swerves from pro-interventionism to anti-interventionism and then back again. Ultimately, the pro-interventionist leadership in the AFL and the CIO undertook a generally successful propaganda campaign to encourage rank-and-file support for President

Roosevelt's foreign and military programs.

There was, however, more at stake than foreign relations and defense. At all times, the AFL and the CIO linked their foreign policy preferences to their on-going or planned domestic programs.

For example, the AFL had dismissed the importance of international trade through most of the 1930s because an emphasis on global commerce seemed to be in conflict with its own proposals for domestic recovery, based on the 30-hour work week and expansion of the domestic market. AFL opposition to United States recognition of the Soviet Union grew partly out of a fear of economic competition with low-wage Soviet labor and a suspicion that Soviet agents would undermine AFL unions. And AFL economic boycotts against Germany, Italy, and Japan were not simply altruistic efforts to force the dictatorships to relent, but were also intended to further the AFL's long-standing "Buy-American," union label campaign. The CIO, meanwhile, used its early anti-interventionism as a method of appealing for domestic political support.

Similarly, the switch to a more interventionist course was tied to labor's domestic priorities. The AFL and the CIO abandoned or revised domestic programs in order to take advantage of the opportunities intervention offered to achieve long-term domestic objectives. The AFL dropped its long-standing reliance on the 30-hour week as a tactic to increase employment in order to support a defense build-up that promised even greater employment. For years the AFL had championed low-cost housing programs and had considered them to be in competition against military programs for government dollars. With the approach of war, the AFL ceased presenting low-cost housing as conflicting with military programs, and instead argued that it was an essential component of a defense effort that needed new dwellings for defense workers. The AFL also sought to use the economic planning necessitated by the defense program as the vehicle to realize its pre-war vision of a national economy spurred by consumer power. And the CIO sought to trade a cooperative attitude on defense for a fundamental restructuring of the industrial process in the United States that would give unions greater influence over policymaking.

At the same time, the AFL and the CIO carried their own bitter, internecine conflict into the international arena. They contended for rank-and-file membership in Canada, forged competing alliances with Latin American labor groups, and vied for influence and prestige in the International Federation of Trade Unions and the International Labor Office.

The AFL and the CIO also attempted to use foreign policy issues to burnish their image at home as well as to malign each other and their opponents outside the labor movement. The AFL trumpeted its emerging support for internationalism as verification of its patriotism, as proof that anti-union legislation to guarantee defense production was unnecessary, and as contrast to what it claimed was the CIO's disloyalty. The CIO for a time appealed for political support by stressing isolationism, and always likened its domestic enemies to the dictators in Europe. By contributing to the national defense effort and publicizing the repression of organized labor by fascist governments abroad, the American labor movement in general attempted to weaken or outmaneuver anti-labor forces at home.

Between 1932 and 1941, America's relationship with the rest of the world underwent a revolution. In 1932, the traditions of isolationism and continentalism—i.e., avoiding entangling alliances with other counties and concentrating economic, political, and military energies in the North American continent and the Western Hemisphere—remained cardinal principles of American statecraft, as they had been for most of the country's history. By the end of 1941, however, the United States had entered a global alliance to fight a war in Europe, Asia, and Africa. It would emerge from that war as the strongest power on earth, prepared to reject its isolationist past even in peacetime through membership in the United Nations, commitment to permanent military alliances, and the development of foreign aid programs on an unprecedented scale. It was a revolution not only in international circumstances and governmental policy, but also in national mood.

The American labor movement became caught up in that

revolution. A microcosm of American society, organized labor reflected America's evolving attitudes. It became committed to a more active role in international affairs at it came to believe that America's new internationalist direction could advance labor's domestic interests.

Notes

1. Wayne S. Cole, *Determinism and American Foreign Relations During the Franklin D. Roosevelt Era* (Lanham, Md.: University Press of America, 1995), p. 102; "Labor Official Blames Clinton for Rift," *Washington Post,* November 22, 1993, p. A5.

2. Ronald Radosh, *American Labor and United States Foreign Policy* (New York: Random House, 1969), pp. 4-8, 72.

3. Ibid., pp. 4-8, 72-6, 101-2, 137-38, 150-52; James Weinstein, *The Corporate Ideal in the Liberal State, 1900-1918* (Boston: Beacon Press, 1968), pp. 218-19. The rank-and-file did not always share Gompers' enthusiasm for internationalist policies and military preparedness. See Simeon Larson, "The American Federation of Labor and the Preparedness Controversy," *Historian* XXXVI (November 1974): 67-81.

AWARENESS WITHOUT INVOLVEMENT: THE AFL'S PERSPECTIVE ON INTERNATIONAL AFFAIRS, 1932-1936

PART 1

Political Threats, Military Security, and Isolationist Impulses

CHAPTER 2

Buddy Myer smacked Freddy Fitzsimmons' pitch hard against the chill, gray sky above Washington's Griffith Stadium. It fell for a double that scored Ozzie Bluege from third, in the Senators' four-nothing victory over the New York Giants in the third game of the 1933 World Series. Delegates to the American Federation of Labor's Annual Convention were in the stands that day to cheer on their favorites. The convention was meeting in the Nation's Capital that week, but had adjourned early the afternoon of the game to enable interested delegates to make their way out to the ballpark. As he gavelled the day's session to a close, AFL President William Green happily announced that Series tickets—"at box office prices"—were on sale at the back of the meeting hall.[1]

For most of the convention, delegates were preoccupied with matters every bit as domestic as baseball—the National Recovery Act, collective bargaining, the right to organize, unemployment, child labor, public works, minimum wage laws, and jurisdictional disputes between unions. Yet convention-goers were also alert to events overseas. Just hours before the ballgame, for example, they heard James Rowan of the British Trades Union Congress warn of the terrible threat that Germany's new chancellor, Adolph Hitler, posed to organized labor.[2]

The 1930s presented the United States with tempting

opportunities and frightening challenges in the international arena, and Americans argued lustily over possible responses. The rise of dictators in Europe and disillusionment with America's role in the First World War renewed controversy over the country's proper relationship to the rest of the world, and the Great Depression prompted a reassessment of America's international economic policies. The immigration question continued to trouble the country, as it had for decades. Organized labor avidly took part in all those debates and others, despite its primary concern with domestic issues.

Three principles animated the AFL's response to foreign affairs between 1932 and 1936: fierce anti-Fascism, fierce anti-Communism, and a determination that American diplomacy reinforce the position of organized labor at home. Those principles were reflected in the AFL's boycott of Nazi Germany, its sympathy for the victims of European Fascism and for the western European democracies, its opposition to United States recognition of the Soviet Union, its economic nationalism, its readiness to work with multilateral organizations in seeking global solutions to the problems of labor, and its pleas to shut the door on immigrants. Sometimes, however, the AFL found itself at cross-purposes on foreign relations issues—as when its anti-Fascism conflicted with its insistence on pro-labor foreign policy, thereby resulting in the Federation's ambivalence on the subject of American military preparedness. Still, foreign affairs were an important matter to the labor movement, and there were few international controversies on which the AFL was silent.

Further, events in foreign countries gave the AFL a useful perspective on events in the United States. The AFL monitored labor relations elsewhere in the world to see how foreign labor movements tried to solve common problems. Also, the AFL found that attacks on organized labor by European dictatorships illuminated attacks on labor in the United States. At the same time the Nazis were moving to subjugate the German labor movement, a special United States Senate committee was investigating the use of spies, strikebreakers, and private militias by American corporations to intimidate unions in the United States. While the Nazis' activities obviously were far more extreme, the AFL could still point to them as a warning of what could happen at home if the anti-union warfare were not curbed.

Between 1932 and 1936, the international tensions that would produce World War II were building, and the fragile security system erected after World War I by the Treaty of Versailles was crumbling. Embarking upon a quest for hegemony throughout the Far East, Japan seized Manchuria in 1931 and turned its back on the world community the following year by withdrawing from the League of Nations. Meanwhile, Benito Mussolini, the Fascist dictator of Italy since 1922, was bent on establishing an empire in East Africa. The most ominous developments were in Germany, where Adolph Hitler and the Nazi Party assumed absolute power in 1933. They crushed domestic opposition, including the labor movement. After disregarding Versailles by rearming its military, remilitarizing the Rhineland, introducing universal conscription, and taking itself out of the League of Nations, Germany was poised for conquest. Various diplomatic initiatives, such as the Four Power Pact, failed to ensure European stability. Thereafter, France and Great Britain felt compelled to answer the arms buildups of Japan, Italy, and Germany with arms buildups of their own.[3]

Throughout the period, the AFL sought to arouse American revulsion against the policies of the fascist states—particularly Germany—and simultaneously to cultivate sympathy for the European democracies—particularly Great Britain. It gathered and publicized information on the anti-labor activities of the Nazis and Fascist; in 1936, for example, Metal Trades Department President John Frey embarked upon a fact-finding tour of Europe, partly to study the impact of totalitarian rule on the workers of Germany and Italy.[4] It collected funds to assist the victims of European fascism, offered British labor leaders a forum in the United States in which to plead for American support, and endorsed economic boycotts and limited collective security measures against the fascists. At the heart of the AFL's policy lay three convictions, uttered repeatedly by AFL publications, by AFL leaders, and in AFL conventions: that Germany was anti-labor, that Great Britain was pro-labor, and that unless Germany's anti-labor policies were checked they would soon endanger the rights and privileges of American labor.

Before Hitler's accession to power, the German labor movement was possibly the strongest and most influential in the world. Its two wings—the Social Democrats and the Communists—boasted total membership of approximately 6 or 7 million in their unions, published over 200 daily newspapers and more than 20 weeklies, commanded enormous wealth, and, through their political parties, enjoyed considerable success at the polls. Hitler required only a few short months to destroy that labor movement through intimidation and outright terror.[5] The AFL seized upon that as its foremost reason for opposing Nazi Germany.

The AFL's first line of communication with its rank and file was the *Weekly News Service*—a clip sheet containing articles, columns, and editorials that were reprinted in labor-oriented newspapers from coast to coast. The AFL used that medium relentlessly to paint a bleak picture of working class life in Germany. In numerous articles, the *Weekly News Service* reported the shocking details of Hitler's campaign against organized labor: raids on union offices, confiscation of union property, prohibition of strikes, suppression of union publications, and even the dissolution of unions. It also told of the arrest and murder of union officials and their families, the revocation of collective bargaining, 80-hour work weeks, compulsory labor, the right of employers to fix wages, the inability of the Nazi government to reduce unemployment, cuts in relief payments, cuts in wages, and the loss of working class buying power. The AFL sought to evoke compassion for the workers of Germany by arguing that German unions, before Hitler laid siege against them, had been similar to American unions. The AFL claimed a "bond of fraternity" between American and German labor and accused Hitler of trying to save the "profits and privileges" of German capitalists by reducing German labor to "physical and mental slavery."[6].

The Nazis, of course, were guilty of many other abuses: the establishment of one-party rule, the suppression of academic freedom, and, most infamously, the brutal persecution of the Jews.

The AFL condemned the Nazis on all those points. In particular, the AFL frequently called attention to the plight of German Jews and the Hitler regime's war upon them. But those were secondary issues for the AFL. The primary emphasis, in issue after issue of the Weekly News Service, as well as in convention resolutions and the statements of Federation leaders, was the catastrophic German labor situation. William Green recited the chilling facts at the 1933 AFL Convention. He spoke of the security and strength of his own organization and suggested that it was unimaginable that a labor movement as well-entrenched as the AFL could be crushed "over night." Yet, he said, "that is the very thing that happened in Germany. An organization as powerful as ours, as well-officered as ours, led by men that measure up to the men here," was simply "wiped out."[7]

On three or four occasions between 1932 (when the Nazis first became a major force in the Reichstag) and 1936, the AFL did express favor for particular policies affecting German workers. In 1933, for example, it praised a "job-making plan" in Germany that it likened to the National Industrial Recovery Act in the United States. But they were but a handful of exceptions in an avalanche of official AFL policies protesting against labor practices in Nazi Germany.[8]

Similarly, the AFL decried labor policies in the other European dictatorships. While occasionally complimenting Mussolini for sponsoring public works projects to relieve unemployment or for encouraging the 40-hour work week, the Federation more typically characterized his government as "anti-labor" for permitting joblessness to increase, opposing child labor reforms, and sending union officials to prison. Likewise, the AFL castigated the government of Austrian Premier Englebert Dollfuss for arresting labor leaders and using artillery against strikers.[9]

In contrast, the AFL frequently praised labor relations in England and throughout the British Empire, and associated itself whenever possible with the British labor movement. Continuing a decades-old tradition, the AFL and the British Trades Union Congress (BTUC) sent fraternal delegates to each other's annual conventions. BTUC head Sir Walter Citrine addressed American workers every Labor Day over a nationwide radio hookup. At an economic security conference called by President Franklin D. Roosevelt in 1934, an AFL representative congratulated the British government for its social service programs and called for the United States to follow Britain's example. And in scores of articles and editorials, the *Weekly News Service* proclaimed the many successes of the vigorous British labor movement. It reported on better working conditions and higher wages won through strikes or collective bargaining; it lauded the political achievements of labor parties in Britain and elsewhere in the Commonwealth; it kept American workers abreast of reductions in unemployment in the British Empire and of notable advances in relief, public works, and unemployment insurance for those who remained out of work; it told of desirable low-cost housing projects for workers; it complimented progressive British employers who instituted shorter work weeks to prevent layoffs following the introduction of labor-displacing machinery; and it ran stories on the successes of workers' cooperatives. At the same time, the AFL applauded the strong democratic tradition of the BTUC and its opposition to Fascism and Communism alike.[10]

At times, the AFL also could be critical of labor relations in Great Britain and the Commonwealth. Through its *Weekly News Service*, the AFL deplored the British practice of requiring relief applicants to submit to means tests, reported on labor disputes and protests involving pay cuts, joblessness, and strikebreakers, and condemned the policies of Conservative Party governments that appeared to victimize the working classes. It also reported on British governmental and employer resistance to shorter work weeks, on official British opposition to International Labor Organization conventions supported by the AFL, on the malevolence or excessive power of certain British banks and corporations, on the introduction of labor-displacing machinery, and on the allegedly unfair practices of British companies operating in Latin America. Nonetheless, the AFL directed far less criticism than praise at British labor policies. Many of the problems the AFL pointed to were no different than the problems faced by

American unions and were a far cry from the anti-union warfare raging in Germany. Moreover, implicit in the criticism of British labor policies was evidence of the good health of the British labor movement. Most of the critical reports were prompted by union members going out on strike, Labour Party lawmakers speaking out frankly on the floor of Parliament, or union leaders issuing public protests. Even in its criticism of the British Empire, in other words, the AFL seemed to underscore the common ideals, goals, and tribulations of Britain and the United States, as well as the unchallenged right of British labor to organize and to protect its own interests.[11]

Almost as soon as Hitler came to power, the BTUC began attempting to enlist the support of American labor. Only a few months after Hitler became chancellor, a BTUC representative told the 1933 AFL convention that democratic government and free trade unions had been abolished in Germany, suggested that Hitler was receiving funds from American and French capitalists, and warned that powerful, anti-labor elements were ready to support Nazi-like movements in other countries in order to destroy "democracy and liberty."[12]

The following year, the director of the BTUC travelled to America to plead the British case. Speaking at the AFL convention in 1934, Sir Walter Citrine called upon American labor to assist in the "fight against Fascism and to secure that free institutions should be restored to the people of the world." Asserting that the battle for democracy was being waged in Europe, Citrine appealed to organized labor in the United States for "all possible financial and material support" against the Fascists. Underscoring his plea for help from across the Atlantic, Citrine argued that "Hitlerism in Germany" was not an "isolated phenomenon." In a statement made in Britain but reprinted in the American labor press, Citrine stated that Hitlerism "is a part of the widespread reaction against Parliamentarianism, and of the reassertion of capitalist dominance in all spheres. It involves a denial of liberty of speech, the right of public assembly, and the freedom and independence of the workers' political and industrial organizations."[13]

AFL leaders needed little prodding from Citrine and the

BTUC. After Citrine's address to the 1934 convention, AFL President William Green asked him to tell the workers of Europe "that their cause is our cause." Green and the Federation's Executive Council were keen to the threat that Fascism posed to labor organizations throughout the world. From 1933 on, they urged the rank and file to identify with the Fascists' victims in the European labor movement, and to understand that free labor movements everywhere were imperiled. In a 1935 report, AFL Vice President Matthew Woll sought to express the fraternity and the unity of purpose between American workers and European workers when he said of oppressed unionists in Germany, Austria, and Italy: "They are our people, they were workers in the same trades, organized along identical or similar lines, and with identical or similar objectives. They are blood relations of millions of our members." Woll's report transmitted shocking figures on executions and prison sentences meted out to German, Austrian, and Italian union officials, and warned: "Their persecutors and oppressors would extend their system to this country and persecute and oppress us if they had the power." That they intended to do just that seemed even more certain when Woll later publicized evidence that Berlin was preparing to unleash a propaganda campaign in the United States.[14]

In September 1933, Green cautiously suggested that American labor consider joining European labor groups in observing an anti-German boycott. With "terrorism in Germany" reaching "wilder and wilder extremes," Green said, verbal protests were no longer enough. According to Green, "a boycott is the only thing that will bring home to the German tyrants the abhorrence in which their rule is held by the rest of the world." The boycott would not be against the German people, Green insisted, millions of whom opposed the Nazis. Rather, by showing the German masses "the true state of world opinion," a boycott would compel them "to tear the grip of Nazi dictatorship from their throats."[15]

A month later, following Executive Council endorsement of the idea, the AFL Convention unanimously declared a boycott against German goods and services until the German government ceased persecuting trade unionists and Jews. "We love the

German people," Green told the Convention, and it was out of love and admiration for the German people that it was American labor's duty to "hearten and strengthen and encourage" them through a boycott that would "strike at the heart of this terror." After the Convention, Green seized upon German withdrawal from the League of Nations and from the World Disarmament Conference at Geneva as further justification for the action.[16]

The Federation implemented the boycott by issuing circulars to labor bodies throughout the country, publishing announcements in the labor press, and organizing local boycott committees. While recognizing that the Nazis extended their persecution of Jews and labor leaders in spite of the boycott, the Federation nevertheless concluded that the policy was "effective" and reaffirmed it annually at its conventions. In 1936, the AFL supplemented its endorsement of an economic boycott of Germany with an unsuccessful call for a boycott of the 1936 Berlin Olympics.[17]

In 1934, one year after inaugurating the boycott, the AFL Convention voted to establish the Labor Chest for the Liberation of Workers in Europe. The Chest had two functions: to raise funds for the relief of victims of Nazi and Fascist persecution, and to expand upon the AFL's campaign of anti-Nazi publicity.[18]

Woll, as vice chairman of the Chest, was the principal spokesman, but much of the AFL's top leadership was involved. Green served as chairman, AFL vice president David Dubinsky was treasurer, and other AFL vice presidents, including Sidney Hillman, John L. Lewis, and John Coefield, were members of the Executive Committee. In its first year of operation, the Chest raised $46,000, distributing about two-thirds of it through the International Federation of Trade Unions and the Modigliani Fund to victims of German Nazism and Italian Fascism. In May 1936 it raised $20,000 in one night, at an all-star benefit at New York's Madison Square Garden. While most donations came from New York City area unions, the Chest established local committees to seek contributions nationwide.[19]

In addition, the Chest published pamphlets, issued press releases and "special bulletins," undertook a series of radio broadcasts, and distributed posters. As many as 50,000 copies each of such Chest publications as "Labor, Democracy, and Fascism," "Persecution of European Labor," "Labor Under Hitler," and "Hitler Terror in 1935" told of the horrifying labor conditions and the destruction of trade unions in Germany, Italy, and Austria, and stressed the importance of adhering to the boycott. Articles and reports produced by the Chest, meanwhile, were reprinted not only in labor newspapers but in the general press as well. The Chest also repulsed attempts by the Nazis to propagandize in the United States, persuading the National Recreation Association of America and the Conference of Mayors not to participate in events in Hamburg and Berlin, respectively, that would have engendered favorable publicity for Germany. And, in October 1936, it organized a 7-city speaking tour for Sir Walter Citrine and International Federation of Trade Unions Secretary Walter Schevenels to discuss labor conditions in Europe and generate opposition to the fascists.[20]

Beyond the voluntarism of boycotts and contributions to the Chest, the AFL advocated collective security and other governmental measures to curb the fascists. On October 3, 1935, the Italian Army invaded Ethiopia, in an offensive that would conclude with the fall of Ethiopia in May 1936. Under the guise of neutrality, the Roosevelt Administration quickly moved to hinder Italy through an embargo on strategic goods. In a parallel move, the League of Nations declared Italy's invasion of Ethiopia to be a violation of the League Covenant and imposed economic sanctions. The collective response, however, weakened by the reluctance of Britain and France to participate, failed to halt Mussolini's advance.[21]

The AFL, meeting in its regular annual convention only days after the initial attack, immediately branded Italy an "outlaw nation," and over the succeeding months urged retaliation against the aggressor. To an extent, the AFL couched its response in the language of isolationism: an embargo would ensure American neutrality, guarantee the safety of American seamen, and keep the United States from being sucked into the hostilities. But collective security action directed against Italy was the AFL's unmistakable objective. From the first, the AFL lauded the Kellogg Pact and the

League of Nations Covenant, and castigated Italy for violating them. It concurred with the League's sanctions against Italy and endorsed Roosevelt's actions. In November, Green not only reiterated organized labor's support for the Roosevelt Administration's ban on exports of strategic materials to Italy, but even warned that AFL unions were prepared to take drastic steps to compel reluctant industrialists to comply with the ban. In addition, the Federation called upon the United States government to become actively involved as a mediator.[22]

About the same time, in mid-1935, AFL leaders began calling for United States government intervention against the Nazis, as well. Saying that "the hour has arrived when our own Government ought to take appropriate action," Green urged an official, nation-wide American economic boycott against Germany. It was not enough for "labor and its friends" to oppose the Nazis, he announced; the federal government should also demand that the "brutality and fiendish persecution" of the Hitler regime come to an end.[23]

The AFL, then, followed political events in Europe closely, was deeply troubled by them, and took steps to influence them. As soon as Hitler came to power in Germany, the AFL began to monitor and publicize his attacks on organized labor. The Federation moved closer to the British labor movement in response to the activities in Germany, invited British labor leaders to speak in the United States on the anti-labor threat of Nazism, and followed the British lead in instituting a boycott against Germany, collecting funds for the relief of European labor, and distributing anti-Nazi literature. In 1935, when Ethiopia was attacked by Europe's other great fascist power, Italy, the AFL advocated the application of limited collective security measures against the invader.

The AFL response to the rise of Fascism in Europe, however, was measured. The AFL was careful to ensure that its positions on foreign affairs issues did not conflict with its existing policies. In fact, sometimes those positions even advanced existing policies. The boycott against Germany, for example, meshed perfectly with the AFL's on-going "Buy American" campaign; the

Federation's Union Label Department simply added the boycott as one more factor to buttress its argument in favor of buying union-made products. On the other hand, the Federation, despite its oft-stated compassion for the victims of Nazi persecution, flatly rejected a proposal for the United States to admit political refugees from Europe into the country in greater numbers. At the 1935 Convention, the International Ladies' Garment Workers' Union (ILGWU) offered a resolution stating that America had always been a refuge for those fleeing economic, political, and religious tyranny, and endorsing the admission of European refugees. The AFL, however, was a fanatic guardian of immigration exclusion laws. The resolutions committee killed the ILGWU proposal because it would have conflicted with those cherished immigration restrictions.[24]

The AFL was opposed not only to the European fascist powers, Germany, Italy, and Austria. It also severely condemned the Soviet Union. The AFL traditionally was anti-communist. Early in its history it rejected Marxism, and for decades it fought attempts by Communists and Socialists to gain control of the American labor movement. Instead of espousing programs of class struggle, the AFL opted to accept the principles of a capitalist economy, disassociate itself from radical elements in order to attain broader respectability, and seek accommodation with the business community. The AFL hoped to achieve labor's ends through business-like collective bargaining rather than political revolution.[25]

In the area of American foreign relations, the AFL's anti-communism manifested itself in an unshakable opposition to United States diplomatic recognition of the Soviet Union.

By 1932, however, the national mood was shifting in favor of recognition. Business interests hoped that trade with Russia would help revive industries in the grip of depression, and even conservatives were ready to dismiss the specter of Soviet-spawned revolution. As newspaper publisher Roy Howard commented, "I think the menace of Bolshevism in the United States is about as great as the menace of sunstroke in Greenland or chilblains in the Sahara."[26]

The AFL, however, continued to fight recognition. After Democratic presidential nominee Franklin Roosevelt discussed the advisability of recognition during the 1932 campaign, William Green immediately sought assurances from the candidate that he would not commit himself to that course. Following Roosevelt's election, the AFL intensified its protests against recognition. Despite AFL resistance, the United States extended diplomatic recognition to the Soviet Union in November 1933. Thereafter, the AFL called in vain for withdrawal of that recognition.[27]

The AFL fought recognition for several reasons, most of which were similar to its reasons for criticizing the fascist states. It considered labor conditions in the Soviet Union to be intolerable, and feared that goods produced under such conditions could undersell goods produced by American labor, should trade between the two countries be reintroduced. The AFL condemned political repression, denial of civil liberties, and compulsory military service in Russia. Most of all, it feared the Soviet Union as a threat to American institutions—including the AFL itself. The United States should never recognize the Soviet Union, argued the AFL, as long as it controlled the Comintern and was committed to the doctrine of world revolution. Recognition would give the Soviet Union the privilege of opening diplomatic posts in the United States, from which the AFL believed it could carry out subversive activities. With recognition, according to the AFL, Russia would be able to strengthen its propaganda effort—prompting Green to warn that the United States government "cannot afford to expose its suffering people to the destructive philosophy preached and practiced by the Soviet Union." Even outright Soviet invasion of the United States was a possibility, as an American Army general suggested in a statement that the AFL publicized. Soviet subversion was particularly menacing to trade unions, which, according to Green, "have been the special object of attack by . . . forces which receive their instructions from Moscow." The AFL contended that Soviet spies worked in U.S. factories and belonged to AFL unions, with the intention of radicalizing the labor movement. Undemocratic and anti-labor policies within the Soviet Union and the danger of Soviet propaganda and subversion in the United States caused the AFL to oppose recognition of the Soviet Union almost as vehemently as it criticized Nazi Germany.[28]

Closely related to the issue of increasing uneasiness in the world due to the rise of dictators in Europe was the question of America's possible military response. Interventionist forms of diplomacy were facing intensified public scrutiny between 1932 and 1936. Organized labor was one of many groups that questioned military preparedness and aggressive foreign policies.

In the aftermath of the First World War, Americans had grown cynical about their country's motives for entering the conflict, and disillusioned with the war's outcome. In books and articles published throughout the 1920s and 1930s, journalists, social scientists, and historians such as John Turner, Harry Elmer Barnes, C. Hartley Grattan, Charles Beard, Walter Millis, and Charles Tansill put forth a variety of arguments critical of American involvement in the war. The barrage included assertions that American intervention could have been avoided altogether, that President Woodrow Wilson, despite his rhetorical observance of American neutrality, had pursued a deliberately pro-British and anti-German policy before 1917, that the thesis of German war guilt was incorrect, and that British propaganda had tricked Americans into supporting the Allied cause. There were further charges that the war effort had harmed domestic reform movements and that the Treaty of Versailles was unjustly punitive and incapable of promoting peace and self-determination.[29]

Especially provocative was the thesis that American business interests had played a critical role in maneuvering the United States into World War I. American industrialists sold goods to the Allies that were purchased on the credit extended by American bankers and financiers. The businessmen pushed the United States into war, so the interpretation went, in order to protect their markets and investments. While Barnes, Beard, and Millis were fairly balanced in their writings along those lines, less restrained authors put the argument with much greater relish in a series of sensational publications in 1933 and 1934 about an international "blood brotherhood" of munitions makers that fomented arms races and wars in order to increase profits. The anti-business sentiment that prevailed during the Great Depression aided the popularity of that view.[30]

A resurgence of both isolationism and pacifism coincided with the reassessment of America's role in World War I. Rejecting Wilsonian internationalism and fearing future involvement in European conflicts, the country pursued generally nationalistic foreign policies from the 1920s until well into the Roosevelt presidency. Meanwhile, the American peace movement was as vigorous as it ever had been, organizing such influential bodies as the League of Nations Association and the War Resisters League in the years after the war, and encouraging United States participation in several futile disarmament conferences and arbitration agreements.[31]

A watershed in the reaction against World War I and the movement towards isolationism was the United States Senate's formation of the Special Committee on Investigation of the Munitions Industry in 1934. Chaired by North Dakota Republican Gerald P. Nye, the committee's inquiries reflected the concerns of anti-business, isolationist, Western, agrarian, progressive senators such as George Norris, Robert LaFollette, Jr., and Nye himself. At the same time, the committee was a response to agitation by pacifists, most notably Dorothy Denzer of the Women's International League for Peace and Freedom.[32]

Broadening its scope beyond the munitions industry to consider the effect economic interests in general had on America's role in World War I, the committee spent almost two years sifting through the records of munitions makers and financiers, reviewing government documents, and hearing testimony. Its findings captured the headlines and shocked the nation. The Nye Committee's revelations seemed to validate earlier accusations that profiteers had engineered United States intervention for their own selfish purposes. Senator Nye even charged that American soldiers who risked their lives on the battlefields of Europe had "little thought that they were there and fighting to save the skins of American bankers who had bet too boldly on the outcome of the war and had two billions of dollars of loans to the Allies in jeopardy." The committee exposed the huge wartime profits of munitions makers, price-fixing deals between American and British arms manufacturers, unscrupulous arms sales techniques, attempts of arms manufacturers to lobby and even bribe government officials to support higher military budgets, the provision of loans to belligerents in a way that was harmful to American neutrality, and the existence of War Department "industrial mobilization" plans. The committee called for price controls and high taxes to limit wartime profiteering, recommended that the Navy become less dependent upon private shipyards for the construction of warships, and urged the enactment of neutrality laws that would restrict loans and exports to belligerents.[33]

Partly on the impetus of the Nye Committee's findings, and in an effort to head off American entanglement in the growing crises in Europe, Congress enacted and later modified a series of neutrality acts, starting in 1935. The first Neutrality Act, in 1935, mandated an impartial arms embargo against all belligerents, should the president determine a state of war to exist. It also discouraged Americans from traveling on the vessels of belligerent countries by warning them that they did so at their own risk. A second Neutrality Act the following year strengthened the arms embargo and forbid loans to belligerents. In 1937, a third Neutrality Act extended the temporary strictures of the first two indefinitely, made it illegal for Americans to travel on belligerents' ships, and required belligerents purchasing American goods to do so with cash and to carry them away from American ports in their own vessels. A fourth Neutrality Act in 1939 repealed the arms embargo but made the cash-and-carry provisions more stringent and authorized the President to prohibit the entry of American citizens into war zones.[34]

The neutrality acts aimed to restrict the economic interests that Nye and others blamed for American participation in World War I. The acts were controversial in other respects, as well. Rather than defending neutral rights on the high seas, the neutrality acts relinquished some of them in order to avoid possible confrontations with belligerents. That angered those isolationists who, unlike Nye and his supporters, relied on international law and adherence to the rights and duties of neutrals as methods to insulate the United States from foreign hostilities. Further, the first three neutrality acts prevented the use of discriminatory as opposed to impartial arms embargoes, thereby blocking American participation in collective security activities against aggressors. That angered internationalists, who worried that the neutrality acts would thereby embolden the dictatorships, weaken their victims, and increase the likelihood of war.[35]

The Nye Committee and the first three neutrality acts, then, represented triumphs for three overlapping groups or points of view: those who held that economics was the key factor that threatened to embroil America in wars, those who feared the use of excessive presidential powers in foreign affairs, and those who advocated pacifism instead of the use of force or reliance on traditional concepts of neutrality. Despite its alarm over the rise of fascism in Europe and its willingness the support such limited collective security measures as economic boycotts, the AFL proved extremely sympathetic to the recommendations of the Nye Committee and the goals of the early neutrality acts. In many respects, its official views were consistent with the era's burgeoning pacifism and the economic interpretation of wars.

By the early 1930s, a strong anti-war movement had emerged in the United States, composed of the many pacifist and internationalist organizations that appeared after the First World War. The AFL, even as it declared its "militant" opposition to the European dictatorships, adopted an anti-war stance, rejected the use of force in international affairs, and even talked of aligning itself with the peace movement. At its 1936 Convention, the AFL determined to "cooperate actively with those groups that are striving to bring together all the forces of peace in the United States of America today."[36]

The AFL was very congenial to the views of the pacifists. It shared the pacifists' disillusionment with World War I. The United States, according to the AFL's Executive Council, had been "too ready to enter" that war. The disappointment in the war's outcome—the postwar social and economic dislocations and the failure of the Armistice to prevent preparations for further carnage—

strengthened the AFL's resolve to block American entry into another European conflict. William Green declared that labor had "not forgotten the lessons learned during the World War," and one of the lessons was that "the belief . . . that the world would be made for democracy was supplanted by human despair." Not wishing to repeat the World War I mistake, the AFL rejected the use of force in international affairs and held that there was "no moral justification" for a resort to arms. Like many peace groups and some of the isolationists, the AFL wanted to rely on international law to solve future international disputes, and endorsed the Kellogg-Briand Pact which sought to outlaw war. It supported the concept of international arbitration, favored American entry into the World Court, and called for adherence to the mandates of international disarmament conferences.[37]

For the AFL, opposition to war was not simply a moral platitude. It reflected the unique interests of the working class and thus emanated from the basic philosophy of the labor movement. The AFL Executive Council, AFL conventions, and individual AFL leaders frequently cast war in terms of the ongoing struggle of labor. The 1935 AFL Convention declared that "in every war it is the workers serving both victors and vanquished who pay the bill with death, mutilated bodies, and shattered health." AFL General Secretary Frank Morrison echoed that sentiment, saying that when labor observed Memorial Day "we pay tribute largely to our own"[38]

Labor provided the soldiers and sailors who fought in war, as the AFL pointed out; labor performed the toil that produced the implements of war; labor paid the taxes that subsidized war. Long after a war was over and the lives of working men were lost, labor continued to suffer the spiritual demoralization and to carry the burdensome debt created by war. Therefore, in the AFL's view, war was a labor issue. It was the working people and their families who suffered most. The Federation even struck an uncharacteristically ideological note in advocating the international solidarity of working classes against war and suggesting that workers in all countries could block rearmament and prevent future wars by opposing taxes for munitions.[39]

If labor bore the brunt of war, it was clear to the AFL who benefitted from war. Despite its generally conservative, pro-capitalist stance, the AFL identified segments of the American business community as its bête noire in many respects. It attacked unregulated competition, unplanned production, and inequitable distribution of profits. It blamed industry for unemployment and unsatisfactory living standards, and denounced American business for resisting wage hikes, installing labor-displacing machinery, breaking strikes, stockpiling munitions to use against non-submissive employees, and hiring spies to infiltrate unions. Those anti-business attitudes carried over into the foreign policy arena, as the AFL asserted that private profit was one of the chief motivations for war. In a resolution at its 1932 convention, the AFL called for action to block "the sinister activities of the war mongers and patriots for profit" who had a financial stake in military preparedness. At the 1936 convention, the AFL declared that "labor is aware that the chief human factors in precipitating war are the munitions-makers, the bankers and the big industrialists." Also in 1936, the AFL endorsed the position of English labor leader Herbert Morrison, who insisted that there was no quarrel between the workers of different countries, and that wars were the product of capitalist rivalries over trade.[40]

The Nye Committee investigated many of the questions raised by the economic critique of war, yet for the most part the AFL avoided comment on the committee's activities and findings. The 1934 convention did approve a resolution calling upon Senator Nye "to probe in the greatest detail into the munitions industry." Several AFL officials testified to the committee, including John T. Frey, head of the Federation's powerful Metal Trades Department. Frey gave evidence that there was collusion between shipbuilding companies in the submission of bids for Navy Department contacts. Then in 1938, after the committee released its reports, Nye enjoyed William Green's endorsement in his successful reelection bid. Even before the Nye Committee began its work, in fact, Green had looked upon the senator as a friend of labor. And as the Second World War approached, the AFL occasionally cited the Nye Committee as its authority in protesting the profit-seeking of munitions makers and advocating neutrality. Beyond that, however, the AFL seldom referred to the Nye Committee directly, and AFL publications certainly did not give the Nye Committee the sort of extensive and laudatory coverage they gave other congressional committees, such as Senator Robert LaFollette's investigating committee on anti-union activities and the House Un-American Activities Committee.[41]

Nonetheless, the AFL was closely aligned with the Nye Committee on many important issues. Sharing the Nye Committee's view that American businessmen could help guide the country toward war, the AFL's demands for restrictions on war profits paralleled those of the committee. At the 1932 convention and at several succeeding conventions, the AFL came out in favor of government manufacture of war materials—which was also the majority view on the Nye Committee. The AFL contended that concentrating the production of munitions and naval vessels in federal arsenals and navy yards, and removing such activity as much as possible from the hands of private industry, would help eliminate the element of private profit from defense production. The Nye Committee also looked into the question of profiteering, which likewise concerned the AFL. The AFL publicized statements and reports calling for confiscatory taxes on war profits and the "drafting" of capital, although it declined to give its official endorsement to such policies.[42]

Like the Nye Committee, the AFL also worried about would-be war profiteers stirring up war sentiment. The immediate cause of the AFL's campaign to place the production of war materiel in navy yards and arsenals was the 1932 report of a congressional committee that advocated just the opposite: turning defense production over to private industry. In the discussion of that recommendation at the 1932 Convention, Frey stated that the "International Munitions Trust" owned or subsidized newspapers throughout Europe that manufactured war scares in order to ensure high levels of defense production. Frey continued: "We want to keep our country free from that type of sinister propaganda." If defense production were removed from private industry, the AFL reasoned that there would be no more incentive for anyone to "seek to create a sentiment for the production of war munitions so that they may be able to convert national defense into a medium for private profit."[43]

The AFL and the Nye Committee also shared a concern over "industrial mobilization," or the drafting of labor in time of war. The labor movement did not begin to panic over the issue until the late 1930s. But as early as 1932, the AFL voiced its opposition to "industrial conscription" and "compulsory labor under any form or guise whatsoever." In 1936, the AFL Convention passed an anti-war resolution that warned that the "War Department already had plans to draft labor in the event of war, place workers under military law, and appoint a board of employers to decide upon wages, hours, and working conditions without consulting labor representatives."[44]

Further, the AFL supported the neutrality laws of 1935 and 1936. The organization seemed to endorse the concept of relinquishing certain traditional rights of neutrals at its 1932 convention, when it approved in principle a resolution calling upon the United States government to withhold protection of the lives and property of American citizens living abroad. The resolution criticized "wealthy" American expatriates who shirked "real citizenship," caused disputes abroad, and expected United States intervention on their behalf. Later, the AFL called for application of the 1935 Neutrality Act in the Italian-Ethiopian War, "regardless of its effect upon economic and industrial conditions in the United States." And in 1936 it urged that Congress strengthen neutrality legislation.[45]

Yet when it came to taking a stand on military preparedness, the AFL was ambivalent. On the one hand, the AFL held that stockpiles of munitions and the agitation to produce those munitions constituted a powerful inducement toward war. As President Green told an American Legion rally in 1936, "The facts of history disclose that when nations develop war machinery to its maximum strength and create a war spirit and a war psychology . . . war becomes inevitable." Hence, the AFL cheered international disarmament conferences and arbitration pacts and called for legislation to restrict private profits on the production of munitions. Further, the AFL was a staunch opponent of military conscription.[46]

Moreover, the AFL objected to military spending that diverted funds from domestic projects. Housing, for example, was a major component of the AFL's domestic recovery program, and the AFL howled when military appropriations dwarfed those for low-cost housing. "Surely the American government cannot object to spending as much or more from public funds to remedy the housing shortage," proclaimed a 1936 AFL editorial, "as it allocates to the War Department in order to prepare the country to meet a possible attack from foreign governments." That same editorial, which the AFL distributed nationally through its *Weekly News Service,* claimed that the "stupendous" War Department appropriation of nearly $450 million would have been enough to construct over 110,000 houses. An AFL editorial the following year pointed out that the Navy Department's appropriation of $526 million would have been sufficient to build 175,000 homes.[47]

On the other hand, the AFL recognized the validity of preparedness programs—especially with anti-democratic, anti-labor forces on the march in Europe. Emphasizing that it supported defensive preparations only, the AFL asserted that it was imperative for the United States to maintain armed forces that were large enough and strong enough to guard against invasions and repel attacks.[48]

There was also the question of jobs. At the 1932 convention, the powerful Machinists' union offered a resolution advocating that United States naval strength be built up to the maximum levels permitted under the 1930 London Treaty. The resolution cited the national importance of maintaining an adequate defense and being able to engage in diplomatic negotiations with other countries from a position of strength. By far the most prominent component of the Machinists' argument, however, was that military spending would relieve unemployment. It would create jobs, directly or indirectly, in "practically every industry." Further, it would generate enormous purchasing power, it would not raise the taxes of "the bulk of the people," and it would force the wealthy to invest (through their taxes) in a building program at a time when they otherwise might be apt to hoard their money. The argument for the resolution was so blatantly economic that the Machinists' delegate felt compelled to say, "I would be the last person in the world to want to participate in a war for the sake of providing work." Yet he also complained that the AFL's "program of world peace will deprive us of jobs."[49]

The convention upheld the Resolution Committee's rejection of the Machinists' proposal to support naval construction as an unemployment relief measure. But within a scant few months, the Federation's Executive Council conceded the Machinists' point when it came out in favor of a $300 million naval appropriation that would bring United States naval strength up to levels authorized by the 1930 London Treaty. In so doing, the Executive Council cited the justification that it would save existing jobs and create new ones. Not only did the AFL portray future military construction programs as victories for organized labor, it also condemned some military spending cuts for throwing people out of work. In the words of William Green, "Anti-war policies that wipe out men's jobs without adequate provision for their future are not the way to peace."[50]

The AFL did not try to resolve the apparent conflict until later in the decade. During the early and middle 1930s, it supported disarmament, attacked military buildups as the contrivances of profit-seeking munitions makers, and criticized military spending that detracted from domestic spending. Yet at the same time it advocated an adequate national defense and called for increased military spending as a guarantee of greater employment.

Notes

1. "Nats Pepped by Support of Fans," *Washington Post,* October 6, 1933, p. 17; "Play by Play of Game," *Washington Post,* October 6, 1933, p. 17; American Federation of Labor, *Report of Proceedings of the Fifty-Third Annual Convention of the American Federation of Labor* (Washington: Judd & Detweiler, 1933), pp. 211, 251.

2. AFL, *1933 Proceedings,* pp. 41, 71, 73, 78, 86, 108, 110, 114-15; "Hitler Denounced at Labor Session as Capital's Ally," *Washington Star,* October 5, 1933, p. 1.

3. Robert A. Divine, *The Reluctant Belligerent: American Entry into World War II* (New York: John Wiley & Sons, 1965), pp. 4, 13-4; Rene Albrecht-Carrie, *A Diplomatic History of Europe Since the Congress of Vienna* (New York: Harper and Row, 1973), pp. 458, 460, 465-68, 478-79, 488-89.

4. John Frey to Walter Citrine, November 23, 1936, file 68, box 5, John Frey Papers, Manuscript Division, Library of Congress, Washington, DC.

5. Evelyn Anderson, *Hammer or Anvil: The Story of the German Working Class Movement* (London: Victor Gollancz Ltd., 1945), pp. 7-8, 61-3, 120-21, 152-53; Robert Black, *Fascism in Germany: How Hitler Destroyed the World's Most Powerful Labour Movement* (London: Steyne Publications, 1975), p. 1.

6. See, for example, "Hitler Aims To Crush Toilers," *American Federation of Labor Weekly News Service* April 8, 1933; "Green Denounces Hitler's War on Trade Unions of Germany," AFL Weekly News Service , May 13, 1933; "All Germans, Rich, Poor, Must Work," AFL *Weekly News Service,* May 20, 1933; "Hitler's Anti-Labor Policy Denounced," AFL *Weekly News Service,* May 27, 1933; "German Jobs Gain As Pay Cuts Lower Buying Power," AFL *Weekly News Service,* October 14, 1933; "Right to Murder Opponents of Hitler's Fascist Regime Defended by Nazi Judge," AFL *Weekly News Service,* July 22, 1933; "Teachers' Congress Expels German Fascist Delegates," AFL *Weekly News Service,* August 19, 1933; "Hitler's Anti-Labor Terrorism in Action," AFL *Weekly News Service,* December 9, 1933; "Hitler's Terror Drives 60,000 From Germany," AFL *Weekly News Service,* December 30, 1933; "AFL Mobilizes Labor for Boycott of German-Made Goods and Services," AFL *Weekly News Service,* December 30, 1933; "Labor Leaders Jailed and Property Confiscated by Hitler's Government; Nazi Terrorism Also Drives 60,000 Jews into Exile," AFL *Weekly News Service,* January 6, 1934; "Hitler's Law Abolishing German Trade Unions Denounced by Green," AFL *Weekly News Service,* January 20, 1934; "Green Indicts Hitler for Persecution of Jews and German Trade Unions," AFL *Weekly News Service,* February 17, 1934; "Labor Service Drills German Youth for Army," AFL *Weekly News Service,* April 6, 1935; "AFL Council Condemns Hitler's Nazis for Killing Miners' Union Official," AFL *Weekly News Service,* May 11, 1935; "Hitler's Nazis Torture and Impose Long Prison Terms on Union Leaders," AFL *Weekly News Service,* April 18, 1936; "Nearly 2,000,000 Workers Unemployed in Nazi Germany," AFL *Weekly News Service,* May 23, 1936.

Actually, the AFL began attacking the labor policies of the German government as early as 1932—before Hitler had become Chancellor, but after the Nazis had acquired power in the Reichstag and were promoting anti-labor measures. See, for example, "70 to 80 Hour Week Imposed on German Railway Employees," AFL *Weekly News Service,* September 3, 1932; "Gov't Dictatorship Menaces German Labor," AFL *Weekly News Service,* October 15, 1932; "Labor in Germany Condemns Wage Cuts," AFL *Weekly News Service,* January 16, 1932; "Germany Cuts Idle Benefits to Near-Starvation Basis," AFL *Weekly News Service,* June 25, 1932.

7. "Green Pledges U.S. Labor to Work for End to Nazi Attacks on Jews,"

AFL *Weekly News Service,* April 1, 1933; "Nazi Head to Continue Warfare Against Jews," AFL *Weekly News Service,* November 11, 1933; "Labor Leaders Jailed and Property Confiscated by Hitler's Government; Nazi Terrorism Also Drives 60,000 Jews into Exile," AFL *Weekly News Service,* January 6, 1934; "Hitler's Law Abolishing German Trade Unions Denounced by Green," AFL *Weekly News Service,* January 20, 1934; "Green Indicts Hitler for Persecution of Jews and German Trade Unions," AFL *Weekly News Service,* February 17, 1934; "Labor Chest for European Workers Names H.L. Franklin as Executive," AFL Weekly News Service, February 9, 1935; "All Jewish Writers Will Be Suppressed by Hitler," AFL *Weekly News Service,* April 6, 1935; AFL, 1933 Proceedings, pp. 141-42, 465-73; American Federation of Labor, *Report of Proceedings of the Fifty-Fourth Annual Convention of the American Federation of Labor* (Washington: Judd and Detweiler, 1934), p. 443; American Federation of Labor, *Report of Proceedings of the Fifty-Fifth Annual Convention of the American Federation of Labor (*Washington: Judd and Detweiler, 1935), pp. 598-99.

8. "Union Pay and 40-Hour Week for German Idle," AFL *Weekly News Service,* December 31, 1932; "Germany's Job-Making Plan Achieves Success," AFL *Weekly News Service,* July 22, 1933; "Germany Plans 16,000 Homes for Unemployed," AFL *Weekly News Service,* April 30, 1932; "East Prussia Government Aids Unemployed Youths," AFL *Weekly News Service,* August 26, 1933.

9. "$200,000,000 Idle-Relief Public Works in Italy," AFL Weekly News Service, April 30, 1932; "Labor Office Studies Italy's 40-Hour Week," AFL *Weekly News Service,* October 8, 1932; "Italian Government Aids International 40-Hour Week; AFL *Weekly News Service,* October 15, 1932; "500,000 Italian Workers Get Ten Per Cent Wage Increase," AFL *Weekly News Service,* August 15, 1936; "Jobless Increase Under Mussolini's Dictatorship," AFL *Weekly News Service,* "14-Year Limit for Child Labor Fought in italy," AFL *Weekly News Service,* December 16, 1933; "Hitler's Agents Have Murdered 17 Union Officials," AFL *Weekly News Service,* October 19, 1935; "Premier Dolfuss' Warfare Against Austrian Workers Flayed by Green," AFL *Weekly News Service,* February 24, 1934; "Vienna Socialist Thwarts Street Sweeping Penalty," AFL *Weekly News Service,* March 28, 1936.

10. See, for example: "Fair Wage Award Won by Transport Workers," AFL *Weekly News Service,* July 30, 1932; "$52,500,000 for Relief of Jobless in Australia," AFL *Weekly News Service,* September 3, 1932; "Melbourne Government Workers Maintain Wages by Strike," AFL *Weekly News Service,* September 24, 1932; "Scottish Cooperative Lands 400,000 Bacon Wrapper Order," AFL *Weekly News Service,* October 22, 1932; "Railway Company Pays Dismissal Wage to Workers," AFL *Weekly News Service,* November 12, 1932; "A Labor Poet Laureate," AFL *Weekly News Service,* December 31, 1932; "Australian Labor Official Placed on Industrial Court," AFL *Weekly News Service,* March 4, 1933; "British Unemployment Conditions Are Better," AFL *Weekly News Service,* June 30, 1934; "Western Australia Voters Elect Labor Government," AFL Weekly News

Service, April 15, 1933; "British Chemical Concern Restores Wage Cut," AFL *Weekly News Service,* May 13, 1933; "British Fraternal Delegates to A.F. of L. Convention Sail," AFL *Weekly News Service,* September 30, 1933; "British Laborites Gain in Municipal Elections, AFL *Weekly News Service,* November 14, 1933; "Brick Makers Win Pay Boost," AFL *Weekly News Service,* November 18, 1933; "Unions Protect Labor in Accident Cases," AFL *Weekly News Service,* November 18, 1933; "Low-Rent Housing Opened for Use of British Workers," AFL *Weekly News Service,* December 2, 1933; "Auto Drivers Get Proper Rest Periods in England," AFL *Weekly News Service,* December 9, 1933; "12,883,000 British Workers Carry Idle Insurance," AFL *Weekly News Service,* December 9, 1933; "3,000,000 Houses Mostly for Persons with Small Incomes Built in England," AFL *Weekly News Service,* August 29, 1936; "General Workers Union Adds 30,000 Members," AFL *Weekly News Service,* December 16, 1933; "Bus Drivers Block Ballot Scheme Imposed by Bosses," AFL *Weekly News Service,* December 23, 1933; "British Cooperatives in Sound Condition," AFL *Weekly News Service;* "Greenwood, Ex-Labor Minister, Returns to British Parliament," AFL *Weekly News Service,* April 30, 1932; "Economic Security Conference Assures Interest and Early Action," AFL *Weekly News Service,* November 17, 1934; "Labor Government's Unicameral Parliament in Queensland, Australia, is Efficient," AFL *Weekly News Service,* August 31, 1935; "Labor's Control of New Zealand," AFL *Weekly News Service,* May 2, 1936; "Wage Fixing," AFL *Weekly News Service,* May 9, 1936; "Advantages of High Wages and Short Hours," AFL *Weekly News Service,* May 2, 1936; "New Zealand Labor Government's Policy Includes Many Plans to Benefit Masses," AFL *Weekly News Service,* June 27, 1936; "Coal industry Nationalization Placed Before British Trades Union Congress," AFL *Weekly News Service,* August 22, 1936; "Labor Day Speeches on the Air," AFL *Weekly News Service,* September 5, 1936; "Unemployed Workers Number 1,613,940 in Great Britain,"

AFL *Weekly News Service,* September 12, 1936; "British Unions Reject Communist United Front," AFL *Weekly News Service,* September 19, 1936; "New Zealand Railway Men Inter 44-Hour Ashes in Inauguration of 40-Hour Week," AFL *Weekly News Service,* November 28, 1936; "British Textile Workers

Gain Increase in Wages," AFL *Weekly News Service,* January 2, 1937; "Communist United Front is Refused by British Labor," AFL *Weekly News Service,* February 22, 1936; "AFL Fraternal Delegates," AFL *Weekly News Service,* October 26, 1935.

11. See, for example, "Social Misery Increased by British Government," AFL *Weekly News Service,* July 9, 1932; "Steel Reorganization Does Not Protect Labor," AFL *Weekly News Service,* July 9, 1932; "Social Service Cuts Hit Mothers, Mrs. Bevin Says," AFL *Weekly News Service,* July 2, 1932; "New Zealand Abolishes Enforced Arbitration," AFL *Weekly News Service,* July 9, 1932; "British Labor Leaders Hit Higher Food Prices," AFL *Weekly News Service,* August 13, 1932; "Unemployment Insurance Means Test," AFL *Weekly News Service,* August 13, 1932; "Wages Must Be Raised to Restore Prosperity," AFL *Weekly News*

Service, August 6, 1932; "Insured Idle in England Victims of Pauper Policy," AFL *Weekly News Service,* September 19, 1932; "Bank of England Assailed by British Labor Party," AFL *Weekly News Service,* October 8, 1932; "Unemployment Cuts Trade Union Membership in Australia," AFL *Weekly News Service,* September 3, 1932; "Jobless in Belfast Protest Dole Slash," AFL *Weekly News Service,* October 15, 1932; "Disfranchising the Unemployed," AFL *Weekly News Service,* October 22, 1932; "British Jobless Marchers Demand Means Test Repeal," AFL *Weekly News Service,* October 29, 1932; "British Employers Blamed for Jobless," AFL *Weekly News Service,* December 3, 1932; "Ten Policemen Injured; Seven Labor Members of Glasgow Council Suspended for Favoring Jobless," AFL *Weekly News Service,* December 31, 1932; "London Labor Defends Social Services and Salaries," AFL *Weekly News Service,* March 11, 1933; "British Employers Fear 40-Hour Week," , April 22, 1933; "Rationalization of Industry is Scourge to British Workers," AFL *Weekly News Service,* October 14, 1933; "Financiers Victimize the Workers by Strangle Hold on Government," AFL *Weekly News Service,* October 14, 1933; "Sweatshop Wages Paid British Store Employees," AFL *Weekly News Service,* November 18, 1933; "'Labor-Saving' Machinery Kills Carpenters' Jobs," AFL *Weekly News Service,* December 16, 1933; "Mexican Workers Strike," AFL *Weekly News Service,* June 2, 1934; "British Government Uses Means Test of Unemployed Insurance Act to Persecute Jobless Workers," AFL *Weekly News Service,* April 2, 1932; "New Zealand Unemployed Protest Against Wage Cut," AFL *Weekly News Service,* May 14, 1932; "Repression Instead of Food and Work," AFL *Weekly News Service,* May 21, 1932; "Budget Bludgeoning the Workers," AFL *Weekly News Service,* May 21, 1932; "New Zealand Wage Cuts Create Unemployment and Pauperism," AFL *Weekly News Service,* May 28, 1932; "International 40-Hour Week Blocked by British Government and Employers," AFL *Weekly News Service,* August 18, 1934; "Lloyd George Urges Dole's End for Idle," AFL *Weekly News Service,* February 9, 1935; "Strikebreakers Are Hired by Australian Shipowners," AFL *Weekly News Service,* January 4, 1936; "British Civil Service Faces 'Stay-in' Strike," AFL *Weekly News Service,* July 4, 1936; "40-Hour Week in Australia Curbed by States' Rights," AFL *Weekly News Service,* August 1, 1936; "Many Measures Benefitting Seamen Adopted by World Maritime Parley," AFL *Weekly News Service,* November 21, 1936; "Workers Strike to Force Observance of Agreement," AFL *Weekly News Service,* March 11, 1933; "Caravan of Jobless Steelworkers Arrives in England," AFL Weekly News Service, November 7, 1936; "Brazilian Strikers Win Audit of Railways Books," AFL Weekly News Service, April 14, 1934; "Argentina Wins," AFL Weekly News Service, December 8, 1934.

12. AFL, *1933 Proceedings,* pp. 237-39.

13. "Walter M. Citrine Flays Dictatorships and Appeals for Aid of European Workers," AFL *Weekly News Service,* October 13, 1934; "British Labor Condemns Dictatorship," AFL *Weekly News Service,* June 3, 1933.

14. AFL, *1934 Proceedings,* p. 442; "Hitler's Agents Have Murdered 17 Union Officials, Woll Says," AFL *Weekly News* Service, October 19, 1935; "Woll

Opposes Nazi Use of U.S. Radio Chains," AFL *Weekly News Service,* October 31, 1936. On another occasion, Green intoned: "I am confident that the American labor movement will stand with the labor movement of Great Britain and with the labor movements of the world in opposition to the oppressive tactics used by dictators wherever they may be found." AFL, *1933 Proceedings,* p. 251.

15. "Green Urges German Goods Boycott As Reprisal Against Destruction of Unions by Hitler's Barbarians," AFL *Weekly News Service,* September 30, 1933.

16. "German Goods Boycott Urged by AFL Council," AFL *Weekly News* Service, October 2, 1933; "Labor Votes Boycott of German Products," AFL *Weekly News Service,* October 21, 1933; "AFL Council Acts to Push Union Drive and Boycott of Reich Goods," AFL *Weekly News Service,* October 21, 1933.

17. "Labor Leaders Jailed and Property Confiscated by Hitler's Government," AFL *Weekly News Service,* January 6, 1934; "Boycott to Strike Hard Blow at Nazis," AFL *Weekly News Service,* October 28, 1933; "Committee Reports Nazi Boycott is Effective," AFL *Weekly News Service,* October 13, 1934; "Morrison Urges Firm German Goods Boycott," AFL *Weekly News Service,* August 31, 1935; "Firm Ban on German Goods Urged by AFL," AFL *Weekly News Service,* October 26, 1935; AFL, 1935 Proceedings, pp. 169, 794; American Federation of Labor, *Report of the Fifty-Sixth Annual Convention of the American Federation of Labor* (Washington: Judd and Detweiler, 1936), p. 592.

18. AFL, *1935 Proceedings,* pp. 385-86.

19. AFL, *1935 Proceedings,* p. 385; "Labor Chest for European Workers Names H.L. Franklin as Executive," AFL *Weekly News Service,* February 9, 1935; "Amalgamated Clothing Workers Give Anti-Fascist, Anti-Nazi Fund $2,500," AFL *Weekly News Service,* June 29, 1935; "Labor Chest Seeks $50,000 for Victims of Notorious European Dictatorships," AFL *Weekly News Service,* April 4, 1936; "Labor and Liberals Score Dictatorships," AFL *Weekly News Service,* May 9, 1936; "New York Labor Chest Benefit Nets $20,000," AFL *Weekly News Service,* June 6, 1936.

20. AFL, *1935 Proceedings,* pp. 385-86; "Amalgamated Clothing Workers Give Anti-Fascist, Anti-Nazi Fund $2,500," AFL *Weekly News Service,* June 29, 1935; "Annual Report of the Labor Chest," November 9, 1936, "Labor Chest Memorandum" from William English Walling, May 27, 1936, folder 19, box 76, Sidney Hillman Papers, ACW Archives, Labor-Management Documentation Center, Cornell University, Ithaca, NY; Citrine to David Dubinsky, September 1, 1936, Dubinsky to Morris Bialis, September 28, 1936, Dubinsky to Sam Otto, September 28, 1936, bile 1B, box 47, David Dubinsky Papers, ILGWU Archives, Labor-Management Documentation Center, Cornell University, Ithaca, NY.

21. Divine, *Reluctant Belligerent,* pp. 23-6.

22. "Green Warns Against War Participation," AFL *Weekly News Service,* October 12, 1935; "Labor and the War," AFL *Weekly News Service,* October 26, 1935; "Green Supports Curb on Shipments of Materials Used in War to Italy," AFL *Weekly News Service,* November 23, 1935; AFL, *1935 Proceedings,* pp. 496-97.

23. "U.S. Should Check Hitler, Green Says," AFL *Weekly News Service,*

August 3, 1935.

24. "Union-Made Goods Boosted by Ornburn," AFL *Weekly News Service,* December 14, 1935; "Convention Proceedings Summarized," AFL *Weekly News Service,* November 16, 1935; AFL, *1935 Proceedings,* pp. 140, 268, 603.

25. Philip Taft, *The A.F. of L. from the Death of Gompers to the Merger* (New York: Octagon Books, 1970), p. 430; James Weinstein, *The Corporate ideal in the Liberal State, 1900-1918* (Boston: Beacon Press, 1968), pp. 21, 172; Robert H. Wiebe, *The Search for Order, 1877-1920* (New York: Hill and Wang, 1967), pp. 124-25.

26. William E. Leuchtenburg, *Franklin D. Roosevelt and the New Deal, 1932-1940* (New York: Harper and Row, 1963), pp. 205-6; Taft, *The A. F. of L. from the Death of Gompers,* p. 430.

27. William Green to Ralph Easley, July 27, 1932, Ralph M. Easley Papers, Herbert Hoover Presidential Library, West Branch, Iowa; Green to Easley, November 21, 1932, "National" file, box 5, series 11B, William Green Papers, AFL Collection, Wisconsin State Historical Society, Madison, Wisconsin; "A.F. of L. Convention Proceedings Summarized," AFL *Weekly News Service,* December 10, 1932; "Green Opposes Soviet Union Recognition," AFL *Weekly News Service,* February 4, 1933; "Soviet Recognition Protested," AFL *Weekly News Service,* April 15, 1933; "U.S. Recognition of Soviet Russia Militantly Opposed by A.F. of L.," AFL *Weekly News Service,* April 22, 1933; "Recognition of Soviet Union Opposed Unless Guarantees Are Given Against Subversive Acts," AFL *Weekly News Service,* November 18, 1933; "Labor Planks Submitted by American Federation of Labor to the Republican National Convention," AFL *Weekly News Service,* June 13, 1936.

28. "Hushing Scourges Communists for Attacks on Organized Labor," AFL *Weekly News Service,* January 14, 1933; "Soviet Union Sets Up New Work Conditions," AFL *Weekly News Service,* January 28, 1933; "Green Opposes Soviet Union Recognition, AFL *Weekly News Service,* February 4, 1933; "Communists and Trade Unions," AFL *Weekly News Service,* April 15, 1933; "U.S. Recognition of Soviet Russia Militantly Opposed by A.F. of L.," AFL *Weekly News Service,* April 22, 1933; "Recognition of Soviet Union Opposed Unless Guaranteed Are Given Against Subversive Acts," AFL *Weekly News Service,* November 18, 1933; "Activities of Communists Pictured by American Federation of Labor," AFL *Weekly News Service,* January 13, 1934; "Garment Workers Attack Soviet for Civil Liberty Repression," AFL *Weekly News Service,* May 14, 1932; "Delafield Visions Soviet Union Invading the United States," AFL *Weekly News Service,* June 4, 1932; "Convict Labor Builds Soviet Union Railroad," AFL *Weekly News Service,* December 28, 1935; "Labor Planks Submitted by American Federation of Labor to the Republican National Convention," AFL *Weekly News Service,* June 13, 1936; "Life in the Soviet Union," AFL *Weekly News Service,* October 10, 1936; "Soviet Union Drafts Youth for Military Service," AFL *Weekly News Service,* August 22, 1936.

29. Gerald N. Grob and George Athan Billias, ed., *Interpretations of*

American History: Patterns and Perspectives (New York: Free Press, 1982), II: 211-16, 224-33; Divine, *Reluctant Belligerent,* p. 10; Arthur A. Ekirch, Jr., *Ideas, Ideals, and American Diplomacy: A History of their Growth and Interaction* (New York: Appelton-Century-Crofts, 1966), pp. 120-21, 128; Charles DeBenedetti, *The Peace Reform in American History* (Bloomington: Indiana University Press, 1980), pp. 110, 111; Selig Adler, "The War Guilt Question and American Disillusionment, 1918-1920," in Lawrence E. Gelfand, ed., *Essays on the History of American Foreign Relations,* (New York: Holt, Rinehart and Winston, 1972), pp. 283, 290-310.

30. Grob and Billias, *Interpretations,* II: 228-30; Divine, Reluctant Belligerent, pp. 8-10; Charles A. Beard, "The Devil Theory of War," in Jerald A. Combs, ed., *Nationalist, Realist, and Radical: Three Views of American Diplomacy* (New York: Harper and Row, 1972), pp. 343-48; Leuchtenberg, *Roosevelt and the New Deal,* p. 217; Wayne S. Cole, *Roosevelt and the Isolationists, 1932-45* (Lincoln: University of Nebraska Press, 1983), pp. 142, 145.

31. DeBenedetti, *Peace Reform,* pp. 108-9, 125-26; Divine, *Reluctant Belligerent,* pp. 2-3.

32. Cole, *Roosevelt and the Isolationists,* pp. 141-43; DeBenedetti, *Peace Reform,* p. 126.

33. Cole, *Roosevelt and the Isolationists,* pp. 149, 159-62; DeBenedetti, *Peace Reform,* p. 126; Leuchtenberg, *Roosevelt and the New Deal,* pp. 217-18; Divine, *Reluctant Belligerent,* p. 9; John E. Wiltz, *In Search of Peace: The Senate Munitions Inquiry, 1934-36* (Baton Rouge: Louisiana State University Press, 1963), pp. 114-16; United States, Congress, Senate, *Munitions Industry: Naval Shipbuilding; Preliminary Report of the Special Committee on Investigation of the Munitions Industry,* S. Report 944, 74th Congress, 1st Session, 1935, pp. 11-12.

34. Alexander DeConde, *A History of American Foreign Policy,* 2nd ed. (New York: Charles Scribner's Sons, 1971), pp. 567-69; Divine, *Reluctant Belligerent,* pp. 21, 68-71.

35. John C. Donovan, "Congressional Isolationists and the Roosevelt Foreign Policy," in Gelfand, ed., *Essays,* pp.343-46; Ekirch, *Ideas, Ideals,* pp. 142-44; DeBenedetti, *Peace Reform,* pp. 127-28, 135.

36. DeBenedetti, *Peace Reform,* pp. 108-9, 122; "America Must Not Become involved in European Wars," AFL *Weekly News Service,* September 26, 1936; "A.F. of L. Convention Proceedings Summarized," AFL *Weekly News Service,* January 9, 1937.

37. "Green Warns Against War Participation," AFL *Weekly News Service,* October 12, 1935; "America Must Not Become Involved in European Wars, Green Declares," AFL *Weekly News Service,* September 26, 1936; "Italian-Ethiopian War Hit By AFL," AFL *Weekly News Service,* August 10, 1935; "Roosevelt's Plan for Infusing New Blood in Supreme Court is Supported by A.F. of L., Green Declares," AFL *Weekly News Service,* March 20, 1937; "Labor Opposes Settling National Disputes With Arms, Green Says," AFL *Weekly News Service,* November 2, 1935;

"International Peace," AFL *Weekly News Service,* May 9, 1936; "Labor and the War," AFL *Weekly News Service,* October 26, 1935; "Time for Action, *American Federationist* 39 (April 1932): 379-80; "A Phase of Disarmament," *American Federationist* 38 (August 1931): 179-80; Frederic C. Smedley, "A Practical Program for Peace and Diplomacy," *American Federationist* 40 (February 1933): 150-56; Burr Price, "The Human Side of the World Court," American Federationist 38 (July 1931), 38: 865-67; American Federation of Labor, *Report of Proceedings of the Fifty-Second Annual Convention of the American Federation of Labor* (Washington: Judd and Detweiler, 1932), pp. 73-4; AFL, *1935 Proceedings,* p. 9.

38. "Labor and the War," AFL *Weekly News Service*, October 26, 1935; "Peace in Industry Urged by Morrison," AFL *Weekly News Service*, June 6, 1936.

39. "Labor Opposes Settling National Disputes With Arms, Green Says," AFL *Weekly News Service*, November 2, 1935; "President Green Sounds Warning Against All War," AFL *Weekly News Service,* October 13, 1934; Smedley, "A Practical Program," pp. 150, 156.

40. "International Peace," AFL *Weekly News Service,* May 9, 1936; "National Income is Unjustly Distributed, Green Declares," AFL *Weekly News Service,* September 1, 1934; "Menace of Unregulated Competition," AFL *Weekly News Service,* February 15, 1936; "AFL Survey Hits Profit Motive," AFL *Weekly News Service,* November 30, 1935; "Unemployment Greater than Last Year," AFL *Weekly News Service,* December 1, 1934; "Business, Profits Are Boosted," AFL *Weekly News Service,* April 25, 1936; "Advantages of High Wages and Short Hours," AFL *Weekly News Service*, May 2, 1936; "Quebec Bars New Pulp Mill," AFL *Weekly News Service*, October 31, 1936; "Price Profiteering is Condemned by A.F. of L. as Injury to Workers," AFL *Weekly News Service*, May 15, 1937; "A.F. of L. Convention Proceedings Summarized," AFL *Weekly News Service*, January 9, 1937; AFL, *1932 Proceedings,* pp. 388-89; "Labor Spy Inquiry," AFL *Weekly News Service,* May 23, 1936.

41. AFL, *1934 Proceedings*, pp. 630-31; AFL, *1936 Proceedings*, pp. 203-4; "Facing the Facts with Philip Pearl," AFL *Weekly News Service*, September 9, 1939; Wiltz, *In Search of Peace,* pp. 105-12, 129; Wayne S. Cole, *Senator Gerald P. Nye and American Foreign Relations* (Minneapolis: University of Minnesota Press, 1962), p. 146; Green to Selma Borchardt, November 15, 1932, file: "Equal Rights," box 2, series 11B, Green Papers.

42. "A.F. of L. Convention Proceedings Summarized," AFL *Weekly News Service,* January 9, 1937; "Take the Profits Out of War," AFL *Weekly News Service*, October 28, 1933; "Convention Proceedings Summarized," AFL *Weekly News Service,* November 16, 1935; "Hayes Says Legion Wants Profit Taken Out of War," AFL *Weekly News Service*, June 16, 1934; "Preventing War," AFL *Weekly News Service,* June 4, 1938; "War Policies Board Asks 95% Tax on War Profits," AFL *Weekly News Service,* March 12, 1932; AFL *1932 Proceedings,* pp. 388-89; AFL, *1933 Proceedings*, p. 497; AFL, *1936 Proceedings*, p. 105; Wiltz, *in Search of Peace,* pp. 117.

43. AFL, *1932 Proceedings*, p. 388; "A.F. of L. Convention Proceedings

Summarized," AFL *Weekly News Service,* January 9, 1937.

44. "Green Presents American Labor's Political Program to Republican National Convention," AFL *Weekly News Service*, June 18, 1932; "A.F. of L. Convention Proceedings Summarized," AFL *Weekly News Service*, January 9, 1937; also see Wiltz, *In Search of Peace*, pp. 128-29.

45. AFL, 1932 Proceedings, pp. 396-97; "America Must Not Become Involved in European Wars," AFL Weekly News Service, September 26, 1936; "A.F. of L. Convention Proceedings Summarized," AFL Weekly News Service, January 9, 1937; Green to Nason, August 30, 1935, "Magazine" file, box 13, series 11E, Green Papers.

46. AFL, *1932 Proceedings*, pp. 73-4, 370-71; "America Must Not Become Involved in European Wars," AFL *Weekly News Service*, September 26, 1936; "Labor and the War," AFL *Weekly News Service*, October 26, 1935; AFL Secretary (Frank Morrison) to F.G. Barlow, March 15, 1932, "Disarmament" file, box 2, series 11B, Green Papers; Green to *Christian Science Monitor*, February 16, 1930, Ibid; Taft, *A.F. of L. from the Death of Gompers*, p. 204.

47. "Preparedness and Housing," AFL *Weekly News Service* February 29, 1936; "What Naval Preparedness Would Mean in Housing," AFL *Weekly News Service,* March 13, 1937.

48. "America Must Not Become Involved in European Wars," AFL *Weekly News Service*, September 26, 1936; AFL *1932 Proceedings*, pp. 393-95.

49. AFL, *1932 Proceedings,* pp. 393-96.

50. AFL, *1932 Proceedings*, p. 396; "A.F. of L. Convention Proceedings Summarized," AFL *Weekly News Service*, December 10, 1932; "Roosevelt's Labor Record as President," AFL *Weekly News Service*, October 24, 1936; "AFL Council Asks $300,000,000 for Naval Construction Projects," AFL *Weekly News Service,* May 6, 1933; "Over 12,000 to Lose Jobs by U.S. Army Budget Slash," AFL *Weekly News Service*, June 3, 1933; Statement of William Green, December 28, 1936, document no. F-609, "News Releases" file, box 9, series 11E, Green Papers.

Economic and Social Aspects of Foreign Relations

CHAPTER 3

Significant as the argument over military production was, the principal public policy debate during the first Roosevelt Administration was over the means for ending the Depression and restoring economic stability. Foreign relations figured prominently in that debate. Economic nationalists argued that greater economic self-sufficiency was the only guarantee of prosperity, and called for programs that would limit the country's overseas economic involvement. Internationalists countered that the countries of the world were economically interdependent, and that the United States could prosper only by strengthening its global economic ties. On very rare occasions, the AFL during the pre-World War II period championed the development of world markets and held that international trade expansion would benefit labor.[1] In most instances, however, the AFL came down firmly on the side of the economic nationalists.

Western progressives, midwestern farmers, and isolationists typically supported policies of economic nationalism. The chief spokesmen in the federal government for the economic nationalists were Assistant Secretary of State Raymond Moley and Agricultural Adjustment Act Administrator George Peek, who also served as Roosevelt's Special Advisor on Foreign Trade.[2]

Although there were differences of opinion and emphasis among the economic nationalists, they were in general agreement that the country should direct its efforts toward strengthening the domestic market. They believed that the federal government should protect the domestic market through tariffs, quotas, and quarantine regulations. If properly insulated and balanced, the domestic market could promote vigorous economic activity, absorb surpluses, guarantee a free exchange of products between all groups, and maintain high levels of employment. In the words of historian Charles Beard, who was a strong advocate of economic nationalism in the 1930s, the United States needed to establish "the Open Door at home," and concentrate on "tilling its own garden."[3]

Economic nationalists did not ignore foreign markets, but they were extremely wary of them. Foreign markets could be a dangerous chimera, unable to live up to their promise of absorbing surpluses and never accounting for a very high percentage of United States sales. The economic nationalists held that increased international trade took jobs away from Americans and interfered with the domestic market by upsetting the vital balance between agricultural interests and industrial interests, and by disturbing the equilibrium between production and consumption. Therefore, economic nationalists advocated only limited and cautious government efforts to foster overseas commerce. They insisted upon bilateral as opposed to multilateral trading arrangements, to ensure that no trading concession would be granted without getting one directly in return and to guarantee balanced trade with each individual trading partner. They wished to restrict government efforts at trade expansion to bartering and subsidies intended strictly to ensure a supply of the commodities not available at home and to permit the dumping of surplus American products in foreign markets.[4]

Further, many economic nationalists believed that national economic planning and federal regulation were essential to the maintenance of a fair and healthy domestic market. During the First New Deal, they feared that increased foreign trade would counteract the efforts of such newly-established planning bodies as the National Recovery Administration and the Agricultural Adjustment Administration.[5]

Finally, economic nationalists saw a correlation between

international trade and war. Many blamed America's international commercial ties for dragging the country into the First World War. If American interests abroad were limited, they reasoned, the country would be less likely to take up arms in order to protect the bankers, or industrialists, or farmers, or whatever group found its livelihood in jeopardy due to external developments.[6]

Southern planters, industrialists, and northern liberals, meanwhile, advocated international economic expansionism. Their most important spokesmen in the Administration were Secretary of State Cordell Hull and Secretary of Agriculture Henry Wallace. They scoffed at economic nationalists for failing to grasp the sophisticated economic relationships between countries that made imports as well as exports essential preconditions for national prosperity. Trade expansionist William Culbertson even charged "economic illiteracy" on the part of those who advocated "Peekinese Economics."[7]

The economic internationalists admitted that exports accounted for only a small percentage of American sales, overall. But they pointed out that even at a rate of ten percent, such sales could spell the difference between profit and loss. Moreover, many industries relied upon exports for twenty to sixty percent of their sales. Without access to foreign markets, those industries would fail, with disastrous results for American economic well-being in general. Overseas sales, in turn, improved domestic purchasing power, permitting sellers to buy more American goods, make more investments, and hire more employees. Conversely, unsold surpluses, by glutting the domestic market, demoralized prices, promoted unemployment, and destabalized the internal economic balance. That, in turn, reduced purchasing power and made it necessary for the government to intervene to offset losses. Imports, meanwhile, were just as important as exports. Many consumer, capital, and strategic goods, necessary for American economic efficiency, military security, and high living standards, were not available in sufficient quantities at home. Also, contrary to the assertions of the nationalists that dollars spent abroad were lost to the American economy, the economic internationalists argued that those dollars actually created credits for the United

States, because they had to be returned for the purchase of American goods or services. Most important, exports were impossible without imports; by purchasing foreign products, Americans gave foreigners the wherewithal to purchase American products. To sell, it was necessary to buy.[8]

To guarantee access to foreign markets as well as an inflow of imports, economic internationalists advocated abandonment of bilateral, preferential bargaining methods in favor of a multilateral, most-favored nation approach. Under the latter scheme, liberal access to the American market negotiated with any trading partner automatically would be extended to all other countries that did not discriminate against American goods. Such a policy was, in the words of George Peek, "unilateral economic disarmament." The internationalists, though, held that preferential bargaining through the use of tariffs, quotas, and barter was self-destructive in the long-run. Bilateral policies did not comprehend the concept of triangularity, which demonstrated that third countries inevitably were important to any bilateral relationship. If the United States ran a favorable balance of trade with another country, that other country had to redress the balance by running a favorable balance of trade with a third country. The reverse, of course, was also true. No country could hope to run favorable balances with all its trading partners. Instead, all countries had to have a mix of favorable and unfavorable balances, while striving for a favorable balance in the aggregate. Bilateral agreements inhibited that process; the multilateral approach encouraged it. According to the internationalists, by granting exclusive trading privileges to one state in return for like concessions, preferential bargaining implicitly discriminated against every country except those making the agreement. That invited retaliation, in the form of new and higher trade barriers. Trade expansion with one country via a preferential agreement, therefore, risked trade reduction with all other countries. And trade reduction, claimed the internationalists, risked economic disaster for the United States. For the internationalists, United States prosperity was tied to world prosperity, world prosperity was dependent upon the expansion of international trade, and economic nationalism would strangle trade with its manifold restrictions.[9]

As did the economic nationalists, the internationalists believed that the economic policies they espoused had favorable political ramifications. At home, many saw trade expansion as an alternative to government economic regulation. Assistant Secretary of State Francis B. Sayre wrote that economic nationalism would involve "national regimentation and strait-jacketing of all trade and business," with federal control of prices, investment, and production to ensure self-sufficiency. International trade expansion would make that unnecessary. Internationalists predicted that the most favored nation formula would lower tariff barriers around the world, thereby easing friction between countries, restoring international stability, and reducing the likelihood of war.[10]

The AFL was in close harmony with the ideas of George Peek and the economic nationalists. Throughout the early and middle 1930s, the AFL consistently pursued a program that hinged on a wholly domestic interpretation of the economic crisis. It stressed the domestic causes of the Depression, and, more to the point, it insisted upon domestic solutions. The AFL rejected arguments that asserted the importance of world trade and international economics because they detracted from the domestic interpretation and weakened the Federation's program.

Primacy of the domestic market was the central feature of the AFL's legislative and economic program. Developing that market was the key to economic recovery. To do so required a higher aggregate income, and achievement of that goal would create more jobs. Thus, the two paramount goals of the AFL—higher wages and lower unemployment—were wedded to the domestic market concept. According to the AFL's analysis, the chief cause of the Depression was the fact that the ability to produce had outstripped the ability to consume. If American consumers enjoyed greater "purchasing power"—that is, if workers received higher wages and could purchase more goods—the domestic market would flourish. More purchases in the domestic market required higher levels of production, which, in turn, necessitated the hiring of more workers. The entire scheme could be carried out within America's borders.[11]

The AFL relied upon the thirty-hour week as the most important tool for achieving its economic objectives. Until the eve of World War II, AFL leaders maintained that the thirty-hour week was the Federation's most important goal, and the most prominent resolutions at the AFL's national conventions concerned the thirty-hour week. The AFL proposed the thirty-hour week as the antidote to "technological unemployment." The AFL held that machines in the workplace had increased production per man-hour dramatically. Greater automation glutted the market at the same time as it permitted employers to cut back on labor, which in turn reduced purchasing power and accelerated the economic decline. Placing workers on a thirty-hour week, without reducing the salaries they had received for forty or forty-eight hour weeks, would mitigate the effects of increased productivity per worker due to automation, increase employment, strengthen national consumer purchasing power, expand the domestic market, and bring about prosperity.[12]

For the AFL during the first Roosevelt Administration, the thirty-hour week seemed a virtual panacea. Given "the enormous increase in the output of labor under machine production . . . the alarming persistency of the long work week and low wages and a large unemployed army," the 1936 AFL Convention held "that the five-day week and the six-hour day is the only means of mastering the unemployment problem and protecting society against further depressions."[13]

Accordingly, the AFL made its quest for the thirty-hour week the centerpiece of its legislative program. It campaigned tirelessly for passage of the Black-Connery Bill, which would have prohibited interstate shipment of goods produced by labor that worked more than thirty hours per week. Other pieces of economic legislation that the AFL favored also conformed to the reliance of economic nationalism upon domestic solutions. The AFL's prescription called for heavy doses of public works spending, with a particular emphasis on low-cost housing, and large federal relief appropriations for the unemployed. The AFL also called for national economic planning, with representatives of organized labor to play a prominent role.[14] Later, as World War II approached, the AFL saw that many of its economic goals could be achieved through global rather than domestic policies, and thus dropped or altered some of its economic strategies. Until then, however, the Federation's economic programs were based on a domestic economic determinism.

With its inward-looking perspective, the AFL resisted suggestions that economic matters elsewhere in the world could have much effect on the American economy, either positive or negative. The AFL *Weekly News Service* happily quoted Albert Einstein's assertion that "the severe economic depression is to be traced back . . . to internal economic cases," and that arguments blaming America's depression on European economic dislocations were not only incorrect but were also dangerous in that they encouraged international animosities.[15]

In particular, the AFL opposed economic revival policies based on expansion of foreign trade. Textile manufacturer Austin T. Levy captured the AFL's point of view perfectly, and the *Weekly News Service* reprinted his remarks, when he said that foreign trade was relatively unimportant compared to the $20 billion worth of domestic sales that were lost due to unemployment. It was the domestic market that was America's salvation, and to develop it required the thirty-hour week. In 1936, William Green testified to a Senate committee that "Foreign trade offers but slim prospect of further expansion. The only hope of securing a balanced economic program lies in measures which will achieve some degree of redistribution of our national income, placing into the hands of the low income groups sufficient purchasing power.[16]

The AFL, then, had a carefully crafted program for more jobs and higher wages that was intertwined with national economic planning and development of the domestic market. If foreign trade expansion were adopted as an alternative, then surplus production could be absorbed without the thirty-hour week, the increased employment, and the increased purchasing power upon which the AFL pinned its hopes. Moreover, foreign trade expansion would mean an influx of imports, which would undermine domestic economic planning. The success of the National Industrial Recovery Act depended upon strict adherence to production codes and other regulations. Imports were not produced under that system, and hence were a threat to it.[17]

The AFL thus saw foreign trade more as a threat than an opportunity. At least in part, that may have been because America's export trade in the 1930s, by and large, did not benefit AFL union members directly. American exports were greatest in agriculture, textiles, steel, and automobiles—enterprises whose workers remained largely unorganized by the AFL. Few of the longshoremen whose livelihoods were dependent upon a vigorous foreign trade were members of AFL unions, either. In many industries that were organized by AFL unions—including processed foodstuffs, paper manufacturing, lumber, silk and pottery—imports offset or surpassed exports.[18]

The AFL did admit that the American economy was dependent upon imports of raw materials for manufacturing, and called for federal policies to ensure an uninterrupted flow of such commodities. As a rule, however, the Federation staked out a pro-tariff position, and characterized foreign trade liberalization as reactionary and anti-social.[19]

The 1934 Trade Agreements Act authorized the president to reduce tariffs through bilateral, reciprocal agreements that guaranteed similar tariff reform by the other state. Tariff reductions achieved in that manner would be extended to all countries enjoying "most favored nation" status in their commercial relations with the United States. Three years later, the Act was renewed. The legislation was highly controversial, prompting a bitter political debate in the United States. Agricultural interests spearheaded the opposition to the measure, concerned that it would enrich industry at the expense of farmers by permitting greater agricultural imports as the cost of expanding industrial exports.[20]

Supporters of reciprocity argued that it would benefit organized labor. They asserted that only a fraction of American workers profited from the maintenance of high tariffs, pointed out that many American industries depended upon exports for their economic survival, and held that protectionism retarded the expansion of American industries, thereby preventing job growth. According to Assistant Secretary of State Francis B. Sayre, one of the administration's leading spokesmen on reciprocity, "labor in the United States is not helped but is definitely injured by embargo tariffs. The overwhelming majority of the workers in this country unquestionably stand to gain from a policy of tariff moderation."[21]

Organized labor, however, remained wary of reciprocity. Although the AFL avoided taking a stand in the debate over passage of the Trade Agreement Act itself, it frequently was critical of the tariff-reducing agreements the legislation spawned. It attacked reciprocal agreements in aluminum, lumber, brewing, and other industries. It blamed reciprocal agreements for debasing wage standards and for "menacing" or "threatening" the very existence of affected industries.[22]

Opposition to specific reciprocal trading agreements was part of a larger campaign against imports conducted by the Federation's Union Label Trades Department. The Department's primary responsibility was to advance union organization by promoting products and services made or provided by union members. The Department's two main messages were "Buy Union" and "Buy American."[23]

The secretary-treasurer of the Union Label Trades Department was I.M. Ornburn. In 1932-33, Ornburn was the AFL's representative on the United States Tariff Commission. A fellow commission member later pronounced Ornburn "the most extreme protectionist who ever sat on the Tariff Commission." As the most publicly visible official in the Union Label Trades Department, Ornburn tirelessly fought imports of foreign-made products. Internationalists argued trade expansion would reinvigorate the domestic market, that increases in imports correlated with increases in domestic employment, and that imports would not reduce American wage levels because high American productivity would ensure that United States products could undersell even those foreign goods produced by low-wage labor. But Ornburn and the AFL would have none of it. To them, imports inescapably were harmful to American workers.[24]

The Union Label Trades Department objected to imports for several reasons. Most important, it argued that imports undercut American workers and wages. Foreign workers earned less than their American counterparts, and the AFL maintained that the goods they produced could therefore sell for less than goods produced by unionized American labor. Foreign products had an unfair competitive edge due to lower labor costs. Buying foreign-made goods was the equivalent of buying non-union, scab-made goods. Further, an expanded import market meant a constricted domestic market, and, with fewer American-made goods being sold, fewer Americans would be employed to produce them. It also meant decreased purchasing power. Dollars spent on American-made goods stayed at home, being re-spent and generating more economic activity and more employment. Dollars spent on foreign goods went overseas, and their value was lost to the American economy. In a radio address on purchasing power, Ornburn gave the "Buy American" campaign equal billing with the thirty-hour work week as essential elements in creating purchasing power and increasing employment.[25]

AFL Vice President Matthew Woll, in testimony before the Tariff Commission, argued that tariff protection was as crucial to American well-being as were immigration restrictions. "We exclude Asiatics," Woll exclaimed, incredulously, "but we welcome—we give preference to—products of Asian labor at the expense of American workmen." Ornburn summed up the AFL's perspective on increased foreign trade when he said that American workers "cannot better their condition by buying foreign-made products and merchandise of chiselers who employ child labor and women at coolie wages in some of the industries of our own land . . . . We cannot have prosperity in America and put the purchasing power fuel into foreign engines."[26]

Beyond the strictly economic arguments, Ornburn and the AFL criticized the quality of foreign-made goods. They warned consumers that imports were "shoddy" and "unsanitary."[27]

Thus, the AFL opposed foreign trade expansion during the 1930s. It fought reciprocal trade agreements, called for anti-dumping legislation, and demanded higher tariffs on oil, pottery, footwear, cement, farm products, apparel, glass, aluminum, and lumber, among other products. The AFL not only opposed imports; it also opposed exports, to the extent that they diverted support from what it considered the more promising and socially-just policies of domestic economic planning and the thirty-hour week.[28]

The AFL may have cherished its position on tariffs as much as any stance it took on international issues. When the two were in conflict, for example, the tariff could take precedence over friendship. Frequently, the AFL lavished praise on Britain for its enlightened labor relations. In opposing reciprocal trade agreements with that country, however, the AFL reversed itself and denounced British goods as the product of "low-wage labor." Likewise, friendship with Canada and the fact that a great many Canadian union locals were affiliated with the AFL were forgotten when tariffs were at stake. The AFL charged that reciprocity agreements permitted low-wage Canadian lumber and aluminum to flood the United States, jeopardizing American enterprises, destroying wage standards, stealing jobs, and—in the case of aluminum—weakening American military defenses by discouraging self-sufficiency in strategic metals.[29]

By the same token, certain AFL positions on international affairs could reinforce its pro-tariff policy, and vice-versa. In one sense, the AFL's boycott against Nazi Germany was a measure short-of-war designed to put pressure on the dictatorship. In another sense, it was a convenient prop for the long-standing AFL policy against imports. In a 1935 radio address on the importance of buying union label goods, Ornburn recited the traditional arguments against imports. He said they were unsanitary and promoted unemployment. Then he added one more reason for buying American-made, union label products: "When Americans buy imported European goods," Ornburn said, "they are helping the dictatorships that are rapidly increasing and spreading through the Old World, whether it be [sic] a Hitler, a Mussolini, or a Stalin.

By spending American dollars abroad our citizens are enriching the nations which support Nazism, Fascism, and Communism."[30]

In 1935, the AFL successfully demanded that the Works Progress Administration (WPA) revoke its rule allowing contractors to purchase foreign-made goods that were priced at least 15 percent below comparable American goods. The WPA began requiring that virtually all materials used in its projects be American-made after the AFL pointed out that "Nazi products"—i.e., German steel—were being used to construct the Triborough Bridge in New York.[31]

Similarly, in 1933 the trade issue was a weapon in the AFL's arsenal against United States recognition of the Soviet Union. William Green denounced selfish, profit-seeking industrialists and financiers for endorsing recognition as a way of gaining access to the Soviet market. Green belittled the sales potential of American exports to the Soviet Union and warned that Soviet imports would harm American workers. "If more manufactured goods are sold to Russia, we must, in turn, buy from them," Green said. "That would mean that Labor in the United States would suffer through importation of goods produced and manufactured by Russian labor under intolerable conditions of employment and at an indefensible, low rate of wages." As an example, the AFL President cited imports of Russian anthracite coal, which was selling in the United States at a price below the costs of production in the Eastern Pennsylvania coal fields.[32]

One facet of economics where the AFL departed from its traditional nationalism was labor relations. Partly as a matter of self-preservation, the AFL became increasingly involved in the international labor movement during the first part of the 1930s, primarily through participating in the activities of the International Labor Organization (ILO), the Pan American Federation of Labor (PAFL), and the International Federation of Trade Unions (IFTU). The AFL hoped to derive benefits from that course of action in three ways. First, the international labor movement could offer direct services to the AFL, mainly in the way of providing technical information about social services and the establishment of standards in particular industries. Second, the international labor movement could have a favorable political effect abroad, by fostering the development of labor unions congenial to the AFL, discouraging the radicalization of labor organizations, and helping unions in foreign countries fight anti-labor dictatorships that ultimately could threaten American workers. Third and most important, the international labor movement sought to improve wages and employment conditions in other countries, which in turn helped protect American workers from having to compete against cheap foreign labor.[33]

Actually, the AFL was returning to the international labor movement in the early 1930s, after having shunned it for a number of years. The AFL had joined the IFTU (then called the International Secretariat of Trade Union Centers) in 1910, and in 1919 long-time AFL President Samuel Gompers had been instrumental in founding the ILO. After World War I, however, the AFL broke with the IFTU over the largely socialist orientation of the European membership, a rules change that would have made IFTU decisions binding upon all affiliates, and an increase in annual dues assessed against the AFL. Meanwhile, AFL interest in the ILO had waned, and during the 1920s the Federation declined to campaign for United States membership in that international body. With the advent of the Great Depression, however, the AFL renewed its interest in international labor activities.[34]

The ILO was a semi-autonomous component of the League of Nations. Established as part of the Versailles Treaty that ended World War I, its goal was to raise living standards and working conditions throughout the world, and thereby ameliorate the social unrest and international economic rivalries that led to war. It sought to codify an international labor code by convening representatives of labor, management, and government from each member state to develop conventions setting minimum labor standards which, if adopted by the legislatures of the individual countries, acquired treaty status. In addition, the ILO conducted investigations to secure compliance with ratified conventions, furnished direct assistance to governments undertaking to improve labor conditions, and carried out research on labor problems that involved collecting and analyzing data and issuing studies, reports, periodicals, and statistics.[35]

Despite American involvement in a pre-World War I predecessor body to the ILO, the International Association for Labor Legislation, and even though the United States government and the AFL participated prominently in the founding of the ILO, the United States refused to become a charter member of the organization. When the Senate rejected the Versailles Treaty, it simultaneously rejected membership in the ILO, whose constitution was contained as a provision in the treaty. Between 1919 and 1933, the United States worked to a limited degree with the ILO: the Department of Labor regularly exchanged information with the ILO, the federal government sent official representatives to a few special committees, and private citizens and civic groups participated in the technical work of the ILO. Yet the United States held back from seeking full membership, partly due to resistance to the notion of using legislation to raise labor standards, partly due to a perception of the ILO as being ineffective, and partly due to incorrect assumptions that ILO conventions were automatically binding on member states and that League of Nations membership was a prerequisite for ILO membership.[36]

The 1919 and 1920 AFL Conventions had urged United States membership in the ILO, but for the balance of the twenties the AFL was apathetic towards the organization. Official correspondence passed between the AFL and the ILO, the AFL bought furnishings for a room at the ILO headquarters in Geneva that the ILO had dedicated to Samuel Gompers, and when William Green became President of the AFL in 1924, he spoke favorably of the ILO. Nonetheless, the AFL refused to participate in ILO activities and made no effort to persuade the United States to become a member. One AFL union, the Seamen's union, expressed open hostility towards the ILO, fearing that ILO conventions would undermine existing international agreements on seamen's rights. In 1929, AFL interest in the ILO began to revive. But as late as 1930, AFL leader Matthew Woll opposed closer United States ties to the ILO, citing the ILO's reliance on the state to protect labor—

a position at odds with the AFL's philosophy of rejecting political activity in favor of independent collective bargaining.[37]

The AFL altered its philosophy somewhat as the Depression wore on, looking more than ever to the government to help the workingman. Consistent with that change of course was a new-found interest in the ILO. The 1931 and 1932 AFL Conventions approved a series of resolutions calling for United States membership in the ILO. One of the 1932 resolutions stated that ILO conventions on child labor, shorter hours, workmen's compensation, and "other humane conditions of work" were already protecting high American labor standards by raising standards in other countries. Meanwhile, the AFL intensified its publicity on ILO initiatives, especially in the area of hours. A few weeks before the 1932 convention, Teamsters' union President Dan Tobin declared that international action was necessary to improve living standards and adjust to the machine age. Striking a clear internationalist note, Tobin said that "the basic impulse of the labor movement the world over is . . . international because of the universal character of the industrial civilization of which it is a part." Making points that would become routine in AFL pronouncements on the ILO throughout the mid-1930s, Tobin portrayed the ILO as Gompers' brainchild, cited AFL support for international arbitration extending as far back as 1887, and praised the role of immigrants in AFL unions for giving the AFL a cosmopolitan perspective. As if to reinforce the glowing internationalism expressed by Tobin, the AFL also publicized a statement by British labor leader Ernest Bevin that "employers are using nationalism to keep the workers of various countries separated" and unable to effect necessary reforms.[38]

In 1933, the incoming Franklin Roosevelt Administration shared the AFL's favorable view of the ILO and labor internationalism. The new secretary of labor, Frances Perkins, believed that American labor standards would put the United States at a trade disadvantage by causing proportionately higher industrial costs, unless they were matched by improvements in labor standards world-wide. ILO membership, she decided, could help accomplish that. Meanwhile, Roosevelt's State Department saw American membership in the ILO as a means of encouraging international cooperation at a time of escalating world tensions, and thus as a tool for averting war. Adroit maneuvering by the Administration secured House and Senate approval of a joint resolution endorsing American entry in June 1934, and the United States formally accepted membership in the world labor body two months later.[39]

Ironically, as the United States moved closer to involvement in the International Labor Organization, the role of the AFL grew somewhat murky. State Department official William McClure argued that it would be undesirable, politically, for the Administration to become tied too closely to the Federation during the negotiations leading up to ILO membership. Accordingly, the Administration's timing of its acceptance of ILO membership may have been calculated to minimize any appearance of AFL influence in the decision.[40]

After the United States became a member of the ILO, delicate questions remained concerning budget appropriations to support United States activity in the organization and the seating of the various components of the United States delegation on the ILO's Governing Board. Labor Secretary Perkins deemed AFL support indispensable in both areas, but, at that critical juncture, the Federation suddenly became taciturn.[41]

The Governing Board was prepared to extend membership to the United States, commencing in April 1935. Perkins considered AFL participation on the board to be critical to the success of the ILO Convention on the Reduction of Hours. Further, she believed that the absence of AFL support would jeopardize the ILO appropriation before Congress. Yet in December 1934 and January 1935 the AFL's position was that it would not take part in the negotiations for United States seats on the Governing Board. Moreover, not only was AFL support of the appropriation in doubt, but at least one leading figure in the AFL—United Mine Workers President John L. Lewis—may have been lobbying actively against the appropriation.[42]

Perkins was mystified by the AFL's unexpected ambivalence regarding the ILO, now that the United States was a member. She thought that part of the problem was the delay of several months in seating all three American groups—representatives of government, labor, and management—on the Governing Board. She thought that the AFL, Lewis in particular, might have been offended by that and for that reason refused to send representatives who would merely advise the government delegate. Also, Perkins theorized that the AFL might have been fearful of being drawn into the affairs of the IFTU, which it still considered too socialistic.[43]

Nonetheless, Perkins was confident that she could prevail over the AFL to participate in the ILO and in the April 1935 meeting of the Governing Board. She reasoned that the opportunity to advance a convention to reduce hours would hold too much importance for the AFL to pass up, and she devised strategies with ILO chief Harold Butler on how best to approach the AFL.[44]

As expected, the ILO offered seats on its Governing Board for all components of the United States delegation, including the labor delegate. The AFL accepted the labor seat and sent International Ladies' Garment Workers President David Dubinsky to Geneva for the meeting of the Governing Board in April. Two months later, Teamsters' President Dan Tobin served as the United States labor delegate to the 16th session of the regular ILO conference.[45]

The 1935 ILO conference approved conventions on social security, the reduction of child labor, and the prohibition of female labor in mines. From the AFL's standpoint, the most important convention approved during the conference was one that endorsed the forty hour week in principle.[46]

The American labor delegation argued strongly in favor of the forty-hour convention. Citing America's successful experience in implementing the forty hour week, an advisor to the delegation stated during the general discussion that the forty hour week had not hindered production in the United States, that psychological barriers rather than social, technical, or economic ones were the primary impediments to shorter hours, and that shorter hours were necessary to ensure employment for all workers in an age of technological advancement. He concluded that American labor saw the forty hour week "as nothing more or less than a way-station in labour's steady progress towards the universal thirty hour week."[47]

Technical information on the application of the forty hour week in the United States was critical to the success of the convention, which endorsed the forty hour week as a general concept and called for additional conventions to apply the forty hour rule in specific industries. The conference, however, rejected draft resolutions on shorter hours in the glass bottle industry, mining, construction and civil engineering, and the iron and steel industry—although it did agree to reconsider conventions on the forty hour week in all those industries at the 1936 conference.[48]

In the year following the 1935 ILO conference, the Governing Body met four times: in October 1935, February 1936, April 1936, and June 1936. The AFL was represented at those four meetings, respectively, by John Possehl, president of the International Union of Operating Engineers, George Harrison, president of the Brotherhood of Railway Clerks, Robert Watt, secretary of the Massachusetts Federation of Labor, and Emil Rieve, president of the American Federation of Hosiery Workers. They continued to press forward on the forty hour issue, and succeeded in placing consideration of shorter hours in the printing and chemical industries onto the agenda for the 1937 conference.[49]

The 1936 ILO Conference, with Rieve representing American labor, considered 8 draft conventions. Five of those draft conventions concerned shorter hours, but only one—calling for a forty hour week on public works projects—was adopted. Conventions to reduce hours in mining, construction and civil engineering, and iron and steel, won majority approval but failed to achieve the mandatory two-thirds vote. A forty hour convention for the textile industry was also defeated. The conference did request the Governing Body to convene technical committees to consider shorter hours in all those industries.[50]

The 1936 ILO Conference adopted a convention calling for paid holidays, a minor victory for the labor delegations. Also, it approved three resolutions introduced by the United States, recommending studies of industrial diseases, freedom of association by workers, and the effects of technological advances on employment.[51]

The first two ILO conferences following the admission of the United States, then, achieved little. Despite strong support from the United States, only two of the conventions to reduce hours were adopted. A handful of lesser conventions and non-binding resolutions favored by the United States also won approval. Given those modest results, the AFL Executive Council had to admit that the 1936 ILO Conference "did not succeed."[52]

Yet the AFL retained its optimism regarding tho ILO. It heralded the conventions on the forty hour week in public works and paid holidays as great victories for the workers' delegations. It expressed surprise and gratification at how close the other forty hour conventions had come to adoption, given the strength of the opposition. And it explained that the lack of progress was the result of unsettled world conditions, and held out hope that the ILO could make more progress once the threat of war dissipated and governments were no longer reluctant to bind themselves to conventions that would curtail hours of production in war-related industries.[53]

Moreover, AFL leaders continued to trumpet the general principles of the ILO and the value of the ILO to the American worker. Always pointing to the ILO as the legacy of Samuel Gompers, AFL leaders pressed hard for rank-and-file acceptance of the world labor body. In a coast-to-coast radio broadcast at the time of the 1935 ILO Conference, David Dubinsky explained that ILO efforts to raise labor standards world-wide were necessary "not only from a humane point of view" but also in order to protect labor standards in the United States. Higher labor standards and shorter hours for European workers, according to Dubinsky, offered greater security for American workers than the protective tariff. Characteristically taking a somewhat more messianic approach, John L. Lewis proclaimed that the ILO was the instrument with which the United States could mobilize the world against economic autocracy. The social and economic revolution that Lewis professed to see in progress at home could only be successful if there were international cooperation, and international cooperation could be achieved by using the ILO to advance the interests of organized labor and batter down European dictatorships. "The real significance" of American entry into the ILO, Lewis intoned, was "that the American labor movement has again taken up the torch of international leadership."[54]

Besides the quarterly Governing Body meetings and the annual ILO conferences, the ILO began to hold regional and technical conferences in 1935, at the behest of the United States. A tripartite technical conference convened in November 1935 and again in October 1936 to consider maritime issues. In 1936, ILO members from the Americas sent representatives to Santiago, Chile, for a regional conference on labor problems in the Western Hemisphere.[55]

Andrew Furuseth, President of the International Seamen's Union, represented American labor at the November 1935 Maritime Conference. Furuseth had been a firm opponent of United States entry into the ILO, and his appointment as a delegate to the Maritime Conference had been pushed by isolationist Senator Hiram Johnson. Secretary Perkins thought it necessary to admonish Furuseth to confine himself to matters on the agenda, and to remember that he could speak as an official representative on no other subjects. Paul Scharrenberg of the California Federation of Labor represented American labor at the October 1936 Maritime Conference.[56]

The Maritime conferences proved highly successful. Following preliminary discussions at the first conference, the second conference agreed upon six conventions to improve the conditions of merchant seamen in such areas as wages, hours, medical insurance, and paid vacations. Pleased with the outcome of the Maritime Conference, the United States delegation called successfully for a tripartite conference on the textile industry, to be convened in 1937.[57]

Carpenters' Brotherhood President and AFL Vice President William L. Hutcheson was the American labor delegate to the ILO's Pan American Labor Conference in Santiago, Chile. President Franklin Roosevelt clearly was unhappy with Hutcheson, a prominent Republican and highly vocal opponent of the New Deal. The AFL insisted upon his appointment, however, with President Green issuing a statement that politics should not be a factor determining the appointment of ILO emissaries. In fact, Hutcheson's appointment may have had more to do with internal Federation wrangling than anything else. The burly Hutcheson was leader of one of the most influential craft unions in the country, and the AFL hierarchy may have selected him for the prestigious ILO appointment as a slap at the budding industrial union movement that would soon tear the AFL asunder.[58]

The Santiago Conference produced few tangible accomplishments. It heard reports from committees on social insurance and on employment conditions for women and children. It adopted resolutions requesting the ILO to establish an information service on social insurance matters, recommending an inquiry into agricultural employment in the Americas, and calling for rural and vocational education, better housing for workers, and the establishment of children's labor bureaus in national labor ministries. In addition, it ascertained the extent to which states in the Western Hemisphere were complying with ILO conventions and resolutions.[59]

On the other hand, the conference largely ignored such women's labor issues as wages, hours, and working conditions, and refused to endorse a minimum age requirement of 16 years for child labor. Further, South American opposition to the concept was so extensive that the United States delegation decided against even proposing a resolution favoring the forty hour week in the textile industry.[60]

Frieda Miller, an official with the New York State Department of Labor, represented the United States government at the Santiago Conference. In her opinion, "the ground covered and the actions taken were about all that one would have any basis for expecting from such a 'first' conference." The United States failed to make real progress toward reaching its cherished goal of the forty hour week. But the conference was "worthwhile," according to Miller, because it brought representatives from twenty Western Hemisphere countries together to discuss labor issues, enhanced the positions of struggling labor organizations in Latin America, established personal contacts between the Latin Americans and officials of the ILO, and clarified for the Latin

Americans what services the ILO could provide. The latter two points were of particular interest to the United States, which had to thwart a move to establish a completely independent Pan American Labor Office by South American countries who had little interest in United States and European matters and little appreciation for the value of attempting to deal with labor's controversies on a global scale. ILO Director Harold Butler added that "the fruitful part of [the] conference was that it gave a platform for the first time to representatives of [Latin American] labor to stand up and say what they thought." Even though some of those representatives were chastised later in their home countries, and even though at least one labor representative was disavowed by his country's labor movement as a foil for the government, many Latin American labor delegates used the conference as an opportunity to issue harsh denunciations of labor conditions in their countries.[61]

Indeed, labor conditions in much of Latin America were deplorable. The wages of South American workers were a mere fraction of those of North American workers. Political dictatorships in many Latin American countries denied labor the right to organize freely. The AFL followed events in Latin America closely, reporting on strikes, wages, and levels of employment, condemning the exploitation of Latin American workers by native capitalists as well as by those from Britain and the United States, expressing sympathy for Latin American workers suffering under political tyranny, and praising the rare labor reforms espoused by such political leaders as President Lazaro Cardenas of Mexico.[62]

Hopeful of ameliorating the dismal Latin American labor situation, the AFL was a member of the Pan American Federation of Labor (PAFL). Unlike the ILO, which was an association of governments, the PAFL was an affiliation of national federations of labor unions. It was founded in 1918 by the AFL and the Mexican labor movement. The PAFL sought to encourage labor organization in the Western Hemisphere, cultivated friendlier relations between labor movements in the Americas, worked to improve labor conditions, circulated information (mainly from the AFL) on tactics and programs, and served, to a limited degree, as a political counterweight to Latin American dictators who tried to repress labor and to radical movements that tried to lure it.[63]

The PAFL, however, had been dormant since holding its Fifth Congress in 1927. Many labor movements in Latin America were in disarray or under governmental control. The worldwide economic depression virtually had wiped out the treasuries of Latin American union federations. Military uprisings and political revolutions caused even greater instability. Those financial, organizational, and political distresses, as well as an ideological gulf between the AFL and its less conservative Latin American counterparts, had caused the PAFL to postpone its Sixth Congress year after year. Member bodies could do no more than correspond with each other.[64]

Anxious to raise labor standards in Latin America, and fearful that communist trade unions or European-style fascism would take hold south of the border, the AFL moved to reinvigorate the moribund PAFL. It called for the Sixth Congress to convene as early as possible, and in July 1935 agreed to join with the Mexican Federation of Labor in sending goodwill ambassadors to meet with labor leaders throughout Latin America and to encourage affiliation with the PAFL. It was not until 1939 that an AFL representative began canvassing Latin American labor movements. Also, it was not until 1939 that the PAFL Executive Council met to discuss the reorganization of the PAFL and the prospects for a Sixth Congress. But as early as the mid-1930s, the AFL had begun the spade work for a revival of the PAFL—a revival that never actually came to pass.[65]

A third international labor association with which the AFL had dealings was the International Federation of Trade Unions (IFTU). A one-time member of the IFTU, the AFL cancelled its membership in 1922, although it maintained relatively cordial relations with the group thereafter. Nonetheless, it would not reaffiliate with the group, and as late as 1932 refused to participate in an IFTU-sponsored world economic conference.[66]

But by the mid-1930s, the AFL was moving closer to rejoining the IFTU. Trade union solidarity seemed increasingly urgent as fascism spread through Europe, and the AFL had already begun to forge links with foreign trade unions as their delegates worked together at the ILO. Craft unionists in the AFL also believed that IFTU affiliation would strengthen them in their domestic battle against industrial unions. The AFL monitored and reported to its members on IFTU activities and policies, relied on the IFTU for information about fascist attacks on trade unions in Europe, and in 1936 entered into exploratory talks with the IFTU concerning possible reaffiliation.[67]

Its participation in the activities of the ILO and the PAFL, and its intensifying interest in the IFTU, revealed the AFL in perhaps its most internationalistic posture. Its attitudes regarding immigration, however, revealed the AFL at its most insular.

Although the rank-and-file included large numbers of immigrants and first generation Americans, the AFL since the early 1890s had been a fervent advocate of laws to restrict immigration. The fear that immigrants who worked for low wages would take jobs from union members and demoralize labor standards was the chief argument advanced by the AFL in favor of immigration restriction, and AFL insistence upon restriction intensified during periods of economic distress when jobs were scarce. Moreover, the AFL feared, language differences would undermine labor solidarity. The AFL argument, in common with all nativist sentiment, had a strong ethnic and cultural bias, as it claimed that immigrants—particularly those from Asia and Eastern Europe—did not have the racial characteristics or the political values necessary to assimilate into American society. The Chinese, for example, were dismissed as too prone to submit to political tyranny, and hence were considered unfit for citizenship in a democracy. And Slavic peasants who sought employment in American steel mills were seen as too docile or transient to participate in the meaningful, collective activity of unionized labor.[68]

The AFL continued its campaign against immigration into the 1930s. During the Great Depression, the AFL was concerned not only that aliens would take jobs away from native-born workers but also that unemployed aliens would absorb relief funds. An editorial in the *Weekly News Service* called immigration a "prolific source of job destruction for American workers," and demand-that Congress adopt "every reasonable measure" to ensure jobs for American citizens.[69]

In addition, the AFL remained skeptical of aliens' qualifications for citizenship and wary of their ability to become assimilated. It considered aliens who held radical political philosophies to be a threat to democracy and the trade union movement and urged their deportation. A "yellow peril" mentality also pervaded the AFL. In a 1932 radio address outlining the AFL's position on immigration, an official of the Postal Clerks' Federation advocated prohibiting the immigration of "races considered incapable of assimilation into American life." Testifying in 1935 to a Senate committee, a Seamen's Union executive warned that Asian seamen on American merchant vessels were "the entering wedge in the domination by the yellow race over the white."[70]

The AFL pursued its anti-immigration philosophy on several fronts. First, it defended existing restrictions and doggedly resisted any liberalization of the immigration statutes. It lobbied in Congress to that effect and every election year petitioned the major parties to include pro-restriction planks in their platforms. As part of its hold-the-line attitude on immigration laws, the AFL opposed a quota system that would have had the effect of increasing Japanese immigration and also opposed emergency exceptions to permit European refugees fleeing fascist persecution to enter the country.[71]

Second, the AFL followed the lead of Andrew Furuseth and his Seamen's Union in calling for legislation to restrict the number of alien crew members on American-owned merchant ships. Not only did alien seamen take jobs from American seamen, but, the AFL argued, alien seamen left their ships as soon as they docked to take jobs illegally in the United States. The AFL bristled at the British ambassador and the United States Department of State for being against proposed measures restricting the hiring of alien seamen. In 1936, after 13 years of lobbying by organized labor, legislation finally was enacted mandating minimum percentages of United States citizens for the crews of certain types of ships.[72]

Third, the AFL fought immigration from the Philippines. Because the Philippines became a commonwealth of the United

States, Philippine exporters enjoyed access to American markets and Filipino nationals were permitted to work in the United States. Chafing under what it considered unfair competition from the Philippines, organized labor demanded independence for the Philippines, under which that country would lose privileges it enjoyed as a commonwealth. The 1934 Tydings-McDuffie Act granted independence to the Philippines under terms not entirely satisfactory to the AFL, inasmuch as independence was not scheduled to be given until 1944. Nonetheless, the AFL defended the Tydings-McDuffie Act, arguing, among other things, that an independent Philippines would not be imperiled by Japan. In 1935 and 1936, the AFL applauded Congress for appropriating funds to pay for up to 50,000 Filipinos to return to their homeland.[73]

Of somewhat less importance were two other items on the AFL's anti-immigration agenda. For years, Mexican immigration had been a sore point with the AFL. Starting in the 1920s and continuing through the 1930s, the AFL attempted to ameliorate that problem by encouraging the Mexican government to follow a policy of voluntary emigration restriction. And, as early as 1934, there was sentiment within the AFL favoring the mandatory registration of aliens—an initiative that gained momentum later in the decade, as the country moved closer to war.[74]

AFL leaders occasionally praised the role of the foreign-born in building American trade unions or recalled the ethnic roots of the rank-and-file when expressing sympathy for the relatives of American union members who were still living in fascist Europe. But as a matter of policy, the AFL was committed to keeping the foreign-born in the United States to a minimum. As one union official explained, "Labor's immigration policy is its 'tariff wall,'" and was necessary for the protection of the American worker.[75]

Finally, the AFL followed events in other countries as a reflection of America's own experiences. In strictly labor-related matters, there were many parallels. Foreign labor movements struggled for shorter hours, greater purchasing power, solutions to technological unemployment, low-cost housing, and public works projects, just as the AFL did. The similarities in problems and goals may have helped validate the AFL's own policies. The threat of mechanized production and the resulting need to increase employment by cutting hours and increasing consumption, for example, was not the concern of the AFL alone; it was, as the AFL reported in its *Weekly News Service* and other media, an issue of global significance, and the response of foreign labor was much the same as that of the AFL itself. Even America's immigration restrictions, supported so strongly by the AFL, could enjoy the imprimatur of similar immigration restrictions in Britain. Further, the foreign labor experience could offer instruction as well as validation: the AFL studied and praised innovative solutions to common problems devised overseas, such as cooperatives, minimum wage laws, and better methods of calculating unemployment.[76]

In particular, the AFL used the rise of fascism in Europe to illuminate ominous events in the United States. Many people and organizations, including the AFL, perceived that civil liberties in America were under attack during the Depression. Congress and state legislatures considered anti-sedition legislation. Some corporations employed private militias, spies, and other means to thwart labor organizations, in what the AFL characterized as a direct threat to freedom of speech and freedom of assembly. The AFL endorsed legislation to combat those abuses, opposed legislation that would have brought greater restrictions upon labor, and supported the work of Senator Robert LaFollette's Senate investigating committee that was seeking to expose unfair and anti-constitutional labor activities on the part of so-called "employer dictators." In urging democratic vigilance, the AFL often cited analogies in fascist Europe. Speaking at the Convention of the Ohio Federation of Labor in 1934, Green said "we become . . . alarmed as we look across the sea and there see the loss and surrender of freedom and democracy." He referred to the "atrocities" in Europe, he said, "only to show you what might happen if we are not vigilant." "Upon the ruins of the American Federation of Labor," he warned, "there would be built an organization more destructive than those erected upon the ruins of the Organized Labor Movement in the nations of Europe." The AFL may have been worried about the spread of fascism abroad, but it was probably more concerned about the rise of home-grown fascism, and its consequences for labor.[77]

The AFL's positions on foreign policy issues between 1932 and 1936 may have seemed divergent and contradictory. The AFL could espouse internationalist policies in one situation and isolationist policies in the next. It could even endorse internationalist policies in such a way as to achieve isolationist goals—as when its boycott of Nazi Germany served to advance the policy of economic nationalism.

The one constant that held true was that the AFL supported foreign policies that would promote the interests of organized labor. The AFL hoped that American labor standards would be raised through the isolationist policy of concentrating on the domestic market just as it hoped they would be protected through the internationalist policy of working with the ILO.

Throughout the period, the AFL was keenly aware of events beyond America's borders and how they could affect American labor. Yet it held back from making strong commitments to global action. Sometimes it supported isolationist policies. Even the internationalist policies it supported involved little real sacrifice or effort on the part of the AFL and made few demands upon American diplomacy.

Before 1937, the AFL was able to judge each foreign policy issue on its own merits. Then a new element came into play. The Congress of Industrial Organizations, which had begun as a splinter group within the AFL, had emerged fully as a rival national labor center. Thereafter, foreign relations matters were, in part, a factor in the warfare between the two labor organizations. Foreign policy positions were weighed to determine their possible influence over that warfare, which, in turn, helped push organized labor to supporting greater activism in American diplomacy.

Notes

1. See, for example, "Major Benefits of Recovery Appropriated by Employers," AFL *Weekly News Service*, November 7, 1936, and William Green statement, April 10, 1936, document no. G-491, "Magazine" file, series 11E, box 13, Green Papers.

2. Wayne S. Cole, *Roosevelt and the Isolationists, 1932-45*,(Lincoln: University of Nebraska Press, 1983), pp. 101-3; William Leuchtenberg, *Franklin D. Roosevelt and the New Deal, 1932-1940*, (New York: Harper and Row, 1963), pp. 199, 204;William S. Culbertson, *Reciprocity: A National Policy for Foreign Trade* (New York: Whittlesey House, 1937) p. 129; Lloyd C. Gardner, *Economic Aspects of New Deal Diplomacy* (Madison: University of Wisconsin Press, 1964) pp. 14, 24-5; Henry J. Tasca, *The Reciprocal Trade Policy of the United States: A Study in Trade Philosophy* (Philadelphia: University of Pennsylvania Press, 1938) pp. 85-6.

3. Culbertson, *Reciprocity*, pp. 126-37, 145-6; Gardner, *Economic Aspects*, pp. 9, 43-4; Charles A. Beard, *The Devil Theory of War: An Inquiry into the Nature of History and the Possibility of Keeping Out of War* (Westport, Conn.: Greenwood Press, 1972), pp. 120-24.

4. Gardner, *Economic Aspects*, pp. 24-8, 40-3; Culbertson, *Reciprocity*, pp. 126-37, 145-6.

5. Gardner, *Economic Aspects*, pp. 9, 27-8. 6Beard, *Devil Theory of War*, p. 124; Charles A. Beard, *The Idea of National Interest: An Analytical Study in American-Foreign Policy* (Chicago: Quadrangle Books, 1966), p. 438; George R. Leighton, "Beard and Foreign Policy," in Howard K. Beale, ed., *Charles A. Beard: An Appraisal*, (Lexington: University of Kentucky Press, 1954), pp. 166-67; Robert A. Divine, *The Reluctant Belligerent: American Entry into World War II* (New York: John Wiley and Sons, 1965), pp. 16-8.

7. Culbertson, *Reciprocity*, p. 131; Cole, *Roosevelt and the Isolationists*, p. 101; Leuchtenberg, *Roosevelt and the New Deal*, p. 204.

8. Culbertson, *Reciprocity*, pp. 132-33, 144-50; Adlai Stevenson speech, "The United States and Foreign Trade," May 18, 1936, box 2, Adlai E. Stevenson Papers, Seeley Mudd Library, Princeton University, Princeton, N.J.

9. Culbertson, *Reciprocity*, pp. 142-44; Leuchtenberg, *Roosevelt and the New Deal*, p. 204; Stevenson speech, "The United States and Foreign Trade," May 18, 1936, box 2, Stevenson Papers; Stevenson speech at Carlton College, October 23, 1936, Walter Johnson, ed., *The Papers of Adlai E. Stevenson* (Boston: Little, Brown and Company, 1972), I:342.

10. Gardner, *Economic Aspects*, pp. 39-40; Francis B. Sayre, *The Way Forward: The American Trade Agreements Program* (New York: Macmillan, 1939), pp. 29, 35; Richard N. Kottman, *Reciprocity and the North Atlantic Triangle, 1932-1938* (Ithaca, N.Y.: Cornell University Press, 1968), p. 5. Secretary of State Hull also hoped that reciprocal trading agreements between the United States and Great Britain would substantiate an Anglo-American harmony that would dissuade the Axis powers from aggression and deter war. See Kottman, *North Atlantic Triangle*, pp. 272-73.

11. "Jobless Millions and Low Wages Cause Nation's Ills, Green Says," AFL *Weekly News Service*, April 14, 1934; "Larger Buying Power for Employed Labor Urged by AFL to Relieve Unemployment," AFL *Weekly News Service*, August 4, 1934; "Frey Places Blame for Depression on Machinery and Inadequate Pay," AFL

Weekly News Service, May 21, 1932; "Raising Wages Only Way to Bring Real Recovery, Labor Points Out," AFL *Weekly News Service*, October 1, 1932; "Raise Consumer Buying Power!," AFL *Weekly News Service*, October 1, 1932; "William Green Testimony to Senate Committee on Education and Labor," April 21, 1936, document no. H-26, box 15, series 11E, Green Papers.

12. "Frey Places Blame for Depression on Machinery and Inadequate Pay," AFL *Weekly News Service*, May 21, 1932; "Shorter Work Week is the Only Real Unemployment Remedy," AFL *Weekly News Service*, June 19, 1937; "Green Urges Thirty-Hour Week . . . for the Cotton Textile Industry," AFL *Weekly News Service*, July 1, 1933; "Labor Saving Machinery Brought on Depression," AFL *Weekly News Service*, January 28, 1933; "30 Hour Week Made Labor's Paramount Objective by A.F. of L. Convention," AFL *Weekly News Service*, December 5, 1936; "Complete Support of Recovery Act to Provide Work and Wages for Idle Millions Urged by President Green," AFL *Weekly News Service*, September 2, 1933.

13. A.F. of L. Convention Proceedings Summarized," AFL *Weekly News Service*, January 9, 1937. Emphasis added.

4. "Shorter Work Week is the Only Real Unemployment Remedy," AFL *Weekly News Service*, June 19, 1937; "A.F. of L. Convention Proceedings Summarized," AFL *Weekly News Service*, January 9, 1937; "30-Hour Bill is Introduced," AFL *Weekly News Service*, January 19, 1935; "Government Fund for Unemployment Relief Necessary, Green Declares," AFL *Weekly News Service*, January 30, 1932; "AFL Asks Billion for Public Works," AFL *Weekly News Service*, May 21, 1932; "AFL Council Urges Roosevelt to Push 30-Hour Week and Five Billion Dollar Public Works Program," AFL *Weekly News Service*, May 6, 1933; "Millions of Jobs for Unemployed Created by Public Highways," AFL *Weekly News Service*, June 24, 1933; "A.F. of L. Survey Hits Profit Motive," AFL *Weekly News Service*, November 30, 1935; "Federal Housing Act is Stressed by Woll," AFL *Weekly News Service*, May 30, 1936.

15. "Labor-Saving Machines Brought On Depression; Professor Einstein Discounts influence of War Debts on Economic Conditions," AFL *Weekly News Service*, January 28, 1933.

16. "Manufacturers Favor Thirty-Hour Week," AFL *Weekly News Service*, January 14, 1933; William Green testimony to Senate Education and Labor Committee, April 21, 1936, document no. H-26, box 15, series 11E, Green Papers.

17. United States, Congress, House of Representatives, Ways and Means Committee, *Reciprocal Trade Agreements*, 73rd Congress, 2nd Session, March 1934, p. 261; Gardner, *Economic Aspects*, p. 27. John Frey further buttressed the anti-import argument with his assertion in 1928 that foreign loans could increase domestic foreign competition, enabling foreign companies to eat into America's domestic markets. See John P. Frey, "Foreign Loans and National Prosperity," *American Federationist* (July 1928), copy in file 127, box 9, John Frey Papers, Manuscript Division, Library of Congress, Washington, DC.

18. United States, Department of Commerce, *Statistical Abstract of the*

United States, 1940 (Washington: U.S. Government Printing Office, 1941), pp. 492-99; Arthur J. Goldberg, *AFL-CIO Labor United* (New York: McGraw-Hill, 1956), p. 26; Joseph G. Rayback, *A History of American Labor* (New York: Free Press, 1966), pp. 303, 355.

19. "Raising Wages Only Way to Bring Real Recovery, Labor Points Out," AFL *Weekly News Service*, October 1, 1932; "Big Business Reiterates its Unsocial Policies," AFL *Weekly News Service*, December 22, 1934.

20. Cole, *Roosevelt and the Isolationists*, pp. 102, 107-9; Gardner, *Economic Aspects*, pp. 41-2; Selig Adler, *The Uncertain Giant, 1921-1941; American Foreign Policy Between the Wars*, (New York: MacMillan Co., 1965), pp. 118-20.

21. Sayre, *The Way Forward*, pp. 139-41; Culbertson, *Reciprocity*, pp. 145-46; Raymond Leslie Buell, *The Hull Trade Program and the American System* (New York: National Peace Conference and Foreign Policy Association, 1938), pp. 26-7.

22. "Reynolds Metals Co. Grants Pay Boost Despite Foreign Aluminum Foil Dumping," AFL *Weekly News Service*, September 5, 1936; "Aluminum Tariff Cut Opposed by A.F. of L.," AFL *Weekly News Service*, April 2, 1938; "Deluge of Canadian Lumber Victimizes American Labor in the Northwestern United States," AFL *Weekly News Service*, November 20, 1937; Reduced Tariff on Canadian Aluminum Hit by A.F. of L.," AFL *Weekly News Service*, April 16, 1938; "Reciprocal Trade Pacts Menace Brewing Industry, Says Ornburn," AFL *Weekly News Service*, November 19, 1938.

23. See "Continued Drive Against Sweatshop and Foreign Goods Urged by Ornburn," AFL *Weekly News Service*, January 7, 1939.

24. United States, House of Representatives, *Reciprocal Trade Agreements*, p. 389; Sayre, *The Way Forward*, pp. 129, 135-38.

25. "Woll Urges Tariff Boosts to Bar Cheap Labor Imports," AFL *Weekly News Service*, February 4, 1933; "American Federation of Labor Convention Proceedings Summarized," AFL *Weekly News Service*, November 16, 1935; "Union Labor Goods Stressed by Ornburn," AFL *Weekly News Service*, January 2, 1937; "Thirty Hour Work Week Urged As job Creator for All," AFL *Weekly News Service*, January 25, 1936.

26. "Woll Urges Tariff Boosts to Bar Cheap Labor Imports," AFL *Weekly News Service*, February 4, 1933; "Union Labor Goods Stressed by Ornburn," AFL *Weekly News Service*, January 2, 1937.

27. "Union Label Goods Urged to Bar Foreign Products, AFLWNS, February 11, 1933; "Union Label Leagues Urged by Ornburn," AFL *Weekly News Service*, December 28, 1935.

28. "A.F. of L. Favors Tariff to Protect Oil Industry," AFL *Weekly News Service*, January 14, 1933;" "Woll Urges Tariff Boosts to Bar Cheap Labor Imports," AFL *Weekly News Service*, February 4, 1933; "American Federation of Labor Convention Proceedings Summarized," AFL *Weekly News Service*, November 16, 1935;" "Control of Prices, Wages, and Hours Recommended by

Industrial Council," AFL *Weekly News Service*, March 28, 1936; "Dumping Cheap Labor Clothing in Foreign Markets Subsidized by Polish Government," AFL *Weekly News Service*, December 9, 1933; "Japanese Glass Making American Workers Idle," AFL *Weekly News Service*, November 3, 1934; "Reynolds Metals Co. Grants Pay Boost Despite Foreign Aluminum Foil Dumping," AFL *Weekly News Service*, September 5, 1936; "Aluminum Tariff Cut Opposed by A.F. of L.," AFL *Weekly News Service*, April 2, 1938; "Deluge of Canadian Lumber Victimizes American Labor in Northwestern States," AFL *Weekly News Service*, November 20, 1937.

29. "Aluminum Tariff Cut Opposed by A.F. of L.," AFL *Weekly News Service*, April 2, 1938; "Deluge of Canadian Lumber Victimizes American Labor in Northwestern States," AFL *Weekly News Service*, November 20, 1937; "Reduced Tariff on Canadian Aluminum Hit by A.F. of L.," AFL *Weekly News Service*, April 16, 1938.

30. "Union-Made Goods Boosted by Ornburn," AFL *Weekly News Service*, December 14, 1935.

31. "German Steel Curb Decreed by Ickes," AFL *Weekly News Service*, November 18, 1935.

32. "U.S. Recognition of Soviet Russia Militantly Opposed by A.F. of L.," AFL *Weekly News Service*, April 22, 1933; "Green Opposes Soviet Union Recognition by the United States," AFL *Weekly News Service*, February 4, 1933.

33. American Federation of Labor, *Report of Proceedings of the Fifty-Second Annual Convention of the American Federation of Labor* (Washington: Judd and Detweiler, 1932), p. 439; American Federation of Labor, *Report of Proceedings of the Fifty-Fourth Annual Convention of the American Federation of Labor* (Washington: Judd and Detweiler, 1934), pp. 168-70; "Dubinsky Outlines Functions and Work of International Labor Organization," AFL *Weekly News Service*, June 1, 1935; "United States Must Take Leadership in Economic Freedom, Lewis Declares," AFL *Weekly News Service*, July 13, 1935.

34. John E. Windmuller, *American Labor and the International Labor Movement, 1940 to 1933*, (Ithaca, N.Y.: Cornell University Institute of International Industrial and Labor Relations, 1954), pp. 7, 11-13; Gary B. Ostrower, "The American Decision to Join the International Labor Organization," *Labor History* 16 (Fall 1975): 498; "Labor Backs All international Action That Aids Human Welfare," AFL *Weekly News Service*, October 1, 1932; John Bruce Tipton, *Participation of the United States in the International Labor Organization* (Urbana,: University of Illinois Institute of Labor and Industrial Relations, 1959), pp. 22, 25.

35. Tipton, *Participation of the United States*, pp. 4, 5, 10, 11; Antony Alcock, *History of the International Labour Organization* (London: MacMillan, 1971), pp. 25, 125.

36. Tipton, *Participation of the United States*, pp. 15-17, 22, 25-31, 35, 37, 40; Alcock, *International Labour Organization*, p. 125.

37. Tipton, *Participation of the United States*, pp. 32-4.

38. Ibid., pp. 33-4; AFL *1932 Proceedings*, pp. 439-40; "Labor Backs All

International Action that Aids Human Welfare," AFL *Weekly News Service*, October 1, 1932; "World's Unemployed Total 30,000,000," AFL *Weekly News Service*, February 4, 1933; "Machinery and Unemployment," AFL *Weekly News Service*, February 18, 1933; "World Hours-Cut Drive by Transport Workers," AFL *Weekly News Service*, September 3, 1932.

39. Ostrower, "American Decision to Join," pp. 498-503.

40. Ibid., pp. 502-3.

41. Memorandum of conversation between Francis Perkins and Harold Butler, January 9, 1935, file: "ILO, October and November 1934," box 74, Francis Perkins Subject Files, Labor Department Records, Record Group 174, National Archives, Washington, DC.

42. Ibid.; Wyzanski to the Secretary, December 24, 1934, file: "ILO, December 1934," box 74, Perkins Subject Files, RG 174.

43. Memorandum of conversation between Perkins and Butler, January 9, 1935, file: "ILO, October and November 1934," box 74, Perkins Subject Files, RG 174.

44. Ibid.

45. American Federation of Labor, *Report of Proceedings of the Fifty-Fifth Annual Convention of the American Federation of Labor* (Washington: Judd and Detweiler, 1935), p. 150.

46. Ibid., pp. 152, 155.

47. International Labor Organization, *Provisional Record, 19th Session, Geneva, 7th Sitting, June 7, 1935, General Discussion of Hours of Work*, June 7, 1935, pp. 97-9.

48. AFL, *1935 Proceedings*, pp. 152, 155-56, 696.

49. American Federation of Labor, *Report of Proceedings of the Fifty-Sixth Annual Convention of the American Federation of Labor*, (Washington: Judd and Detweiler, 1936), pp. 187-88.

50. Ibid., pp. 189-91.

51. Ibid., pp. 190-92; Perkins to Emil Rieve, May 19, 1936, file: "ILO-Maritime Conference, 1936," box 75, Perkins Subject Files, RG 174.

52. AFL, *1936 Proceedings*, p. 195; Tipton, *Participation of the United States*, p. 48.

53. AFL, *1936 AFL Proceedings*, p. 195; "40-Hour Week on Public Works Treaty Adopted by Geneva Labor Conference," AFL *Weekly News Service*, July 25, 1936. The AFL even hailed the mere consideration of a forty hour convention in the textile industry as a victory. See "American Labor Wins Victory in Geneva," AFL *Weekly News Service*, October 26, 1935.

54. "Dubinsky Outlines Functions and Work of International Labor Organization," AFL *Weekly News Service*, June 1, 1935; "United States Must Take Leadership in Economic Freedom, Lewis Declares," AFL *Weekly News Service*, July 13, 1935.

55. Tipton, *Participation of the United States*, p. 48.

56. AFL, *1936 Proceedings*, p. 188; Hiram Johnson to Perkins, October 21,

1935, file: "ILO: Maritime Conference—1935," box 74, Perkins Subject Files, RG 174; Perkins to Andrew Furuseth, November 9, 1935, file: "ILO, January-June, 1935," box 74, Ibid.

57. AFL, *1936 Proceedings*, p. 188; "Shall Seamen Have Holidays with Pay?," AFL *Weekly News Service*, October 10, 1936; "Merchant Ship Hours and Manning," AFL *Weekly News Service*, October 10, 1936; "United States Asks 3-Watch Ship Plan," AFL *Weekly News Service*, October 10, 1936; "48-Hour Week Voted by Sea Labor Parley," AFL *Weekly News Service*, October 31, 1936; "Many Measures Benefitting Seamen Adopted by World Maritime Parley," AFL *Weekly News Service*, November 21, 1936; "World Textile Meeting in U.S. is Held Likely," AFL *Weekly News Service*, November 14, 1936; "Green, Goodrich, and Dennison Are Among ILO Delegates to World Textile Parley," AFL *Weekly News Service*, March 13, 1937.

58. Maxwell C. Raddock, *Portrait of an American Labor Leader: William L. Hutcheson* (New York: American Institute of Social Science, 1955), pp. 188-91.

59. "Report to the Secretary of Labor on the First Pan-American Labor Conference . . . January 2-14, 1936," (23-page version), n.d., file: "ILO: Santiago Conference," box 47, Perkins Subject Files, RG 174; AFL *1936 Proceedings*, p. 189.

60. "Report to the Secretary of Labor on the First Pan-American Labor Conference . . . January 2-14, 1936," (23-page version), n.d., file: "ILO: Santiago Conference," box 47, Perkins Subject Files, RG 174.

61. Ibid.; Raddock, *Hutcheson*, p. 191.

62. Raddock, *Hutcheson*, p. 191; AFL, *1932 Proceedings*, p. 438; AFL, *1933 Proceedings*, pp. 138, 537-38; AFL, *1934 Proceedings*, pp. 169-70, 725; AFL, *1935 Proceedings*, p. 162; "American Capitalists Exploit Cuban Workers," AFL *Weekly News Service*, August 19, 1933; "Havana Dock Workers Win Union Recognition Strike," AFL *Weekly News Service*, August 26, 1933; "Labor Supports Cuban Struggle for Liberty," AFL *Weekly News Service*, November 4, 1933; "Colombian Railway Workers Strike Over Hours and Wages," AFL *Weekly News Service*, November 18, 1933; "Brazilian Strikers Win Audit of Railway's Books," AFL *Weekly News Service*, April 14, 1934; "Mexican Jobless Ask Relief," AFL *Weekly News Service*, January 23, 1932; "Government Troops Called in Mexican Miners' Strike," AFL *Weekly News Service*, March 19, 1932; "10,000 Jobless in Argentina," AFL *Weekly News Service*, April 2, 1932; "Tobacco Monopoly Planned by Government of Uruguay," AFL *Weekly News Service*, June 11, 1932; "Mexican Sugar Companies Fight Wage Boost Edict," AFL *Weekly News Service*, April 21, 1934; "Argentina Wins," AFL *Weekly News Service*, December 8, 1934; "Employers Must Be Fair to Labor, President Cardenas of Mexico Says," AFL *Weekly News Service*, May 11, 1935; "Chilean 'Socialism' Becomes Economic Planning," AFL *Weekly News Service*, September 10, 1932; "Telephone Strike Cost Cuban Company," AFL *Weekly News Service*, June 15, 1935.

63. AFL, *1932 Proceedings*, pp. 115, 438; AFL, *1934 Proceedings*, pp. 169-70, 725; AFL, *1935 Proceedings*, pp. 160-61; Sinclair Snow, *The Pan-American Federation of Labor* (Durham, N.C.: Duke University Press, 1964), pp.

36-8, 147.

64. AFL, *1932 Proceedings*, p. 115; AFL, *1933 Proceedings*, pp. 137-38; AFL, *1934 Proceedings*, pp. 170, 725; "A.F. of L. Convention Proceedings Summarized," AFL *Weekly News Service*, January 9, 1937; Snow, *The Pan-American Federation of Labor*, pp. 133, 142-43, 148-49.

65. AFL, *1933 Proceedings*, pp. 138, 537; AFL, *1934 Proceedings*, pp. 170, 725; "A.F. of L. Proceedings Summarized," AFL *Weekly News Service*, January 9, 1937; "Mexican Labor Delegation, Headed by Morones, Confers With Green," AFL *Weekly News Service*, July 20, 1935; "Facing the Facts with Philip Pearl," AFL *News Service*, May 27, 1939; "Inglesias Will Make Survey of Labor Movement in Latin-American Nations," AFL *News Service*, October 14, 1939; "Pan American Labor Federation Surveys Trade Union Movements In Latin America," AFL *Weekly News Service*, November 25, 1939.

66. Windmuller, *American Labor and the International Labor Movement*, pp. 11-13; "AFL Council Vetoes World Labor Parley," AFL *Weekly News Service*, February 6, 1932.; AFL, *1935 Proceedings*, pp. 156-59.

67. Windmuller, *American Labor and the International Labor Movement*, pp. 13-15; AFL, *1935 Proceedings*, pp. 158-60; "A.F. of L. Convention Proceedings Summarized," AFL *Weekly News Service*, January 9, 1937; "A.F. of L. Joins World Labor Body," AFL *Weekly News Service*, July 10, 1937; "Hitler's Anti-Labor Policy Denounced," AFL *Weekly News Service*, May 27, 1933.

68. John Higham, *Strangers in the Land: Patterns of American Nativism, 1860-1925*, (New York: Atheneneum, 1973), pp. 71-2, 163, 305-6, 321-22; David Brody, *Steelworkers in America: The Nonunion Era*, (New York: Harper and Row, 1969), pp. 136-37; Alexander Saxton, *The Indispensable Enemy: Labor and the Anti-Chinese Movement in California* (Berkeley: University of California Press, 1971), pp. 276-77.

69. "Smuggled Aliens and Unemployment," AFL *Weekly News Service*, May 27, 1933; "Roosevelt's Labor Record as President," AFL *Weekly News Service*, October 24, 1936; "Necessity for Rigid Immigration Restriction Explained by Flaherty," AFL *Weekly News Service*, October 29, 1932.; "6 to 9 Million Aliens in U.S., Dies Claims," AFL *Weekly News Service*, January 11, 1936; "Would Restrict All 'Commuting Aliens," AFL *Weekly News Service*, February 23, 1935; "Copper Company Dumps Idle Mexicans on County," AFL *Weekly News Service*, April 23, 1932.

70. "Unemployed Seamen Increase; Enactment of King-Dies Bill Would Give Them Jobs," AFL *Weekly News Service*, June 24, 1933; "A.F. of L. Declares War on Reds in the American Labor Movement," AFL *Weekly News Service*, August 25, 1934; "Aliens Rounded Up and Pickets Jailed in Outlaw Coal Strike," AFL *Weekly News Service*, March 26, 1932; "Necessity for Rigid Immigration Restriction Explained by Flaherty," AFL *Weekly News Service*, October 29, 1932; "Domination of American Shipping by Yellow Races Visioned," AFL *Weekly News Service*, April 27, 1935; "Labor Planks Submitted," AFL *Weekly News Service*, June 13, 1936. Also see AFL, *1933 Proceedings*, pp. 429-30.

71. "Republican, Democratic Platforms Are Both Unsatisfactory to Labor," AFL *Weekly News Service*, July 23, 1932, "Green Presents American Labor's Political Program to Republican National Convention," AFL *Weekly News Service*, June 18, 1932; "Labor Planks Submitted," AFL *Weekly News Service*, June 13, 1936; AFL, *1933 Proceedings*, pp. 103, 430; AFL, *1934 Proceedings*, pp. 87-8, 553; AFL, *1935 AFL Proceedings*, pp. 140, 268, 603.

72. "State Department and the Seamen's Bill," AFL *Weekly News Service*, August 10, 1935; "Roosevelt's Labor Record as President," AFL *Weekly News Service*, October 24, 1936; "Ship Subsidy Bill Aids Sea Workers," AFL *Weekly News Service*, June 27, 1936; "Smuggled Aliens and Unemployment," AFL *Weekly News Service*, May 27, 1933.

73. AFL, *1933 Proceedings*, pp. 429-30; AFL, *1935 Proceedings*, pp. 141-42; "Canadian Immigration Discussed by Hushing," AFL *Weekly News Service*, March 5, 1932; "Roosevelt's Labor Record as President," AFL *Weekly News Service*, October 24, 1936; DeConde, *History of American Foreign Relations* pp. 533-34.

74. "Mexico Divides 22,000 Acres Among Unemployed Workers," AFL *Weekly News Service*, June 11, 1932; Snow, *Pan-American Federation of Labor*, pp. 129-31; "Over 100 Resolutions Reach Great A.F. of L. Convention," AFL *Weekly News Service*, October 6, 1934.

75. "Walter M. Citrine Flays Dictatorships," AFL *Weekly News Service*, October 13, 1934; "Green Pledges U.S. Labor to Work for End to Nazi Attacks on Jews," AFL *Weekly News Service*, April 1, 1933; "Necessity for Rigid Immigration Explained by Flaherty," AFL *Weekly News Service*, October 29, 1932.

76. See, for example, "British Workers Must Secure Shorter Hours," AFL *Weekly News Service*, February 18, 1933; "Unemployment is Britons' Curse, British Union Official Says; Urges 40-Hour Week," AFL *Weekly News Service*, July 22, 1933; "English Labor Leader Hits Bosses' Hostility to Shorter Work Week for Jobless Relief," AFL *Weekly News Service*, August 15, 1933; "Labor-Saving Machine Kills Carpenters' Jobs," AFL *Weekly News Service*, December 16, 1933; "Shorter Hours Without Wage Reductions Asked," AFL *Weekly News Service*, March 26, 1932; "6-Hour Day Urged to Help Problem of Unemployment," AFL *Weekly News Service*, June 25, 1932; "European Employers Block 40-Hour Week," AFL *Weekly News Service*, August 11, 1934; "Wages," AFL *Weekly News Service*, August 11, 1934; "Labor's Control of New Zealand," AFL *Weekly News Service*, May 2, 1936; "Advantages of High Wages and Short Hours," AFL *Weekly News Service*, May 2, 1936; "Wage Fixing," AFL *Weekly News Service*, May 9, 1936; "New Zealand's Government's Policy Includes Many Plans to Benefit Masses," AFL *Weekly News Service*, June 27, 1936; "New Zealand Labor Asks Shorter Hours," AFL *Weekly News Service*, July 14, 1936; "Millions of Immigrants Here Illegally is Claim," AFL *Weekly News Service*, March 7, 1936; "3,000,000 Houses, Mostly for Persons with Small Incomes, Built in England," AFL *Weekly News Service*, August 29, 1936; "Canadian Labor Insists Workers Shall Share Increased Output Under Machine Production," AFL *Weekly News Service*,

January 16, 1937; "Unemployment Census in England," AFL *Weekly News Service*, March 18, 1939; "Scottish Cooperative Lands 400,000 Bacon Wrapper Order," AFL *Weekly News Service*, October 22, 1932; "Swedish Drill Helps British Idle," AFL *Weekly News Service*, October 22, 1932; "Low-Rent Housing Opened for Use of British Workers," AFL *Weekly News Service*, December 2, 1933; "Lottery Loan to Provide Funds for Public Works," AFL *Weekly News Service*, December 2, 1933; "Cooperatives Bar Fascism in England," AFL *Weekly News Service*, August 8, 1936; "Public Works Plan Started in France,"' AFL *Weekly News Service*, May 26, 1934; "Explanation of New French Labor Laws," AFL *Weekly News Service*, July 4, 1936; "Electricity Takes Over French Village," AFL *Weekly News Service*, January 23, 1937; "Danish Unions Resist 20 Per Cent Wage Cut," AFL *Weekly News Service*, March 5, 1932; "Belgian Unions Ask Wage Raise and 40-Hour Week," AFL *Weekly News Service*, March 12, 1932; "Polish Government Cuts Idle Insurance Benefits," AFL *Weekly News Service*, March 12, 1932; "48-Hour Edict Issued by Hungary to Quiet Labor," AFL *Weekly News Service*, July 6, 1935; "Cooperative System Aids Swedish Masses," AFL *Weekly News Service*, November 30, 1935; "Spanish Shipping Strike," AFL *Weekly News Service*, May 16, 1936; "Spanish Miners Win," AFL *Weekly News Service*, June 20, 1936; "Irish Unions Demand Public Works for Idle," AFL *Weekly News Service*, August 22, 1936; "Chilean 'Socialism' Becomes Economic Planning," AFL *Weekly News Service*, September 10, 1932.

77. Green speech to Ohio F.L., July 9, 1934, document no. B-311, "Speeches" file, box 2, series 11E, Green Papers; "Strike Right Affirmed," AFL *Weekly News Service*, June 23, 1934; "Union-Smashing and Strike-Breaking Activities of Detective Agencies and Labor Spies Exposed by Green," AFL *Weekly News Service*, April 18, 1936; "Labor Spy Inquiry," AFL *Weekly News Service*, May 23, 1936; "Full Right of Labor to Organize Urged by Federal Church Council," AFL *Weekly News Service*, September 5, 1936; "Alabama Labor Opposes Anti-Sedition Measure," AFL *Weekly News Service*, June 13, 1935; "A.F. of L. Convention Proceedings Summarized," AFL *Weekly News Service*, January 9, 1937; "$200,000 For Continuing LaFollette Labor Spy Probe Asked by American Federation of Labor," AFL *Weekly News Service*, January 30, 1937.x0

FOREIGN POLICY AS HANDMAIDEN: THE AFL AND THE CIO USE DIPLOMACY TO FIGHT A WAR, 1937-1938

PART II

Responding to the Rise of Totalitarianism

CHAPTER 4

William Hutcheson, President of the Brotherhood of Carpenters and Joiners, and John L. Lewis, President of the United Mine Workers, were both big, barrel-chested, middle-aged labor executives who were ready to poke somebody in the snoot when they had to. They were alike in many respects, bar one: Hutcheson was one of the labor movement's most adamant defenders of craft unionism, and Lewis was one of its most impassioned advocates of industrial unionism.

When Hutcheson used parliamentary procedure to try to silence a speech favoring industrial unionism at the 1935 American Federation of Labor (AFL) Convention, Lewis became agitated. Lewis and Hutcheson first exchanged angry words and then exchanged punches. Lewis suffered a torn shirt in what by all accounts was a personal victory; Hutcheson stalked out of the hall with a bloodied face and a fat lip.[1]

The scuffle between Lewis and Hutcheson accented long-simmering differences in the American working class movement. By 1938, the dispute had sundered the AFL and produced a rival association of labor unions: the Congress of Industrial Organizations (CIO). The split influenced organized labor's position on international affairs in at least two ways.

First, each of the labor organizations—but particularly the

AFL—attacked its rival for the positions it adopted concerning American foreign policy. Thus, foreign policy positions figured in the propaganda war between the AFL and the CIO as each body sought members and supporters within the United States. Certainly, the AFL and the CIO had different emphases or interests in the area of American diplomacy. The CIO stressed the importance of Latin America more than the AFL did, while the AFL was more oriented towards European matters than was the CIO. The AFL issued strong denunciations of the Soviet Union, whereas the CIO avoided almost any mention of that country. Both organizations took a generally favorable view of Great Britain, but the CIO was more likely to criticize Britain on occasion. The AFL, which was larger, older, and more stable, was able to take stands on many foreign policy issues about which the fledgling CIO remained silent. In truth, however, the AFL and the CIO differed little on global issues. On the dominant international theme of the era—the gathering war clouds in Europe and the Far East—the two labor federations were in agreement. They both unequivocally recognized the threat to world peace and even to the United States posed by the dictatorships (especially Nazi Germany), and they both groped for methods to halt the dictators' advance without drawing the United States into hostilities.

Second, the AFL and the CIO collided head on over international labor matters. The CIO fought with partial success for representation on the United States delegation to the International Labor Organization, but failed to win representation equal to that of the AFL. The AFL rejoined the International Federation of Trade Unions, largely in order to block CIO membership in that body. The CIO struggled to establish a toehold in Canada by chartering unions in that country. The AFL, which had organized extensively north of the border, fought back ruthlessly—and, to some extent, in disregard of the feelings and rights of the Canadians themselves. In Latin America, the CIO became an enthusiastic presence and allied itself with newly-formed labor organizations that were trying to displace established organizations that enjoyed AFL endorsement. In confronting each other across national borders, the AFL and the CIO were seeking dues-paying members for certain of its international unions, attempting to develop converts to their divergent philosophies of union organization, and trying to win whatever status and power came with recognition by international groups.

⊕ ⊕ ⊕

Traditionally, the AFL had been governed by a weak executive and composed of strong individual unions that enjoyed exclusive jurisdiction within narrowly-defined crafts or trades, such as carpentry, bricklaying, plumbing, and machine-building. That situation was well-suited to the economic system that existed in the late 19th century, in which highly-skilled and specialized craftsmen performed a limited number of functions, using simple technology, in small shops.[2]

American business evolved dramatically in the decades following the AFL's formation. Alongside small shops that each employed a few specialized craftsmen, sprawling and highly-automated factories appeared, employing hundreds or even thousands of workers in a wide variety of occupations and at all levels of skill. Industrial combines formed as mass production corporations tried to dominate a market for their products or ensure a source for their supplies. That meant that a steel worker in Pittsburgh could be toiling for the same employer as a coal miner in West Virginia. The new economic system put terrible strains on the AFL's form of organization. As job definitions blurred, craft-oriented unions fought each other for the right to organize skilled workers in different industries. Further, they typically failed to organize workers in mass production industries, despite their increasing significance in the modern workplace. As craft unions quarrelled, an alternative theory of labor organization was gaining popularity. It called for workers to organize themselves on an industrial basis rather than along craft lines. In a radio factory, for example, the industrial organization theory held that the carpenter who built the cabinet, the electrician who installed the tubes and wiring, and the laborer who packed the finished products into boxes should all belong to a single union. Under the craft alternative, however, the first employee would belong to the Carpenters'

Union, the second to the Electricians' Union, and the third to no union at all.[3]

Several unions within the Federation strongly favored industrial organization, including the United Mine Workers (UMW), Amalgamated Clothing Workers (ACW), International Ladies' Garment Workers' Union (ILGWU), United Auto Workers (UAW), and United Rubber Workers (URW). In addition, new federal legislation in the 1930s tended to facilitate industrial organization. Under the National Labor Relations Act, non-union workers were guaranteed the opportunity to organize. When they did, they overwhelmingly voted to join industrial rather than craft unions. As the AFL issued charters to new, industrially-organized Federal Labor Unions (FLUs), the opposing forces within the Federation debated whether those FLUs should be fused into permanent, industrial unions, or absorbed into existing craft organizations.[4]

Led by UMW President John L. Lewis, the industrial unions pressed the AFL for formal endorsement of the concept of industrial organization. The AFL's stormy 1935 convention, which got to see the Lewis-Hutcheson brawl, defeated several major resolutions calling for recognition of broad industrial jurisdictions. Immediately after the convention, Lewis met with other proponents of industrial organization, including David Dubinsky of the ILGWU, Sidney Hillman of the ACW, and Max Zaritsky of the Hat and Millinery Workers. They formed the Committee for Industrial Organization to promote industrial unionizing of workers in mass production industries. Although the Committee avowedly intended to carry out its educational and advisory functions within the AFL and according to the Federation's by-laws, craft union hardliners declared that the Committee's activities constituted an "insurrection." In September 1936 they prevailed upon the Executive Council to suspend all unions affiliated with the Committee. Over the next year, peace negotiations between the rival factions failed to heal the rift. Meanwhile, in March 1937, the Committee inaugurated organizing campaigns in the oil and textile industries and began chartering its own city and state branches, in direct competition with AFL branches.[5]

The Committee finally reconstituted itself as the Congress of

Industrial Organizations in October 1938, formally becoming a competitor to the AFL. But the CIO really had been an independent and competing body since its decision to start issuing charters the year before.

Throughout 1937, as the CIO progressed from a loose and renegade committee within the AFL to an autonomous association of labor unions, it acquired the machinery and prerogatives of an on-going enterprise. It hired staff, rented office space, collected dues, developed and began carrying out long-term strategies, and established its own weekly newspaper, the *CIO News.* It also began taking stands on political issues and international affairs.

Interestingly, when drawing the battle lines in his speech to the 1935 AFL convention, Lewis cited the international scene to justify the expansion of the industrial organization movement. For years, the AFL had been seriously disturbed by the fascist offensive against organized labor in Europe. In his speech, Lewis stated that if American labor did not strengthen itself, it would risk being wiped out just as organized labor had been wiped out in Germany and Italy. And industrial unionism, Lewis held, was a sure way of strengthening the American labor movement. In the ensuing years of struggle against the AFL, one of the CIO's favorite themes was that it furnished a bulwark against fascism by offering labor strong and aggressive leadership.[6]

Perhaps the first official pronouncements made by the CIO on international affairs appeared in December 1937. In one of the earliest issues of its national weekly, the CIO News, it condemned the Japanese invasion of China that had taken place earlier that year. Like similar AFL protests against the expansionism of the dictatorships, the CIO's criticism of Japan carried an obvious aspect of self-interest. The criticism of Japan was leveled by UAW President Homer Martin, who was also chairman of the CIO's Toy and Novelty Workers' Organizing Committee. His call to boycott Japanese-made toys during the Christmas season was hardly disinterested. A boycott obviously would lead to increased sales of American-made toys. "A Japanese-made toy for an American child," he intoned, "is a bomb for a Chinese child."[7]

The CIO credited its boycott with causing sharp reductions

in Japanese imports, particularly in toys, novelties, porcelain, and crockery. And it justified the boycott on both economic and political grounds, charging that competition from goods produced in Japanese sweatshops caused lowered wages for American workers.[8]

CIO opposition to Japan, of course, was not based solely on trade issues. In addition to protesting Japan's brutal imperialism, it also condemned the Japanese government for its anti-democratic character and for its attacks upon Japan's trade union movement. If all that were not enough, Japan was tainted further by its unholy alliance with one of the CIO's most hated domestic enemies—fervently anti-union industrialist Henry Ford, whose Japanese subsidiary invested in Japanese war bonds.[9]

The CIO denounced the fascist powers in Europe on much the same grounds as it denounced Japan. In the statements of its officials, editorials in its newspaper, and resolutions at its first convention (held in 1938), the CIO condemned Italy and Austria for suppressing organized labor, reducing its people to "economic and political bondage," and denying civil and religious liberties.[10]

The CIO reserved its sternest criticism for Nazi Germany. Calling German Chancellor Adolph Hitler a "mad, bloodthirsty wolf," John L. Lewis told the 1938 CIO convention that Nazi attacks upon the Jews were among "the most appalling events in history." He observed that the persecution of the Jews was preceded by the destruction of Germany's labor unions and warned that Hitler might have designs upon the Western Hemisphere. CIO Director John Brophy decried the "barbarities" and "savageries" inflicted by the Nazis not only upon the Jews but upon Catholics and other minorities as well. A cartoon in the *CIO News* in November 1938 showed the CIO and President Franklin D. Roosevelt armed with rifles and defending American democracy from a wolf that bore a swastika and was surrounded by skeletons labelled "religious and racial minorities" and "labor unions."[11]

The CIO held that the fascist threat was not confined to Europe or East Asia. As it condemned Japan's invasion of China, Italy's conquest of Ethiopia, Germany's absorption of

Czechoslovakia's Sudetenland, and the insurrection of Spanish fascists under Colonel Francisco Franco that threatened to topple republican government in that country,[12] the CIO expressed concern that fascist aggression might soon imperil the United States.

The CIO was as alert as the AFL to the menace of domestic groups and individuals that it considered to be pro-fascist and anti-labor. It charged that businessmen such as Tom Girdler of Republic Steel and Henry Ford, politicians such as Gerald L.K. Smith and Jersey City Mayor Frank Hague, governmental bodies such as the Un-American Activities Committee of the United States House of Representatives, and vigilante groups such as the Silver Shirts, the Black Legion, the Ku Klux Klan, and the Associated Farmers of California sought to intimidate organized labor. The means at their disposal included labor spies, private munitions arsenals, violent strike-breaking, company unions, false testimony, so-called "relief camps" for the unemployed, and anti-strike legislation. Also, the CIO was quick to point out—as was the AFL—that labor unions suffered the first attacks whenever fascism sought to crush democracy. Lewis stated on several occasions during 1937 and 1938 that although "reactionary employers . . . in great corporations" had not resorted to an open fascist offensive "as yet," the "outright dictatorship of big business" was a clear possibility for the United States. Philosophy, methods, and even direct communications linked American big business with the European and Japanese dictatorships. As an editorial in the *CIO News* argued, "embryonic" fascist organizations already were present in the United States, and "reactionary corporate interests" in America that fought organized labor at home were welcoming the advance of fascism abroad. Germany subsidized the Nazi Bund in the United States. Henry Ford not only trafficked in Japanese war bonds, he also had connections with the German government, which, the CIO headlined, decorated him with the Grand Cross of the German Eagle. The CIO had to endure strong criticism in the United States during its early years of existence, and it made a connection between that criticism and the growing strength of Berlin and Tokyo. Fascism, the CIO maintained, linked reactionaries in all countries, and the resistance faced by the CIO at home was allegedly part of a world-wide onslaught against democracy.[13]

Moreover, the fascist powers were gaining actual toeholds in the Western Hemisphere—specifically, in Latin America—and the CIO expressed grave concern over that. The CIO was acutely aware of circumstances in Latin America because of its close and deeply-valued ties with certain elements of the Latin American labor movement. The Confederacion de Trabajadores de Mexico (CTM) was a left-wing organization of industrial unions, based on the CIO model. Its leader, Vincente Lombardo Toledano, was called the "John L. Lewis of Mexico." Lombardo Toledano was active throughout Central and South America, and in 1938 he was elected president of the newly-formed Confederacion de Trabajoadores de America Latina (CTAL), a regional labor body. The CIO considered Lombardo Toledano, the CTM, and the CTAL to be important allies, and it supported them in their conflicts with Latin American labor groups that were friendly with the AFL.[14]

Taking such an active interest in Latin America, the CIO grew alarmed by the extent of fascist penetration in that part of the world. It reported on the ominous developments in the pages of the *CIO News* and in a major resolution approved at the 1938 convention. It pointed out that German, Japanese, and Italian commercial interests were "planting seeds of Fascism" with increasing amounts of capital investment in Latin America. It reported that one of Peru's most prominent bankers reputedly was an Italian Fascist and that the German counsel in El Salvador was head of the National Farm Loan Bank there. The CIO expressed alarm over the anti-Semitic and anti-democratic handbills from Germany that were flooding Brazil and Uruguay and the fact that German schools operated in Argentina. According to the CIO, Nazi cells were being organized in Brazil, Uruguay, Guatemala, and El Salvador, and some members even dared to wear their Nazi uniforms in public. Further, schools in southern Chile were operated by the German Ministry of Education and students there belonged to the Hitler Youth Movement; a labor organization inspired by the Nazi's German Labor Front was growing in Argentina; and European fascists had bankrolled unsuccessful political uprisings in Brazil and Mexico.[15]

The CIO responded in several ways to the growing fascist threat at home and abroad. Part of its response centered on domestic legislation, thereby dovetailing neatly with its economic reform program. The CIO argued that to stave off fascism in the United States it was necessary to attain economic democracy and to end the Depression. The CIO espoused a variety of measures to those ends, including federal jobs programs (such as the Works Progress Administration), housing subsidies, enhanced Social Security, wage and hour legislation, price ceilings, capital gains taxes, corporate debt regulation, and increased protection for organized labor under the Wagner Act. In 1938, UMW Vice President Philip Murray went so far as to assert that the economic legislation endorsed by the CIO had "saved" the United States from collapse. John L. Lewis, saying that fascism "feed[s] upon hunger," claimed CIO-backed proposals were necessary for American democracy to survive. And John Brophy credited the CIO with thwarting dictatorship by helping American citizens acquire material sufficiency. Thus, as Americans watched dictatorships claim much of Europe, the CIO trumpeted that it had saved American democracy by forestalling the economic collapse that would have invited fascism.[16]

If the looming specter of international fascism could be brought into play as a justification for domestic economic reform, then it also could help advance the CIO's campaign against the AFL. Just as "Fascism sprout[ed] from economic collapse [and] domestic strife," according to the CIO, it typically won its first victories against weak labor movements. If the United States were to avoid the fate suffered by European countries that had gone fascist after their labor unions had been crushed, it required a solidly organized labor movement with aggressive and determined leadership. The CIO argued that it could provide that kind of labor movement, but that the AFL could not. CIO Publicity Director Len DeCaux expressed that concept in a positively dazzling exhibition of mixed metaphors when he wrote, "the leadership of labor no longer rests in the faltering hands of a hidebound craft bureaucracy which would spinelessly bow before the storm and offer its neck as a stepping stone for Fascists to climb to power."[17]

Not only did the AFL fail to offer much security against fascism due to its craft-based organizational weaknesses; it was also a bad bet in the struggle, according to the CIO, because its top officials actually sympathized with the fascists! The CIO implied that AFL executives were in cahoots with reactionary businessmen and "Tory" politicians. Desperate to sustain outmoded craft organizations, the AFL allegedly engaged in such fascist tactics as strike-breaking and union-busting where industrial organization existed. It also opposed some of the pro-labor legislation that the CIO endorsed and refused to work for peace and unity in labor's ranks—again, supposed evidence of the AFL's fascist leanings. Although many of the disputes were quite parochial and limited to the very specific needs and desires of the two rival labor organizations, the CIO nonetheless put its contest with the AFL into an international context by associating the AFL with the worldwide fascist menace.[18]

When World War II erupted in Europe in 1939, the CIO's initial response was to demand that the United States maintain absolute neutrality. For more than a year, the CIO expressed growing dissatisfaction with the Franklin D. Roosevelt Administration, which it claimed was seeking to push the United States into the coalition against the Axis powers. In 1937-38, however, the CIO generally was supportive of the policies of the Franklin Roosevelt Administration. War was still only a prospect, the fledgling labor group felt threatened by fascism at home and abroad, and CIO Communists were not yet constrained by the German-Soviet Non-Aggression Treaty to oppose interventionism. Thus, the CIO endorsed Roosevelt's cautious leanings against the totalitarian states. But while some individual components of the CIO were quite specific about their objectives and the particular policies they endorsed, the national CIO was somewhat vague in the positions it took on foreign policy matters. It did not make the sort of commitment to anti-fascist initiatives that the AFL did.

In 1938, the CIO's first national convention approved several foreign policy resolutions that deplored fascism without offering specific prescriptions or making commitments. In one resolution, the CIO expressed its accordance with President Roosevelt's recent scathing denunciation of Nazi persecution of the Jews and subscribed "to the President's determination to prevent Nazism from gaining a foothold in the Western Hemisphere." In another resolution, entitled "Protection of Democracy," the convention cited the intention of Germany, Italy, and Japan "to impose their domination over weaker nations," and also discussed how those governments had denied civil liberties to their own citizens. The resolution then stated that the United States "should not give any aid or comfort . . . to these aggressor nations," and pledged "full support to legislation that would be formulated by the Federal Administration which would effectively carry through such a program." Finally, the resolution called upon President Roosevelt and the United States government to "cooperate with all other democratic nations in the protection and strengthening of democracy and democratic institutions."[19]

The "Protection of Democracy" resolution at the 1938 convention thus implied that the CIO favored a boycott of the fascist states (no "aid or comfort"), wanted changes in the neutrality laws so that the United States could aid in resisting the fascists ("full support to legislation" prohibiting aid or comfort), and supported the concept of collective security ("cooperate with all other democratic nations"). Advanced as those notions may have been in 1938, the CIO made no concrete policy recommendations and undertook no commitments. The CIO response to the fascists was confined primarily to protests leveled in convention resolutions and in the public statements of Lewis, Brophy, and its other leading officials.[20]

Except for its endorsement of an embargo against Japanese toys and novelties, and pro-boycott sentiments expressed by Lewis, the CIO did not officially organize or publicize any on-going boycotts of goods or services sold by fascist countries. In contrast, the AFL had ordered a full boycott against Germany in 1933, and in 1937 imposed one against Japan. Similarly, the CIO urged international cooperation against the fascists without pinning itself down as to what form that cooperation should take. The CIO's publicity director captured the CIO's spirit when he wrote that "the democratic countries need to draw closer together against their common peril" if "Fascist imperialism" were to be checked. And Lewis himself insisted that the United States could not "huddle within" its own borders and ignore "Fascist aggression in Spain, Fascist aggression in Austria, the dismemberment of Czechoslovakia, the rape of Ethiopia, [or] the Japanese aggression in China." He announced that "I stand forthright and openly committed to the proposition that only a policy of collective security can attain peace and defeat Fascism throughout the world." But nowhere did the CIO specify what such policies would entail.[21]

There were, however, a few references to the idea of international labor cooperation against fascism. Newspaper Guild President Heywood Broun, in his weekly *CIO News* column, criticized "mental isolation" and stated that "all American trades unionists should keep a weather eye on the affairs of Europe." But Broun's strain of internationalism rejected conventional diplomacy and even the League of Nations, calling instead for a "League of Labor" to take a hand in global affairs. And Lewis spoke of coordinated "popular action" and "labor action" world-wide to block fascism through boycotts against fascist products, refusal to manufacture or transport war materials to "aggressor nations," and resistance to fascist propaganda campaigns.[22] Beyond that, CIO pronouncements about international cooperation were not accompanied by systematic or clearly articulated policy proposals.

While the national CIO frequently was vague on foreign policy matters, individual components of the organization sometimes took more definite stands. The ILGWU's Dubinsky, in fact, opposed Nazi anti-Semitism as vigorously as anyone in the American labor movement. When the Nazis unleashed the "Kristallnacht" pogrom in November 1938, he and the ILGWU Executive Board tried to initiate a "thundering protest" by world labor "against these barbaric orgies." Dubinsky also cabled President Roosevelt, asking him to denounce the Nazi atrocities. More than two years earlier, Dubinsky helped organize the World Labor Athletic Carnival in New York City, in an effort to direct attention away from the 1936 Olympic Games that Adolph Hitler was using to showcase his Third Reich.[23]

In a controversial and dramatic speech in October 1937, President Roosevelt warned that fascist aggression made "escape through mere isolation or neutrality" impossible and might require the United States to cooperate with other law-abiding countries in imposing a "quarantine" against aggressors. Although Roosevelt was ambiguous about what form a quarantine would take, the speech indicated a clear-cut determination that the United States play a more positive role in international affairs and represented a break with the isolationists, who roared their disapproval. The national CIO avoided any official comment on the Quarantine Speech, but at least two affiliates of the CIO—the Woodworkers' Union and the Indiana State Industrial Union Council—explicitly endorsed it.[24]

Other specific policies were put forth by CIO affiliates. The Marine and Shipbuilding Workers and the Pennsylvania Industrial Union Council joined the Indiana Council and the Woodworkers in urging a revision of the Neutrality Act to permit the sale of arms to Republican Spain, for use in the battle against the fascist insurgency. The Rochester, N.Y., Industrial Union Council and the Cleaners and Dyers Union of New York City demanded a trade embargo against Nazi Germany. CIO Longshoremen in San Francisco on at least one occasion refused to load scrap iron on a vessel bound for Japan. The Amalgamated Clothing Workers, the International Ladies' Garment Workers' Union, and other groups raised relief funds or otherwise sought to aid European refugees. The Amalgamated, for example, was a regular contributor to the Joint Distribution Committee, which helped spirit refugees out of Nazi Germany, and also contributed to United China Relief. ILGWU President Dubinsky, meanwhile, was a trustee of the Refugee Relief Fund of the Coat and Suit Industry, which distributed hundreds of thousands of dollars to such groups as the Hebrew Immigrant Aid Society and the Pope Pius XII Catholic Relief Fund. The ILGWU also made sizeable donations—one as large as $30,000—to aid the anti-fascist Loyalist forces in the Spanish Civil War, and appropriated funds to assist the underground labor movements in Germany and Italy. The CIO did not adopt any of those assistance policies on the national level, but it may have at least shown concurrence with some of those policies to the extent of publicizing them in the pages of the *CIO News.*[25]

A rare example of national CIO support for a specific foreign policy in response to the fascist threat occurred when the 1938 CIO convention came out in favor of economic aid to Latin America. Central and South American countries could "thwart economic and political penetration of . . . Germany, Italy, and Japan," predicted the resolution, if the United States government extended credits that would enable those countries to purchase United States commodities. That, in turn, would elevate living standards in Latin America, "build up industry and agriculture in those countries, and provide a bulwark of American democracy."[26]

By equating the protection of democracy with the overseas sale of American products, the CIO may have implied a greater affinity than the AFL for economic internationalism. To be sure, the CIO championed many of the same domestic economic reforms espoused by the AFL—housing subsidies as pump primers, WPA and relief appropriations, enhancement of purchasing power, and job creation through shorter hours and regulation of machinery in the workplace. But the CIO was not as willing as the AFL to denigrate the significance of foreign markets as compared to the domestic market.[27]

The CIO did not issue any major policy statements on trade, perhaps because the battle over reciprocity already had been fought and the trade controversy was not as volatile in 1937 and 1938 as it had been a few years earlier. But it hinted at its appreciation of international trade. In a speech in September 1938, John L. Lewis stated that the United States was "unable to dispose of its products in [its] internal markets," that it had to "search out markets elsewhere," and that the "external activity of the economic system of the United States most certainly brings us into Europe and into Asia." In December 1938, Kathryn Lewis was a member of the United States Delegation to the Eighth Pan American Conference in Lima, Peru. Miss Lewis, daughter of the CIO president and an official of the organization in her own right, praised Secretary of State Cordell Hull, who was chairman of the delegation and the architect of reciprocity. She proclaimed that one of the most important achievements of the Lima Conference was the passage of a resolution to reduce trade barriers. And, in early 1937, the Steel Workers Organizing Committee (SWOC)—a primary component of the CIO and a bellwether of national CIO policy—countenanced the decision by United States Steel and Bethlehem Steel to join German, French, and Belgian steel companies in an international steel cartel, the Entente Internationale de L'Acier. The SWOC agreed to that in order to ensure the higher steel rates necessary for higher wages, and as a quid pro quo for union recognition and collective bargaining in the steel mills.[28]

As a final aspect of its response to the rise of fascism, the CIO's position on defense issues was ambivalent. To an extent, the CIO appeared to endorse greater military preparedness. Not only did the CIO recognize the threat posed to the United States by the fascist powers, it also anticipated a job boom—in certain industries, at least—and its unions were eager to capitalize on the situation. When the CIO championed non-interventionism in 1939-40, however, it expressly denied the likelihood of a job boom. Nevertheless, the Industrial Union of Marine and Shipbuilding Workers, at its 1938 convention, happily deliberated over ways and means for using the anticipated "great increase in employment" in shipbuilding to complete its organizing of workers in the field. Indeed, shipbuilding expanded as international tensions escalated. Workers at the New York, Brooklyn, Hercules, and Bethlehem shipyards enjoyed many gains: an end to the open shop in some yards, the elimination of company unions, the successful negotiation of pay raises and desirable contracts, and the introduction of collective bargaining.[29]

Still, the CIO knew that munitions production was a double-edged sword. Preparedness, in the words of the *CIO News*, gave employers the chance "to hide . . . anti-union activities behind an American flag." Even companies with federal contracts sought to evade mandates of the Wagner Act on the pretext of maintaining high levels of defense production. The War Department and the Navy Department opposed labor legislation that might delay defense orders. In response, the CIO sought assurances that all defense contractors comply with the National Labor Relations Act and demanded that labor have a voice in defense planning. Especially ominous, in the view of the CIO, was the Sheppard-Hill or "Industrial Mobilization" Bill (later known as the May Bill), which the House and Senate considered in 1937 and 1938. The legislation proposed to grant the military sweeping control over labor in time of war, would have authorized the government to dictate hours and wages, and would have outlawed strikes. Claiming that the bill would have conscripted labor and calling it "an attempt to subject American labor to a fascist regime in wartime," the CIO helped organize protests against it. Congress did not pass the law, but the issue of industrial mobilization continued to cause the CIO to be wary of military buildups.[30]

In addition, there was the ever-present conflict between defense spending and domestic spending. The significance of that question abated somewhat as time passed and the benefits of defense spending spread to non-defense industries, but in 1938 the CIO was concerned that preparedness might undercut the interests of its constituency. Money appropriated for defense appeared to be a loss for social reconstruction. The Southern Tenant Farmers' Union, for example, which belonged to the CIO's Cannery and Agricultural Workers, passed a resolution urging that a $1.25 billion appropriation for armaments be earmarked instead for the rehabilitation of landless farmers. And a resolution passed at the 1938 CIO convention asserted that "full employment" was America's "best natural defense," vowed to oppose curtailment of federal social services, and demanded that defense spending "be made above and beyond the full appropriations necessary" for the Works Progress Administration, the Public Works Administration, the housing program, and Social Security.[31]

Finally, the CIO championed an anti-war ideology, based on labor's unique concerns, not unlike that which the AFL had propounded for years. Essentially, it held that the working classes never benefitted from wars, that "wire-pullers" and diplomats and capitalists engineered wars, that workers toiled in the munitions factories and fought in the trenches without suitable rewards, and that wartime profits were siphoned off by the privileged. In the words of John L. Lewis, "The workers of this country will never make anything out of war. They will merely work and sweat and fight and die. Someone else takes the profits." From that perspective, preparedness could seem threatening. CIO representatives joined union officials from around the world in a 4-day anti-war congress in Mexico City in 1938, and the CIO publicized the anti-preparedness arguments of such international labor leaders as Leon Jouhaux of France, who maintained that workers should compel their governments to preserve peace by refusing to work for corporations that manufactured or transported implements of war.[32]

Corresponding with its revulsion against the fascist states was the CIO's generally indulgent attitude towards Europe's two great democracies, Britain and France. Not surprisingly, the CIO tended to focus on labor relations when looking at those countries—as it did when it looked at Germany and Italy.

The CIO frequently praised Britain for having among the most enlightened labor relations in the world. Unlike American employers, British employers did not hire labor spies or strike-breakers, according to the CIO. Moreover, the concept of collective bargaining was universally accepted in Britain, employers respected the right of workers to organize, and British unions, unlike those in the United States, were not subject to labor injunctions or anti-trust suits. An anti-strike law was on the books in Great Britain, passed in the wake of the traumatic 1926 General Strike. In the United States, opponents of the Wagner Act suggested that the British law could serve as a model for revising (and weakening) the Wagner Act. The CIO prized the Wagner Act highly, and took an immediate interest in the controversy. It pointed out that the British law was not applicable to the situation in the United States, that principles embodied in the Wagner Act were long-established in Britain, and that British labor relations, despite the anti-strike law, were more progressive than those in the United States. A presidential commission that visited Great Britain to study the anti-strike law concurred with the CIO's assessment, and the Wagner Act remained unsullied.[33]

Yet the CIO did not consider Great Britain to be entirely praiseworthy. While it applauded the strength of the British labor movement, it was also leery of the British Trades Union Congress (BTUC)—a craft-based organization with close ties to the AFL. It was critical of British economic interests overseas, particularly in Latin America. And in a caustic swipe at both the foreign and domestic policies of Britain's Conservative government, the CIO called upon Prime Minister Neville Chamberlain to start "appeasing" the growing ranks of unemployed Englishmen.[34]

Similarly, while occasionally criticizing the French government for such actions as its attack on the forty-hour work week, the CIO presented labor relations in France in a generally favorable light. In particular, the CIO established a rapport with France's national union center, the Confederation Generale du Travail (CGT). There were several reasons for CIO-CGT compatibility. Communists were well represented in both organizations. Industrial unions predominated in the CGT as they did in the CIO. In 1937 and 1938, the CGT was at least as ambivalent as the CIO was about military preparedness—unlike the British TUC, which was growing increasingly bellicose toward the fascist powers. The CIO reacted approvingly to CGT policies (and vice versa), welcomed CGT President Leon Jouhaux to the United States in 1938, joined the CGT in support of Mexico's CTM, and, at its first convention, exchanged fraternal greetings with the CGT. In controversies within the international labor community, the CGT became the CIO's ally against the AFL and the British TUC.[35]

The foreign countries that the CIO monitored most assiduously, however, were those of Latin America. Its involvement with fellow confederations of industrial unions in Latin America gave the CIO its first wholly positive exposure to the international labor movement. Moreover, the CIO recognized that the economic well-being of its own members was affected by the economic well-being of Latin American workers. It also saw that Latin American workers faced many of the same opponents as did workers in the United States—i.e., the Ford Motor Company, Standard Oil, and other multi-national corporations.[36]

CIO interest in Latin America centered on Mexico's CTM—

the organization of industrial unions led by Lombardo Toledano, who was Latin America's most charismatic labor leader. The CIO and the CTM believed they had many common interests. As John Brophy said, "Every time the Mexican workers make an advance . . . it is an advance for [CIO workers]." Organizational gains and higher standards of living for Mexican workers, in other words, helped secure organizational gains and higher living standards for workers in the United States. Thus, the CIO and the CTM collaborated with each other. They supported each other's strikes, exchanged fraternal delegates, and praised social reform legislation enacted in each other's countries.[37]

The CIO's interest in Latin America extended beyond labor relations in Mexico. It gave encouragement to the struggling labor movement in Cuba, and in January 1939 sent a delegate to the first National Congress of Cuban Workers to be held in many years. It participated in the development of the Lombardo Toledano-inspired regional labor organization, the CTAL. It urged the reduction of trade barriers and the extension of foreign aid to Latin American countries in order to facilitate commerce between the United States and Latin America. And, of course, it warned of ominous moves in Latin America by Germany, Italy, and Japan.[38]

In 1937 and 1938, then, the main themes in the CIO's pronouncements on world affairs concerned Latin America, the gathering war clouds in Europe and Asia, and the state of labor relations in the chief fascist and democratic states of Europe. Except for those issues, the CIO took little notice of events in other countries—except for a handful of references to labor advances in other countries, such as Sweden, and extensive attention to labor relations in Canada, where it was actively chartering union locals.[39]

Particularly conspicuous by its absence was a CIO position on the Soviet Union. During its first two years of existence, the CIO avoided making official comments on the Soviet Union's role in European diplomacy, its labor movement, or its relations with the United States.[40]

The CIO may have been circumspect with regard to the Soviet Union because it was in a highly sensitive position on the issue of communism. Calling for more radical reforms than the AFL, the CIO was attractive to many American Communists and communist-sympathizers. Eager to supplement membership rolls, the CIO encouraged its unions to recruit Communists. Communists soon dominated several CIO unions, including the Mine, Mill, and Smelter Workers, the West Coast maritime unions, and elements of the United Electrical Workers. They enjoyed substantial influence in many other unions. Confident that they could purge the Communists once the CIO was on its feet, anti-communist CIO leaders such as Lewis filled important jobs at CIO headquarters with Communists who offered the young organization badly-needed executive experience. Among them were Lee Pressman, who became the CIO's General Counsel, and CIO Publicity Director Len DeCaux.[41]

As a result, the CIO found itself subject to stinging criticism. Thrown on the defensive by red-baiting, the CIO was forced to issue denials that it was a communist organization and to plead for recognition of its patriotism. "The CIO," protested Heywood Broun, "need not play second fiddle to any group in its devotion to Americanism." The CIO also launched an attack upon the House Un-American Activities Committee, whose probes—sometimes aided by the AFL—zeroed in on both real and imagined communist influences in the CIO. Yet at the same time, the CIO had to protect Communists in top positions in order to avoid destabilizing the entire organization.[42] Given the CIO's vulnerability on the issue of communism, its leaders apparently considered it prudent to refrain from discussing the Soviet Union.

For the AFL, on the other hand, the Soviet Union—and its contacts with the CIO—was a favorite topic. When the CIO was formed at the pivotal 1935 AFL convention, John L. Lewis argued that industrial unionism promised a better defense against fascism than did craft unionism. In response, AFL conservative John Frey told the convention that industrial unions were the tools of dictatorships, including those in Germany, Italy, and the Soviet Union. In its dispute with the CIO, the AFL liked to assert that the CIO was undemocratic—Lewis being portrayed as American labor's version of a European strongman—and that the CIO was riddled with Soviet influence.[43]

Just as the CIO attempted to associate the AFL with the European fascists,[44] the AFL tried to associate the CIO with the Soviet Union. But whereas the CIO relied on analogies, the connection of AFL leaders with domestic right-wing spokesmen, and claims that craft unionism was a weak defense against fascism, the AFL pointed to direct ties between the CIO and Moscow. The AFL charged that the CIO and its political cohort, Labor's Non-Partisan League, were both under the domination of "Moscow-trained Reds" who took orders from the Comintern and who were seeking to overthrow the United States government. It accused top CIO leaders such as Lewis and Broun, who were not actually Communists, of being communist stooges. The 1937 AFL convention asserted that "lurking within . . . the CIO is not only an alien philosophy" but also a determination to cause the United States "to bow to the will of an alien government." The sit-down strike and other controversial tactics, in the estimation of the AFL, were aided by the Communist Party of the United States in order to set the stage for a revolutionary uprising and the establishment of the dictatorship of the proletariat. In contrast with the CIO, the AFL was a vigorous supporter of the House Un-American Activities Committee, and in 1938 AFL Metal Trades Director John Frey furnished the committee with the names of hundreds of CIO officials that he alleged were Communists or communist sympathizers.[45]

Communist influence within the CIO was not merely a threat to domestic stability, the AFL argued; it also menaced America's international relations. The AFL raised the specter of pro-communist CIO unions abetting Soviet foreign policies, thereby endangering American diplomacy. As an example, the AFL suggested that in the event of a war between the Soviet Union and Japan, CIO longshoremen on the West Coast might contribute to the Soviet war effort by refusing to handle goods bound for Japan.[46]

Linking the CIO with the Soviet Union was part of a larger campaign that held that the conflict between the AFL and the CIO was not one of craft organization versus industrial organization. Rather, the dispute involved democracy versus dictatorship.

The AFL maintained that it was an organization based on the principle of majority rule, whereas the CIO was an autocracy that wanted to extend autocratic rule to the entire labor movement and even to the country as a whole. By virtue of its alleged anti-democratic stance, the CIO was analogous to all the European tyrannies—Communist, Fascist, or Nazi. Not only, then, did the AFL link the CIO with Moscow, it also likened it to Berlin and Rome. At the 1937 AFL convention, John L. Lewis was called "The Man on Horseback." Lewis Hines, the well-known social critic of the Progressive Era who, in 1938, was the AFL's Director of Organization, said the CIO president was "a combination of the arrogance of Hitler and the impudence of Mussolini." At the same time that the AFL charged that the CIO's sit-down strikes were the work of Communists, it also argued that sit-down strikes were a tactic of fascism. Coupled with assertions such as those were warnings that fascist tactics presaged fascist labor unions, and fascist unions spelled the end of free labor organization. "There are no democratic trade unions in Italy," AFL President William Green reminded delegates to the 1937 AFL convention. Earlier, at a meeting of aluminum workers, Green had said that the AFL was fighting against Lewis and the CIO to ensure that there would not be "a Hitler or a Mussolini in the labor movement in America."[47]

The CIO responded that it, and not the AFL, represented the majority views of American labor. The AFL leadership—with its "Tory" policies—was badly out of step with its own rank and file. According to the CIO, the "democracy versus autocracy" struggle as portrayed by the AFL was false.[48] But the CIO did not match the expertise and determination of the AFL in tying its opponent's tactics and philosophies into the chilling events taking place overseas.

AFL contentions that the CIO was an ally of Moscow coincided with the AFL's campaign against the Soviet Union. In addition to claiming that the Soviet Union was responsible for labor unrest involving the CIO, the AFL castigated the Soviet Union for being a dictatorship that was no different from those in Germany and Italy, for being a threat to American security, for prohibiting free labor organization among its own people, and for imposing unfair working conditions on labor. In 1938, the AFL blocked the entry of Russian trade unions into the international labor community.[49]

The AFL's attitude towards the Soviet Union in 1937 and 1938, then, was the same as it had been earlier in the decade. The same was true of the AFL's attitude towards the fascist powers. The AFL expressed its horror over the terrorism of Spanish Fascist leader Francisco Franco and protested Italy's destruction of domestic trade unions and its invasion of Ethiopia. William Green called Adolph Hitler a "desperate madman" for imposing a "reign of terror" upon his people, obliterating freedom in Germany, and ruthlessly persecuting the Jews and Catholics. As in previous years, AFL leaders emphasized the brutal suppression of the German labor movement and the horrible conditions under which Germany workers suffered. In 1937 Green cabled a personal but vain plea to the German Chancellor to spare the lives of two German union executives who had been sentenced to death. In a 1938 radio address, shortly after Germany had forced the partition of Czechoslovakia, AFL Vice President Matthew Woll warned that the Nazis threatened everyone, not just Jews, and urged that the American people join in building a "moral ring" that would isolate Germany until Hitler's "murderous dictatorship" collapsed.[50]

The AFL continued to rely on a trade boycott as the weapon that would bring Germany to heel. It urged individual unions to lend a hand by forming their own boycott committees against German goods and services. The AFL had instituted its boycott in 1933. Five years later, with no apparent sense of irony, Green argued that the effectiveness of the boycott in creating economic distress in Germany was proved by Hitler's decision to seize Jewish assets.[51]

In 1937, the AFL announced a boycott against Japan. Adopted with the encouragement of the British TUC, the AFL boycott was intended to protest Japanese invasion of China. It was a "moral weapon," Green said, against the "aggressive, indefensible" war Japan was waging, punctuated by air raids upon innocent civilians. Refusing to buy Japanese products would have a telling impact, according to the AFL, because Japan was able to finance its war effort against China "only through dumping into the United States and other countries the products of exploited workers who are paid the equivalent of less than 5 cents per hour."[52]

Faith in the mechanism of the trade boycott reflected an unsophisticated economic determinism that pervaded AFL thinking on the issue of relations with the fascist states. William Green even reduced Hitler's motives for persecuting the Jews to simple economic blackmail. Hitler was "holding the German Jews captive like a kidnapper," the AFL president suggested, in order to exact "ransom" from the rest of the world in the form of advantageous trading arrangements! And when the AFL extended the boycott to include Japan as well as Germany, it cited, of course, Japan's brutal invasion of China. But it laid greatest stress upon Japan's increasingly serious economic competition against the United States. Calls to stanch the flow of commercial profits to the Japanese war machine were replete with condemnations of Japanese economic policies. Bicycles, pottery, and other products of what the AFL misnamed "coolie labor" flooded American markets. According to the AFL, Japanese fishing fleets invaded American waters and threatened the Northwest salmon industry. Further, Japan restricted American imports, with devastating effects upon West Coast lumber workers in particular. The Boilermakers' delegate to the 1937 AFL convention pointed out that even the souvenirs sold as "Colorado stone" at Rocky Mountain resorts were made in Japan. Ohio ceramics workers had long chafed under Japanese competition; when they inaugurated the boycott in December 1937, they lit huge bonfires of Japanese merchandise "to emphasize their resentment against Japan"—and perhaps to underscore their relief at having an excuse to take action.[53]

The boycotts were compatible with the AFL's position on international commerce, which was highlighted by a continued opposition to reciprocal trading arrangements. Indeed, "Buy American" banners waved alongside "Boycott Japan" banners at union rallies. The Federation's skepticism about benefits to be derived from increased foreign trade reflected its renewed commitment to the belief that prosperity was dependent on domestic factors. The AFL reasserted that its program of housing subsidies, price controls, shorter hours, increased purchasing power, and buying American-made union goods, was more essential for the country's economic health than international trade.[54]

Complementing its boycotts against Germany and Japan, the AFL operated relief programs for the victims of fascist aggression and offered praise to the democratic countries that might one day face aggression themselves. Since 1934, the AFL had managed the Labor Chest for the Liberation of Europe, which dispensed aid to refugees and issued publications exposing the villainy of Nazi Germany and Fascist Italy. In January 1938, it established a parallel organization to assist Chinese war victims, Labor's Committee for Civilian Relief in China. Matthew Woll was chairman of the committee, Green was honorary chairman, and nearly 100 AFL executives were members of the committee. In November 1938, the AFL announced its sponsorship of another anti-totalitarian relief organization, the League for Human Rights, Freedom, and Democracy. Also chaired by Woll, the League intended "to support freedom and democracy and to oppose every attempt to promote autocracy or to deny human rights" anywhere in the world. Asserting that "Democracy can make no compromise with autocracy," Woll said the group would uphold the principles of the United States Constitution against Communism, Fascism, and Nazism alike.[55]

Meanwhile, the AFL reminded its rank and file of the interests that the European democracies and the United States shared by contrasting the oppression of labor in the fascist countries with the generally enlightened labor relations in France and Britain. Beyond cultivating sympathy for them in the United States, the AFL gave direct encouragement to the European democracies. In a shortwave radio transmission to the United Kingdom in April 1938, Green declared that the AFL stood "with the working people of the British Empire in a common cause for world decency and in defense of economic, racial, religious, and political freedom." At its annual conventions, the AFL provided a friendly forum for representatives of the Britain's national labor center, the TUC. They used the opportunity to state the British case and even call for rearmament and the application of collective security measures involving the United States against the fascists.[56]

In at least one area, however, the AFL registered opposition to British diplomatic policy. The AFL was a strenuous advocate of a Jewish homeland in Palestine—perhaps because it would help solve the plight of European refugees whom the AFL was loathe to admit into the United States. Great Britain, which had held the mandate over Palestine since the World War, cautiously had endorsed the idea of Jewish homeland in the Balfour Declaration of 1917. The 1923 partition of Palestine that created an Arab Transjordan had whittled down the potential Jewish homeland, and in 1937 the British proposed another partition that would have reduced further the area available for Jewish settlement. Calling the partition an "inexcusable act of political surgery" and "an act of cruel persecution" against the Jews, William Green disputed British contentions that Palestine had been Arab territory before the war and pointed to the vast improvements the Jews had made to Palestine since the war. He said that the United States had consented to the British mandate only because it promised a national homeland for the Jews. The AFL leader urged "the Christian people of the United States" to take "militant action" against the partition proposal. "Instead of permitting Palestine to become a haven of refuge for the oppressed Jews of Poland, Germany, Romania, and elsewhere," said Green, "Great Britain proposes to limit the Jews to a small territory scarcely large enough for those who have already settled there." At the same time, the AFL insisted that no refugees be allowed into the United States over and above existing immigration quotas.[57]

As it did in the earlier part of the decade, the AFL equivocated on the issues of military preparedness and the official, governmental response to fascist aggression. It endorsed concepts of international law but shied away from governmental efforts to enforce them. It decried excessive military spending but upheld the importance of national security. It called for American neutrality but rejected the pleas of some of its member unions to adhere explicitly to isolationist policies.

In 1937 and 1938, the AFL criticized large appropriations for naval preparedness and argued that the money would be better spent on public housing. Expressing alarm over the escalating international armaments race in 1938, the Federation pledged "to work actively with the labor movements of the world" to promote disarmament. It urged national economic planning that would avoid "unnecessary production" of armaments and instead create jobs in industries that produced consumer goods. Echoing the CIO, the AFL opposed the Sheppard-Hill legislation being considered by Congress in 1937 and 1938, on the grounds that it would impose conscription of labor for war production and eliminate protections accorded workers in defense industries under the Walsh-Healey Act and the National Labor Relations Act. The AFL continued to propound a mildly class-conscious interpretation of war, holding that workers suffered most and capitalists benefitted most from war. It proposed heavy taxes on war profits, called for the construction of naval vessels in government shipyards rather than privately-owned ones, and endorsed a congressional proposal to draft money and property in wartime. And even as the AFL advocated "concerted action between free peoples" to ensure international security and defend the peace against countries that would violate international laws and treaties, it demanded that the United States reaffirm its tradition of avoiding entangling alliances and that Congress strengthen the neutrality laws.[58]

Moreover, the AFL resisted efforts to propel its opposition to the fascist powers beyond simple condemnations and voluntary boycotts. At the 1937 convention, the predominately black Brotherhood of Sleeping Car Porters pushed for the predominately white AFL to adopt stern measures against Italy for its occupation of Ethiopia. It wanted the AFL to go on record as insisting upon Italian withdrawal from that African country and demanding the restoration of Emperor Haile Selassie's throne. Further, Sleeping Car Porters' President A. Philip Randolph argued that "Italy ought to be boycotted, just as Germany is boycotted," and "if we can boycott Japan . . . we ought to develop a boycott against Italy." The Resolutions Committee, however, sidetracked the proposals, stating that the provisions of the railroad porters' resolution were too broad to be achieved by AFL action. It further explained that the Federation had already expressed its sympathy for Ethiopia and had protested the invasion. Also at the 1937 convention, the Resolutions Committee blocked a recommendation that the Federation endorse a proposed government-imposed boycott of Japan, considering it inappropriate to "add to the heavy and critical responsibility of the Department of State at this time."[59]

In January 1938, the AFL Executive Council refused an invitation from French labor leader Leon Jouhaux to send a representative to the World Boycott Conference. At the same time, it rejected a proposal from the International Federation of Trade Unions to enlist governments in the embargo against Japan, explaining that it opposed any step that might involve the United States in a war. Then, at the 1938 convention, the Resolutions Committee killed two resolutions offered by the Hotel and Restaurant Employees' Alliance and the Bartenders' League to support intergovernmental cooperation to quarantine aggressors, supposedly in the spirit of President Roosevelt's "quarantine speech." The Resolutions Committee said that the resolutions were unsound, unworkable, and likely to precipitate military action.[60]

If the AFL stymied efforts to push it into adopting an explicitly interventionist posture, it also rejected an isolationist course. In 1937, Americans debated a constitutional amendment proposed by United States Representative Louis Ludlow that would have required a public referendum before Congress could declare war. Although the House of Representatives buried the amendment by a narrow vote in January 1938, public opinion polls showed that upwards of 73 percent of the American people supported the measure. At the 1937 AFL convention, the Chicago Federation of Labor and the Illinois State Federation of Labor introduced a resolution in support of the Ludlow Amendment. The Resolutions Committee squelched the move. At that same convention, the AFL rejected other isolationist resolutions. The International Printing Pressmen's Union called unsuccessfully for the collection of wartime debts owed the United States by its allies from the World War—an action that inevitably would have weakened the European democracies. The Resolutions Committee expressed "complete sympathy" with the spirit of the resolution, but flatly announced that it was "not prepared to take definite steps" to collect the debts. And the California State Federation of Labor offered a resolution demanding that the manufacture of war materials be prohibited, excepting those to be used for the defense of the United States. The convention voted the resolution down, with the Resolutions Committee claiming that it was impractical. According to the Resolutions Committee, "every article of life"—from chemicals to surgical instruments to pig iron—could be identified as war material. Finally, the AFL set aside its criticisms of defense spending to praise military construction projects carried out in accordance with the Walsh-Healey Act, and the Executive Council announced its opposition to the proposal of some labor groups to call a general strike in the event of war.[61]

Whereas some components of the AFL began to dissent slightly from the Federation's policies on military preparedness and the American response to the tensions in Europe and East Asia, there seemed no weakening of the AFL's anti-immigration consensus. One aspect of that, of course, was the AFL's objection to the raising of immigration quotas in order to permit an influx of European refugees. The AFL also supported legislation to prohibit alien employment on relief projects and to require merchant marine crews to be made up of United States citizens. The AFL was most strident in its opposition to Asian immigration. On a least one occasion, an AFL union staged a march to protest the alleged anti-union sympathies of those of Oriental extraction. The AFL battled against efforts to weaken the 1924 Asiatic Exclusion Law and applauded a special appropriation to the Labor Department in 1937 to pay travel expenses for Filipinos in the United States who agreed to return to their native land. In addition, the AFL came out in 1937 against statehood for Hawaii, on the grounds "that a great majority of the population are Asiatics of doubtful loyalty to American ideals and of equally doubtful material for citizenship."[62]

The immigration issue was a point of contention in the struggle between the AFL and the CIO. The CIO generally was more favorable to immigration than the AFL, urging protection for the civil liberties of aliens and supporting reduction in naturalization fees. When it urged changes in the immigration laws to permit the naturalization of Filipinos, so that they could qualify for jobs aboard American vessels, the CIO drew AFL criticism. The CIO position threatened the jobs of thousands of American seamen, claimed the AFL. Moreover, it reopened the whole question of Asiatic exclusion. "If Filipinos are granted the right to naturalize," warned Paul Scharrenberg, legislative representative of the AFL's International Seamen's Union, "such privilege must obviously be granted to the Asiatic, including the Japanese." The AFL Executive Council added that if Filipino seamen were granted "special rights of naturalization then "American opponents of Asiatic exclusion would have a new alibi for a campaign to modify our present effective exclusion laws."[63]

The global interests of the AFL and the CIO were not limited to issuing comments on world affairs and using foreign policy issues to attack each other. The AFL and the CIO were both actively involved in the international labor movement and they competed for power and influence in Latin America and Canada.

Notes

1. "Labor: A.F. of L. Meeting Ends in Words, Blows, and Finally Peace," *Newsweek*, October 26, 1935, p. 11.

2. Irving Bernstein, *Turbulent Years: A History of the American Worker, 1933-1941* (Boston: Houghton-Mifflin, 1970), pp. 352-53.

3. Ibid., pp. 353-63.

4. Ibid., pp. 355, 359, 368, 398; Philip Taft, *The A.F. of L. From the Death of Gompers to the Merger* (New York: Harper and Brothers, 1959), p. 178.

5. Bernstein, *Turbulent* Years, pp. 359-68, 386-401; Taft, *Gompers to the Merger*, pp. 162, 165-67, 173-78, 183, 187, 190, 193-98.

6. Bernstein, *Turbulent Years*, p. 391; "Looking Ahead," *CIO News*, December 7, 1937, p. 2.

7. "Union Group Urges Boycott of Jap Toys," *CIO News*, December 22, 1937.

8. "Jap Exports Down," *CIO News*, February 26, 1938, p. 4; "30 Cents-a-Day

Pay for Kids," *CIO News*, July 16, 1938, p. 7.

9. Congress of Industrial Organizations, *Proceedings of the First Constitutional Convention of the Congress of Industrial Organizations* (Pittsburgh: CIO, 1938), pp. 261, 275; "Arrest of Jap Labor Leaders Brings Protests," *CIO News*, January 22, 1938, p. 3; "CIO Calls For Unity of Democracies," *CIO News*, November 21, 1938, p. 12; "Ford Aids War," *CIO News*, December 29, 1937, p. 1.

10. CIO, *1938 Proceedings*, p. 261; "Hands Across the Rio," *CIO News*, November 17, 1938, p. 4; "A Message Heard Around the World," *CIO News*, March 19, 1938, p. 4; "'Heil Hague!,'" *CIO News*, June 11, 1938, p. 4.

11. "Lewis Scores Nazi Barbarism," *CIO News*, November 21, 1938, p. 6; "Brophy Hits Nazi Terror," *CIO News*, November 28, 1938, p. 3; "Keeping the Wolf From the Door" (cartoon), *CIO News*, November 28, 1938, p. 4.

12. CIO, *1938 Proceedings*, pp. 262-63. Also see "Rochester CIO Raps Hitler," *CIO News*, October 8, 1938, p. 7; "State Council Convention Hails Kennedy for Governor," *CIO News*, April 2, 1938, p. 3, and "Shipyard Workers Prepare for Boom in Organization," *CIO News*, September 17, 1938, p. 3.

13. CIO, *1938 Proceedings*, pp. 262-63; "Flivver King Gets Nazi Tribute," *CIO News*, August 6, 1938, p. 8; "Labor Board Knocks Ford Policies Again," *CIO News*, August 6, 1938, p. 8; "Steel Barons Fight Steel Workers," *CIO News*, August 6, 1938, p. 6; "Lewis Aids Anti-Fascist Drive," *CIO News*, September 17, 1938, p. 5; "Hands Across the Rio," *CIO News*, September 17, 1938, p. 4; "Lewis Scores Nazi Barbarism," *CIO News*, November 21, 1938, p. 6; "Lewis Warns Steel Union of Fascist Danger," *CIO News*, December 22, 1937, p. 3; "'Heil Hague!,'" CIO *News*, June 11, 1938, p. 4; "A Message Heard Round the World," *CIO News*, March 19, 1938, p. 4; "On Freedom of the Press," *CIO News*, April 2, 1938, p. 4; "National Guard Under Fire in Minnesota," *CIO News*, April 9, 1938, p. 7; "4,000,000 Words," *CIO News*, April 16, 1938, p. 1; "Republic Steel's Use of Violence Bared by Labor Board," *CIO News*,, April 16, 1938, p. 2; "Industrial Armaments Knocked by Cummings," *CIO News*, April 30, 1938, p. 8; "Hague Sees Red," *CIO News*, June 18, 1938, p. 2; "Anti-Hague Fight Opens," *CIO News*, June 4, 1938, p. 5; "Relief Camps Seen as Scab Nests," *CIO News*, June 11, 1938, p. 1; "Blackleg and Blackshirt Models," *CIO News*, June 11, 1938, p. 4; "Reactionaries' Hate of Progress Reaching New Low Levels," *CIO News*, June 25, 1938, p. 7; "Attack on Rubber Workers is Flop; Audience Deserts Gerald L.K. Smith, *CIO News*, June 25, 1938, p. 8; "Now It Can Be Told, *CIO News*, July 23, 1938, p. 4; "What Crimes in Liberty's Name!," *CIO News*, October 22, 1938, p. 4; "Dies Spies Flock Back to Capitol," *CIO News*, October 22, 1938, p. 8; "Modern Witch Burners," *CIO News*, July 9, 1938, p. 4.

14. "Toledano Warns of Fascist Danger," *CIO News*, July 2, 1938, p. 1; "CTM and CIO," *CIO News*, July 2, 1938, p. 4; "Latin American Labor Body Formed," *CIO News*, September 10, 1938, p. 5.

15. "Swastikas to the South; Fascists Active in Latin America," *CIO News*, December 19, 1938, p. 6; "Plan Three Labor Meets in Latin America," *CIO News*,

August 6, 1938, p. 5; "CTM and CIO," *CIO News*, July 2, 1938, p. 4; CIO, *1938 Proceedings*, p. 275.

16. "Recovery Bill Will Ease Suffering," *CIO News*, May 7, 1938, p. 3; "CIO Saved the U.S., Murray Declares," *CIO News*, May 14, 1938, p. 2; "Report Offers 7-Point Program for Lasting Prosperity," *CIO News*, November 14, 1938, p. 2; "Need Urgent for More WPA Funds," *CIO News*, February 19, 1938, p. 1; "CIO Has Plan to Fight Business Depression," *CIO News*, February 19, 1938, p. 3; "Start Housing Program," *CIO News*, April 30, 1938, p. 2; "Fight to Strengthen Wagner Act Will Continue," *CIO News*, June 18, 1938; "Building A Floor Under Wages,'" *CIO News*, October 15, 1938, p. 5; "The Church and the CIO," *CIO News*, May 7, 1938, p. 69; "The CIO—A Mighty Force for Freedom," *CIO News*, November 14, 1938, p. 5.

17. "The CIO—A Mighty Force for Freedom," *CIO News*, November 14, 1938, p. 5; "A Message Heard Round the World," *CIO News*, March 19, 1938, p. 4.

18. "Green's Attack on CIO Sputters in Ohio," *CIO News*, October 8, 1938, p. 7; "Fortune Magazine Sees AFL Heads as Bosses' Allies," *CIO News*, October 1, 1938, p. 5; "Revolt Grows in AFL Against Green's Tory Politics," *CIO News*, September 24, 1938, p. 2; "British Experience Backs CIO Stand," *CIO News*, September 10, 1938; "Sour Grapes," *CIO News*, July 30, 1938, p. 4; "Green With Envy" (cartoon associating AFL President Green with company unions), *CIO News*, July 30, 1938, p. 4; "The AFL in Jersey," *CIO News*, June 11, 1938, p. 3; "Green Resignation Accepted by UMWA," *CIO News*, May 28, 1938, p. 7; "Los Angeles CIO Bucks War on Unions," *CIO News*, March 5, 1938, p. 3; "Police Nab Leaders of 'War' on CIO," *CIO News*, February 12, 1938, p. 4; "You Think You Got Troubles?," *CIO News*, January 29, 1938, p. 4; "Green to Get Treason Trial," *CIO News*, February 5, 1938, p. 1; "Why Peace Talks Failed," *CIO News*, January 22, 1938, p. 2; "Meanest Trick of the Year," (cartoon showing AFL President Green allied with "Southern Reactionaries"), *CIO News*, December 22, 1937, p. 2; "Wage-Hour Bill Defeat," *CIO News*, December 22, 1937, p. 1; "AFL Rejects Unity," *CIO News*, December 22, 1937, p. 1.

19. CIO, *1938 Proceedings*, pp. 18O, 261.

20. Ibid. For examples of protests, see "Brophy Hits Nazi Terror," *CIO News*, November 28, 1938, p. 3 and "Democracy Keynote of Convention," *CIO News*, November 21, 1938, p. 8.

21. CIO, *1938 Proceedings*, pp. 261-63; "Union Group Urges Boycott of Jap Toys," *CIO News*, December 22, 1937, p. 1; "CTM and CIO," *CIO News*, July 2, 1938, p. 4; "Lewis Aids Anti-Fascist Drive," *CIO News*, September 17, 1938, p. 5.

22. "Heywood Broun on World Peace," *CIO News*, March 26, 1938, p. 3; "Lewis Aids Anti-Fascist Drive," *CIO News*, September 17, 1938, p. 5.

23. David Dubinsky to Walter Schevenels and Walter Citrine, November 11, 1938, and miscellaneous newspaper clippings, file 3B, box 6, David Dubinsky Papers, ILGWU Archives, Labor-Management Documentation Center, Cornell University, Ithaca, NY.

24. Robert A. Divine, *The Reluctant Belligerent: American Entry into*

World War II (New York: John Wiley and Sons, 1965), p. 45; Wayne S. Cole, *Roosevelt and the Isolationists, 1932-45* (Lincoln: University of Nebraska Press, 1983), pp. 233-38, 243-46; "18th CIO Council Formed in Indiana," *CIO News*, May 28, 1938, p. 7.

25. "CIO Woodworkers Hit Anti-Labor Attacks," *CIO News*, September 24, 1938, p. 5; "Shipyard Workers Prepare for Boom in Organization," *CIO News*, September 17, 1938, p. 3; "State Council Convention Hails Kennedy for Governor," *CIO News*, April 2, 1938, p. 3; "Gotham Dyers Protest Nazi Brutality," *CIO News*, December 19, 1938, p. 3; "Rochester CIO Raps Hitler," *CIO News*, October 8, 1938, p. 7; "Clothing Workers to Give $250,000 to Refugees," *CIO News*, January 2, 1939, p. 1; "Chinese Drop Picket Line Around Boat for Japan," *CIO News*, January 2, 1939, p. 2; "Aid Refugees, Honor Hillman," *CIO News*, January 16, 1939, p. 8; "Ask Aid for Italian Refugees," *CIO News*, July 9, 1938, p. 8; Sidney Hillman to Paul Baerwald, May 2, 1940, folder 1, box 68, Sidney Hillman Papers, ACW Archives, Labor-Management Documentation Center, Cornell University, Ithaca, NY; James G. Blaine to Hillman, October 14, 1941, folder 18, box 69, Ibid.; various letters re. Refugee Relief Fund, file 6C, box 6, Dubinsky Papers; Harry Uviller to ILGWU, September 19, 1940, J.N. Rosenberg to Dubinsky, October 14, 1941, file 1A, box 7, Ibid.; George D. Smith to Dubinsky, August 25, 1941, file 2D, box 174, Ibid.; ILGWU Press Release, November 12, 1936, Schevenels to Dubinsky, March 25, 1937, Dubinsky to Schevenels, June 19, 1937, file 2B, box 47, Ibid.; Dubinsky to Freda Kirchwey, May 16, 1938, file 3B, box 6, Ibid.; "Mrs. Roosevelt, Bishop, Hail Donors at Dinner," *New York World-Telegram*, April 19, 1940, "Refugee Fund Distributed at Historic Coat Event," *Women's Wear Daily*, April 19, 1940 (clippings in file 6C, box 6, Ibid.).

26. CIO, *1938 Proceedings*, p. 275

27. "CIO Has Plan to Fight Business Depression," *CIO News*, February 19, 1938, p. 3; "Unions Rally to Support Kennedy's Bid," *CIO News*, March 12, 1938, p. 5; "Wage-Hour Bill Delay Deepens Depression," *CIO News*, March 12, 1938, p. 4; "Jobs for All is CIO Demand," *CIO News*, March 19, 1938, p. 1; "CIO Backs New Deal Program for Relief and Recovery," *CIO News*, April 23, 1938, p. 3; "Start Housing Program," *CIO News*, April 30, 1938, p. 2; "The New Relief and Recovery Bill," *CIO News*, June 2, 1938, p. 5; "'Dead Ends' on Down Grade as U.S. Housing Drive Gains," *CIO News*, August 6, 1938, p. 5; "Forum Hears CIO Plea for Better Housing Program," *CIO News*, October 15, 1938, p. 6; "Report Offers 7-Point Program for Lasting Prosperity," *CIO News*, November 14, 1938, p. 2.

28. Richard A. Lauderbaugh, 'Business, Labor, and Foreign Policy: U.S. Steel, the International Steel Cartel, and Recognition of the Steel Workers Organizing Committee," *Politics and Society* 6, no. 4 (1976): 433-57; CIO, *1938 Proceedings*, pp. 262-63; "Miss Lewis Deplores Small Labor Voice at Lima Confab," *CIO News*, January 23, 1939, p. 5. On the other hand, the CIO also could call for trade restrictions when they served the needs of one of its unions. In 1939, CIO executive John Brophy testified to a Senate committee in support of legislation favored by the Woodworkers Union that would have permitted the president

to prevent importation of logs used for making plywood. See Diary entry for May 2, 1939, box 1B, John Brophy Papers, Catholic University, Washington, DC.

29. "Shipyard Workers Prepare for Boom in Organization," *CIO News*, September 17, 1938, p. 3; "Shipyard Gains New Election Victories," *CIO News*, March 5, 1938, p. 4; "Open Shop Near End at Newport Shipyard," *CIO News*, August 20, 1938, p. 1; "NLRB Kills Fake Union at Shipyard," *CIO News*, September 3, 1938, p.8; "Hercules Weakens," *CIO News*, September 3, 1938, p. 8; "220 Shipbuilders to Get $40,000 in NLRB Award," *CIO News*, September 10, 1938, p. 7; "Shipyard Union Gets New Pact," *CIO News*, October 8, 1938, p. 8; "Shipyard Workers Lift Pay," *CIO News*, October 22, 1938, p. 2.

30. CIO, *1938 Proceedings*, p. 252; "'Patriotism' Argument Fails; Electric Boat Must Obey Wagner Act," *CIO News*, June 11, 1938, p. 2; "Capital Closeups," *CIO News*, June 11, 1938, p. 5; "CIO Asks Protests on Hill-Sheppard Bill," *CIO News*, February 5, 1938, p. 1; "Brophy Asks Unions Protest War Labor Bills," *CIO News*, February 12, 1938, p. 3; "Sheppard-Hill Bill Little Changed in May Measure," *CIO News*, February 19, 1938, p. 3; "Kill the May Bill," *CIO News*, March 5, 1938, p. 2; "Labor's League Presents—A Program of Action for American Workers," *CIO News*, April 9, 1938, P. 5.

31. "SFTU Passes Anti-War Resolution," *CIO News*, April 2, 1938, p. 2;CIO, *1938 CIO Proceedings*, p. 252.

32. "Lewis Scores Nazi Barbarism," *CIO News*, November 21, 1938, p. 6; "Workers Can Stop War, Says Jouhaux," *CIO News*, September 24, 1938, p. 6; "Lewis Aids Anti-Fascist Drive," *CIO News*, September 17, 1938, p. 5; "Unity Keynotes Mexican Congress," *CIO News*, September 10, 1938, p. 5; "Heywood Broun on World Peace," *CIO News*, March 26, 1938, p. 3; "Lewis Receives Invitation to Appear at Mexican Labor Parley," *CIO News*, May 7, 1938, p. 2; "Depression is Worst in U.S., Says ILO," *CIO News*, June 4, 1938, p. 2.

33. "Blackleg and Blackshirt Models," *CIO News*, June 11, 1938, p. 4; "English Labor Law," *CIO News*, June 25, 1938, p. 3; "The British Trades Dispute Act Not a Model for U.S.," *CIO News*, July 23, 1938, p. 6; "British Experience Backs CIO Stand," *CIO News*, September 10, 1938, p. 4.

34. "CIO Backs Mexican Workers," *CIO News*, March 19, 1938, p. 1; "CTM and CIO," *CIO News*, July 2, 1938, p. 4; "Unity Keynotes Mexican Congress," *CIO News*, September 10, 1938, p. 5; "Two Pittsburgh Conventions," *CIO News*, November 14, 1938, p. 4; "English Jobless in Protest," *CIO News*, , January 9, 1939, p. 7.

35. Val P. Lorwin, *The French Labor Movement* (Cambridge, Mass.: Harvard University Press, 1954), pp. 25, 70, 146; Henry W. Ehrmann, *French Labor: From Popular Front to Liberation* (New York: Oxford University Press, 1947), pp. 102, 105-6, 109, 114; Michael R. Gordon, *Conflict and Consensus in Labour's Foreign Policy, 1914-1965* (Palo Alto, Cal.: Stanford University Press, 1969), pp. 76, 77, 79; Henry Pelling, *A History of British Trade Unionism* (London: MacMillan, 1972), p. 203; William Rayburn Tucker, *The Attitude of the British Labour Party Towards European and Collective Security Problems,*

1920-1939 (Geneva: Imprimerie du Journal de Geneve, 1950), pp. 204-6, 209, 244; David L. Sallach, *Enlightened Self-Interest: The Congress of Industrial Organizations' Foreign Policy, 1935-1955*, doctoral dissertation, Rutgers University, 1983 (Ann Arbor, Mich.: University Microfilms International, 1983), pp. 9-11; CIO, *1938 Proceedings*, p. 234; "CTM and CIO," *CIO News*, July 2, 1938, p. 4; "Jouhaux, French Union Praises Gains of Labor in United States," *CIO News*, August 27, 1938, p. 8; "Jouhaux Gets Welcome," *CIO News*, August 27, 1938, p. 1; "Unity Keynotes Mexican Congress," *CIO News*, September 10, 1938, p. 5; "Hands Across the Rio," *CIO News*, September 17, 1938, p. 4.

36. See, for example, "CTM and CIO," *CIO News*, July 2, 1938, p. 4; "Miss Lewis Deplores Small Labor Voice at Lima Confab," *CIO News*, January 23, 1939, p. 5; "Toledano Warns of Fascist Danger," *CIO News*, July 2, 1938, p. 3; "Mexican Workers Don't Like Ford, Either," *CIO News*, May 14, 1938, p. 3; "CIO Backs Mexican Workers," *CIO News*, March 19, 1938, p. 1. Also see Sallach, *Enlightened Self-Interest*, pp. 15-9.

37. Sallach, *Enlightened Self-Interest*, pp. 16-7; "Mexican Labor Meeting Hears Lewis Urge Unity," *CIO News*, September 10, 1938, p. 1; "Unity Keynotes Mexican Congress," *CIO News*, September 10, 1938, p. 5; "Toledano Warns of Fascist Danger," *CIO News*, July 2, 1938, p. 3; "UAW Backs Mexican Ford Strike," *CIO News*, May 14, 1938, p. 3; "CIO Backs Mexican Workers," *CIO News*, March 19, 1938, p. 1; "Lewis Receives Invitation to Appear at Mexican Labor Parley," *CIO News*, May 7, 1938, p. 2; "5,000 Hear Toledano in Texas," *CIO News*, July 9, 1933, p. 2; "Mexican Leaders Tour U.S.," *CIO News*, July 2, 1938, p. 5; "Mexican Labor Plans Chain of Coop Food Stores," *CIO News*, November 28, 1938, p. 7; "Mexico Gives Print Shop to Workers," *CIO News*, January 9, 1939, p. 2.

38. Sallach, *Enlightened Self-Interest*, p. 16; CIO, *1938 Proceedings*, p. 275; "CIO Pledges Aid to Cuban Unions," *CIO News*, January 30, 1939, p. 7; "Miss Lewis Deplores Small Labor Voice at Lima Confab," *CIO News*, January 23, 1939, p. 5; "CIO Pledges Aid to Latin America," *CIO News*, November 21, 1938, p. 4; "Cuban Trade Unions Fight Uphill Battle," *CIO News*, October 8, 1938, p. 8; "Swastikas to the South," *CIO News*, December 19, 1938, p. 6; "Seamen Give Big Reception to Lewis," *CIO News*, October 8, 1938, p. 6; "Latin American Labor Body Formed," *CIO News*, September 10, 1938, p. 5; "Lewis Aids Anti-Fascist Drive," *CIO News*, September 17, 1938, p. 5; "Plan Three Labor Meets in Latin America," *CIO News*, August 6, 1938, p. 5.

39. "Commission Reports: Swedish Employers Bargain," *CIO News*, October 1, 1938, p. 5; "CIO Opens Drive in Canadian Gold Fields," *CIO News*, March 5, 1938, p. 4; "CIO Unions Grow Fast in Canada," *CIO News*, January 23, 1939, p. 3; "Canadian Labor Keeps Unity, Refuses to Oust CIO Unions," *CIO News*, September 24, 1938, p. 5.

40. This assertion is based upon a review of the CIO's *Proceedings* for 1938 and each issue of the *CIO News* for 1937 and 1938.

41. David J. Saposs, *Communism in American Unions* (New York: McGraw-Hill, 1959), pp. 119-22, 130-35.

42. "Brophy Challenges Critics of CIO," *CIO News*, August 20, 1938, p. 6; "Outside Agitators," *CIO News*, April 30, 1938, p.3; "Frey's Red Scare Talks About CIO," *CIO News*, August 20, 1938, p. 3; "The Un-American Committee," *CIO News*, August 20, 1938, p. 4; "LNPL Bares Past of Dies Prober as Fascist Spy," *CIO News*, August 27, 1938, p. 3; "Modern Witch Burners," *CIO News*, July 9, 1938, p. 4; "Lewis Defends Wagner Act," *CIO News*, November 5, 1938, p. 3; "Two Pittsburgh Conventions," *CIO News*, November 14, 1938, p. 4. Also see Saposs, *Communism in American Unions*, pp. 20-1.

43. Bernstein, *Turbulent Years*, pp. 391, 393. Also see, for example, several articles on the topic in the July 31, 1937 and August 7, 1937 issues of the AFL *Weekly News Service*.

44. See, for example, "Dictators in Glass Houses," *CIO News*, January 30, 1939, p. 4; "Green's Attack on CIO Sputters in Ohio," *CIO News*, October 8, 1938, p. 7; "Revolt Grows in AFL Against Green's Tory Policies," *CIO News*, September 24, 1938, p. 2; "The AFL in Jersey," *CIO News*, June 11, 1938, p. 3; "A Message Heard Round the World," *CIO News*, March 19, 1938, p. 4.

45. "Labor Trouble in U.S. is Laid to 'Reds in the CIO,'" AFL *Weekly News Service*, February 15, 1938; "CIO Is Supported by Communists with Revolutionary Aims, Green Says," AFL *Weekly News Service*, May 29, 1937; "Green Declares Broun is 'Stooge' for Avowed Communists in CIO," AFL *Weekly News Service*, July 24, 1937; "Ross Denounces CIO Before Mississippi Labor Convention," AFL *Weekly News Service*, July 31, 1937; "Communists Lead CIO is Charge," AFL *Weekly News Service*, July 31, 1937; "Bold Plot to Communize Transit Workers is Thoroughly Exposed," AFL *Weekly News Service*, August 21, 1937; "CIO Unions Hire Reds, Green Asserts," AFL *Weekly News Service*, August 28, 1937; "AFL Unions Urged by Green to Leave Lewis' Labor League," AFL *Weekly News Service*, February 5, 1938; "CIO Is Under Communist Domination, Frey Declares," AFL *Weekly News Service*, August 20, 1938; "AFL Convention Outlines Controversy With the CIO," AFL *Weekly News Service*, October 23, 1937; text of William Green CBS radio broadcast, October 4, 1937, document B-362, box 3, series 11E, William Green Papers, American Federation of Labor Collection, Wisconsin State Historical Society, Madison, Wis.

46. "AFL Convention Outlines Controversy with the CIO," AFL *Weekly News Service*, October 23, 1937.

47. "CIO Hitlerism Assailed by Green," AFL *Weekly News Service*, April 10, 1937; "Relentless War on CIO Urged by Green," AFL *Weekly News Service*, October 9, 1937; "Lewis Dictatorship Assailed by Hines," AFL *Weekly News Service*, April 16, 1938; "Dictatorship Condemned by Green," AFL *Weekly News Service*, March 26, 1938; "Preservation of Democracy in Organized Labor is Only Issue in Controversy," AFL *Weekly News Service*, March 19, 1938; "CIO Dictatorship Denounced by Frey," AFL *Weekly News Service*, March 12, 1938; "AFL Convention Outlines Controversy with the CIO," AFL *Weekly News Service*, October 23, 1937; "AFL Stands for Democracy's Defense, Green Says," AFL *Weekly News Service*, July 31, 1937; "President Green Declares That Preservation

of Majority Rule in Labor Movement is the Real Issue," AFL *Weekly News Service*, March 20, 1937; "Industrial vs. Craft Unionism is Not Involved in Controversy with the CIO," AFL *Weekly News Service*, August 8, 1936.

48. "Sour Grapes," *CIO News*, July 30, 1938, p. 4; "Revolt Grows in AFL Against Green's Tory Policies, *CIO News*, September 24, 1938, p. 2; "AFL Members Refuse to Aid 'War' on CIO," *CIO News*, January 6, 1938, p. 1; "AFL 'Drive' in Tailspin," *CIO News*, April 2, 1938, p. 8; "Revolt Spreads in AFL Against Tory Policies," *CIO News*, October 15, 1938, p. 3.

49. "Speed-Up Order Issued by Soviet Government," AFL *Weekly News Service*, May 1, 1937; "Bold Plot to Communize Transit Workers," AFL *Weekly News Service*, August 21, 1937; "AFL Convention Outlines Controversy with the CIO," AFL *Weekly News Service*, October 23, 1937; "Soviet Artists Given Wage Reductions," AFL *Weekly News Service*, November 20, 1937; "Russian Unions Hit by AFL Council," AFL *Weekly News Service*, February 5, 1938; "Labor Trouble in U.S. is Laid to Reds in the CIO," AFL *Weekly News Service*, February 5, 1938; text of William Green radio address on "The Labor Parade," March 23, 1938, document B-370, box 3, series 11E, Green Papers.

50. "Hitler Denounced as Brutish Caesar and Desperate Madman," AFL *Weekly News Service*, November 26, 1938; "Nazi Germany's Persecution of Jews is Deliberate Savagery, Says Woll," AFL *Weekly News Service*, November 26, 1938; "German Idle Suffer Home Work Slavery," AFL *Weekly News Service*, January 7, 1939; "Engineering Workers Speeded Up by Nazis," AFL *Weekly News Service*, November 7, 1939; "Nazi Persecution of Jews Condemned by AFL," AFL *Weekly News Service*, November 19, 1938; "German Miners Flee From Nazi Paradise," AFL *Weekly News Service*, April 16, 1938; "Nazi Death Decrees Protested by Green," AFL *Weekly News Service*, June 19, 1937; "Bombing Civilians in Wartime," AFL *Weekly News Service*, March 36, 1938; AFL, *1937 Proceedings*, pp. 12, 422; AFL, *1938 Proceedings*, pp. 504-6; Green speech, "Labor Renews its Protest Against the Hitler Dictatorship," January 31, 1937, document B-357, box 2, series 11E, Green Papers.

51. "Hitler Denounced as Brutish Caesar and Desperate Madman," AFL *Weekly News Service*, November 26, 1938; "Green Urges All AFL Unions to Appoint Committees to Promote Militant Boycott," AFL *Weekly News Service*, November 25, 1938.

52. AFL press release, December 16, 1937, document F-665, box 9, series 11E, Green Papers; AFL, *1937 Proceedings*, pp. 302-3, 504-5; "Japanese Boycott Voted by AFL," AFL *Weekly News Service*, October 16, 1937; "AFL Convention Proceedings Summarized," AFL *Weekly News Service*, December 18, 1937.

53. "Hitler Denounced as Brutish Caesar and Desperate Madman," AFL *Weekly News Service*, November 26, 1938; "Larger Lumber Exports Urged by Green," AFL *Weekly News Service*, July 30, 1938; "Fisherman's Union Protests Japanese Invasion of U.S. Fishing Interests," AFL *Weekly News Service*, November 27, 1937; "AFL Convention Proceedings Summarized," AFL *Weekly News Service*, December 18, 1937; "Japanese Boycott Pressed by Labor," AFL

Weekly News Service, December 19, 1938; AFL press release, December 16, 1937, document F-665, box 9, series 11E, Green Papers; AFL, *1937 AFL Proceedings*.

54. "Union Label Goods Stressed by Ornburn," AFL *Weekly News Service*, January 2, 1937; "Deluge of Canadian Lumber Victimizes American Labor," AFL *Weekly News Service*, November 20, 1937; "Printing Trades Oppose Pending Copyright Treaty," AFL *Weekly News Service*, January 1, 1938; "Clarksburg Unions Boycott Jap Goods," AFL *Weekly News Service*, April 2, 1938; "Aluminum Tariff Cut Opposed by AFL," AFL *Weekly News Service*, April 2, 1938; "Reduced Tariff on Canadian Aluminum Hit by AFL," AFL *Weekly News Service*, April 16, 1938; "Reciprocal Trade Pacts Menace Brewing Industry," AFL *Weekly News Service*, November 19, 1938; "Brewers Association Urges Use of American Barley and Malt," AFL *Weekly News Service*, November 26, 1938; "Shorter Hours to Make Jobs for the Idle," AFL *Weekly News Service*, January 30, 1937; "Prompt Passage of Federal Billion Dollar Housing Bill Urged by Green," AFL *Weekly News Service*, April 17, 1937; "Price Profiteering is Condemned by AFL," AFL *Weekly News Service*, May 15, 1937; "Shorter Hours and Wage Protection Urged," AFL *Weekly News Service*, January 15, 1938.

55. "AFL Group Plans Chinese Aid," AFL *Weekly News Service*, January 15, 1938; "Green Becomes Honorary Chairman," AFL *Weekly News Service*, January 15, 1938; "Woll Sponsors Group to Aid the Victims of European Totalitarian Governments," AFL *Weekly News Service*, November 19, 1938; "Woll's League to Aid Democracy Progresses," AFL *Weekly News Service*, December 3, 1938; "Human Rights League Will Protect Democracy and Freedom, Says Woll," AFL *Weekly News Service*, December 17, 1938.

56. "Pay Increases Secured by Many Paris Workers," AFL *Weekly News Service*, January 30, 1937; "Collective Bargaining in England," AFL *Weekly News Service*, April 10, 1937; "Public Control of Coal Industry Begun in Great Britain," AFL *Weekly News Service*, April 16, 1938; "Brash Organized Labor Aids Millions of Workers," AFL *Weekly News Service*, April 16, 1938; "British Employers Do Not Use Guns or Gas to Fight Organized Labor," AFL *Weekly News Service*, October 15, 1938; AFL, *1937 Proceedings*, pp. 294-5, 302-3; Green radio address, April 19, 1938, document B-372, box 3, series 11E, Green Papers.

57. "British Plan to Partition Palestine Hit by Green as Persecution of Jews," AFL *Weekly News Service*, July 24, 1937; "America Must Mobilize Democracy to Safeguard Liberty, Says Green," AFL *Weekly News Service*, December 10, 1938; "Haven in U.S. for Political Refugees Favored by AFL," AFL *Weekly News Service*, April 2, 1938; Rene Albrecht-Carrie, *A Diplomatic History of Europe Since the Congress of Vienna* (New York: Harper and Row, 1973), pp. 338, 404.

58. AFL, *1937 Proceedings*, pp. 13, 172-73, 302, 219; "War and Treaty Violations Condemned by AFL," AFL *Weekly News Service*, October 23, 1937; "Construction of Battleships by U.S. Navy Yards, AFL *Weekly News Service*, July 17, 1937; "What Naval Preparedness Would Mean in Housing" AFL *Weekly News Service*, March 13, 1937; "The Billion Dollar Navy Bill," AFL *Weekly News*

Service, May 28, 1938; "Preventing War," AFL *Weekly News Service*, June 4, 1938; "AFL Pledges Efforts to Maintain World Peace," AFL *Weekly News Service*, August 27, 1938; "National Planning Board Supported by the AFL," AFL *Weekly News Service*, January 7, 1939.

59. AFL, *1937 AFL Proceedings*, pp. 421-23, 505.

60. AFL, *1938 Proceedings*, pp. 503-5; "World Embargo Against Japan Rejected by AFL," AFL *Weekly News Service*, January 29, 1938.

61. Divine, *Reluctant Belligerent*, pp. 48-9; Cole, *Roosevelt*, p. 253; AFL, *1937 Proceedings*, pp. 448-49, 512-14; AFL, *1938 Proceedings*, p. 170; "Labor Standards in Naval Construction," AFL *Weekly News Service*, November 20, 1937; "AFL Pledges Efforts to Maintain World Peace," AFL *Weekly News Service*, August 27, 1938.

62. AFL, *1937 Proceedings*, p. 318; AFL, *1938 Proceedings*, pp. 168-69; "Oriental Workers Opposed by Yakima Culinary Union," AFL *Weekly News Service*, August 21, 1937; "Labor Laws Gained by AFL Non-Partisan Political Policy," AFL *Weekly News Service*, December 3, 1938; "Haven in U.S. for Political Refugees Favored by AFL," AFL *Weekly News Service*, April 2, 1938; "Admission of Refugees Favored by AFL," AFL *Weekly News Service*, February 11, 1939.

63. AFL, *1938 AFL Proceedings*, p. 168; "Fools Rush In," AFL *Weekly News Service*, August 21, 1937; "CIO Favors Filipinos to Man American Ships," AFL *Weekly News Service*, April 9, 1938. Also see "CIO Fights Anti-Alien Proposal," *CIO News*, April 28, 1941, p. 8, "Heywood Broun on 'Outside Agitators,'" *CIO News*, April 30, 1938, p. 3, and "Lewis Aids Anti-Fascist Drive," *CIO News*, September 17, 1938, p. 5; Diary entry, May 13, 1939, box 1B, Brophy Papers; Secretary of American Committee for Protection of Foreign-Born (Dwight C. Morgan) to Hillman, May 11, 1938, folder 22, box 66, Hillman Papers.

The AFL and CIO Compete in Latin America and Canada

CHAPTER 5

America's two national labor centers did not confine their warfare against each other to the United States. Unions of the American Federation of Labor (AFL) and the Congress of Industrial Organizations (CIO) competed face-to-face in Canada. In Latin America, the AFL and the CIO battled each other by proxy.

The CIO's only notable successes in international labor circles during the period came in Latin America. There, the CIO aligned itself with vigorous, new labor organizations that eclipsed older organizations with which the AFL was associated.

In Mexico, the AFL for many years had maintained ties with a federation of craft-based unions, the Confederacion Regional Obera Mexicana (CROM). Until the mid-1930s, the CROM was the dominant labor organization in Mexico. Starting in the late 1920s, however, it had gone into a decline. It lost the support of the Mexican government, individual unions cancelled their affiliation, and a group of left-wing unions began to coalesce. In 1936, those left-wing unions formed an organization to rival the CROM, called the Confederation de Trabajadores de Mexico (CTM).[1]

Led by a Marxist, Vicente Lombardo Toledano, the CTM quickly amassed power and influence. It forged a strong alliance with the government of President Lazaro Cardenas, which then was embarked upon a controversial program of social and economic reform. Meanwhile, the CROM was so discredited that its president, Luis Morones, was forced into a brief exile in the United States (although he was able to return to Mexico in 1937).[2]

Yet the AFL continued to stand by the CROM. Traditionally, the AFL had supported the CROM for two reasons: first, the conservative CROM opposed the spread of radical sentiments among the Mexican working classes; and, second, the CROM exercised its influence to persuade the Mexican government to curb the emigration of Mexican nationals to the United States. By the 1930s, its influence with the government having dissolved, the CROM no longer was effective at curbing emigration. But the CROM retained some value for the AFL because of its anti-communist stance. Further, it was the only counterweight to the CTM and the only available brake on CIO designs in Mexico.[3]

Thus, the AFL welcomed Morones to the United States in 1936 when he was driven out of his homeland. It proclaimed the CROM as the true, democratic representative of Mexican workers, and compared the CROM's tribulations to those of the German trade unions that were being crushed by an anti-labor dictatorship. It denounced the CTM as a communist organization and vowed to fight any CTM attempts to undermine existing labor groups in Latin America.[4]

Meanwhile, however, the CTM replaced the CROM as Mexico's preeminent labor organization and the CIO was cementing close ties with it. The CIO and the CTM were ideologically compatible, they battled against the same multinational corporations, and they had similar backgrounds as renegade groups that had rebelled against conservative labor federations. Moreover, their leaders—Lewis and Lombardo Toledano—were great admirers of each other, and they became warm friends.[5]

In 1937, Lombardo Toledano was an honored guest at the United Mine Workers' convention, and the following year he returned to the United States with a delegation of CTM officials to meet with CIO leaders and speak under CIO auspices. Then, in September 1938, Lewis journeyed to Mexico City to address a huge anti-war, anti-fascist rally organized by Lombardo Toledano. In their appearances in each other's countries, Lewis and

Lombardo Toledano spoke of their organizations' common goals and interests and urged close cooperation between the CIO and the CTM.[6]

Beyond simply giving each other encouragement and a taste of international recognition, the CIO and the CTM found practical ways to cooperate. The CTM tried unsuccessfully to aid the CIO by blocking AFL entry into the International Federation of Trade Unions. Also, the CIO and the CTM supported each other's strikes. In 1937, CTM dockworkers supported a CIO longshoremen's strike by refusing to unload American ships. The following year, CTM oil workers went on strike against British and American owned petroleum companies. The companies imposed a boycott against Mexican oil to avoid compliance with a government-mandated strike settlement that was favorable to the CTM. A CTM victory in the dispute was assured when John L. Lewis personally brokered a deal whereby the Mexican government obtained oil tankers from Italy, enabling it to undercut the British and American oil companies and break the boycott.[7]

In addition, the CIO and the CTM saw each other as allies against the spread of fascism. When they visited the United States, CTM officials told American audiences that German, Italian, and Japanese interests were making gains in Latin America and warned that fascists could use Latin American countries as "stepping stones" to the United States. For its part, the CIO expressed grave concern over the extent of fascist penetration into Latin America. Leaders of the CIO and the CTM pledged to work together to stem fascist advances in the Western Hemisphere. Underscoring the common interests of the CTM and the CIO was the concern that each had for domestic fascism. The CIO praised the progressive social legislation of the Cardenas Administration in Mexico and the CTM praised that of the Roosevelt Administration in the United States. The CIO and the CTM likened the two governments to each other, and they both felt a responsibility to defend their respective governments' reforms against the incursions of home-grown reactionaries, as well as those from Europe.[8]

The CTM quickly moved into regional labor activities.

Concurrent with his rally against war and fascism, Lombardo Toledano chaired a conference to organize a new amalgamation of Latin American labor unions, the Confederacion de Trabajadores de America Latina (CTAL).[9]

The CTAL was an alternative to the old Pan-American Federation of Labor (PAFL). The PAFL had been in its heyday in the 1920s, and could boast of a number of accomplishments. It had worked with some success to advance the interests of Latin American workers, to improve labor organization in Latin America, and to cultivate better relations between labor unions throughout the hemisphere. By the time of the CTAL's establishment in 1938, however, the PAFL was moribund. The PAFL had not held a congress of its members in ten years, although there had been unsuccessful attempts to convene one at various times in the early 1930s. Co-founded by the AFL, the PAFL alienated many Latin Americans because it appeared to be dominated by the United States. Finally, the PAFL was too conservative for many Latin American unions. Because of the ideological differences, some of Latin America's most important labor organizations—such as those in Argentina, Chile, and Uruguay—refused to join the PAFL.[10]

The CTAL, on the other hand, reflected the interests and tastes of the Latin American labor movement more accurately, and it immediately surpassed the PAFL. It was more radical than the PAFL and it attracted more and stronger affiliates. Although it welcomed international support and recognition, it was a regional entity, not a hemispheric one. Only Latin American organizations could belong, thereby precluding the charges of United States domination that had so wounded the PAFL. Soon, the CTAL was more powerful and influential than the PAFL had ever been, even at its height.[11]

The AFL, however, reasserted its commitment to the PAFL. It alleged that the CTAL was a communist organization bent on destroying democratic trade unions. At its 1938 convention, the AFL announced its intention to reorganize the PAFL. The AFL soon began preparations to survey labor conditions in Latin America and to dispatch a commission to Latin America in 1939 as part of the effort to revive the PAFL. The effort was destined to fail, although the PAFL would linger as a paper organization into the 1940s.[12]

In contrast, the CIO supported the CTAL enthusiastically. Lewis spoke at the organizing conference of the CTAL. Another speaker was Lewis' and Lombardo Toledano's European counterpart, President Leon Jouhaux of the France's industrially-organized Confederation Generale du Travail. Two months later, at its 1938 convention, the CIO congratulated the CTAL for taking "the first step towards the unity of the workers of the Western Hemisphere" and declared "its support (for) the efforts of the masses of Latin American workers to achieve economic and political democracy" via the CTAL. By establishing friendly ties with the CTAL, the CIO was not only lending support to a like-minded organization. It was also challenging, once again, AFL supremacy. Further, involvement with the CTAL meant enhanced international recognition for the CIO. "I wish you could have seen the enthusiasm for the CIO at (the CTAL) convention," a delighted Lewis told maritime workers upon his return from Mexico City.[13]

In December 1938, official delegations from the countries of the Western Hemisphere met in Lima, Peru, for the Eighth International Conference of American States. The conference adopted resolutions calling for Inter-American cultural exchange, improved housing and working conditions, and reductions in trade barriers within the hemisphere. In addition, the conference promulgated a Declaration of American Principles that proscribed territorial conquest, mandated respect for international law and treaty obligations, called for racial and religious tolerance, and included provisions for common defense against invaders from outside the hemisphere. The CIO and the AFL each was represented by one individual on the American delegation: Kathryn Lewis for the CIO, and Daniel Tracy, President of the International Brotherhood of Electrical Workers, for the AFL.[14] For the AFL and the CIO to be on such an equal footing in Latin America, however, was the exception rather than the rule.

In fact, the CIO stole a march on the AFL south of the border. It established important relationships with two vibrant, influential organizations: the regional CTAL and the CTM of Mexico. It left the AFL far behind, trying unsuccessfully to breathe life back into the PAFL and the CROM.

North of the border, in Canada, the activities of the AFL and the CIO were extensions of their domestic activities. AFL and CIO unions actually operated within Canada—chartering locals, organizing workers, and negotiating with employers.

Canada's main national federation of labor unions was the Trades and Labour Congress (TLC). Many of the TLC's affiliates were the Canadian subsidiaries of unions headquartered in the United States and chartered by the AFL. Among them were the Mine, Mill, and Smelter Workers, the United Mine Workers, the Amalgamated Clothing Workers, the International Union of Quarry Workers, and the United Automobile Workers—all of which joined the CIO and lost their AFL charters. In addition, the CIO opened an office in Toronto in 1937, and the CIO's important Steel Workers Organizing Committee began operations in Canada as an affiliate of the TLC. The CIO embarked upon organizing campaigns in other Canadian industries as well, including electrical products and lumber. By 1938, CIO unions in the TLC claimed well over 20,000 rank-and-file members.[15]

At first, CIO unions and AFL unions co-existed in the TLC. Considerable sentiment favoring industrial unionism had existed in Canada for many years, and the TLC's membership wanted to avoid a split in their organization like the one that had taken place in the American labor movement. The 1938 TLC convention overwhelmingly approved a resolution calling for continued harmony between craft unions and industrial unions, and insisting that CIO unions be permitted to retain their TIC affiliation. Local labor federations (i.e., local trades councils), public opinion polls, and editorials in leading Canadian newspapers largely opposed the idea of expelling CIO unions from the TLC. TLC Vice President D.W. Morrison declared that there could be "no greater injury to the trades unions of Canada than to divide the ranks of labor." TLC President P.M. Draper insisted that his organization's constitution left the question of whether to organize on a craft basis or an industrial basis entirely to the discretion of individual unions.[16]

Citing jurisdictional disputes and asserting that Canadian workers did not want CIO units operating in their midst, the AFL started pressuring the TLC to expel the CIO unions. AFL President William Green told the TLC's fraternal delegate to the 1938 AFL convention that the TLC should follow AFL policy and deny membership to CIO unions. The AFL convention itself passed a resolution that strongly criticized the TLC for chartering CIO unions. TLC leaders responded by acknowledging the AFL's authority over jurisdictional matters while begging the AFL to recognize the autonomy of the TLC and the local trades councils in decisions regarding membership.[17]

The AFL, however, threatened to pull its unions out of the TLC and the local trades councils unless its demand was met. The majority of the TLC's rank and file belonged to AFL unions. To lose them and the dues they paid would have been catastrophic for the TLC. In January 1939, the AFL's gambit paid off. The TLC's Executive Committee reluctantly suspended the CIO unions. In its notice of suspension, the Executive Committee noted the AFL's insistence upon expulsion, yet expressed the desire that CIO and AFL unions in Canada maintain their cordial relations. It stated that "we reaffirm our friendliness and good spirit" toward the CIO. "We are not declaring war on the CIO," said acting TLC President R.J. Tallon. Several months later. after a lengthy debate, the 1939 TLC convention upheld the Executive Committee's decision, and the expulsion of the CIO unions became final.[18]

Outmaneuvered but undaunted, the CIO continued to organize in Canada, particularly in steel and mining. In September 1940, CIO locals that the TLC had expelled joined a competing federation of unions. An industrial organization of railway employees had formed the basis for the All-Canada Congress of Labor. The CIO locals merged with that group to form the new Canadian Congress of Labor, to rival the TLC.[19]

The AFL thwarted CIO aspirations in Canada. CIO influence in Latin America, however, displaced that of the AFL. Another battlefield upon which the AFL and the CIO fought extended beyond the Western Hemisphere: the international labor movement.

Notes

1. Harvey A. Levenstein, *Labor Organizations in the United States and Mexico: A History of Their Relations* (Westport, Conn.: Greenwood Publishing Co., 1971), pp. 146-48.

2. Ibid., pp. 148-51, 161.

3. Ibid., pp. 116-20, 128, 134-36, 142-43.

4. William Green Statement, April 26, 1936, document F-577, box 9, series 11E, William Green Papers, American Federation of Labor Collection, Wisconsin State Historical Society, Madison, Wis.; "AFL Spurns Labor Congress in Mexico City," AFL *Weekly News Service*, August 27, 1938.

5. Levenstein, *United States and Mexico*, pp. 149-59; "CTM and CIO," *CIO News*, July 2, 1938, p. 4.

6. "Toledano Warns of Fascist Danger," *CIO News*, July 2, 1938, p. 3; "Mexican Leaders Tour U.S.," *CIO News*, July 2, 1938, p. 5; "5,000 Hear Toledano in Texas," *CIO News*, July 9, 1938, p. 2; "Lewis Aids Anti-War Fascist Drive," *CIO News*, September 17, 1938, p. 5; David L. Sallach, *Enlightened Self-Interest: The Congress of Industrial Organizations' Foreign Policy, 1935-1955*, doctoral dissertation, Rutgers University, 1983 (Ann Arbor, Mich.: University Microfilms International, 1983), p. 16.

7. Sallach, *Enlightened Self-Interest*, pp. 9, 16-7; "CIO Backs Mexican Workers," *CIO News*, March 19, 1938, p. 1; "UAW Backs Mexican Food Strike," *CIO News*, May 14, 1938, p. 3; "Philadelphia CIO Backs Mexican Oil Action," *CIO News*, July 2, 1938, p. 2.

8. "Mexico Gives Print Shop to Workers," *CIO News*, January 9, 1939, p. 2; "Hands Across the Rio," *CIO News*, September 17, 1938, p. 4; "5,000 Hear Toledano in Texas," *CIO News*, July 9, 1938, p. 2; "CTM and CIO," *CIO News*, July 2, 1938, p. 4; "Toledano Warns of Fascist Danger," *CIO News*, July 2, 1938, p. 3; "Swastikas to the South," *CIO News*, December 19, 1938, p. 6; "Plan Three Labor Meets in Latin America," *CIO News*, August 6, 1938, p. 5. Also see Levenstein, *United States and Mexico*, pp. 153-56.

9. Sinclair Snow, *The Pan-American Federation of Labor* (Durham, N.C.: Duke University Press, 1964), p. 145.

10. Ibid., pp. 144-50.

11. Ibid., p. 145; Levenstein, *United States and Mexico*, p. 160.

12. American Federation of Labor, *Report of Proceedings of the Fifty-Eighth Annual Convention of the American Federation of Labor* (Washington: Judd and Detweiler, 1938), p. 63; "Reorganization of Pan-American Federation of Labor is Planned," AFL *Weekly News Service*, October 22, 1938; "AFL Considers Latin-American Labor," AFL *Weekly News Service*, February 11, 1939; "Pan-American Labor Federation Will Be Revived by AFL," AFL *Weekly News Service*, p. 146; Snow, *Pan-American Federation of Labor*, p. 146; Sallach, *Enlightened Self-Interest*, p. 17.

13. Congress of Industrial Organizations, *Proceedings of the First*

Constitutional Convention of the Congress of Industrial Organizations (Pittsburgh: Congress of Industrial Organizations, 1938), p. 247; "Mexican Labor Meeting Hears Lewis Urge Unity," *CIO News*, September 10, 1938, p. 1; "Unity Keynotes Mexican Congress," *CIO News*, September 10, 1938, p. 5; "Latin American Labor Body Formed," *CIO News*, September 10, 1938, p. 5; "Seamen Give Big Reception to Lewis on Trip From Mexico," *CIO News*, October 8, 1938, p. 6.

14. Donald Marquand Dozer, *Are We Good Neighbors? Three Decades of Inter-American Relations, 1930-1960* (Gainesville: University of Florida Press, 1959), pp. 24-5, 39, 53; "Miss Lewis Deplores Small Labor Voice at Lima Confab," *CIO News*, January 23, 1939, p. 5; "Roosevelt Names Tracy to Attend Lima Parley," AFL *Weekly News Service*, November 19, 1938.

15. Jack Williams, *The Story of Unions in Canada* (n.p. [Canada]: J.M. Dent and Sons, 1975), pp. 158-59; "CIO Unions Grow Fast in Canada," *CIO News*, November 23, 1939, p. 3; "CIO Opens Drive in Canadian Gold Fields," *CIO News*, March 5, 1938, p. 4.

16. Mary V. Jordan, *Survival: Labour's Trials and Tribulations in Canada* (Toronto: McDonald House, 1975), pp. 211-31; Williams, *Unions in Canada*, pp. 156-58; "Canadian Labor Keeps Unity, Refusing to Oust CIO Unions," *CIO News*, September 24, 1938, p. 5; "Canadian Unions Work for Unity, Snub AFL Demand," *CIO News*, October 22, 1938, p. 2; "Canadian Labor Congress Clings to Unity Course Despite AFL Threats," *CIO News*, January 2, 1939, p. 2.

17. "AFL Unions Plan Canadian Maritime Unit," AFL *Weekly News Service*, November 6, 1937; "CIO Ban Asked of Canadian Labor," AFL *Weekly News Service*, October 15, 1938; "Curb on Canadian Trades and Labor Congress Charters Asked by AFL," AFL *Weekly News Service*, November 12, 1938; "Canadian Unions Work for Unity, Snub AFL Demand," *CIO News*, October 22, 1938, p. 2; "Urges Labor Unity in Canada," *CIO News*, January 16, 1939, p. 3. Also see Jordan, *Survival*, p. 241.

18. Jordan, *Survival*, p. 242; Williams, *Unions in Canada*, pp. 158-59; "Green Forces Split Between CIO, AFL in Canada," *CIO News*, January 16, 1939, p. 3.

19. "Canadian CIO Strikes Blow at AFL Splitters," *CIO News*, May 20, 1940, p. 8; "The New Canadian Congress of Labor," *CIO News*, September 9, 1940, p. 7; "Form United Labor Body in Canada," *CIO News*, September 16, 1940, p. 3; "Canadian CIO Unions Form National Council," *CIO News*, October 23, 1939, p. 2; "Toronto in First CIO Steel Strike," *CIO News*, November 6, 1939, p. 6; "Quick Victory—SWOC-CIO Wins," *CIO News*, November 13, 1939, p. 8; "Canadian Labor Congress Elects Leaders, Plans Drive," *CIO News*, September 23, 1940, p. 8; "Canadian Steel Workers Vote CIO, 20-1," *CIO News*, October 7, 1940, p. 8; "Canadian Unions Plan Merger Soon," *CIO News*, June 24, 1940, p. 8; "Canadian CIO Head Urges Organizing Drive," *CIO News*, July 1, 1940, p. 2; "Conciliators Urge Canadian Mine Recognize Union," *CIO News*, July 8, 1940, p. 8; "Form New CIO Council in British Columbia," *CIO News*, July 15, 1940, p. 2; "CIO Man on Canada's Labor Board," *CIO News*, July 29, 1940, p. 2; "Canadian Steel Union Wins Bonuses," *CIO News*, July 29, 1940, p. 7; "Canadian Workers Fined in Smear Trial,"

CIO News, July 28, 1941, p. 7; "Canadian Gold Mine Workers Vote Strike," *CIO News*, December 11, 1939, p. 7; "Canadian Miners' Strike Gets Support," *CIO News*, November 27, 1939, p. 8; "Canadian CIO Launches Drive," *CIO News*, November 13, 1939, p. 2.

Carrying the Fight into the International Labor Arena

CHAPTER 6

The international labor movement was concerned over the rift between the American Federation of Labor (AFL) and the Congress of Industrial Organizations (CIO). Lillian Herstein was an official of the Chicago Federation of Labor, an AFL affiliate, who served as an advisor to the 1937 United States delegation to the International Labor Organization (ILO). Before departing for Geneva to attend the 1937 session, the child labor expert said she "boned up" on all agenda items. She did not, however, "anticipate the great interest Europeans had in the CIO-AFL controversy." She wrote that she "developed a conventional smile and a conventional answer. I got so that I said automatically, 'This is a quarrel in the family of Labor in America which I am sure will soon be settled.' I developed an expression as enigmatic and inscrutable as that of the Sphinx or of Mona Lisa."[1]

In general, however, the AFL and the CIO were anything but enigmatic in pleading their cases to world audiences. In a radio broadcast to Great Britain in 1938, for example, AFL President William Green told British trade unionists that the AFL was America's only true labor congress and that it was a democratic organization, whereas the CIO was an autocratic, dual movement that sought to evade the principle of majority rule. "Suppose that a group in the British Trades Union Congress" had rebelled as the

CIO had rebelled, asked Green; "Would the British labor movement submit?" As the AFL was appealing for sympathy from British workers, the CIO was appealing for sympathy from Latin American workers. To embarrass the AFL, CIO leaders spoke at Latin American labor conferences that AFL leaders refused to attend, and emphasized the common interests between American workers in the CIO and Latin American workers.[2] Not only did the AFL and the CIO vie in the court of world labor opinion, they also contested for status in such bodies as the ILO and the International Federation of Trade Unions (IFTU).

The AFL had been a reluctant supporter of United States entry into the ILO in 1934, and AFL representatives served on the American delegations to the ILO in 1935 and 1936.[3] By 1937, however, the CIO was clamoring for a voice in the ILO.

The first skirmish came over the selection of the United States workers' delegate to the 1937 ILO session. The AFL's choice was its vice president, Matthew Woll, and AFL leaders thought that Woll's appointment was assured. But with John L. Lewis demanding consideration for a CIO candidate, President Franklin D. Roosevelt passed over Woll. Besides, Woll had spoken out against the New Deal, and the Administration might have preferred not to send him to Geneva in any event. As a compromise, Roosevelt selected Robert J. Watt as United States workers' delegate. Watt was secretary-treasurer of the Massachusetts State Federation of Labor, and hence an official of the AFL. But he was not one of the anti-CIO firebrands and the Administration reasoned that he would be acceptable to both sides. The CIO accepted Watt's appointment because he was preferable to Woll, but the AFL was infuriated. It threatened to lobby for United States withdrawal from the ILO, pointedly declined to invite Secretary of Labor Frances Perkins to its convention that year, and sent Woll as William Green's substitute at a session of the ILO Governing Body—a move that brought ILO complaints that the AFL did not take the work of the ILO seriously.[4]

In addition to Watt, the American delegation to the ILO included several labor advisors. As part of the compromise, the Administration appointed a CIO representative to one of those posts. In 1937, Francis Gorman of the Textile Workers Organizing Committee represented the CIO as a labor advisor. The AFL, on the other hand, was represented by Marion Hedges of the International Brotherhood of Electrical Workers, Lillian Herstein of the Chicago Federation of Labor, and Frank Martel of the International Typographical Union. The following year, with Watt reappointed as American Workers' Delegate, the CIO again placed but one representative on the delegation as an advisor: A.D. Lewis, brother of John L. Lewis and a member of the United Mine Workers. The AFL was represented by two advisors: Hedges and George Googe, who was the AFL's chief organizer in the southern states. Under CIO protests, the AFL was represented on the ILO's Governing Body, to the exclusion of the CIO.[5]

In spite of the divisions among the representatives of organized labor, by 1937 and 1938 the work of the American delegation to the ILO was starting to bear fruit. The United States was a leading champion of the 40-hour week, and it won a significant victory at the 1937 conference with the adoption of a 40-hour convention in the textile industry. Forty-hour conventions in the chemical and printing industries, however, were rejected. The United States delegation at the 1937 conference also worked successfully for adoption of a resolution outlining standards in public works employment, approval of several measures mandating safer conditions in the construction industry, and adoption of measures raising the minimum age for employment in industrial, non-industrial, and family work.[6]

In 1938, after lobbying by the AFL's Legislative Committee, the United States Senate approved and the president ratified five ILO conventions specifying minimum labor standards for merchant seamen. The conventions had been drafted in October 1936 at the ILO's special Maritime Conference. AFL representatives had played an important role at that conference. The five maritime conventions were the first ILO measures to be ratified by the United States. Also in 1938, an American—John Winant, former governor of New Hampshire—was elected director of the ILO. One reason that the CIO accepted a less than favorable compromise on representation might have been to avoid any overt disharmony within the American delegation that might have cost Winant the election.[7]

1938 ILO conference, however, proved disappointing. While the 40-hour work week continued to be of primary importance to the United States delegation, the European countries that were preparing for impending war could not countenance the productivity losses that shorter hours might have entailed. The 1938 session passed but one minor convention, relating to the collection of statistics on wages and hours. Discussion of more important or controversial issues, such as a universal reduction of hours, the transnational recruitment of migrant workers, and vocational education, was deferred to the 1939 session.[8]

After the close of the 1938 session, the CIO signalled that it was no longer satisfied with its subordinate position within the American delegation. The ILO seemed to be moving toward consideration of issues of special interest to the CIO—in particular, labor standards in the coal industry. CIO representative A.D. Lewis had served on an ILO technical committee on the coal industry just before the regular ILO session, and the subject of hours in the coal industry was placed on the 1939 ILO agenda. Further, the CIO professed to discern great interest in and sympathy for its activities from among the other delegations at the 1938 ILO Conference. The CIO decided that it was no longer acceptable for the AFL to dominate the American workers' delegation to the ILO. At its 1938 convention, the CIO vowed to fight for equal representation at future ILO meetings.[9]

Again at its 1939 convention, the CIO registered its dissatisfaction with the Labor Department's refusal to grant the CIO full representation at the ILO. In November 1939, however, the CIO did get to share a vote with the AFL at a regional ILO conference in Havana, Cuba. CIO Secretary-Treasurer James B. Carey represented American labor jointly with George Harrison, president of the AFL's Brotherhood of Railway Clerks. Carey used the occasion to stress "the importance of the closest economic and financial cooperation between the nations of the American Continent." Several AFL and CIO officials, including Kathryn Lewis, accompanied the delegation as advisors. The Havana Conference developed guidelines to facilitate the emigration of non-political refugees, recommended the abolition of monopolistic land-holding systems in Latin America, and passed resolutions on occupational diseases, unemployment insurance, and child labor.[10]

After the Havana Conference, the ILO entered a period of dormancy for the duration of the war. Operating with a skeleton staff, the ILO relocated from Geneva, Switzerland to Montreal, Canada. There, it awaited its revival, which came in 1944 as the Allied powers began planning for postwar international organization.[11]

If the AFL enjoyed a qualified victory over the CIO in the International Labor Organization, it scored a complete rout over its rival in the International Federation of Trade Unions (IFTU). The AFL had withdrawn from the IFTU in 1920 and in the succeeding years had spurned several opportunities to rejoin. The increasing power of fascist dictators and the increasing vulnerability of the European labor movement in the mid-thirties rekindled AFL interest in IFTU membership. The emergence of the CIO finally spurred the AFL to reaffiliate with the international labor union body.[12]

The IFTU admitted only one trade union center per country. If the CIO were admitted, it would give that organization considerable international prestige and shut the AFL out of the IFTU. To be sure, that appealed to many members of the IFTU, who opposed craft organization and wanted to encourage the CIO. On the other hand, AFL reaffiliation would prevent CIO membership and deal a blow to CIO aspirations.[13]

In June 1937, a confident Matthew Woll traveled to Warsaw, Poland, to present the IFTU General Council with the AFL's application for membership. He expected immediate approval of the application. The CIO, however, had two allies at Warsaw: the French Confederation Generale du Travail (CTG) and the Mexican Confederacion Trabajodores de Mexico (CTM). The CTG and the CTM both favored industrial organization and had ties to the Left, and thus were sympathetic to the CIO. John L. Lewis and

Sidney Hillman, President of the CIO's Amalgamated Clothing Workers Union, persuaded the CTG and the CTM to try to block the AFL's affiliation.[14]

Joined by the Belgian delegation, the French and Mexican delegations called for the General Council to postpone consideration of the AFL's application until the IFTU was able to review the split between the AFL and the CIO. The AFL's principal ally, the British Trades Union Congress (BTUC) saved the day. The BTUC had a special session convened where it prevailed upon the General Council to approve AFL membership. Ironically, the BTUC's trumpcard was a statement by CIO leader David Dubinsky to the effect that the AFL should be admitted to the IFTU because the CIO was only a "temporary organization" within the AFL, and not an on-going, dual labor movement.[15]

The IFTU hoped that admission of the AFL would "help to unite all sections of the United States trade union movement," and cautioned that its decision "should not be taken as approval or condemnation of the form of organization" of either the AFL or the CIO. But the AFL was quick to hail its "unqualified acceptance" by the IFTU as a defeat for advocates of the "destructive policy" of the CIO. For its part, the CIO expressed resentment over the "deal" that had been engineered by the "old guard leaders of the British labor movement," and resolved at its convention the following year to seek full CIO membership in the IFTU.[16]

With its three million members and considerable resources, the AFL brought significant power and prestige to the IFTU. Upon entering the IFTU, the AFL was not reluctant to use that power and prestige to attain its goals—one of which was the denial of IFTU membership to the Soviet labor movement. In 1938 and early 1939, the French and Mexican delegations—eventually joined by the British delegation—led a campaign to admit the Soviet labor unions into the IFTU. The AFL had always been critical of the Soviet Union and was convinced that the CIO was influenced by Moscow. It battled relentlessly against the effort to bring the Soviet labor movement into the IFTU, arguing that Soviet trade unions were not free trade unions but were part of the administrative machinery of a dictatorial government, no different from the unions of Italy and Germany. Woll threatened that the AFL would pull out of the IFTU if the Soviet trade unions were admitted, saying "it was an impossible situation to fight against the Fascist dictatorships in partnership with other dictatorships." In a series of votes over a period of several months, the AFL mustered enough support from such members as Poland, Belgium, the Netherlands, Sweden, and Switzerland to keep the Soviet Union out of the IFTU.[17]

Although the AFL had succeeded in keeping the CIO out of the IFTU, the two national labor centers would resume their contest in the international labor movement after World War II. In 1945, the CIO joined a newly-organized rival to the IFTU, the World Federation of Trade Unions (WFTU). The WFTU included Communist labor unions, and the AFL joined forces with the United States Department of State to weaken it. Partly because of the American pressure, the WFTU broke up after only four years.[18]

◍ ◍ ◍

The most important issue in the American labor movement in 1937 and 1938 was the split between the AFL and the CIO. The struggle went far beyond the union halls and shop floors of the United States, reaching even into other countries.

The AFL held a slight upper hand over the CIO at the International Labor Organization, forced the Canadian Trades and Labour Congress to oust CIO unions, and rejoined the IFTU at least partly in order to prevent CIO membership In that body. The CIO, meanwhile, made impressive strides in Latin America, while the AFL's position in that part of the Western Hemisphere eroded.

The AFL and the CIO both advocated American foreign policies that could further their own domestic agendas. In supporting trade embargoes against the fascists, the AFL was furthering its "Buy American" campaign and its program for economic revival based on domestic reforms. The CIO urged vigilance against the fascist dictatorships and offered its own domestic reform program as a way of defending the country. Further, each labor federation presented itself as better able than its opponent to strengthen

America's global position. The CIO tried to link the AFL to the fascist powers and held that industrial union organization would furnish stronger resistance against outside dictators than craft organization. The AFL argued that the CIO was dominated by Communists and alleged that the CIO would undercut American diplomacy out of sympathy for Moscow.

In truth, there was little to distinguish the AFL's foreign policy views from the those of the CIO. Both the AFL and the CIO were deeply troubled by the burgeoning power and increasing aggressiveness of Germany, Italy, and Japan, and both believed that those countries posed direct threats to organized labor and to the United States. While the AFL went somewhat further than the CIO by participating in boycotts and relief efforts, both organizations advocated some kind of American response to the dictators. Yet they both shied away from endorsing any kind of military or meaningful collective security response. In their opinions on world affairs, perhaps, the AFL and the CIO were a microcosm of American society. They exemplified what historian Robert Divine described as a "nation (that) was stalled at dead center—torn between paralysing fear of war . . . and the dawning realization that world events menaced the United States."[19]

One reason the CIO and the AFL were stalled at dead center may have been that their affiliates were beginning to pull in opposite directions. Some voices called for stronger action in international affairs, some for greater caution. Those discordant voices would grow louder between 1939 and 1941, as the United States moved closer and closer to war.

Notes

1. Lillian Herstein to Frances Perkins, September 13, 1937, file: "International Labor Office, 1937," box 75, Frances Perkins Subject Files, Labor Department Records, Record Group 174, National Archives and Records Administration, Washington, DC.

2. William Green radio address, April 19, 1938, document no. B-372, box 3, series 11E, William Green Papers, American Federation of Labor Collection, Wisconsin State Historical Society, Madison, Wis.; Harvey A. Levenstein, *Labor Organizations in the United States and Mexico: A History of Their Relations*

(Westport, Conn.: Greenwood Publishing Co., 1971), p. 157; "Unity Keynotes Mexican Congress," *CIO News*, September 10, 1938, p. 5; "Toledano Warns of Fascist Danger," *CIO News*, July 2, 1938, p. 3.

3. See Chapter 3, above.

4. John Bruce Tipton, *Participation of the United States in the International Labor Organization* (Urbana: University of Illinois Institute of Labor and Industrial Relations, 1959), p. 60.

5. "Twenty-Third Session of International Labor Conference," June 1937, file: "International Labor Office, 1937," box 75, Perkins Subject Files; Perkins to Cordell Hull, May 7, 1938, file: "ILO Conference—Geneva—June 1938," box 75, Ibid.; Lewis to Perkins, June 1, 1937, file: "International Labor Office, 1937," box 75, Ibid.; American Federation of Labor, *Report of Proceedings of the Fifty-Seventh Annual Convention of the American Federation of Labor* (Washington: Judd and Detweiler, 1937), p. 197; "Shorter Hours Needed, A.D. Lewis Tells ILO Confab at Geneva," *CIO News*, June 25, 1938, p. 3.

6. Perkins to Robert Watt, May 18, 1937, file: "International Labor Office, 1937," box 75, Perkins Subject Files; AFL, *1937 Proceedings*, pp. 197-98.

7. "Five Labor Treaties Ratified by Senate," AFL *Weekly News Service*, June 18, 1938; American Federation of Labor, *Report of Proceedings of the Fifty-Eighth Annual Convention of the American Federation of Labor* (Washington: Judd and Detweiler, 1938), pp. 191-95; Tipton, *Participation of the United States*, p. 60.

8. Tipton, *Participation of the United States*, pp. 52-3; AFL, *1938 Proceedings*, pp. 192-93; "Miss Perkins Attends Geneva Labor Parley," AFL *Weekly News Service*, June 11, 1938.

9. "A.D. Lewis Back from Geneva, Tells of World Coal Confab," *CIO News*, July 30, 1938, p. 5; Congress of Industrial Organizations, *Proceedings of the First Constitutional Convention of the Congress of Industrial Organizations* (Pittsburgh: Congress of Industrial Organizations, 1938), p. 247; Tipton, *Participation of the United States*, pp. 60-1.

10. John P. Windmuller, *American Labor and the International Labor Movement, 1940 to 1953* (Ithaca, N.Y.: Cornell University Institute of International Industrial and Labor Relations, 1954), p. 28; "CIO Gets Position on ILO Delegation to Havana," *CIO News*, November 27, 1939, p. 3; Havana Conference Considered Many Questions Affecting Labor," AFL *Weekly News Service*, December 16, 1939; "Memorandum Concerning Economic and Financial Cooperation Between the Nations of the American Continent," November 1939, file: "International Labor Office, 1939-53," box 132, James Carey Papers (Records of CIO Secretary-Treasurer), Reuther Library, Wayne State University, Detroit, Mich. Also see CIO Press Release, June 14, 1939, file: "International Labor Office," box 4B, John Brophy Papers, Catholic University, Washington, DC, for further evidence of the CIO's anger over what it considered "discriminatory" treatment by the Labor Department in selecting ILO representatives.

11. Walter Galenson, *The International Labor Organization: An*

American View (Madison: University of Wisconsin Press, 1981), p. 7; Antony Alcock, *History of the International Labour Organization* (London: MacMillan, 1971), pp. 158-61.

12. Windmuller, *American Labor and the International Labor Movement*, pp. 12-15; Lewis L. Lorwin, *The International Labor Movement: History, Politics, Outlook* (New York: Harper and Brothers, 1953), pp. 180-81.

13. Lorwin, *International Labor*, p. 181; David L. Sallach, *Enlightened Self-Interest: The Congress of Industrial Organizations' Foreign Policy, 1935-1955*, doctoral dissertation, Rutgers University, 1983 (Ann Arbor, Mich: University Microfilms International, 1983), p. 9.

14. Sallach, *Enlightened Self-Interest*, pp. 9-10.

15. Ibid., pp. 9-10.

16. "AFL Joins World Labor Body," AFL *Weekly News Service*, July 10, 1937; CIO, *1938 Proceedings*, p. 248; "CTM and CIO," *CIO News*, July 2, 1938, p. 4.

17. "Russian Unions Hit by AFL Council," AFL *Weekly News Service*, February 5, 1938; "International Federation of Trade Unions Bans Russian Labor Group," AFL *Weekly News Service*, July 15, 1939; AFL, *1938 Proceedings*, pp. 197-99; Lorwin, *International Labor Movement*, p. 181, 184; Sallach, *Enlightened Self-Interest*, pp. 11-14.

18. Peter Weiler, "The United States, International Labor, and the Cold War: The Breakup of the World Federation of Trade Unions," *Diplomatic History* 5 (Winter 1981): 1-22; David Dubinsky, "Rift and Realignment in World Labor," *Foreign Affairs* 27 (January 1949): 232-33.

19. Robert A. Divine, *The Reluctant Belligerent: American Entry into World War II* (New York: John Wiley and Sons, 1965), p. 49.

CROSS CURRENTS TO CONSENSUS: ORGANIZED LABOR'S CONFLICTING PERSPECTIVES ON FOREIGN AFFAIRS, 1939-1941

PART III

Points of Agreement in the Debate Over Intervention

CHAPTER 7

Phil Spitalny and his All-Girl Orchestra went on the air at 10:00 P.M. on January 26, 1941, over the National Broadcasting Company's Red Network. In New York City, the broadcast was carried by flagship station WEAF. O.L. Sprague might well have tuned into that program. He was a guest that evening at New York's Hotel Times Square, an establishment that proudly proclaimed it was equipped with a radio in every room.[1]

Sprague was in New York on behalf of the America First Committee, which was the leading pressure group opposing United States intervention in World War II. A representative of a health insurance company, the Benefit Association of Railway Employees, Sprague periodically attached himself to political campaigns as an expert on labor issues—even though his main union contacts were with such nondescript organizations as the Joint Association of Postal Employees of Western and Central Pennsylvania and the Independent Union of Allis-Chalmers Employees. Sprague had hired on with America First to help present that group's position to labor as part of its effort to block passage of the Lend-Lease bill, which sought to make the United States a virtual ally of Great Britain in its war against Nazi Germany.[2]

For several weeks in January 1941, Sprague travelled around the country, staying at posh hotels in New York, Florida,

Washington, Cleveland, Indianapolis, and elsewhere. He busied himself by organizing a national labor conference—that never actually took place—to protest Lend-Lease. He sent telegrams, wrote progress reports on hotel stationery, and made claims about his contacts with prominent labor executives whose names he sometimes misspelled. More importantly, he submitted numerous expense vouchers for himself and his two operatives, and managed to check out of hotels just in the nick of time to avoid receiving wires and phone calls from distressed America First officials who were trying to ascertain what, exactly, he was up to.[3]

William R. Castle was a former undersecretary of state who served on the National Committee of America First. When he encountered Sprague one day at America First headquarters, "doing a great deal of telephoning and apparently considering himself very important," he was aghast. Castle immediately dashed off a letter to America First Chairman Robert E. Wood, warning him that Sprague had been a "nuisance" for years around partisan groups and public interest committees, passing himself off as being very influential with organized labor. In fact, Castle reported, Sprague had "as far as we have been able to make out, no standing with either the CIO or the American Federation [of Labor]."[4]

Exasperated by the lack of results and the abundance of expense vouchers, the America First Committee dispensed with Sprague's services on January 28, 1941—simultaneously sending him one last expense check for $400. Evidently Sprague did not take the point immediately. In April, after learning that Sprague was "under some misapprehension as to [his] connection with the America First Committee," the national director of America First had to fire a note to his erstwhile colleague demanding that he cease using America First stationery.[5]

The resilient Mr. Sprague was not down for long. By May he turned up on the payroll of the Committee to Defend America by Aiding the Allies as a consultant on labor issues. That organization was the leading pressure group supporting intervention in World War II and the leading foe of the America First Committee. Sprague busied himself by sending telegrams, attending meetings, outlining ambitious plans to organize pro-intervention labor groups throughout the West and Midwest, and submitting expense vouchers for himself and his two operatives. Sprague subsequently vanished from the Committee to Defend America by Aiding the Allies as quickly as he had appeared, and on June 4 the meager paper trail of his abortive effort to establish pro-intervention labor groups was neatly and permanently filed away in the Committee's archives.[6]

If their choice of O.L. Sprague was not particularly astute, the committees' intention of swaying organized labor was. The Committee to Defend America by Aiding the Allies and the America First Committee were battling over the most controversial issue of the day. Whichever side could win labor's support would score a major coup. Upwards of 10 million workers belonged to unions affiliated with the American Federation of Labor (AFL) or the Congress of Industrial Organizations (CIO), and they and their families represented a sizeable bloc of votes.

Organized labor, however, was anything but monolithic. Its members lived in all sections of the country and were employed in fields as diverse as aviation and mining, pipe fitting and photo engraving, barbering and shipbuilding. They represented different ethnic groups, worshipped at different churches, and voted for different political parties. They were a cross section of an American public that was badly divided over the direction of American diplomacy.

Thus, there was no readily apparent labor perspective on foreign policy in 1939, 1940, and 1941 any more than there was a clear national point of view. The AFL and the CIO attempted to define positions on foreign affairs. They had to lead cautiously, however, because organized labor's rank and file were as divided over foreign policy as the rest of the country was. When a foreign policy consensus finally seemed to emerge within the labor movement, it came only as it had come among the American public as a whole—after a spirited and painful debate, and after Nazi Germany's power, intentions, and threat to the Western Hemisphere began to appear undeniable.

When Nazi forces attacked Poland on the morning of

September 1, 1939, the war that had been brewing in Europe for most of the decade was finally at hand. France and Britain declared war on Germany on September 3, and Canada followed suit within one week. Nine months later, Italy entered the fray as an ally of Germany. Americans, meanwhile, argued among themselves over how their country should respond to the events across the Atlantic Ocean.

Isolationists or non-interventionists argued that it was more important for the United States to stay out of the war than it was for the European democracies to prevail over the Axis powers. Generally suspicious of Europe, they viewed the war as nothing more than a continental power struggle in which the United States had no legitimate interest. Non-interventionists opposed giving American aid to Britain, partly because some of them were Anglophobic, but primarily because they were convinced that the United States would be drawn into the war if it provided assistance to a belligerent. Further, some believed that American aid would be worse than useless, because Britain was no match for the powerful Germans. Many non-interventionists hoped that the war would end quickly so that Western Europe could re-unite as a bulwark against the Soviet Union and they feared that would be impossible if American aid to Britain prolonged the war. Finally, non-interventionists were concerned that American involvement in the war would lead to political regimentation at home.[7]

Non-interventionism was strongest in the Middle West and Great Plains states, in Western mining states, and in such occupations as agriculture, light manufacturing, and service industries. It was people in those regions of the country and in those enterprises who felt most likely to be hurt rather than helped by foreign markets and least likely to discern any interests of their's being at stake in European struggles. Among numerous groups formed to express non-interventionist viewpoints and lobby against United States involvement in the war, the most important was the America First Committee.[8]

Interventionists, on the other hand, believed that the defeat of the Axis powers was essential to the security and well-being of the United States. They maintained that the Fascists and Nazis were determined to destroy democracy throughout the world. In particular, they feared that if Britain fell, the United States would be placed in the gravest peril. A victorious Germany, in control of the European continent and strengthened by the plundered resources of France and Britain, would pose an immediate military threat to the United States. Economically, a victorious Germany would harm the United States by denying it access to European markets and competing for trade with Latin America. American survival, the interventionists held, might well depend upon the ability of Britain to defeat Germany. To achieve that goal, many interventionists advocated United States assistance to Britain, in the form of loans and war materials. Some interventionists even called for the United States to enter the war as an ally of Britain.[9]

Greatest support for interventionism came from the Northeast and South, urban areas, and heavy industry, where there was greater susceptibility to trans-Atlantic influences, a keener sense of being threatened by European instabilities, and a notable presence of ethnic groups whose kinsmen were victims of the European dictators. The Committee to Defend America by Aiding the Allies championed the cause of aid to the European democracies. It was also known as the White Committee, after its founder and first chairman, Kansas newspaper editor William Allen White. The Century Group and Fight for Freedom, Incorporated, meanwhile, favored an immediate United States declaration of war against Germany.[10]

At the local and state levels, organized labor sometimes appeared confused or naive in its reactions to developments in Europe. The *Southern Labor Review,* for example, which was the official organ of AFL-affiliated trades councils in several cities in Alabama, published some of the country's most muddled assessments of the international scene. The *Review* seemed unaware that what monarchies existed in Europe were constitutional rather than absolute, once babbling that "Prime Ministers must now shake in their shoes for 'the King can do no wrong.'" On more than one occasion the *Review* implied that a root cause of World War II was that Britain and France desired to reintroduce monarchy throughout Europe. In a major front page editorial about the war in Europe, the *Review* expressed the fear that the United States would become a "protectorate" of Britain and Germany (although apparently what it meant was that Britain and Germany would become protectorates of the United States). It also adopted contradictory positions—denouncing Britain but supporting aid to that country, for instance, and opposing entangling alliances while endorsing internationalist policies.[11]

The ramblings of the *Southern Labor Review* notwithstanding, organized labor's rank and file followed international affairs avidly and perceptively. Union members debated foreign policy in statewide federations, citywide councils, and local unions, and they issued resolutions. They read about world developments in the pages of labor newspapers, which devoted increasing space to international events. Not only were labor newspapers publishing more and more locally-written editorials on international topics, they also printed speeches and news reports and ran regular, nationally syndicated features and columns that dealt with those issues.[12]

The response of organized labor to the war in Europe reflected national patterns. That is, opinion on whether or not the United States should intervene in any way in the hostilities broke down along regional and occupational lines, as it did throughout the country.

⊕ ⊕ ⊕

While divided on the subject of intervention, organized labor was in agreement on two related issues. First, organized labor opposed sending American troops to Europe. Second, organized labor opposed Adolf Hitler and the Nazis.

Especially during the first year of the European hostilities, the issue that divided American labor was not precisely that of going to war versus staying out of war. It was true that by the middle of 1941 the pro-war Fight For Freedom organization had won the endorsements of several labor groups. Still, even the most fervent pro-interventionist elements in the labor movement usually gave at least pro-forma support to the ideal of American neutrality, and only espoused assistance to Britain that fell short of actual American entry into the war. A poll conducted by the Federated Press in December 1940 revealed that 91 percent of the editors of labor newspapers opposed United States entry into the war. As late as May 1941, a Federated Press poll indicated widespread anti-war sentiment among the labor editors.[13]

Defense industries were major employers in Los Angeles, and union members in that city generally supported Britain and military preparedness programs—but they also urged the United States to stay out of the war.[14] Even as it condemned pacifists and appeasement and edged toward support of aiding Britain, the Topeka Federation of Labor warned against sending American forces to Europe.[15] Well after it had become one of the stronger voices in midwestern labor circles favoring preparedness and aid to the Allies, the *Labor News* of South Bend and Fort Wayne, Indiana, continued to rail against "war mongers" who sought to "enmesh" the United States in the European war, to remind labor of how it had been "betrayed" after the First World War, and to warn of the misfortunes that would befall labor if the United States entered the Second World War.[16]

Even the Atlanta Federation of Trades and Allied Unions—surely one of the most consistently pro-interventionist, pro-preparedness, and anti-isolationist labor groups in the country—urged the United States to keep its troops at home. It praised the Neutrality Act of 1937 as an effective defense against foreign entanglements, criticized Europe for its reliance on "power politics," and stated that the experience of World War I proved "that war settles nothing."[17]

If American labor was fairly unified in its opposition to war, it was just as unified in its revulsion against Adolf Hitler and Nazi Germany. Obviously, interventionists in the labor movement spoke out loudly against the treachery of the Nazis and Fascists in Europe.[18] Yet their anti-Nazi sentiments were matched by those of isolationists in the labor movement. In that respect, labor isolationists were not unlike isolationists in other walks of life. Although there were some pro-Nazi and anti-Semitic elements among the isolationists, the vast majority of isolationists did not side with Hitler. As leading isolationist United States Senator Burton K. Wheeler said in response to a union resolution accusing him of having Nazi sympathies, "I know of no American who does not hate Hitler and Nazism and all they symbolize."[19]

Anti-interventionist labor groups in Cincinnati and Chicago, for example, frequently expressed anti-Nazi views. They assailed Nazi Germany for destroying German democracy, despoiling Europe, and seeking to "paganize the Western world." They attacked the racial hatred and religious persecution that had taken hold in Germany.[20]

An essential factor that gave rise to the anti-Hitler consensus within organized labor was the widespread understanding that Hitler and Italian dictator Benito Mussolini were anti-labor. Following the lead of the AFL and the CIO, official publications of city and state labor organizations in all parts of the country carried a steady stream of reports and editorials recounting and denouncing Nazi and Fascist mistreatment of labor. The dissolution of free trade unions in Germany and Italy, the establishment of government-controlled, bogus labor organizations to replace the unions, the disappearance of collective bargaining, the introduction by the Nazis of compulsory labor, the "speed-up" of labor, and the abolition of unions in counties invaded by Germany were seen by all elements of American labor as evidence that European labor was being driven into a "condition approaching serfdom." American unions also condemned Germany's use of prisoners of war as forced labor, the exploitation of child labor, the drastic reduction of wages and cuts in social services, the dire need for food and clothing among workers in areas under Axis control, and the apparently increasing wealth and power of German capitalists.[21] The labor press carried critical references to Japan once in a while, but the overwhelming interest was in the European dictators and their anti-union policies.

State labor organizations passed resolutions and issued statements condemning the Nazis—particularly for their hostility toward labor. Likewise, anti-Nazi sentiments were expressed by individual unions, from the anti-interventionist Carpenters (AFL),

Pressmen (AFL), and United Mine Workers (CIO) to the pro-interventionist United Auto Workers (CIO) and Restaurant Employees (AFL). All segments of organized labor in the United States seemed to perceive that European dictatorships were anti-labor and that they turned "human beings . . . into slaves." As early as 1935, the Milk Wagon Drivers of Indiana grasped that concept when they successfully submitted a resolution to the convention of the Indiana State Federation of Labor that stated that Hitler's "reign of terror" had "wiped out the free trade unions [and] imprisoned, tortured, and murdered trade union leaders and thousands of the working population." As the president of the New York State Federation of Labor declared in 1940, "Dictatorships and a Labor Movement as we Americans know it are in direct contradiction to each other. There is no such thing as a Labor Movement existent in the countries of the dictators or those countries they have conquered."[22]

The labor press feared that Hitler's war on unions would reach beyond Europe and affect American labor. That fear emanated partly from the concern that Hitler might one day attack the United States. Shortly before the United States entered the war, some labor newspapers ran "In Hitler's Own Words"—a lurid series distributed by Fight for Freedom that sought to depict an America under Nazi rule. One installment bore a headline paraphrased from Hitler's *Mein Kampf*: "Labor unions are ridiculous." Decorated with photographs of terrified American workingmen and their even more terrified wives cowering beneath a glowering, whip-brandishing storm trooper, the feature warned that Hitler was out to destroy unionism in America, repeal the gains American labor had won, and "reduce man to an animal state."[23]

American labor felt the Nazi threat in more immediate ways. Low wage labor and slave labor in Nazi-occupied Europe could undercut American exports and create unemployment in the United States. German interests were reported in 1941 to be purchasing American holdings in Europe, further putting the American economy at risk. And in 1939 and 1940, tongues were set wagging in labor circles when an anti-union, German-controlled Czech footwear company, Bata shoes, attempted to open a plant in Maryland—a step potentially laced with danger for American unions.[24]

Reinforcing Hitler's anti-labor image were innumerable analogies drawn by unionists between the German dictator and union-baiting industrialists and reactionary politicians in the United States. The Pressman's local in Topeka accused American corporate leaders of admiring the Nazis for crushing German unions and labeled them "would-be Hitlers." An article in the Hotel and Restaurant Workers' journal described American industry as an "autocracy" similar to the dictatorships of Hitler and Mussolini. The *Lansing Industrial News* editorialized that United States Representative Carl Vinson acted in "the traditional Hitler blitzkrieg method" when he introduced legislation to impose compulsory arbitration in lieu of strikes. Sometimes it was possible to go beyond metaphors and demonstrate links between Hitler and labor's enemies in America that were direct, if weak. Henry Ford, longtime nemesis of organized labor, accepted a medal from Hitler and collaborated with American Nazis on a German exposition in New York. Conservative United States Senator Edward Burke, an opponent of the Wagner Act, was quoted as having praised Hitler and was reputedly a one-time member of an American fascist organization, the Khaki Shirts. The analogies and alleged links were cited commonly by members of organized labor.[25] If the bogeymen of the labor movement were American reactionaries of business and politics, then American reactionaries were like demi-tasse Hitlers, and Hitler was simply an American reactionary on a grand scale.

Even in areas with high concentrations of German-American residents, such as Cincinnati, St. Louis, and Wisconsin, labor circles typically expressed strong anti-Nazi sentiments. For example, the St. Louis Central Trades and Labor Union, headed by people with names such as Brandt, Preisler, Stegman, and Heinrichs, developed a series of radio broadcasts in 1939 to denounce the Nazis and generate local support for the boycott of German goods. One of America's most prominent anti-Nazi labor leaders of German descent was UAW Vice President Walter Reuther.

Another was AFL Vice President Matthew Woll. He joined Fred Rasser, vice president of the Hotel and Restaurant Employees and Bartenders Union, Edward Volz, president of the Photoengravers Union, and William Schrenberg, president of the United Cement, Lime, and Gypsum Workers Union, in an anti-Nazi group, "Loyal Americans of German Descent." Perhaps helping persuade German-American unionists were exiled German labor leaders, including Frederick Stampfer, Gerhardt H. Seger, and Toni Sender, who wrote articles and spoke to labor groups throughout the United States about the anti-labor intentions of the Nazis.[26]

Pro-Nazi organizations in the United States claimed tens of thousands of German-Americans as members, but unionists were seldom among them. Instead, the German-American Bund and similar groups attracted German-Americans who were at loggerheads with organized labor, such as small merchants and recent immigrants who had drifted into unskilled and unorganized occupations.[27]

Mussolini and his Italian Fascists, meanwhile, were enormously influential in the Italian-American community—except among Italian-American unionists. From the time of Mussolini's ascension to power in Italy, labor leaders such as Luigi Antonini of the International Ladies' Garment Workers' Union and August Bellanca of the Amalgamated Clothing Workers fought to stave off Fascist influence in the Italian-American labor movement and to counteract Fascist dominance in the Italian-American community as a whole. The leading anti-Fascist group in the United States, the Mazzini Society, reminded Italian-American workers of how Fascist Italy had exploited Italian labor. Italian-American labor groups spoke out against the Fascists, raised money for Italians who had suffered at the hands of the Fascists, and also condemned the Nazis. One-time labor organizer Anthony Capraro deemed his role in the Italian-American anti-Fascist movement a "holy crusade."[28]

There was consensus in the labor movement, then, on the two very broad issues of opposition to an American declaration of war and opposition to the Nazis and Fascists. On more specific issues, however, there were significant disagreements within organized labor. Labor groups held divergent opinions on Lend Lease, convoys, military conscription, preparedness, Neutrality Act revision, the value of Britain to American security, the role of American business in the war, and the possible effects of wartime measures on American political institutions. Those differences led some labor groups—notably in the Middle West and Far West—to align themselves with the isolationists. Other labor groups, meanwhile—notably in the Northeast and the South—aligned themselves with the interventionists.

Notes

1. *New York Times*, January 26, 1941, section 9, page 11; Sprague to General [Robert Wood], n.d., "Sprague-Spencer" file, box 4, Papers of America First Committee, Hoover Institution Archives, Stanford University, Palo Alto, Calif.; R. Douglas Stuart to Wood, January 27, 1941, Ibid.

2. J.M.R. to Wood, n.d., William Castle to Wood, January 22, 1941, James Callagher to O.L. Sprague, January 21, 1941, George Humphreys receipt, n.d., Sprague to Wood, January 31, 1941, John Chambers to Sprague, January 29, 1941, "Sprague-Spencer" file, box 4, America First Papers.

3. Humphreys to Sprague, January 18, 1941, National Director to Sprague, February 5, 1941, Sprague to Wood, January 31, 1941, Steven Spencer to Sprague, January 30, 1941, "Report on Sprague telegrams," n.d., Sprague to Hoover, January 28, 1941 (plus similar telegraphs to Hutchinson [sic], Vance, and Duffy), Sprague letter (to "Dear Sir"), January 22, 1941, Sprague memo, n.d., Sprague to Stuart, January 20, 1941, Sprague to Wood (Willkie stationery), n.d., Sprague to Stuart, January 25, 1941, J.M.R. to Wood, n.d., Sprague to General [Wood], n.d., Stuart to Sprague, January 31, 1941, Stuart to Wood, January 27, 1941, F.H. Camphausen to Stuart, January 24, 1941, Sprague to Wood, January 24, 1941, Castle to Wood, January 22, 1941, Wood to Whom It May Concern, January 20, 1941, miscellaneous hotel receipts, Postal Telegram Company to Wood, January 24, 1941, "Sprague-Spencer" file, box 4, America First Papers.

4. Castle to Wood, January 22, 1941, "Sprague-Spencer" file, box 4, America First Papers.

5. Wood to Sprague, January 28, 1941, "Sprague-Spencer" file, box 4, America First Papers; Stuart to Sprague, April 1, 1941, file: "S—Jan.-April," box 67, Ibid.

6. Goodwin to Clark Eichelberger, May 6, 1941, Goodwin to Eichelberger, May 9, 1941, Committee to Gibson, May 7, 1941, Gibson to Sprague, May 10, 1941, Chambers to Eichelberger, May 15, 1941, Chambers, Smith, Spencer, and Sprague to Gibson, May 3, 1941, Graves to Gibson, May 3, 1941, R.S.G. to Ericson, June 4,

1941, file: "Admin. Mgmt.—Labor Organizations in the Middle West—Sprague," box 4, Committee to Defend America by Aiding the Allies Archives, Princeton University Library, Princeton, N.J.

7. Wayne S. Cole, *Charles A. Lindbergh and the Battle Against American Intervention in World War II* (New York: Harcourt Brace Jovanovich, 1974), pp. 9-10, 72, 78-84; Wayne S. Cole, *America First: The Battle Against Intervention, 1940-1941* (Madison: University of Wisconsin Press, 1953), pp. 8-10; America First advertisement, *Chicago Daily News*. November 1, 1940 p. 18.

8. Wayne S. Cole, *An Interpretive History of American Foreign Relations*, rev. ed. (Homewood, Ill.: Dorsey Press, 1974), p. 322; Wayne S. Cole, *Roosevelt and the Isolationists, 1932-45* (Lincoln: University of Nebraska Press, 1983), pp. 365, 379; Wayne S. Cole, *Determinism and American Foreign Relations During the Franklin D. Roosevelt Era* (Lanham, Md.: University Press of America, 1995), pp. 3-4, 8-9, 30-2, 77-9.

9. Cole, *Lindbergh*, pp. 8-9, 75, 136-7; Cole, *America First*, pp. 6-8, 37-9, 79-80; Walter Johnson, *The Battle Against Isolation* (Chicago: University of Chicago Press, 1946), pp. 47-8, 79, 86, 132, 223-5; Mark Lincoln Chadwin, *The Hawks of World War II* (Chapel Hill: University of North Carolina Press, 1968), pp. v, 33, 74-5, 156-62.

10. Cole, *Interpretive History*, pp. 323-24; Cole, *Determinism and American Foreign Relations*, pp. 5, 53-6, 79-82.

11. Untitled squib, "A quandary . . .," Birmingham (Ala.) *Southern Labor Review*, April 12, 1939, p. 2; Untitled squibs, "The German-Russian Pact . . . " and "Prime Ministers must . . ." Birmingham *Southern Labor Review*, August 23, 1939, p. 2; "An Open Letter to the People of America," Birmingham *Southern Labor Review*, December 25, 1940, p. 1; Untitled squib, "A military dictatorship . . ." Birmingham *Southern Labor Review*, April 12, 1939, p. 2; "Selfishness of Great Britain," Birmingham *Southern Labor Review*, March 15, 1939, p.2; Untitled squib, "But England seems . . ." Birmingham *Southern Labor Review*, March 15, 1939, p. 2; "Our Place," Birmingham *Southern Labor Review*, March 22, 1939 p. 1; Untitled squib, "Beware of foreign entanglements . . ." Birmingham *Southern Labor Review*, February 14, 1940; Untitled squib, "If allowed a voice . . ." Birmingham *Southern Labor Review*, October 16, 1940, p. 2; "European Situation Befogged," Birmingham *Southern Labor Review*, October 23, 1940, p. 2; "For Our Own Safety, Act Now!," Birmingham *Southern Labor Review*, January 15, 1941. Also see Gerald R. Gordon, *The AFL, the CIO, and the Quest for a Peaceful World Order, 1914-1946*, doctoral dissertation, University of Maine, Orono, 1967 (Ann Arbor: University Microfilms, 1968), p. 107.

12. Syndicated columnists such as Charles Stelzle, Ruth Taylor, Scot Nearing, and features such as "What the Magazines Are Saying," "On the Capital's Cuff," "Legislative News Chatter," "The Washington Scene," "Weekly News Analysis," "Who's News," and "Picture Parade" frequently covered international events and were carried regularly by many labor newspapers, including the Butte *Montana Labor News*, the *Hannibal Labor Press*, the Council Bluffs *Farmer-*

Labor Press, the Duluth *Labor World*, the Des Moines *Iowa Unionist*, the *Lansing Industrial News*, and the Peoria *Labor Temple News*, among others.

13. Labor leaders to Franklin Roosevelt, June 11, 1941, Fight for Freedom Press Release: "More than 1,600 local labor leaders . . ." n.d., "U.S. Labor Gives President Strong Support in 'Stop Hitler' Moves," *Labor News Service*, May 29, 1941, "Labor" file, box 45, Fight for Freedom Archives, Princeton University Library, Princeton, N.J.; "Convoys Opposed by Labor Editors; Poll Reveals Anti-War Sentiment," Portland *Oregon Labor Press*, May 30, 1941, p.l.

14. "War Guns Echo Here," *Los Angeles Citizen*, April 19, 1940, p. 4; "Is Just an Office Holder," *Los Angeles Citizen*, December 27, 1940, p. 4; "Light of Freedom," *Los Angeles Citizen*, February 2, 1940, p. 4; "Armistice Day 1939," *Los Angeles Citizen*, November 10, 1939, p. 4.

15. "Timely Topics," *Kansas Labor Weekly*, February 15, 1940, p. 2; untitled editorials, *Kansas Labor Weekly*, January 25, 1940, p. 2; "Labor Wants Peace," *Kansas Labor Weekly*, September 21, 1939, p. 3; untitled editorials, *Kansas Labor Weekly*, September 7, 1939, p. 2.

16. "War Mongers Work with Daring and Persistency," South Bend/Fort Wayne *Labor News*, January 10, 1941, p. 1; "Labor Betrayed in the Last War," South Bend/Fort Wayne *Labor News*, November 8, 1940, p. 1; "Chaos in the War Boom," South Bend/Fort Wayne *Labor News*, May 9, 1941; "Defense Program May Mean More Poverty," South Bend/Fort Wayne *Labor News*, May 16, 1941; "War Means Lower Living Standards," South Bend/Fort Wayne *Labor News* June 13, 1941, p.l.

17. "Our Foreign Policy," Atlanta *Journal of Labor*, September 8, 1939, p. 4.

18. See, for example, "Labor is Conscripted in Germany," Atlanta *Journal of Labor*, July 22, 1938, p. 1; "War on Children," Atlanta *Journal of Labor*, September 15, 1939, p. 6; "Keep America Out of War," Atlanta *Journal of Labor*, August 23, 1940, p. 2; "Why We Aid British Labor," Atlanta *Journal of Labor*, July 18, 1941, p. 2; "First Take an Active Part," Atlanta *Journal of Labor*, February 3, 1939, p. 2; "Proceedings, Pre-and-Post Convention Meetings, Executive Council," August 19-28, 1941, pp. 79-80, file 25-2, box 25, Series III, Records of the American Federation of Teachers, Walter Reuther Library, Wayne State University, Detroit, Mich.; Zander to Sauthoff, August 1, 1941, file 2, box 104, Records of President's Office, American Federation of State, County, and Municipal Employees, Walter Reuther Library, Detroit, Mich.; Walter Reuther Radio Address, December 28, 1940, file 539-14, box 539, Walter P. Reuther Papers, Walter Reuther Library, Detroit, Mich.; Walter Reuther radio address, October 30, 1940 (transcript dated October 31, 1940), file 539-13, box 39, Reuther Papers.

19. Cole, *America First*, pp. 8-9; Burton Wheeler to Zander, November 28, 1941, folder 2, box 104, President's Office, American Federation of State, Country and Municipal Employees Records.

20. "United Garment Workers' Local 99," Cincinnati *Chronicle*, July 28, 1939, p. 6; "Recreational Tid-bits," Cincinnati *Chronicle*, August 25, 1939, p. 3;

"Mass Meeting Condemns Autocrats of Europe," Cincinnati *Chronicle*, October 13, 1939, p. 5; "Why Did We So Long Back Hitler?" and "Tolerance?," Chicago *Federation News*, July 13, 1940, p. 4; "The Old U-Boat Spirit," Chicago *Federation News*, August 26, 1939, p. 4; "Casualties," Chicago *Federation News*, June 22, 1940, p. 4; "Can Christianity Survive?," Chicago *Federation News*, November 2, 1940, p. 1.

21. "Right to Strike Guarantees Freedom," *Wisconsin Labor*, 1941, p. 47; "Hitler's Rule in Germany Brought Hunger to Many," *Los Angeles Citizen*, September 1, 1939, p. 5; "Slavery of People Under Hitler," *Los Angeles Citizen*, November 24, 1939, p. 4; "Workers Enslaved in Nazi Germany," South Bend/Fort Wayne *Labor News*, September 29, 1939, p. 1; "The German Labor Movement," South Bend/Fort Wayne *Labor News*, March 8, 1940, p. 2; "Nazis Erect Slave State in Pole Area," South Bend/Fort Wayne *Labor News*, May 10, 1940, p. 3; "Trade Unionism Under a Dictatorship," South Bend/Fort Wayne *Labor News*, November 1, 1940; "Workers Enslaved in Nazi Germany—Heil Hitler!," Portland *Oregon Labor Press*, September 22, 1939, p. 3; "War Time Employment Control in Dictatorships and Democracies," Portland *Oregon Labor Press*, August 22, 1941, p. 2; "Big Business Built Hitler," Portland *Oregon Labor Press*, August 1, 1941, p. 2; "Two Symbols," Portland *Oregon Labor Press*, October 17, 1941, p. 2; "Slavery of People Under Hitlerism," *Lansing Industrial News*, November 3, 1939, p. 2; "Labor and the Middle Class Under Hitler," *Lansing Industrial News*, December 8, 1939, p. 2; "Hitlerism Re-Analyzed," Peoria *Labor Temple News*, January 5, 1940, p. 5; "Reveal Home Work New Kind of Slavery in Nazi Germany," Peoria *Labor Temple News*, January 13, 1939, p. 11; "The Weekly Parade," Peoria *Labor Temple News*, March 17, 1939, p. 5; "Prisoner War Slavery Sign of New Dark Ages," Peoria *Labor Temple News*, February 23, 1940, p. 10; "Old Grouch's Column," *Hannibal Labor Press*, November 22, 1940; "French Labor Group Abolished by Petain," *Hannibal Labor Press*, November 29, 1940; "Hitler's Power Means Death to Unions," *Hannibal Labor Press*, October 17, 1941; "Slavery of People Under Hitlerism," Omaha *Unionist*, November 3, 1939, p. 2; "German Labor Under Iron Rule," Omaha *Unionist*, September 27, 1940, p. 3; "Compulsory Labor," Kalispell (Montana) *Treasure State Labor Journal*, May 27, 1941, p. 1; "Americanism and Trade Unionism," Chicago *Federation Labor News*, December 6, 1941, p. 6; "Labor Day and the Future," Toledo *CIO News*, September 2, 1940, p. 1; "Workers Enslaved in Nazi Germany," Cheyenne *Wyoming Labor Journal*, September 29, 1939, p. 7; "Slavery of People Under Hitlerism," Cheyenne *Wyoming Labor Journal*, October 20, 1939, p. 8; "He's a Free Man, Not a Galley Slave," (cartoon), Cheyenne *Wyoming Labor Journal*, July 5, 1940, p. 2; "Googe Back from Geneva Discusses Labor in Europe," Atlanta *Journal of Labor*, July 22, 1938, p. 1; "Labor is Conscripted in Germany," Atlanta *Journal of Labor*, July 22, 1938, p. 1; "Labor and the National Emergency," Topeka *Kansas Labor Weekly*, August 28, 1941, p. 10.

22. Indiana State Federation of Labor, *Official Proceedings of the Fifty-Seventh Annual Convention*, (Evansville: Indiana State Federation of Labor,

1941), pp. 175, 177; Indiana State Federation of Labor, *Official Proceedings of the Fifty-First Annual Convention*, (Muncie: Indiana State Federation of Labor, 1935,) p. 109; Missouri State Federation of Labor, *Proceedings of the Forty-Third Annual and Third Biennial Convention*, (Springfield: Missouri State Federation of Labor, 1939), p. 76; New Hampshire State Federation of Labor, *Fortieth Annual Convention of the New Hampshire State Federation of Labor: Journal of Proceedings*, (Keene: New Hampshire Federation of Labor, 1941), p. 11; New York State Federation of Labor, *1940 Official Proceedings, Seventy-Seventh Annual Convention*, (n.p.: New York State Federation of Labor, 1940), p. 11; "More Airplanes for Defense," Reuther radio address, December 28, 1940, file 539-14, box 539, Reuther Papers; Mahan to Reuther, November 27, 1941 (plus attachment: transcript of Reuther remarks to the 1941 CIO Convention), file 540-3, box 540, *Ibid.*, "Coal Miners in Germany May be Forced to Accept Soldiers' Pay," *United Mine Workers Journal*, December 15, 1939, p. 16; "German Labor is Chain Gang," *Catering Industry Employee*, November 1939, p. 19; "Will Europe Call Hitler's Bluff in 1939?," *Carpenter*, February 1939, pp. 2-4; "The Enslavement of German Workers," *Carpenter*, July 1939, pp. 4-5; "Facing the Facts," *Carpenter*, March 1940, pp. 9-13; "The Test of Democracy," *American Pressman*, February 1939, pp. 19-21; "Two Symbols," *American Pressman*, November 1941, p. 16; "Labor vs. Dictatorship," *Los Angeles Citizen*, September 5, 1941, II:2.

23. "In Hitler's Own Words," Des Moines *Iowa Unionist*, November 21, 1941. Also see "Suppose Hitler Conquered America" Salt Lake City *Utah Labor News*, April 25, 1941, p. 8; "Hitler Would Make Slave of All Workers," *Lansing Industrial News*, June 20, 1941, II:1; "Hitler Victory Would Enslave American Workers," *Hannibal Labor Press*, June 20, 1941; and "Greenwood Tells American Workers that Hitler Victory Would Enslave Them," *Waco Farm and Labor Journal*, July 25, 1941, p. 2; "Gov. Sewall Warns Maine Open to Attack," Boston *Wage Earner*, July 14, 1941, p. 1.

24. "Hitler's Power Means Death to Unions," *Hannibal Labor Press*, October 17, 1941; "Harrison Warns Hitler Will Attack U.S. Trade," *Hannibal Labor Press*, July 12, 1940; "Reveal Additional Hitler Ties of Czech Shoe Czar," Peoria *Labor Temple News*, August 23, 1940, p. 1; "Refugee Industries," *Lansing Industrial News*, May 10, 1940, p. 2; "Germans Take Over American Concerns at Bargain Prices," *Lansing Industrial News*, June 13, 1941, p. 1; "Labor Blocks 'Speedup' Bata," *Carpenter*, March 1940, p. 30; "Objection to Foreign Firm," *United Mine Workers Journal*, December 15, 1939, p. 9.

25. "Just to Keep the Record Straight," Topeka *Kansas Labor Weekly*, September 4, 1941; "Just to Keep the Record Straight," Topeka *Kansas Labor Weekly*, November 27, 1941; "Who Is the Dictator, Organized Labor or the Employer?," *Catering Industry Employee*, March 1940, p. 17; "'Hitler' Invades Coachella Valley, California," *Catering Industry Employee*, November 1941, p. 9; "Attack on Labor," *Lansing Industrial News*, May 2, 1941, p. 2; "What Some in the U.S. Would Like to Have Here," *Los Angeles Citizen*, July 7, 1939, p. 3; "Burke

Sees Merit German Dictator," Omaha *Unionist*, October 7, 1938, p. 2; "Burke Member of Khaki Shirts, Revealed by Former Organizer," Peoria *Labor Temple News*, October 6, 1939, p. 2; "Ford Exhibit in Nazi Show," Peoria *Labor Temple News*, December 23, 1938, p. 5; "Ford and Hitler," *Denver Labor Bulletin*, September 1938, p. 3. For further examples of the analogy, see "Lewis Warns Steel Union of Fascist Danger," *CIO News*, December 22, 1937, p. 3; "CIO Asks Protests on Hill-Sheppard Bills," *CIO News*, February 5, 1938, p. 1; "Heil Hague!", *CIO News*, June 11, 1938, p. 4; "Appeasing the Wolves," *CIO News*, February 20, 1939, p. 4; "NLRB Official Assails Tories in Mexico Speech," *CIO News*, September 10, 1938, p. 5; "Senator Burke, Wagner Act Foe, Praises Hitler," *CIO News*; "Delegates Assail Anti-Labor Policies of Ford, *CIO News*, November 21, 1938, p. 2; "Facing the Facts," AFL *Weekly News Service*, January 6, 1940; "Facing the Facts, AFL *Weekly News Service*, February 10, 1940; "Lyons Warns of Attacks on Rights of Workers," AFL *Weekly News Service*, October 22, 1940; "A.F. of L. Fights Anti-Trust Suits Against Labor Unions," AFL *Weekly News Service*, February 10, 1940; "Facing the Facts," AFL *Weekly News Service*, February 24, 1940; "We Are Thankful We Live in America Where Unions Still Exist," *Sacramento Valley Union Labor Bulletin*, November 3, 1939, p. 1.

26. "Two New Books Repeal [sic] Labor's Plight Under Hitlerized State," *St. Louis Union Labor Advocate*, February 15, 1941, p. 1; "Labor Speaks Against Nazism," *St. Louis Union Labor Advocate*, June 15, 1939, p. 5; "Father Coughlinism," *St. Louis Union Labor Advocate*, June 15, 1939, p. 2; "To Hell With Hitler!," *St. Louis Union Labor Advocate*, September 15, 1939, p. 2; "St. Louis Ideal Center for Airplane Factories," *St. Louis Union Labor Advocate*, June 1, 1940, p. 1; "Old Glory Must Not Take the Wrap," *St. Louis Union Labor Advocate*, July 15, 1940, p. 2; "Central Trades Hear Gerhart Seger Blast Hitler Labor Slavery," *St. Louis Union Labor Advocate*, February 1, 1941, p. 1; "Nazis Strike at Civilization," *St. Louis Labor Tribune*, May 11, 1940, p. 4; "Mass Extermination," *St. Louis Labor Tribune*, November 5, 1941, p. 4; "Right to Work Guarantees Freedom," *Wisconsin Labor*, 1941, p. 47; "Stay Democratic," *Wisconsin Labor*, 1941, p. 59; "President Roosevelt Pleads for Peace," Madison *Union Label News*, March 1939, p. 2; "It Looks Like This," Madison *Union Label News*, October 1939, p. 1; "Hitler is the Meanest Man," Madison *Union Label News*, October 1939, p. 2; "Blessing of Nazism: German Workers Low Living Standard," Madison *Union Label News*, December 1940, p. 3; "United Garment Workers' Local 99," Cincinnati *Chronicle*, July 28, 1939, p. 6; "Activities of Women's Auxiliary to Trades Unions," Cincinnati *Chronicle*, August 25, 1939, p. 5; "Recreational Tid-bits," Cincinnati *Chronicle*, August 25, 1939, p. 3; "Even the U.S. Has Its Troubles," Cincinnati *Chronicle*, September 1, 1939, p. 4; "Both Mean Dictatorship and Terrorism," Cincinnati *Chronicle*, September 8, 1939, p. 4; "Mass Meeting Condemns Autocrats of Europe," Cincinnati *Chronicle*, October 13, 1939, p. 5; "Slavery of the People Under Hitlerism," *Lansing Industrial News*, November 3, 1939, p. 2; "The German Labor Movement," South Bend/Fort Wayne *Labor News*, March 8, 1940; "Facing the Facts," AFL *Weekly News Service*,

February 10, 1940; "The Choice Before Us," n.d. (ca. 1942), file: "Articles by T. Sender," box 5, Toni Sender Papers, Wisconsin State Historical Society, Madison, Wis.; "German-American Congress for Democracy Active in Many Fields," *Intercultural Education News*, October 1941, p. 3, Ibid.; Press Release, July 28, 1941, "Labor" file, Fight for Freedom Archives, Princeton University Library, Princeton, N.J.

27. Sander A. Diamond, *The Nazi Movement in the United States, 1924-1941* (Ithaca: Cornell University Press, 1974), pp. 30-1, 137-39, 146-51, 156.

28. James Edward Miller, *The United States and Italy, 1940-1950: The Politics and Diplomacy of Stabilization* (Chapel Hill, N.C., 1986), pp. 13-15, 25; Anthony Capraro to Editor of *Advance*, September 20, 1943, box 1, Anthony Capraro Papers, Immigration History Research Center, University of Minnesota, St. Paul, Minn.; Capraro to Editor of *New York Times*, June 6, 1941, *Ibid.*, Capraro to *New York Post*, September 24, 1938, Ibid.; Capraro to Rower, January 8, 1946, Ibid.; Capraro to Salvadori, January 3, 1939, box 2, Ibid., Capraro to Poyntz, May 22, 1939, box 4, Ibid.; Typed excerpt from *Il Progresso Italo-Americano*, March 28, 1941, "Antonini" file, box 1, Alberto Cupelli Papers, Immigration History Research Center, University of Minnesota, St. Paul, Minn.; Salvemia to George Quilici, September 24, 1942, folder 17, box 3, George L. Quilici Papers, Immigration History Research Center, University of Minnesota, St. Paul, Minn.; Quilici speech to American Clothing Workers, June 6, 1951, folder 18, box 6, Ibid.; "Italy and the 'Now Order,'" *Mazzini News*, February 14, 1941, box 1, Capraro Papers; "Coagulation or Strangulation," *Mazzini News*, March 5, 1941, Ibid.; "La nostra unione aiutera' divettamente lo vittime italiane profughe all' estero," Jersey City/New York *Giustizia*, August 1941, p. 1; "Mento la follia sanguinaria divampa," Jersey City/New York *Giustizia*, August 1941, p. 12; "Luigi Antonini Protests to Phillip Murray," New York *Il Progresso Italo-Americano*, December 5, 1943, p. 12; "Union Officer Affirms U.S. Italians' Loyalty, AFL *Weekly News Service*, June 18, 1940; "President Green Says Fascism Is Menace on Par with Communism," AFL *Weekly News Service*, February 2, 1935.

The Labor Isolationists

CHAPTER 8

Anti-interventionist sentiment was strongest in the Midwest. That was true for the country as a whole, and it was true for organized labor.

Two of the most successful chapters of the anti-interventionist America First Committee were located in Chicago and Cincinnati.[1] Similarly, two of the most anti-interventionist labor groups in the country were the Chicago Federation of Labor and the Central Labor Council of Greater Cincinnati. They both denied that democracy or American interests were at stake in the European conflict and advocated strict neutrality. Pointing to World War I as an example, they warned that revising the Neutrality Act to permit loans or the sale of war implements to the Allies unquestionably would force the United States into the war by creating an American economic interest in the outcome of the war. Echoing one of the primary arguments of America First, they predicted that American entry into the war would result quickly and unavoidably in the imposition of a military dictatorship that would restrict political liberties in the United States and regiment labor. The two labor groups publicized the activities of America First, denigrated the pro-interventionist White Committee, organized anti-intervention letter-writing campaigns, and endorsed the views of leading isolationist spokesmen such as aviators Charles Lindbergh and Eddie Rickenbacker, historian Charles Beard, and United States Senators Gerald Nye, William

Borah, Pat McCarran, Henrik Shipstead, and Burton Wheeler.[2]

The "Theory of Two Spheres"—the notion that the Old World was inherently different from the New and that the Eastern Hemisphere was corrupt and the Western democratic—was a bedrock principle of American isolationism. That view was reflected in the foreign policy positions of the Chicago Federation of Labor and the Cincinnati Central Labor Council. If the United States attempted to stabilize Europe by force, it would risk its own internal peace and stability. United Garment Workers Local 99, an affiliate of the Cincinnati Central Labor Council, stated that "Europeans know only European principles which have been handed down by tyrants" and that "we cannot lose our faith in preserving America for the Americas. We must make and keep America a utopia of peace forever and ever." Moreover, whenever the United States became involved in European affairs, the Europeans supposedly took advantage of the Americans. In the words of the Cincinnati Central Labor Council, the United States must not enter World War II and once again become Europe's "fall guy."[3]

Accordingly, the country's proper course was to concentrate on the Americas. It should strive for economic self-sufficiency in the Western Hemisphere and devote its military energies to erecting a defensive wall around the hemisphere that forces from the Old World could not breach. The Chicago and Cincinnati labor organizations asserted that such a defensive wall would make collective security with the European democracies unnecessary. In their view, Hitler, Mussolini, and Soviet Premier Josef Stalin did not pose credible threats to invade the United States. A British loss to Germany, undesirable as it might be, would not affect American security. To the contrary, they thought, American entry into the war would weaken the United States and clear the way for future invasions.[4]

The Chicago and Cincinnati groups were joined by labor organizations throughout the West and Middle West that opposed intervention. The Peoria Trades and Labor Assembly, the Minnesota State Federation of Labor, the Duluth Federated Trades Assembly, the Duluth Industrial Union Council, the Ohio

Industrial Union Council, the Kalispell (Montana) Trades and Labor Council, the Oregon Industrial Union Council, the Indiana State Industrial Union Council, the American Federation of Labor (AFL) and Congress of Industrial Organization (CIO) unions in Cheyenne, Wyoming, the Oregon Federation of Labor, the Idaho Federation of Labor, the South Dakota Federation of Labor, the Silver Bow (Montana) Trades and Labor Council, and the AFL unions in St. Louis were among the regional labor bodies that espoused isolationist positions. In addition, labor newspapers in Salt Lake City, Denver, and St. Paul, while not the official organs of the AFL or CIO central bodies in those cities, were strongly anti-interventionist. The labor isolationists expressed their opposition to intervention by passing resolutions, issuing statements, and publishing editorials and news reports that supported isolationist arguments. They also distributed anti-war circulars, publicized the activities of anti-interventionist groups, and staged anti-war rallies.[5]

It was not mere opposition to war that distinguished the anti-interventionist labor groups. Even President Franklin Roosevelt, who was deeply committed to the goal of providing assistance to Britain, expressed opposition to sending an American expeditionary force to Europe. Rather, what made the labor isolationists part of the nationwide anti-interventionist movement was their adherence to many of the tenets of anti-interventionism that went beyond simple opposition to entanglement in the war and formed the intellectual and emotional basis for a national movement.

In common with much of the anti-interventionist movement, for example, the anti-interventionist labor organizations frequently harbored a certain antipathy towards Great Britain. They took populist swipes at the British aristocracy, charged that English industrialists were reaping huge war profits while American workers were making sacrifices, and criticized Britain for not repaying World War I loan debts to the United States. Citing the "100 percent dictatorship" supposedly imposed by the British War Cabinet and Britain's refusal to grant independence to India, South Africa, and other colonial possessions, labor isolationists denied that

Britain was fighting to defend democracy. They accused Britain of having helped cause the war through its diplomatic bungling at Versailles after World War I and through the investments British business had made in Nazi Germany in order to build that country up as a counterweight to the Soviet Union. Finally, they indignantly alleged—with some justification—that the British employed shrewd propaganda campaigns to lure the United States into the war.[6]

Viewing Britain with such suspicion, anti-interventionist elements in the labor movement opposed American loans and other wartime assistance to that country. Some labor groups argued that Britain did not truly need American assistance to stave off the Nazis, and, even if Britain did lose the war for want of American aid, the British loss would not be detrimental to American security. Moreover, they argued that the United States itself easily could get sucked into the war as a full belligerent if it dared furnish aid to Britain. The Cincinnati Central Labor Council ran an editorial in its weekly newspaper that warned, "The belief that we can go halfway into the war and stop at that point is a dangerous assumption which has been discredited on many occasions." Those convictions were not held by anti-interventionists in the labor movement alone. They were shared by all anti-interventionists and were among the standard arguments put forth by America First.[7]

Isolationists waged a particularly bitter (and unsuccessful) battle against the Lend-Lease bill, which authorized the president to sell, exchange, lease, or lend any defense articles he deemed appropriate to Britain or any other countries at war with the Axis powers. Enacted in March 1941, it was the legal basis for American assistance to Britain and its allies. Isolationists fought with greater success to prevent the use of American naval vessels to convoy ships carrying cargo to Britain across the Atlantic. President Roosevelt nearly implemented a proposal to do so, but then decided against the idea. Another major point of contention was America's swap of 50 obsolete navy destroyers to Britain for leases on British military bases. The isolationists opposed that scheme just as they opposed Lend-Lease and convoys.[8]

The AFL supported Lend-Lease, as did the CIO, albeit somewhat more cautiously. In addition, several national labor leaders went on record as being personally in favor of Lend-Lease. Nonetheless, labor groups in Montana, Ohio, Oregon, Minnesota, and elsewhere opposed it. The state CIO organization in Connecticut, for example, called Lend-Lease "an outright act of war" and predicted that it would pave the way for dictatorship in the United States. These groups also opposed convoys and the destroyer deal, in common with isolationists outside the labor movement.[9]

Labor isolationists spoke out against other war-related measures. They criticized defense contracts as tending to generate a vested economic interest in war and for diverting money from domestic activities. When the Burke-Wadsworth Military Conscription Bill was introduced in Congress in June 1940, union opposition was widespread and vehement.[10]

Another issue in the national foreign policy debate was a constitutional amendment proposed by United States Representative Louis Ludlow that would have required a popular referendum before a declaration of war. The House of Representatives effectively killed the Ludlow proposal in 1938 by narrowly defeating a resolution permitting consideration of the amendment. Isolationists in the labor movement continued to champion the idea, though, as late as 1940. The 1939 AFL Convention defeated a pro-Ludlow Amendment resolution. In spite of that, the Minnesota Federation of Labor and other Midwestern labor organizations passed strong resolutions endorsing a war referendum. The official newspaper of the Oregon Federation of Labor argued that a war referendum fought dictatorships by showing faith in democracy. The Council Bluffs, Iowa, *Farmer-Labor Press* asserted that "since the people of this country are going to fight in any war . . . then let the people themselves take a vote before ANYBODY presumes to plunge this country into war" (emphasis in the original). The *Chicago Federation News* declared that opponents of the Ludlow Amendment "cannot consistently claim to be real Americans."[11]

The entire labor movement was concerned that American

involvement in World War II might have adverse political and economic affects that would hurt unions. Even staunchly interventionist labor groups blasted "industrial mobilization" plans and emergency legislation being contemplated by Congress, the military, and state legislatures. They argued that such measures threatened to prohibit strikes, annul union contracts, and conscript labor. Likewise, a wariness of wartime profiteering was common throughout organized labor, as were calls for price controls and excess profit taxes to prevent it (and to harness wealth for the war effort).[12]

Labor isolationists, however, went beyond those basically remediable concerns to question the motives for the war. They echoed the America First argument that United States intervention in the war would imperil civil liberties across the board. Further, they warned that going to war would produce an economic calamity.

A widely-held conviction among American isolationists was that World War I, far from being a crusade to save democracy, was a raw grab for profits engineered by a handful of plutocrats. Senator Gerald P. Nye's investigation into the causes of American intervention in World War I lent credence to that point of view with its conclusion that the United States had entered the war at least in part to protect the economic interests of munitions makers and financiers. A common theme of non-interventionism between 1939 and 1941 was that America should learn from the experiences of 1917 and not be duped into war a second time by greedy businessmen.[13]

Labor isolationists relished the argument that wealthy businessmen were trying to push the country into the European conflict in order to further their own narrow interests. Assertions that America had to help Britain and France save democracy, they said, were a subterfuge. In fact, they argued, the war was simply a contest for scarce economic resources in Europe and one in which American businessmen would attempt to reap profits as they had during the First World War.

Particularly in the upper Midwest, where anti-business radicalism was strong, labor groups argued that industrialists and bankers wanted the United States to enter the war. The *Montana Labor News* editorialized that businessmen were more of a threat to the United States than Hitler, accused America's wealthiest families of conspiring to "drag the United States into war for the glory of war profits," and cited the Nye Committee's findings as proof of the duplicity of American capitalists. The Chicago Federation of Labor warned against allowing American boys to become "cannon fodder . . . for the preservation of America's Dollar Nobility," and charged that American business interests formed an "invisible government" that "exploited [the] citizenry as pawns in its foreign investments and imperialistic designs." The *Farmer-Labor Press* of Council Bluffs, Iowa—which had the endorsement of the Council Bluffs Central Labor Union—reported an "amazing disclosure" concerning "the absolute assurance of Big Business interests that they will be able to do away with our neutrality laws . . . by selling vast supplies of arms and munitions abroad." As another union newspaper put it, "The Standard Oil Company, General Motors, General Electric, Ford, [and] J.P. Morgan have interests abroad to defend. We haven't. If the big boys want to go abroad to defend their investments, let them go."[14]

Also consistent with the views of isolationists generally were the concerns of labor isolationists that United States involvement in the war would have adverse economic and political repercussions for the country. Notions that the war would create a job boom were dismissed. The great profits to be realized from the war by big business would not trickle down to the workers, they argued. Consumer prices would skyrocket. Transfer of government funds from the Works Progress Administration and other federal jobs programs to the War and Navy Departments would, in fact, eliminate much employment. A huge national debt would be incurred, they said, that would inhibit prosperity. Extension of credit to the Allies would reduce the availability of capital for domestic business recovery. Even industries that might be buoyed by the war would collapse at war's end, thereby ushering in a new depression. Far from anticipating more jobs and higher wages in a wartime economy, a substantial portion of the labor community was convinced that intervention would lead to economic hardship.[15]

According to the labor isolationists, involvement in the war also would damage the American political system. Not only would restrictions be imposed on organized labor, but democracy itself would be jeopardized. Prominent isolationist spokesman Charles Lindbergh once declared that "If we enter fighting for democracy abroad, we may end by losing it at home." Similarly, the *Chicago Federation News* warned that anything could happen with the United States Congress out of session and stated that the first result of United States entry into the war would be that "democracy would disappear in this country and be replaced by a military dictatorship." And the Industrial Union Council of Toledo pointed out that one "need only to look at the curbing of democracy by the Allies to prove" that wars and democracy were not compatible.[16]

The fact that many unionists in the Midwest and West expressed strong isolationist sentiment did not mean that labor isolationists were restricted to those parts of the country. Nor did it mean that there was no sympathy for intervention among Midwestern and Western labor organizations.

Anti-interventionist feeling was hardly unknown, for example, in labor circles in the Northeast. In an extraordinary development, given the extreme tension between the two national labor centers, one hundred representatives from AFL and CIO locals in Western Pennsylvania convened in January 1940 to promulgate a "Peace Proclamation of Labor." It condemned American intervention in World War I, accused Wall Street of trying to maneuver the country into the hostilities, opposed the extension of credit to the Allies, denounced war-boom economic expansion as "false prosperity," and declared that WPA appropriations and unemployment benefits should not be slashed to permit greater spending on defense.[17]

In April 1940, the Buffalo Industrial Union Council organized a "Peace Day Demonstration" where speakers warned that intervention would cause economic dislocations. The speakers went on to oppose aid to the Allies and urge that the United States concentrate on domestic markets and not resort to war in an attempt to defend its overseas trade. Also in New York, the Jamestown

Central Labor Council and the Jamestown Labor Union Conference—composed of AFL locals, CIO locals, and unaffiliated locals—followed an anti-interventionist line well into 1941. They opposed military spending, the draft, loans to the Allies, Lend-Lease, and the destroyers for bases deal with Britain. They were doubtful that the United States was in danger of being invaded, skeptical about wartime economic expansion, supportive of isolationist Senators Nye and Wheeler, and suspicious of British intentions. Local labor leaders were instrumental in forming a chapter of the Emergency Peace Mobilization Committee.[18]

By the same token, there were labor groups in the Midwest and West that supported intervention. The Phoenix Labor Temple and the Allied Crafts of Phoenix and Arizona, the Iowa Federation of Labor, the Topeka Federation of Labor, and the Hannibal, Missouri, Trades and Labor Assembly were scarcely jingoistic, but they generally avoided the anti-war rhetoric of the isolationists. They consistently supported Britain and aid for the Allies, attacked the Nazis, espoused preparedness, and lauded the economic benefits to be derived from the defense program. Even when ostensibly arguing for neutrality in the first days of the war, the Topeka Federation of Labor condemned pacifists and urged sympathy for Britain. Heaping scorn on isolationists, the Topeka group held that even if the United States stayed out of the war, it could not help but be affected by it. To emphasize America's peril, it ran a short story in its weekly newspaper concerning a hypothetical Nazi invasion of Kansas. The official organ of the Iowa Federation of Labor, meanwhile, carried articles distributed by Fight for Freedom and editorialized: "Let us realize now and forever—this war is being fought for us by Great Britain and against us by Germany."[19]

Headquartered in the midwestern community of Madison, Wisconsin, the American Federation of State, County, and Municipal Employees (AFSCME) was one union that adopted a staunchly interventionist position. AFSCME's President, Arnold Zander, was a Wisconsin native who felt frustrated over the general expectation that midwestern unionists would automatically favor isolationism. In August 1941, he called Madison's United

States Representative to task for trying "to depict the attitude of the people out here" as anti-interventionist. In an angry letter to Congressman Harry Sauthoff, Zander explained that as a high school boy in Two Rivers, Wisconsin, in 1917 he had opposed United States entry into World War 1. So did his family and most of the people they knew. But after talking to "farm and town folks" in the district, he found that in 1941 "the feeling is different. Those people do not want . . . us to get into war, but they want Hitler stopped and they want him stopped on foreign soil if possible."[20]

Zander went on to comment that the people in the district "must remember that we failed pretty miserably in taking our responsibility at the close of the last war. Midwest isolationist sentiment had a lot to do with that failure." He concluded that "our people" were so adamant that Hitler should be defeated that they were even willing to risk "very direct participation on our part" in the war.[21]

Thus, the regional breakdown within the labor movement on foreign policy issues was not perfect. Many unionists in the Midwest endorsed interventionism, and many outside the Midwest opposed it. But, outside the labor movement, the regional pattern did not hold universally true, either. By the autumn of 1940, isolationists were in the minority in all sections of the country, including the Midwest. Nonetheless, non-interventionism was strongest in the Midwest.[22] The same thing was true for the labor movement. To the extent that union voices were raised in protest against intervention, some of the loudest voices emanated from the Midwest and the western mining states.

Workers in certain occupations tended to join the anti-interventionism chorus. Industries that were unlikely to enjoy immediate economic benefits from defense spending—light manufacturing, mining, and service occupations—were well represented. The Western Pennsylvania unionists who passed the "Peace Proclamation of Labor" included representatives of the Steel Workers' Organizing Committee, but were mainly bank clerks, railway clerks, carpenters, brewers, electrical workers, and miners. The Brewery Workers of Cincinnati passed an anti-interventionist resolution in January 1940, convinced that war would lead to persecution of German-Americans (many of whom worked in the brewing industry). The brewers also feared that prohibition would be re-introduced as a war measure. Especially during the first months of the war, such national unions as the Paper Mill Workers, the Mine, Mill, and Smelter Workers, the United Mine Workers, the Carpenters, and the Printing Pressmen came out against intervention. They cited the usual arguments supporting strict neutrality, opposing Lend-Lease, warning against Allied propaganda, discounting the economic benefits of the war and military spending, dismissing the possibility of invasion, and questioning the role of Britain.[23]

Other labor groups that championed anti-interventionism were those with ties to the Communist Party. Communists were particularly strong in several CIO unions. Although the president of the CIO's United Electrical, Radio, and Machine Workers (UE), James B. Carey, was a staunch anti-Stalinist, many of that union's locals were dominated by Communists. Also in the CIO, the International Longshoremen's and Warehousemen's Union and the National Maritime Union of the Pacific (both of which were controlled by Harry Bridges), the National Maritime Union on the East Coast (under Joseph Curran), the New York City Transit Workers' Union (under Michael Quill), the Mine, Mill, and Smelter Workers' Union, and Plymouth Local no. 51 of the UAW were pro-Communist, as were the Industrial Union Councils of New York City, Milwaukee, Seattle, Cleveland, Texas, and Connecticut. In the AFL, one of the most prominent pro-Communist groups was New York City Local no. 5 of the American Federation of Teachers (AFT).[24]

The Communist-dominated unions followed the Moscow line on foreign policy issues throughout the era leading up to American entry into World War II. They opposed neutrality and called for American action against the Nazis up until August 1939, when the Soviet Union and Germany concluded a non-aggression pact. As long as that treaty was in force, the Communist-dominated unions characterized World War II as merely a struggle between rival imperialists. They argued against neutrality revision, the destroyers-for-bases deal, Lend-Lease, and preparedness. In 1940, CIO Communists were instrumental in establishing an anti-interventionist pressure group, the American Peace Mobilization.[25]

While the Communists were a powerful force for non-intervention—at least for a time—they were not typical of labor isolationists. The archetype of labor isolationists may have been John L. Lewis. A Midwesterner, Lewis was less affected by European influences than his fellow union leaders in the East—especially people such as David Dubinsky and Sidney Hillman, who were immigrants. Like many other natives of the Midwest, he was inclined to view Europe as corrupt and dangerous, and European struggles as none of America's business. He feared Hitler less than entangling diplomatic and military alliances between the United States and European powers, was apprehensive over the domestic political repercussions of entering the war, and his Welsh heritage may have encouraged an antipathy towards Great Britain that he shared with many in the anti-interventionist movement.[26]

Notes

1. Wayne S. Cole, *America First: The Battle Against Intervention, 1940-1941* (Madison: University of Wisconsin Press, 1953), p. 31.

2. "American Opposition to War Justified by Past Experiences," Chicago *Federation News*, September 2, 1939, pp. 88-9; "Says No War in Europe Very Soon; Borah Tells Information is Reliable," Chicago *Federation News*, August 5, 1939, p. 1; "Take National Defense Out of Politics," Chicago *Federation News*, June 1, 1940, p. 4; "American Invasion," Chicago *Federation News*, May 25, 1940, p. 4; "Neutrality,?," Chicago *Federation News*, September 23, 1939, pp. 2, 12; "America Must Remain Neutral," Chicago *Federation News*, September 16, 1939, p. 10; "Quarrels of Europe No Fight of USA," Chicago *Federation News*, June 1, 1940, p. 10; "Free Speech Threatened," Chicago *Federation News*, June 22, 1940, p. 4; "Our War Policy; Comment on Dangers," Chicago *Federation News*, June 15, 1940, p. 1; "Further Steps Toward War Expected," Chicago *Federation News*, November 23, 1940, p. 4; "1917-1940: Think It Over," Chicago *Federation News*, November 23, 1940, p. 4; "U.S. Dictatorship a Possibility; May Be Real Objective of Military Group," Chicago *Federation News*, June 29, 1940, p. 2; "America Keep Out!," Cincinnati *Chronicle*, September 22, 1939, p. 4; "We Repeat: America Keep Out!," Cincinnati *Chronicle*, September 22, 1939, p. 4; "Lest You Forget," Cincinnati *Chronicle*, September 22, 1939, p. 4; "Says War Will Spell Doom of

Democracy," Cincinnati *Chronicle*, July 7, 1939, p. 1; "Foreign Policy Should Not Be In President's Hands," Cincinnati *Chronicle*, July 7, 1939, p. 1; "Something Phony About the War," Cincinnati *Chronicle*, October 13, 1939, p. 4; "America Can Keep Out!," Cincinnati *Chronicle*, October 6, 1939, p. 4; "A. F. of L. Echoes Central Council Demand," Cincinnati *Chronicle*, May 24, 1940, p. 1; "Repeal—Step Toward War," Cincinnati *Chronicle*, October 27, 1939, p. 4; "Teachers Unite in Protest Against War Participation," Cincinnati *Chronicle*, May 31, 1940, p. 4; "How We Go to War," Cincinnati *Chronicle*, May 17, 1940, p. 4; "Hold the Johnson Act!," Cincinnati *Chronicle*, May 31, 1940, p. 4; "Remember 1916 War Hysteria, Billings Cautions Unionists," Cincinnati *Chronicle*, June 28, 1940, p. 1; "Labor in Vanguard Against War Hysterics," Cincinnati *Chronicle*, June 21, 1940, p. 1; "Check the War Jitters," Cincinnati *Chronicle*, June 14, 1940, p. 4; "Stay Out of Europe and Asia," Cincinnati *Chronicle*, June 14, 1940, p. 1; "'Not So Long Ago They Opposed Appropriations for Jobless Workers,' Says Wheeler of Warmakers," Cincinnati *Chronicle*, April 11, 1941, p. 1; "Fish Slated for April 19 at Taft," Cincinnati *Chronicle*, April 11, 1941, p. 1; "Wheeler Slated to Talk Here on Friday Against War Preparation," Cincinnati *Chronicle*, March 28, 1941, p. 1; "Slate Another Nye Talk Here," Cincinnati *Chronicle*, September 12, 1941, p. 4. Also see "Certain as Death," *Duluth Labor World*, July 13, 1939, p. 2.

3. "Quarrels of Europe Not Fight of U.S.A.," Chicago *Federation News*, June 1, 1940, p. 10; "Europe's Cockeyed Methods," Chicago *Federation News*, January 13, 1940, p. 4; "Four Assumptions About the War," Chicago *Federation News*, January 18, 1941, p. 11; "Imperialist Greed European War Cause," Chicago *Federation News*, June 22, 1940, p. 3: "A. F. of L. Echoes Central Council Demand," Cincinnati *Chronicle*, May 24, 1940, p. 1; "United Garment Workers No. 99," Cincinnati *Chronicle*, October 20, 1939, p. 2.

4. "Can Hitler, Mussolini, Stalin . . . Invade the United States?," Chicago *Federation News*, June 22, 1940. p. 3; "Our War Policy; Comment on Dangers," Chicago *Federation News*, June 15, 1940,. p. 1: "Four Assumptions About the War," Chicago *Federation News*, January 18. 1941. p 11; "American Invasion," Chicago *Federation News*, May 25, 1940, p. 4; "Stay Out of Europe and Asia," Cincinnati *Chronicle*, June 14, 1940, p. 1.

5. "Not Inevitable," Peoria *Labor Temple News*, September 22, 1939, p. 5; "The Weekly Parade," Peoria *Labor Temple News*, September 22, 1939, p. 5; "The Horrorscope," Peoria *Labor Temple News*, October 6, 1939, p. 8: "The Weekly Parade," Peoria *Labor Temple News*, May 31, 1940, p. 5; "Shipstead Warns Against Propaganda," Duluth *Labor World*, September 7, 1939, p. 7; "Federation Supports AFL in Controversy with CIO," Duluth *Labor World*, September 14, 1939, p. 2; "'Never Again' Says Nation," Duluth *Labor World*, October 5, 1939, p. 2; "Danger in Hysteria," Duluth *Labor World*, October 5, 1939, p. 2; "Is Right," Duluth *Labor World*, October 5, 1939, p. 2; "St. Paul Labor Opposes Attempt to Amend U.S. Neutrality Law," Duluth *Labor World*, October 5, 1939, p. 1; "The Spot Lite," Duluth *Labor World*, May 9, 1940, p. 1; "The Hope of Americans," Duluth *Labor World*, April 11. 1940, p. 2; "Anti-War Play is Scheduled," Duluth

Labor World, March 28, 1940, p. 6; "Peace Rally Here Saturday," Duluth *Labor World*, April 4, 1940. p. 1; "Labor," *Lansing Industrial News*, October 20, 1939, p. 2; "America's War" *Lansing Industrial News*, December 15, 1939. p. 2; "Inter-American Conferences," *Lansing Industrial News*, December 29, 1939, p.2; "What Price Glory?," *Lansing Industrial News*, November 10, 1939, p. 2; "To Be Mobilized," Kalispell *Flathead Labor Journal*, October 7, 1939. p. 4; "Lest We Forget," Kalispell *Flathead Labor Journal*, October 24, 1939, p. 2; "War Propaganda," Kalispell *Flathead Labor Journal*, November 7, 1939, p. 5; "Picket Line for 1940," Kalispell *Flathead Labor Journal*, January 2, 1940, p. 1; "Youth," Kalispell *Flathead Labor Journal*, March 5, 1940, p. 5; "Seamen Urge No-Transfer of Ships," Toledo *CIO News*, January 13, 1941, p. 1; "Indiana CIO Urge U.S. Avoid War," Toledo *CIO News*, May 27, 1940, p. 7; "War by April is Predicted Says Wheeler," Toledo *CIO News*, March 3, 1941, p. 1; "'Short of War' Bubble Burst by Militarists," Toledo *CIO News*, March 31, 1941, p. 1; "Artists Urge Support of Peace Meeting," Toledo *CIO News*, March 31, 1941, p. 2; "Profits and Poppies vs. Peace and Prosperity," Toledo *CIO News*, June 10, 1940, p. 1; "Peace Committee Pushes Plan for April 6, Rally," Toledo *CIO News*, March 25, 1940, p.1; "Union News," Toledo *CIO News*, March 18, 1940, p. 7; "Anti-War Rally Campaign Launched," Toledo *CIO News*, March 18, 1940, p. 1; "'Yanks Are Not Coming' CIO Council Warns," Toledo *CIO News*, December 25, 1939, p. 1; "'Nothing to Gain from War,'" Toledo *CIO News*, November 27, 1939, p. 2; "Bending Neutrality," Cheyenne *Wyoming Labor Journal*, December 27, 1940, p. 4; "Close Your Ears to War Propaganda," Cheyenne *Wyoming Labor Journal*, May 3, 1940, p. 4; "In War, All Are Losers," Cheyenne *Wyoming Labor Journal*, May 3, 1940, p. 4; "Peace Group Asks President to Act for War Truce," Cheyenne *Wyoming Labor Journal*, October 27, 1939, p. 1; "Keep Out of Europe!," Cheyenne *Wyoming Labor Journal*, October 27, 1939, p. 8; "Idaho Federation Opposes Changed Neutrality Law," Portland *Oregon Labor Press*, September 22, 1939, p. 1; "American Workers, Beware!," Portland *Oregon Labor Journal*, December 9, 1939, p. 1; "Let Us Be On Our Guard," Portland *Oregon Labor Press*, September 8, 1939, p. 2; "Labor Representatives Emphatic in Opinion that Labor Say Out," Portland *Oregon Labor Press*, September 8, 1939, p. 1; "War," Portland *Oregon Labor Press*, September 8, 1939, p. 2; "Neutrality Confusion," Portland *Oregon Labor Press*, September 29, 1939, p. 1; "Allies Better Prepared to Fight Long War Than Is Hitler's Naziland," Portland *Oregon Labor Press*, September 29, 1939, p. 1; "Central Council Opposes War for Nation," Portland *Oregon Labor Press*, October 20, 1939, p. 1; "Drifting Into War," Portland *Oregon Labor Press*, October 20, 1939, p. 2; "A Tribute to the Isolationists," Portland *Oregon Labor Press*, August 9, 1940, p. 1; "Why Not?," Sioux Falls *Union News*, December 1939,; "Did You Ever Hear of an Aggressive War Against the U.S.?," Sioux Falls *Union News*, December 1939; "In Case of War Labor Loses," Sioux Falls *Union News*, February 1940; "Why Do Some Men Want War?," Sioux Falls *Union News*, June 20, 1940; "News of Local Organizations," Sioux Falls *Union News*, July 3, 1940; "Resolutions Adopted at State Labor Meet," Sioux Falls *Union News*, August 29, 1940;

"Happenings of the Central Labor Body," Butte *Montana Labor News*, May 18, 1939, p. 1; "The Imperialist War," Butte *Montana Labor News*, October 19, 1939, p. 4; "News of the Cascade Trades Assembly," Butte *Montana Labor News*, March 14, 1940, p. 2; "Past and Present of the Unemployment Situation," Butte *Montana Labor News*, April 25, 1940, p. 3; "Theme of May Day Meeting," Butte *Montana Labor News*, April 25, 1940, p. 4; "News of Cascade Trades Assembly," Butte *Montana Labor News*, April 25, 1940, p. 4; "For Peace," *St. Louis Union Labor Advocate*, February 1, 1939, p. 4; "Wheeler Hits Back at Iowa Paper Editor," *St. Louis Union Labor Advocate*, September 15, 1939, p. 3; "Wars of Revenge," *St. Louis Union Labor Advocate*, December 1, 1939, p. 2; "If War Comes," *St. Louis Labor Tribune*, June 24, 1939, p. 2; "A New Unholy Alliance," *St. Louis Labor Tribune*, August 26, 1939, p. 2; "Poll or Propaganda," *St. Louis Labor Tribune*, August 26, 1939, p. 2; "Lindbergh Points the Way," *St. Louis Labor Tribune*, September 23, 1939, p. 2; "Good Example to Follow," *St. Louis Labor Tribune*, September 23, 1939, p. 2; "Washington Stirs With War Talk," *St. Louis Labor Tribune*, May 25, 1940, p. 4; "America Keep Out!," Salt Lake City *Utah Labor News*, September 15, 1939, p. 1; "Americans Do Not Desire to Participate in Another World War" Salt Lake City *Utah Labor News*, September 22, 1939, p. 1; "1939-1940 Platform of the Non-Partisan League of Utah," Salt Lake City *Utah Labor News*, October 6, 1939, p. 1; "Will Labor Lose the War?," Salt Lake City *Utah Labor News*, October 6, 1939, p. 8; "Trade Union Women," Salt Lake City *Utah Labor News*, October 13, 1939, p. 3; "Anti-War Mobilization Adopt 6-Point Program," Salt Lake City *Utah Labor News*, June 28, 1940, p. 1; "It's A Mess In Europe," Salt Lake City *Utah Labor News*, June 28, 1940, p. 1; "'Collective Security' for Czechoslovakia" *Denver Labor Bulletin*, June 1938, p. 2; "Between War and Peace," *Denver Labor Bulletin*, August-September 1939, p. 2; "Grab Your Hats, Here We Go Again," *Denver Labor Bulletin*, May 1940, p. 2; "Bad News from Across the Waters," *Denver Labor Bulletin*, May 1940, p. 1; "Norris Opposes Peacetime Conscription," *Denver Labor Bulletin*, August 1940, p. 3; "War Means End of Generation's Liberty, Wheeler Declares," *Denver Labor Bulletin*, August 1940, p. 1; "Look Before You Leap—Into War!," *St. Paul Minnesota Leader*, September 13, 1939, p. 2; "Nation Needs Progressive Leaders As Never Before," St. Paul *Minnesota Leader*, September 30, 1939, p. 1; "Twin Cities People Oppose Taking Part in this World War," St. Paul *Minnesota Leader*, October 1939, p. 1; "'I Am War,'" St. Paul *Minnesota Leader*, October 1939, p. 1; "Farmer-Labor Association Takes Anti-War Position," St. Paul *Minnesota Leader*, June 15, 1940, p. 1; "The Battle for Bread!," St. Paul *Minnesota Leader*, July 15, 1940, p. 2; "American Farmers and Workers Do Not Want War," St. Paul *Minnesota Leader*, December 1940, p. 1; "Convention Shows Solid Peace Front," St. Paul *Minnesota Leader*, February 1941, p. 4; Oregon Industrial Union Council to Lewis, July 1, 1940, item 108, reel 13, Robert H. Zieger, *The CIO Files of John L. Lewis*, Part II (Frederick, MD: University Microfilm Publications of America, 1988); Anne Gerlovich to Lewis, plus attachments, January 20, 1941, item 830, reel 11, *CIO Files of John L. Lewis*, Part II.

6. "United States Must Come First," *Sacramento Valley Union Labor Bulletin*, September 15, 1939, p. 2; "Readers' Column," Cincinnati *Chronicle*, November 10, 1939, p. 4; "God Is Not Responsible," Cincinnati *Chronicle*, June 14, 1940, p. 4; "U.S. Labor Asked to Sacrifice Gains for England; British Industry Boosts Profits by 100 Million," Cincinnati *Chronicle*, January 24, 1941, p. 1; "'To the Last Briton,'" Cincinnati *Chronicle*, May 23, 1941, p. 4; "Lust For Power Basic Cause of War," Chicago *Federation News*, September 2, 1939, p. 1; "Dictation by the Money Masters," Chicago *Federation News*, September 2, 1939, p. 39, p. 67; "Stop-Look-Listen," Chicago *Federation News*, June 8, 1940, p. 9; "Britain Wants U.S. to Enter War," Chicago *Federation News*, November 23, 1940, p. 4; "Taking Advantage of War to Plunder the People," Chicago *Federation News*, June 22, 1940, p. 9; "Britain Gambling on U.S., Says Denny," Chicago *Federation News*, January 4, 1941, p. 4; "For the Ladies," Council Bluffs *Farmer-Labor Press*, October 26, 1939, p. 2; "Labor Broadens Fight Against United States Participation in War," Council Bluffs *Farmer-Labor Press*, March 28, 1940, p. 1; "Second World Conflict Seen as a Civil War," Council Bluffs *Farmer-Labor Press*, August 29, 1940, p. 9; "British Firm's Hindrance of Defense Program Puzzles U.S. Workers," Council Bluffs *Farmer-Labor Press*, July 17, 1941, p. 1; "How About This 'Alien Propaganda,'" *Denver Labor Bulletin*, June 1939, p. 1; "The Editor's Desk," Toledo *CIO News*, May 12, 1941, p. 1; "CIO Under Ban In India!," Toledo *CIO News*, March 3, 1941, p. 1; "British Tune Changes as U.S. War Loans Are Needed," Toledo *CIO News*, January 20, 1941, p. 2; "British Urge Abolition of 40 Hour Week in U.S. Industry," Butte *Montana Labor News*, November 14, 1940, p. 2; "Dies on the Anti-American Fringe," *St. Louis Labor Tribune*, September 23, 1939, p. 2; "Envoy Reveals How Capitalists Helped Hitler Destroy Spain," St. Paul *Minnesota Leader*, November 1941, p. 4; "The Neutrality Act," St. Paul *Minnesota Leader*, October 1941, p. 2; "Lords of the British Empire," St. Paul *Minnesota Leader*, September 1941, p. 2. Also see Selig Adler, *The Isolationist Impulse: Its Twentieth Century Reaction* (New York: The Free Press, 1957), pp. 265-66, 268, 270, 279, 283.

7. "Hold the Johnson Act!," Cincinnati *Chronicle*, May 31, 1940, p. 4; "America Can Keep Out!," Cincinnati *Chronicle*, October 6, 1939, p. 4; "Stay Out of Europe and Asia," Cincinnati *Chronicle*, June 14, 1940, p. 1; "Quarrels of Europe Not Fight of U.S.A.," Chicago *Federation News*, June 1, 1940, p. 10; "Our War Policy: Comment on Dangers," Chicago *Federation News*, June 15, 1940, p. 1; "Allies Better Prepared to Fight Long War Than Is Hitler's Naziland," Portland *Oregon Labor Press*, September 39, 1939, p. 1; "News of the Cascade Trades Assembly," Butte *Montana Labor News*, March 14, 1940, p. 2; "Billions for British Aid; Chicken Feed for Our Unemployed," Butte *Montana Labor News*, April 3, 1941, p. 1; "America, Keep Out!," Salt Lake City *Utah Labor News*, September 15, 1939, p. 1. Also see Adler, *Isolationist Impulse*, pp. 274, 276.

8. Robert A. Divine, *The Reluctant Belligerent: American Entry into World War II* (New York: John Wiley and Sons, 1965), pp. 89-92, 104-6, 126-27.

9. "AFL Endorses Lease-Lend Measure," AFL *Weekly News Service*,

January 21, 1941; "Text of Pres. Murray's Statement to Senate on 'Lease-Lend' Proposal," *CIO News*, February 10, 1941, p. 6; "News of Silver Bow Trades Council," Butte *Montana Labor News*, August 15, 1940, p. 4; "News of the Cascade Trades Assembly, Butte *Montana Labor News*, June 19, 1941, p. 2; "News of the Cascade Trades Assembly," Butte *Montana Labor News*, May 22, 1941, p. 2; "'Don't Lease or Lend Our Lives,' Youth Town Meeting Says," Butte *Montana Labor News*, April 3, 1941, p. 6; "Lease-Lend Bill," Butte *Montana Labor News*, February 13, 1941, p. 1; "Miners Oppose Lease-Lend Bill," Butte *Montana Labor News*, March 6, 1941, p. 1; "Great Falls Unions Ask for Opinion on Lease-Lend Measure," Butte *Montana Labor News*, March 6, 1941; "Miners Auxiliary Protests Convoys," Butte *Montana Labor News*, May 29, 1941, p. 1; "Senate Debates Lease-Lend Bill; F-L Brands It 'War,'" St. Paul *Minnesota Leader*, February 1941, p. 4; "Roseau Warns Against Convoys," St. Paul *Minnesota Leader*, April 1941, p. 1; "Warn War Will Follow Free Munitions to Europe," Cincinnati *Chronicle*, February 21, 1941, p. 1; "Seamen Urge Non-Transfer of Ships," Toledo *CIO News*, January 13, 1941, p. 1; "Peace Conference Urges Defeat of H.R. 1776," Toledo *CIO News*, February 3, 1941, p. 2; "Curran Says H.R. 1776 is Fascist Bill," Toledo *CIO News*, February 24, 1941, p. 1; "Convoys Opposed by Labor Editors," Portland *Oregon Labor Press*, May 30, 1941, p. 1; "The Choice is Still Ours," Portland *Oregon Labor News*, April 11, 1941, p. 2; "Bases May Cost Us Fifty Million," Chicago *Federation News*, January 4, 1941, p. 4; Connecticut State Industrial Union Council Resolution, January 18, 1941, item 419, reel 10, *CIO Files of John L. Lewis*, Part II; Pennsylvania Industrial Union Council Resolution, May 4, 1941, item 693, reel 13, Ibid.

10. "Reasons for Going Slowly in Naval Building," Cincinnati *Chronicle*, March 29, 1940, p. 4; "The Case Against Conscription," Cincinnati *Chronicle*, July 26, 1940, p. 4; "Conscription Vigorously Opposed," Council Bluffs *Farmer-Labor Press*, August 1, 1940, p. 2; "The Beginning of a Program," and "Let the Cannons Eat," Council Bluffs *Farmer-Labor Press*, November 16, 1939, p. 2; "Military Expense Up 67 Per Cent, Domestic Spending Down 15," Council Bluffs *Farmer-Labor Press*, January 16, 1941, p. 1; "All Labor Groups Join Opposition to Conscription," Kalispell (Mont.) *Flathead Labor Journal*, August 20, 1940, p. 1; "Labor Opposition to Conscription," *Denver Labor Bulletin*, August 1940, p. 4; "War Means End of Generation's Liberty, Wheeler Declares," *Denver Labor Bulletin*, August 1940, p.1; "Nearing the Precipice," *Denver Labor Bulletin*, August-September, 1939, p.2; "Against Conscription," Toledo *CIO News*, August 12, 1940, p. 1; "Ohio CIO Board Passes Resolution Against Draft Bill," Toledo *CIO News*, August 26, 1940, p. 7; "Labor Day and the Future," Toledo *CIO News*, September 2, 1940, p. 1; "Draft Repeal Gains Wide Support," Toledo *CIO News*, September 30, 1940, p.2; "Minneapolis Labor Hits Conscription," Portland *Oregon Labor Press*, August 2, 1940, p. 1; "Regimentation For America?," Portland *Oregon Labor Press*, August 9, 1940, p. 2; "Conscription Bill is Condemned," Butte *Montana Labor News*, August 1, 1940, p. 1; "Democracy Betrayed," Butte *Montana Labor News*, August 1, 1940, p. 1; Adler, *Isolationist Impulse*, p. 273.

11. Divine, *Reluctant Belligerent*, pp. 48-9; "Sure, Let the People Vote a War!," Council Bluffs *Farmer-Labor Press*, August 24, 1939, p.2; "The Arms Embargo Act," Council Bluffs *Farmer-Labor Press*, September 21, 1939, p. 2; "Local 554 Demands Peoples' Vote Before Anybody Gets United States Into War," Council Bluffs *Farmer-Labor Press*, November 2, 1939, p. 1; "Minnesota Labor Demands People Be Given Right to Vote on War," Council Bluffs *Farmer-Labor Press*, September 28, 1939, p. 1; "For the Ladies," Council Bluffs *Farmer-Labor Press*, January 11, 1940, p. 3; "Neutrality," *Denver Labor Bulletin*, June 1939, p. 1; "What About the War Referendum?," Portland *Oregon Labor Press*, March 22, 1940, p. 2; "Interesting News of the Trades Council," Butte *Montana Labor News*, April 13, 1939, p. 1; "Happenings of the Central Labor Body," Butte *Montana Labor News*, May 4, 1939, p. 1; "Happenings of the Central Labor Body," Butte *Montana Labor News*, May 18, 1939, p. 1; "Let the People Vote on War, Say Senators," and "Urges War Vote," Duluth *Labor World*, June 1, 1939, p. 4; "Resolutions," Duluth *Labor World*, September 14, 1939; "War's Hate Inspired Propaganda Emphasizes Need of a Referendum," Chicago *Federation News*, September 9, 1939, p. 1.

12. "Mobilization Plan is Dictatorship," Toledo *CIO News*, December 11, 1939, p.1; "General Hershey Scored by CIO Council," Toledo *CIO News*, September 22, 1941, p. 2; "Labor's Rights Menaced," Toledo *CIO News*, August 4, 1941, p. 1; "No Compromise," Toledo *CIO News*, June 30, 1941, p. 1; "Brewer Hits Greedy 'Barons,'" Omaha *Unionist*, October 3, 1941, p. 6; "Green Pledges Convention Action on Profiteers," Omaha *Unionist*, October 6, 1939, p. 1; "State Legislators Continue to Vilify Georgia Unionists, Atlanta *Journal of Labor*, February 28, 1941, p. 2; "3 Anti-Labor Bills Proposed in Georgia General Assembly," Atlanta *Journal of Labor*, March 7, 1941, p. 1; "Union Contracts Accelerate, Not Hinder Defense," Atlanta *Journal of Labor*, March 7, 1941, p. 1; "Oppose Anti-Strike Laws," Atlanta *Journal of Labor*, March 7, 1941, p. 2; "Editorial of the Week," Atlanta *Journal of Labor*, March 14, 1941, p. 2; "Labor Editors See Profiteering Ahead," Madison *Union Label News*, November 1940, p. 1; "War Chiseling," Topeka *Kansas Labor Weekly*, July 11, 1940, p. 2; "Vinson Bill Will Impose Serfdom on American Labor," Topeka *Kansas Labor Weekly*, April 24, 1941, p. 1; "Profits Make Joke of 'F.D.'s' Pledge," Topeka *Kansas Labor Weekly*, November 20, 1941, p. 1; "Real Intent of M-Day Plan Concealed in Secret 'Annexes,'" Chicago *Federation News*, January 6, 1940, p. 11; "A Twenty Year Conspiracy Against American Labor," Chicago *Federation News*, February 24, 1940, p. 8; "No Need to Sacrifice," Kalispell (Mont.) *Treasure State Labor Journal*, September 24, 1940, p. 2; "Just Give American Workers a Chance," Kalispell *Treasure State Labor Journal*, October 8, 1940, p. 2; "Green Denounces Anti-Strike Bill; Says Vinson Measure is Un-American," *Hannibal Labor Press*, May 23, 1941, p. 1; "Would Protect Workers' Rights," and "Old Grouch's Column," *Hannibal Labor Press*, October 25, 1940; "No Basis for Soaring Prices," Des Moines *Iowa Unionist*, October 6, 1939; "Watch the Price Gougers!," Des Moines *Iowa Unionist*, September 29, 1939; "Now Draft the Dollar!," *St. Louis Labor*

Tribune, October 19, 1940, p. 4; "An Alarming Trend," *St. Louis Union Labor Advocate*, April 15, 1941, p.2; "M-Day Plan Needs No O-Kay, Declare Military Men," South Bend/Fort Wayne *Labor News*, December 8, 1939, p.1; "Labor's Role Under 'M-Day' Plans Revealed," South Bend/Fort Wayne *Labor News*, December 20, 1940.

13. Wayne S. Cole, *Charles A. Lindbergh and the Battle Against American Intervention in World War II* (New York: Harcourt Brace Jovanovich, 1974), pp. 164-65; Wayne S. Cole, *Senator Gerald P. Nye and American Foreign Relations* (Minneapolis: University of Minnesota Press, 1962), pp. 65-6, 83-7, 91-6.

14. "War's Hate Inspired Propaganda Emphasizes Need of a Referendum," Chicago *Federation News*, September 9, 1939, p. 1; "U.S. For Economics of Plenty in U.S.," Chicago *Federation News*, June 1, 1940, p. 6; "American Opposition to War Justified by Past Experiences," Chicago *Federation News*, September 2, 1939, pp. 88-9; "Imperialistic Greed European War Cause," Chicago *Federation News*, June 22, 1940, p. 3; "Industry's Strike Against Government Recalls Nye Committee Findings," Butte *Montana Labor News*, December 26, 1940, p. 4; "Is Hitler a Menace?," Butte *Montana Labor News*, September 5, 1940, p. 2; "Dollar Patriotism," Butte *Montana Labor News*, August 15, 1940, p. 2; "The Imperialistic War" Butte *Montana Labor News*, October 19, 1939, p. 4; "Wall Street Bankers Raid Market; Prepare Neutrality Assault," Council Bluffs *Farmer-Labor Press*, September 14, 1939, p. 1; "Sure, Let the People Vote a War!," Council Bluffs *Farmer-Labor Press*, August 24, 1939, p. 2; "They're Plotting a Military Dictatorship," Council Bluffs *Farmer-Labor Press*, September 14, 1939, p. 4; "War—Inside Track," Council Bluffs *Farmer-Labor Press*, October 19, 1939, p. 2; "For the Ladies," Council Bluffs *Farmer-Labor Press*, January 11, 1940, p. 3. Also see "Secret Arms Agreement Disclosed," Toledo *CIO News*, December 9, 1940, p. 8; "Profits and Poppies vs. Peace and Prosperity," Toledo *CIO News*, June 10, 1940, p. 1; "The Editor's Desk," Toledo *CIO News*, October 28, 1940, p. 8; "Peace—It's Terrible," Toledo *CIO News*, April 8, 1940, p. 2; "No Profit—No War," Kalispell (Mont.) *Flathead Labor Journal*, November 21, 1939, p. 2.

15. "Hold the Johnson Act!," Cincinnati *Chronicle*, May 31, 1940, p. 4; "The Workers Pay for War," Cincinnati *Chronicle*, August 23, 1940, p. 4; "How We Go to War," Cincinnati *Chronicle*, May 17, 1940, p. 4; "Watch the Price Gougers," Cincinnati *Chronicle*, September 29, 1939, p. 4; "Who Said 'Profiteering?,'" Cincinnati *Chronicle*, September 29, 1939, p. 4; "World-Wide Increase in Jobless Noted as Result of War," Council Bluffs *Farmer-Labor Press*, January 4, 1940, p. 1; "Four Months of War Deepens Farm Crisis," Council Bluffs *Farmer-Labor Press*, February 8, 1940, p. 4; "Labor Warned Not to Expect Job Boom," Kalispell (Mont.) *Flathead Labor Journal*, November 21, 1939, p. 3; "Ask U.S. Plan Ahead to Aid Unemployed," Toledo *CIO News*, June 10, 1940, p. 7; "Boom Stories Go Boom," Toledo *CIO News*, November 20, 1939, p. 7; "Living Costs Mount," Toledo *CIO News*, June 2, 1941, p. 1; "No War Boom Big Enough to Put All Idle to Work is Likely, WPA Chief Warns Nation," Cheyenne *Wyoming Labor Journal*, October 6,

139,; "War Boom Not Helpful to Worker," South Bend/Fort Wayne *Labor News*, November 24, 1939, p. 1; "Labor Warring to Prevent U.S. Participation in War," South Bend/Fort Wayne *Labor News*, April 5, 1940; "Labor to Lose in War Boom," Duluth *Labor World*, November 9, 1939, p. 1; "War Wrecks Business and Promotes Scarcity," Duluth *Labor World*, August 29, 1940, p. 6; "People to Bear Arms Cost," Jamestown *Tri-County Herald*, November 20, 1940, p. 3. Also see Cole, *America First*, pp. 79-84.

16. "Profits and Poppies vs. Peace and Prosperity," Toledo *CIO News*, June 10, 1941, p. 1; "They're Plotting a Military Dictatorship," Council Bluffs *Farmer-Labor Press*, September 14, 1939, p. 4; "Lest You Forget," Cincinnati *Chronicle*, September 22, 1939, p. 4; "Quarrels of Europe Not Fight of USA," Chicago *Federation News*, June 1, 1940, p. 10; "Our War Policy: Comment on Dangers," Chicago *Federation News*, June 15, 1940, p. 1; "U.S. Dictatorship a Possibility; May Be Real Objective of Military Group," Chicago *Federation News*, June 29, 1940, p. 2; "In War, All Are Losers," Cheyenne *Wyoming Labor Journal*, May 3, 1940; "The Weekly Parade," Peoria *Labor Temple News*, October 4, 1940, p. 5; "War Cry: Regiment Labor," Peoria *Labor Temple News*, October 18, 1940, p. 1; "War Threatens American Civil Liberties, Labor," Butte *Montana Labor News*, May 23, 1940, p. 2; "Free Men Make Best Fighters," *Sacramento Valley Union Labor Bulletin*, September 29, 1939, p. 2; Cole, *Lindbergh*, p. 88.

17. " 'Yanks Are Not Coming,' Says Penn. Labor," Jamestown (N.Y.) *Tri-County Herald*, January 18, 1940, p. 2.

18. "Handsoff Policy Asked by Samuel Carlson in Peace Rally Address," Jamestown (N.Y.) *Tri-County Herald*, April 12, 1940, p. 5; "Column of Independent Thought," Jamestown *Tri-County Herald*, October 12, 1939, p. 2; "Column of Independent Thought," Jamestown *Tri-County Herald*, October 26, 1939, p. 2; "Wanted: Jobs—Not Guns," Jamestown *Tri-County Herald*, January 18, 1940, p. 4; "Central Labor Council Names Standing Groups; Hits Mobilization Plan," Jamestown *Tri-County Herald*, January 25, 1940, p. 1; "Labor Booms Fight on War Drive," Jamestown *Tri-County Herald*, March 22, 1940, p. 4; "The Battle of 1776," Jamestown *Tri-County Herald*, February 7, 1941, p. 3; "Legislative Group Urges Defeat of Lend-Lease Bill," February 7, 1941, Jamestown *Tri-County Herald*, p. 1; "World War—What For?," Jamestown *Tri-County Herald*, April 26, 1940, p. 5; "'Yanks Aren't Coming' Is Theme of Jamestown May Day Celebration," Jamestown *Tri-County Herald*, May 8, 1940, p. 4; "Column of Independent Thought," Jamestown *Tri-County Herald*, May 24, 1940, p. 7; "The War Drums Are Off Key," Jamestown *Tri-County Herald*, May 24, 1940, p. 1; "Column of Independent Thought," Jamestown *Tri-County Herald*, May 31, 1940, p. 5; "No Time for Hysterics," Jamestown *Tri-County Herald*, June 7, 1940, p. 3; "We Explain Our Policy," Jamestown *Tri-County Herald*, June 14, 1940, p. 3; "Britain's Fifth Column Unmasked," Jamestown *Tri-County Herald*, June 21, 1940, p. 3; "The Chances for an Invasion of the United States," Jamestown *Tri-County Herald*, June 21, 1940, p. 3; "U.S. Lives Above Trade—Wheeler," Jamestown *Tri-County Herald*, June 21, 1940, p. 1; "Local Peace Group Organizes to Oppose

Conscription, War" Jamestown *Tri-County Herald*, August 23, 1940, p. 1; "British Loans Seen as Step Toward War," Jamestown *Tri-County Herald*, December 13, 1940, p. 2; "Destroyers for England . . . and War," Jamestown *Tri-County Herald*, September 6, 1940, p. 3; "Wheeler Calls Draft Club Over Labor," Jamestown *Tri-County Herald*, September 13, 1940, p. 2; "What the Admirals Are Thinking," Jamestown *Tri-County Herald*, September 13, 1940, p. 3; "War Boom No Gain for Labor," Jamestown *Tri-County Herald*, October 4, 1940, p. 6; "Will It Take Six Months Again?," Jamestown *Tri-County Herald*, November 15, 1940, p. 3; "The Road We Traveled Once Before," Jamestown *Tri-County Herald*, November 13, 1940, p. 3.

19. "Britain Prepares for Gas and Bombs, Hoping Civilization Will Win Next War," *Phoenix Labor Press*, July 28, 1939; "Slavery of the People Under Hitlerism," *Phoenix Labor Press*, November 24, 1939, p. 6; "Increased Wages Won by British Workers,," *Phoenix Labor Press*, December 29, 1939; "Building Trades Council News," *Phoenix Labor Press*, December 29, 1939; "Arsenals Add 24,000 to Force," *Phoenix Labor Press*, August 30, 1940, p. 19; "Government Armament Program Presages Huge Business Boom," *Phoenix Labor Press*, October 25, 1940; "U.S. Farm Aid to Britain Likely to Pay Benefits," *Phoenix Labor Press*, November 1941; "Woll Declares War Aims Clear Enough for Labor's Choice," *Phoenix Labor Press*, March 1941, p. 2; "Building Trades Council News," *Phoenix Labor Press*, April 1941, p. 1; "Labor's Obligation," *Phoenix Labor Press*, May 1941, p. 8; "President Roosevelt Declares British Labor Aid 'Most Welcome'" *Phoenix Labor Press*, May 1941, p. 1; "Build Huge Plants and Power Dams to Supply 2 Billion Pounds Aluminum for U.S. Defense," *Phoenix Labor Press*, September 1941; "Unless We Help," *Phoenix Labor Press*, November 1941, p. 14; "President Couch Urges Aid to the Allies," Des Moines *Iowa Unionist*, June 14, 1940, ; "An Economic 'Blitzkrieg' by Hitler Would Have a Serious Affect on Free Labor," Des Moines *Iowa Unionist*, June 28, 1940; "National Defense," Des Moines *Iowa Unionist*, October 4, 1940; "Huge Unemployment Slash is Recorded," Des Moines *Iowa Unionist*, November 15, 1940; "Small Arms Project," Des Moines *Iowa Unionist*, June 13, 1941; "Record Payroll at Ordinance Plant," Des Moines *Iowa Unionist*, November 14, 1941; "Troubled Waters," Des Moines *Iowa Unionist*, December 13, 1940; "National Defense Work Reducing Unemployment," Des Moines *Iowa Unionist*, June 27, 1941; "This Is OUR War," Des Moines *Iowa Unionist*, June 6, 1941; "Victory and Then What?," Des Moines *Iowa Unionist*, July 4, 1941; "Labor Leaders Come Out Against Nazis," Des Moines *Iowa Unionist*, July 4, 1941; "Hobson Supports Hull Statement on Finland," Des Moines *Iowa Unionist*, November 14, 1941; "Upsurge of Sabotage Seen in Europe," Des Moines *Iowa Unionist*, November 21, 1941; "In Hitler's Own Words," Des Moines *Iowa Unionist*, November 21, 1941; "In Hitler's Own Words," Des Moines *Iowa Unionist*, November 28, 1941; untitled editorials, Topeka *Kansas Labor Weekly*, September 7, 1939, p. 2; untitled editorials, Topeka *Kansas Labor Weekly*, January 25, 1940, p. 2; "Timely Topics," Topeka *Kansas Labor Weekly*, March 14, 1940, p. 3; "A Warning by Hendrick Van Loon," Topeka *Kansas Labor Weekly*,

May 23, 1940, p. 3; untitled editorials, Topeka *Kansas Labor Weekly*, May 16, 1940, p. 2; "Lease-Lend Bill 'Indispensable,' Pres. Green Tells Committee," Topeka *Kansas Labor Weekly*, January 30, 1941, p. 1; "Two Million New Jobs Predicted in 1941 with Defense Expansion," Topeka *Kansas Labor Weekly*, October 24, 1940, p. 1; "He Knew Hitler," Topeka *Kansas Labor Weekly*, February 6, 1941; untitled editorials, Topeka *Kansas Labor Weekly*, July 31, 1941, p. 2; "Events That Cast Their Shadow," Topeka *Kansas Labor Weekly*, July 31, 1941, p. 2; "Has Germany Weakened?," Topeka *Kansas Labor Weekly*, August 7, 1941, p. 3; "Defense Sidelights," Topeka *Kansas Labor Weekly*, August 28, 1941, p. 9; "Arguing in Ignorance," Topeka *Kansas Labor Weekly*, October 23, 1941, p. 2; "Topeka Falls," Topeka *Kansas Labor Weekly*, November 13, 1941, p. 3; "Who's News This Week," *Hannibal Labor Press*, September 15, 1939; "Old Grouch's Column," *Hannibal Labor Press*, March 24,, 1939; "Old Grouch's Column," *Hannibal Labor Press*, May 23, 1941; "Let's Get Behind British Workers," *Hannibal Labor Press*, June 6, 1941; "Hitler Victory Would Enslave American Workers," *Hannibal Labor Press*, June 20, 1941; "Old Grouch's Column," *Hannibal Labor Press*, June 20, 1941; "All British Labor Spurns Defeatism," *Hannibal Labor Press*, October 17, 1941.

20. Arnold Zander to Harry Sauthoff, August 1, 1941, folder 2, box 104, President's Office Files, American Federation of State, County, and Municipal Employees Papers, Reuther Library.

21. Ibid.

22. Wayne S. Cole, *Roosevelt and the Isolationists, 1932-45* (Lincoln: University of Nebraska Press, 1983), pp.364-65.

23. " 'Yanks Are Not Coming,' Says Penna. Labor," Jamestown (N.Y.) *Tri-County Herald*, January 18, 1940, p. 2; "Readers' Column," Cincinnati *Chronicle*, January 26, 1940, p. 4; "Springfield, Ohio, Pressmen," *American Pressman,*, December 1938, p. 38; "The Test of Democracy," *American Pressman*, December 1938, pp. 19-21; "Let Us Think Together," *American Pressman*, July 1940, p. 18; "Things Which Appear Inevitable," *American Pressman*, August 1940, pp. 17-8; "Importance of Our Industry," *American Pressman*, June 1941, p. 19; "Trade Treaty Closes Everett Shingle Mills," *Carpenter*, February 1939, p. 22; "The Voice of Business," *Carpenter*, October 1939, p. 12; "Americans, Beware!," *Carpenter*, October 1939, pp. 10-11; "Another Economic Cure-All Exploded," *Carpenter*, December 1939, pp. 6-8; "Loop-Holes in the Neutrality Act," *Carpenter*, December 1939, pp. 19-20; "To Believe or Not To Believe," *Carpenter*, February 1940, pp. 2-3; "How the Military Mind Thinks," *Carpenter*, April 1940, p. 14; "The World War and Unemployment," *Carpenter*, February 1940, pp. 14-5; "Caveat Emptor," *Carpenter*, March 1940, p. 34; "'Keep Out' Urges U.S. Ambassador Joe Kennedy," *Carpenter*, March 1940, p. 53; "Views of Americans," *United Mine Workers Journal*, December 1, 1939, p. 8; "President Lewis Bids Labor and Farmers to Cooperate," *United Mine Workers Journal*, September 15, 1939, p. 5; "President Urges the People to Avoid War Excitement," *United Mine Workers Journal*, September 15, 1939, p. 9; "Vital Questions Are Now Before a Special Session of Congress," *United Mine Workers Journal*, October 1, 1939; "No War is Wanted,"

United Mine Workers Journal, October 15, 1939, p. 19; "An Editorial by John P. Burke," *Pulp, Sulphite, and Paper Mill Workers Journal*, January-February 1939, p. 1; "Mark Twain on War," *Pulp, Sulphite, and Paper Mill Workers Journal*, March-April 1939, p. 20; "Unpaid War Debts," *Pulp, Sulphite, and Paper Mill Workers Journal*, March-April 1939, p. 22; "An Editorial by John P. Burke," *Pulp, Sulphite, and Paper Mill Workers Journal*, July-August 1939, p. 3; "Defense Program and Recovery," *Pulp, Sulphite, and Paper Mill Workers Journal*, September-October 1940, p.1; "The Miners' Union and Free Speech," Butte *Montana Labor News*, December 21, 1939, p. 1; "Protest Lease-Lend Bill," Butte *Miner's Voice*, March 1941.

24. LeRoy James Lenburg, *The CIO and American Foreign Policy: 1935-1955*, doctoral dissertation, Pennsylvania State University, 1973 (Ann Arbor, Mich.: University Microfilms, 1974), pp. 46-9, 77; Timothy R. Dzierba, *Organized Labor and the Coming of World War II, 1937-1941*, doctoral dissertation, State University of New York, Buffalo, 1983 (Ann Arbor, Mich.: University Microfilms International, 1984), pp. 44, 51; "Teachers' Union Defeats Red Bloc," AFL *Weekly News Service*, August 27, 1940; "The Line Has Changed Again," (n.d.; ca. July 1941), folder 9-19, box 9, Reuther Papers. Curran and Quill eventually broke with the Communists, but they were allied with them throughout the prewar period. See David J. Saposs, *Communism in American Unions* (New York: McGraw-Hill, 1959), pp. 131, 141, 171, 176.

25. C.G. "Pop" Edelen, "Appeal to Reason," (UAW Local 51 booklet), n.d., pp. 8-11, folder 9-19, box 9, Reuther Papers; Dzierba, *Organized Labor and the Coming of World War II*, pp. 44, 51, 56, 79-80, 103, 125; Lenburg, *The CIO and American Foreign Policy*, pp. 46-9.

26. Robert H. Zeiger, *John L. Lewis, Labor Leader* (Boston: Twayne Publishers, 1988), pp. 107, 129-30.

The Labor Interventionists

CHAPTER 9

In contrast to the labor isolationists, there were other labor groups that were convinced that the United States had a profound interest in the outcome of the war in Europe and doubted the ability or wisdom of the country trying to remain aloof. Reflecting national patterns,[1] there were particularly forceful advocates of that point of view in the South (such as the Atlanta Federation of Trades and Allied Unions), in the Northeast (such as the New York State Federation of Labor), and in areas where defense industries were major employers (such as the Los Angeles Central Labor Union).

Even before the Second World War began, the Atlanta Federation of Trades and Allied Unions condemned appeasement and warned that the Axis powers would prove insatiable. Less than a month into the European war, it asserted that total United States neutrality was "impossible" and that the United States could not keep a "hands-off" attitude. It condescended to isolationists and peace groups, saying they were unrealistic and unable to "face the facts." A May 1940 editorial in the official publication of the Atlanta Federation crystallized the group's internationalist perspective: "It is unnatural for one-half of the world to be on fire and the other half not be scorched. 'Splendid isolation' is a nice phrase. . . . But we cannot be deceived thereby. We are much nearer Europe than some would have us believe. We may be nearer the war than some would have us believe." The Los Angeles

Central Labor Council concurred with the Atlanta group's anti-isolationist position, cautioning against a false sense of security and suggesting that the Atlantic Ocean might be "simply a broad highway" for potential invaders rather than a "mighty protective barrier."[2]

Groups such as the Alabama Federation of Labor, the Birmingham Trades Council, the Atlanta Federation of Trades and Allied Unions, the New York State Federation of Labor, the New Jersey Industrial Union Council, the Nebraska State Federation of Labor, the Philadelphia Industrial Union Council, the Massachusetts Industrial Union Council, and the Los Angeles Central Labor Council went on record in favor of aid programs for the Allies. Many labor interventionists endorsed neutrality revision, the destroyers-for-bases deal, and Lend-Lease. Some even hinted at support for convoys. Also, labor interventionists subscribed enthusiastically to war relief campaigns for the British, such as the AFL's American Labor Committee to Aid British Labor.[3]

Support for aid was based on two assumptions. First was the assumption that Britain and the United States were partners in a common struggle to preserve democracy. According to an editorial in several pro-interventionist labor newspapers, "Today, all of Great Britain is the Army of Democracy and all America is Democracy's civilian front." Whereas the labor isolationists expressed suspicion of the British, the labor interventionists praised them highly for their democratic government and their strong labor movement. Germany's attack upon Britain was seen as an attack upon democracy itself, and the defense of Britain was implicitly a defense of America's own form of government. It was also a defense of organized labor. The labor interventionists were impressed with the support British labor gave to the war effort. They promoted the visits to the United States of British labor leaders and gave them a platform from which to appeal for American support. Fighting to stave off the anti-labor Nazis put British labor in the position of defending free trade unionism everywhere, in the view of the labor interventionists.[4]

The second assumption was that British victory over

Germany was necessary if the United States were to remain at peace, and that the likelihood of a British victory would be enhanced by American assistance. That same idea was advanced by the national interventionist groups, such as the Committee to Defend America by Aiding the Allies. Further, even if Britain were to lose, American aid would have helped weaken the Germans—thereby making them less invincible should they shift their sights to the Western Hemisphere. Similarly, some labor interventionists called for military and economic aid for Latin America, in order to forestall Nazi influence in that region and to assure the United States of allies if Britain were to fall.[5]

In addition to supporting aid for Britain, the labor interventionists applauded the Roosevelt Administration's defense program. They endorsed increased spending for shipbuilding, aircraft construction, and armament production, and even tended to support military conscription. Although virtually the entire labor movement ultimately cooperated with Selective Service once it was law, support from the labor interventionists came earlier and was more enthusiastic than that from their anti-interventionist colleagues. The Los Angeles Labor Temple draft board, for example, boasted that it had one of the largest pools of registrants in Los Angeles County, that it was one of the first to submit its list of registrants to Selective Service authorities, and that it had devised its own efficient methods of processing registrants.[6]

While not necessarily a causal factor, the belief that defense spending would open the door to prosperity usually accompanied the labor interventionists' endorsement of Roosevelt's programs. Pro-intervention regional labor groups encouraged their communities to bid for airports, military bases, shipyards, airplane factories, and arms plants, as well as the myriad construction and supply contracts that went with them. Defense spending at home and the increased exports to Britain made possible by neutrality revision seemed to promise better job training, more employment, and higher wages. Defense industries would be the immediate beneficiaries, but there would be a multiplier effect, too: highways would be built between army camps and defense plans, houses would be built for defense workers, rural electrification projects would be galvanized, and consumer spending would be stimulated by the burgeoning new payrolls. In contrast with the labor isolationists' gloom and doom predictions, many labor interventionists saw the defense program and aid to Britain as an economic bonanza. The Los Angeles Central Labor Council exclaimed, "the business of defense has emphatically come to mean business, jobs, and payrolls to California" That same mood was expressed in Waco, Atlanta, New York, and elsewhere.[7]

State and city union groups were joined by certain national and international unions in support of the Roosevelt Administration's foreign policies and preparedness programs. Two of the most prominent were the Amalgamated Clothing Workers (ACW) of the CIO and the International Ladies' Garment Workers Union' (ILGWU), which began the era as part of the CIO but returned to the AFL in 1940. The needlework trades were not really a defense industry (though they might benefit from contracts for military uniforms and from the consumer purchasing power generated by defense spending). The ACW and the ILGWU, however, fit the interventionist pattern in other ways. They were concentrated in the Northeast. Further, their rank-and-file were largely Jewish, and thus might have felt concerned over Hitler's anti-Semitism as well as his anti-unionism.[8]

Unions that stood to benefit most directly from the expanded defense program also tended to support Roosevelt's policies. Walter Reuther, Vice President of the CIO's United Auto Workers (UAW), spoke out forcefully in favor of aiding the British and devised an ambitious plan to convert auto plants to aircraft factories capable of producing 500 war planes a day. In the AFL, the International Association of Machinists (IAM), the International Brotherhood of Boilermakers, the Metal Trades Department, and the Building and Construction Trades Department advocated increased defense spending and neutrality revision. For machinists, auto workers, shipbuilders, and others, aid to Britain and military preparedness promised hundreds of thousands of new jobs, and their unions sought to guarantee them through pro-defense lobbying and job placement services.[9]

The job boom in defense industries also offered the unions

an opportunity to strengthen themselves by expanding their dues-paying membership. Thus, in 1940 and 1941, they launched vigorous organizational drives. In factory after factory, the UAW (CIO) and the IAM (AFL) fought each other viciously to unionize aviation workers. Meanwhile, the AFL's Boilermakers battled the CIO's Industrial Union of Marine and Shipbuilding Workers to represent shipyard employees. All four unions added significantly to their membership rolls and negotiated lucrative new contracts.[10]

The foreign policy opinions of organized labor, then, appeared to break down along regional and occupation lines that were consistent with national patterns. A Gallup Poll taken on November 2, 1941, revealed how closely union members' opinions paralleled national opinions. When asked about the level of aid that the Roosevelt Administration was providing to Great Britain, 27 percent of the national sample said too much aid was being given, 57 percent said that the right amount was being given, and 16 percent said that not enough aid was being given. Among union members, the percentages were almost identical: 27 percent, 55 percent, and 22 percent, respectively. Likewise, 32 percent of the national sample expressed the conviction that it was more important for the country to stay out of war that it was to ensure the defeat of Germany, as compared with 34 percent of the union members who were polled. Conversely, 68 percent of the national sample asserted that the defeat of Germany was more important than staying out of war, as compared with 66 percent of the union members.[11]

Other polls confirmed that union members reacted to foreign policy issues in much the same way as non-union members. In a composite of polls taken between November 1940 and October 1941, 41 percent of union members and 39 percent of non-union members thought that it was more important for the United States to stay out of war, while 54 percent of union members and 56 percent of non-union members thought that it was more important for the United States to help Great Britain defeat Germany.[12] American opinion was moving away from neutrality. The opinion of labor was moving in the same direction.

Notes

1. Wayne S. Cole, *An Interpretative History of American Foreign Relations,* rev. ed. (Homewood, Ill.: Dorsey Press, 1974), p. 324.

2. "Democracies Again Feed Their Babies to Moloch," Atlanta *Journal of Labor*, September 23, 1938, p. 2; "Hitler Annexes 3,500,00," Atlanta *Journal of Labor*, September 23, 1938, p. 1; "Peace Only Relative," Atlanta *Journal of Labor*, October 14, 1938, p. 2; "Impossible to Remain Unaffected," Atlanta *Journal of Labor*, September 29, 1939, p. 2; "America's Entry Into the War," Atlanta *Journal of Labor*, May 17, 1940, p. 2; "American Women Commended," Atlanta *Journal of Labor*, December 1, 1939, p. 2; "Our Maginot Line," *Los Angeles Citizen*, September 20, 1940, p. 4.

3. Memorandum to Chapter Representatives, February 10, 1941, Lewis to Eichelberger, May 16, 1941, Lewis to Editors of Labor Papers plus attachment, March 7, 1941, folder: "Admin. Mgmt.—Labor Division, box 4, Committee to Defend America by Aiding the Allies Archives, Princeton University Library, Princeton, N.J.; "The Lease-Lend Bill is Law," Omaha *Unionist*, March 14, 1941, p. 2; "The President's Column," Omaha *Unionist*, December 20, 1940, p. 5; "President Roper of the Alabama Federation of Labor Reports on Labor's Cooperation in National Defense," Birmingham *Southern Labor Review*, February 19, 1941; "For Our Own Safety, Act Now!," Birmingham *Southern Labor Review*, January 15, 1941, p. 1; "Lease-Lend Bill 'Indispensable,'" Birmingham *Southern Labor Review*, February 19, 1941; "Georgia Labor Votes to Aid British Labor," Atlanta *Journal of Labor*, April 25, 1941, p. A-4; "The Significance of the Eight Points," Atlanta *Journal of Labor*, September 5, 1941, p. 2; "Southern Labor Will Do Its Part to Aid British—Googe," Atlanta *Journal of Labor*, May 23, 1941, p. 1; "Aid British Labor Tag Day," Atlanta *Journal of Labor*, July 11, 1941, p. 1; "It Is Better to be Prepared," Atlanta *Journal of Labor*, August 16, 1940, p. 2; "Turner Names Six Committees to Aid British Union Labor," Atlanta *Journal of Labor*, June 13, 1941, p. 1; "Neutrality Bill Passes," *Los Angeles Citizen*, November 10, 1939, p. 5; "Outposts of Defense," *Los Angeles Citizen*, September 20, 1940, p. 4; "Islands for Safety," *Los Angeles Citizen*, October 25, 1940, p. 4; "Union's Fashion Show Was a Big Success," *Los Angeles Citizen*, March 7, 1941, p. 4; "A Shield for Safety," *Los Angeles Citizen*, May 23, 1941, p. 4; "Patrols and War," *Los Angeles Citizen*, July 18, 1941, p. 4; "Scottish War Relief in Full Swing," *Los Angeles Citizen*, January 17, 1941, p. 4; "Labor Pledges Support of President's Policy of All-Out Aid," Des Moines *Iowa Unionist*, June 13, 1941, p. 1; "Labor Subscribes for $325,000," Des Moines *Iowa Unionist*, June 13, 1941; "Neutrality and Its Results," Worcester (Mass.) *Labor News*, June 7, 1940, p. 5; "Roosevelt Defies Mussolini," Worcester *Labor News*, June 14, 1940, p. 4; "'Make America the "Arsenal of Democracy,"' Says the President," Worcester *Labor News*, January 3, 1941, p. 4; "Fund to Aid Workers in Britain Gets Good Start at CLU Meeting," Worcester *Labor News*, August 1, 1941, p. 1; *Official Proceedings* (1940), pp. 220, 229-30; Now York State Federation of Labor, *1941 Official Proceedings,*

Seventy-Eighth Annual Convention (n.p.: New York State Federation of Labor, 1941), p. 247, 250-52.

4. "Boot Shop Workers in Britain Win Agreement," *Los Angeles Citizen*, September 1, 1939, p. II:5; "Citrine, British Labor Leader, Is Honored Quest at Local AFL Function,"*Los Angeles Citizen*, January 10, 1941, p. 7; "Los Angeles Labor Greet Their English Brother," *Los Angeles Citizen*, January 17, 1941, p. 1; "'British Labor Will Never Yield,' Bevin Stated in Broadcast to U.S.," *Los Angeles Citizen*, July 18, 1941, p. 6; "British Labor Group to Attend CLC Meeting," *Los Angeles Citizen*, October 10, 1941, p. 1; "This Is Our War," Des Moines *Iowa Unionist*, June 6, 1941; "Britain Has Strikes in Spite of War," Des Moines *Iowa Unionist*, November 14, 1941; "War—By Dynamite and Water," Birmingham *Southern Labor Review*, June 25, 1941, p. 4; "Folks," *Waco Farm and Labor Journal*, February 21, 1941, p. 1; "Vacations with Pay Raise in England," Atlanta *Journal of Labor*, July 29, 1938, p. 1; "Freezing Wages," Atlanta *Journal of Labor*, April 4,1941, p. 2; "President Roosevelt's Significant Statement," Atlanta *Journal of Labor*, July 11, 1941, p. 2; "Southern Labor Will Do Its Part to Aid British—Googe," Atlanta *Journal of Labor*, May 23, 1941, p. 1; "Why We Aid British Labor," Atlanta *Journal of Labor*, July 18, 1941, p. 2; "Arms and Money Are Urged by Bevin to Aid Britain's War for Democracy," Atlanta *Journal of Labor*, August 29, 1941, p. C-3; "British Government Praises Unions," Atlanta *Journal of Labor*, September 26, 1941, p. 2; "England's No. 1 Labor Leader," Atlanta *Journal of Labor*, October 3, 1941, p. 2; "Here and There," Atlanta *Journal of Labor*, November 8, 1940, p. 2; "British Labor Leader Urges Every Effort," Omaha *Unionist*, January 3, 1941, p. 1; "The President's Column," Omaha *Unionist*, January 10, 1941, p. 4; "British Labor is Fighting for Us!," South Bend/Fort Wayne *Labor News*, June 13, 1941; New York State Federation of Labor, *1940 Official Proceedings, Seventy-Seventh Annual Convention* (n.p.: New York State Federation of Labor, 1940), pp- 11-12, 173-74.

5. "A Shield for Safety," *Los Angeles Citizen*, May 23, 1941, p. 4; "Keep America Out of War," Atlanta *Journal of Labor*, August 23, 1940, p. 2; "It Is Better to Be Prepared," Atlanta *Journal of Labor*, August 16, 1940, p. 2; "For Our Own Safety, Act Now!," Birmingham *Southern Labor Review*, January 15, 1941, p. 1; "Comments on the News," *Waco Farm and Labor Journal*, February 16, 1940, p. 1; Walter Johnson, *The Battle Against Isolation* (Chicago: University of Chicago Press, 1946), pp. 94-6, 115-16.

6. "A Good Beginning," Atlanta *Journal of Labor*, January 13, 1939, p. 2; "Our National Defense," Atlanta *Journal of Labor*, February 23, 1940, p. 2; "Registration Day," Atlanta *Journal of Labor*, October 11, 1940, p. 4; "GFL Pledges Full Support for Defense," Atlanta *Journal of Labor*, May 2, 1941, p. 1; "Comments on the News," *Waco Farm and Labor Journal*, June 14, 1940, p. 1; "Folks," *Waco Farm and Labor Journal*, January 17, 1941, pp. 1, 2; "Which Is More Important?," Worcester *Labor News*, June 21, 1940, p. 4; "Would Shame Slackers," Worcester *Labor News*, January 10, 1941, p. 4; "FDR's Message," Worcester *Labor News*, June 7, 1940, p. 4; "Machinists Back Up the President's

Plea for National Defense," *Los Angeles Citizen*, May 31, 1940, p. 3; "Local AFL Unionists Pledge Support of Defense Program," *Los Angeles Citizen*, June 28, 1940, p. 5; "Official Proceedings of Los Angeles Central Labor Council," *Los Angeles Citizen*, July 5, 1940, p. 7; "American Preparedness is Paramount," *Los Angeles Citizen*, September 6, 1940, p. 21; "Relief Rolls Slash Visioned From Draft," *Los Angeles Citizen*, September 20, 1940, p. 4; "General Policy State Federation of Labor on National Defense," *Los Angeles Citizen*, October 4, 1940, p. 1; "First Draftees Are to be Drawn Next Tuesday," *Los Angeles Citizen*, October 25, 1940, p. 1; "National Defense: Our Number One Job," (special section), Birmingham *Southern Labor Review*, February 19, 1941; New York State Federation of Labor, *1940 Official Proceedings*, pp. 11, 220; Nelson Lichtenstein, *Labor's War at Home: The CIO in World War II* (Cambridge: Cambridge University Press, 1982), p. 37.

7. "Chamber of Commerce Seeks Defense Projects," *Waco Farm and Labor Journal*, October 4, 1940, p. 1; "Army Camp for Brownwood," *Waco Farm and Labor Journal*, October 11, 1940, p. 1; "Opportunity is Here for an Airport," *Waco Farm and Labor Journal*, January 10, 1941, p. 4; "Waco Declares for National Defense," *Waco Farm and Labor Journal*, January 17, 1941, p. 1; "Texas Does Big Work for Defense," *Waco Farm and Labor Journal*, November 28, 1941, p. 1; "Pierce Sees Great Increase in Business and Employment," Boston *Wage Earner*, January 13, 1941, p. 2; "Defense Orders Stimulating New England Business," Boston *Wage Earner*, January 13, 1941, p. 6; "Hartford Industry Aided by National Defense Boom," Boston *Wage Earner*, January 27, 1941, p. 6; "Increased Number of Negroes Working In Defense Industries," Boston *Wage Earner*, July 14, 1941; "Ship Bid Offers Indicate Some Early Construction Here," *Los Angeles Citizen*, September 15, 1939, p. 5; "Frey Here to Aid in Shipbuilding Program," *Los Angeles Citizen*, February 23, 1940, p. 1; "Navy Yard Mechanics' Wage Boost Visioned," *Los Angeles Citizen*, May 31, 1940, p. 5; "Apprentice Training in State Defense Program," *Los Angeles Citizen*, July 19, 1940, p. 8; "Plans Lines for Defense," *Los Angeles Citizen*, July 26, 1940, p. 4; "Some Real Jobs With the U.S. Government," *Los Angeles Citizen*, July 26, 1940, p. 5; "Many Millions in Ship Contracts Are Assured Los Angeles," *Los Angeles Citizen*, September 13, 1940, p. 3; "Defense in the West," *Los Angeles Citizen*, September 20, 1940, p. 4; "Budgets and Balances," *Los Angeles Citizen*, November 22, 1940, p. 4; "Unemployment Slash Recorded As Defense Production Expands," *Los Angeles Citizen*, November 22, 1940, p. 4; "Employment Reaches Record Peak," *Los Angeles Citizen*, December 20, 1940, p. 9; "Machine Tool Industry, Transportation, Defense," *Los Angeles Citizen*, December 20, 1940, p. 12; "California Holds Her Own," *Los Angeles Citizen*, January 3, 1941, p. 4; "All-Out Drive," *Los Angeles Citizen*, January 3, 1941, p. 4; "The Navy Looks West," *Los Angeles Citizen*, April 4, 1941, p. 4; "State Employment and Payrolls in Terrific Gain," *Los Angeles Citizen*, April 4, 1941, p. 4; "Are You Registered?," *Los Angeles Citizen*, April 4, 1941, p. 4; "Training for Defense Work," *Los Angeles Citizen*, June 20, 1941, p. 3; "60,000 More Aircraft Workers to be Needed,"

Birmingham *Southern Labor Review*, June 7, 1939, p. 2; "State Capital News," Birmingham *Southern Labor Review*, June 12, 1940, p. 1; "Adequate Transportation Necessary in Defense," Birmingham *Southern Labor Review*, June 12, 1940, p. 1; "State Capital Notes," Birmingham *Southern Labor Review*, June 26, 1940, p. 1; "State News," Birmingham *Southern Labor Review*, July 3, 1940, p. 1; "240,000 Jobless Find Employment in 30 Days," Birmingham *Southern Labor Review*, July 3, 1940, p.1; "New Highway Considered," Birmingham *Southern Labor Review*, July 3, 1940, p. 1; "Business Improvement Continues," Birmingham *Southern Labor Review*, August 28, 1940; "Two Million New Jobs Predicted," Birmingham *Southern Labor Review*, October 23, 1940, p. 1; "Expectation That Six Large New Hospitals Will Be Built," Birmingham *Southern Labor Review*, February 12, 1941, p. 1; "Dark Outlook Seen if Britain Loses," Birmingham *Southern Labor Review*, February 12, 1941, p. 1; "Predict Now Jobs for Idle," Atlanta *Journal of Labor*, October 18, 1940, p. 4; "Leon Wofford Speaks on Labor and National Defense Housing," Atlanta *Journal of Labor*, October 18, 1940, p. 4; "Leon Wofford Speaks on Labor and National Defense Housing," Atlanta *Journal of Labor*, November 8, 1940, p. 2; "Report of T.M. Mickelson," Atlanta *Journal of Labor*, April 25, 1941, p. B-2; "Johnson and Mann Reelected," Atlanta *Journal of Labor*, April 25, 1941, p. A-6; "Small Arms Project," Des Moines *Iowa Unionist*, June 13, 1941, p. 1; "Record Payroll at Ordinance Plant," Des Moines *Iowa Unionist*, November 14, 1941, p. 1; "Vocational Schools Train for Defense," *Los Angeles Citizen*, October 4, 1940, p. 7; New York State Federation of Labor, *1940 Proceedings*, pp. 13, 219, 243.

8. Lichtenstein, *Labor's War at Home*, pp. 36-7.

9. Walter Reuther radio address, September 14, 1941, folder 540-3, box 540, Walter Reuther Papers, Reuther Library, Wayne State University, Detroit, Mich.; *Town Meeting* , March 24, 1941 (pamphlet), pp. 5-12, folder 540-1, box 540, Ibid.; "More Airplanes for Defense," (Reuther radio address), December 28, 1940, file 539-14, box 539, Ibid.; "Building Trades . . . Approve Roosevelt's Ship Deal," *St. Louis Labor Tribune*, September 7, 1940, p. 1; "Metal Trades Ask Revision of Embargo," Duluth *Labor World*, October 5, 1939, p. 4; "Auto Union Head Raps Ford Stall On Making Planes," *CIO News*, July 18, 1940, p. 1; "Shortage of Skilled Labor Denied," AFL *Weekly News Service*, May 28, 1940; "Metal Unions Adopt 'No Strike' Plan," AFL *Weekly News Service*, January 7, 1941; "19 Building Unions Limit Defense Fees and Banish Strikes," AFL *Weekly News Service*, January 14, 1941; "Boilermakers Start Organization Drive," AFL *Weekly News Service*, August 16, 1940; "Metal Trades Heed Plea," *Los Angeles Citizen*, September 12, 1941, p. 2; "Frey Here to Aid in Ship Building Program," *Los Angeles Citizen*, February 23, 1940, p. 1; "Machinists Back Up the President's Plea for National Defense," *Los Angeles Citizen*, May 31, 1940, p. 3; "Labor Heads Offer to Supply 700,000 Men for Armament Jobs," *Los Angeles Citizen*, May 31, 1940, p. 4; "Cooperation—Not Repression," *Lansing Industrial News*, March 21, 1941, p. 1; Resolution of International Association of Machinists, May 16, 1940, folder 25, box 66, Sidney Hillman Papers, ACW Archives. Labor-Management Documentation Center,

Cornell University, Ithaca, NY.

10. "Boilermakers Organizing All Navy Yard Employees," AFL *Weekly News Service*, October 15, 1940; "Machinists Push Aviation Drive," AFL *Weekly News Service*, July 23, 1940; "Boilermakers Start Organization Drive," AFL *Weekly News Service*, August 16, 1940; "Machinists Report Great Progress," AFL *Weekly News Service*, September 17, 1940; "AFL Union Drive in Aircraft Plants Nets 30,000 Members, Higher Pay," AFL *Weekly News Service*, December 10, 1940; "Drive to Unionize Curtiss-Wright," *St. Louis Labor Tribune*, September 14, 1940, p. 1; "50,000 Aircraft Workers Organized by Machinists," Birmingham *Southern Labor Review*, August 20, 1941; "AFL Shipyard Work Advances," *Los Angeles Citizen*, May 31, 1940, p. 1; "Communists and CIO Group Have Lost Shipyard Fight," *Los Angeles Citizen*, May 31, 1940, p. 1; "Machinists Pushing Organization of the Aircraft Plants Here," *Los Angeles Citizen*, August 2, 1940, p. 8; "AFL Unions Sign Ship Agreement," *Los Angeles Citizen*, January 31, 1941, p. 1; "AFL Machinists Drive for Aviation Workers," *Los Angeles Citizen*, February 14, 1941, p. 1; "Machinists 727 and Lockheed Sign New Pact," *Los Angeles Citizen*, September 19, 1941, p. 1; "Shipyard Workers Prepare for Boom in Organization," *CIO News*, September 17, 1938, p. 3; "Sue Coast Shipyard," *CIO News*, June 17, 1940, p. 2; "Shipyard Union Gets Big Gains," *CIO News*, July 1, 1940, p. 2; "Launch Drive in Aircraft," *CIO News*, July 15, 1940, p. 3.

11. George H. Gallup, *The Gallup Poll: Public Opinion, 1935-1971* (New York: Random House, 1972), I: 304.

12. Alfred O. Hero, Jr., and Emil Starr, *The Reuther-Meany Foreign Policy Dispute: Union Leaders and Members View World Affairs* (Dobbs Ferry, N.Y.: Oceana Publications, 1970), pp. 79-80, 231-32 (table 3-1).

The Emerging Interventionist Consensus

CHAPTER **10**

Labor opinion concerning the war adhered to national patterns in several crucial respects. It reflected regional and occupational variations similar to the rest of the country. And, over time, it became more and more interventionist.

When the war in Europe began, most Americans opposed intervention, even though they typically sympathized with Great Britain. Yet over the next two years, Americans gradually came to support aid to the Allies, even if it meant risking war. By autumn 1940, interventionists were in the majority. By mid-to-late 1941, those who went beyond simple interventionism to advocate an immediate declaration of war were a steadily increasing minority.[1]

Meanwhile, the same transformation was taking place within the labor movement. Labor groups that had endorsed neutrality, opposed aid to the Allies, and disagreed with rearmament initiatives, eventually moderated their anti-interventionism or reversed course entirely. Four factors contributed to that phenomenon: first, the progress of the war in Europe and the impact it had on American thinking; second, the realization that defense spending would not ruin the economy but instead would create jobs; third, the effectiveness of interventionist pressure groups in appealing to labor (and the relative ineffectiveness of America First); and, fourth, the influence over the rank-and-file of national labor leaders and the two national labor centers.

Shortly after the war in Europe began, the combatants settled down to several months of comparative inactivity. Then, in May 1940, the German war machine sprang into action. Within six weeks it had overrun several countries, including France, leaving Britain virtually alone to face the Nazis. The sudden turn of affairs caused many Americans to reassess their position on the country's foreign policy and to conclude that some form of intervention might be necessary, if only to protect American shores from the Axis onslaught.

Events in Europe were equally sobering for organized labor. Starting in the summer and autumn of 1940, labor groups in Peoria, Lansing, Cheyenne, St. Louis, Duluth, Missoula, and elsewhere, gradually moved away from their initial anti-interventionism. They expressed support for British aid and for President Franklin D. Roosevelt's defense program, abandoned their anti-British rhetoric, and criticized isolationist spokesmen whom they had praised only months or weeks earlier. When the once anti-interventionist St. Louis Central Trades Council (AFL) passed a resolution in early 1941 endorsing Lend-Lease, the *St. Louis Union Labor Advocate* reported the Council's sense "that America's national security calls for all possible aid to England in that country's struggle against Hitlerism, and that our country would face a problem, should England fall and Hitler get hold of the powerful British Navy."[2]

Another turning point in the war had a similar effect upon the pro-Communist unions. In June 1941, Hitler broke his non-aggression pact with Moscow and German troops invaded the Soviet Union. Maritime workers on both coasts, the United Electrical, Radio, and Machine Workers Union, the New York City Industrial Union Council, and other groups that had opposed intervention ever since the non-aggression treaty had been signed two years earlier immediately became perhaps the most vehement proponents of intervention in the entire labor movement.[3]

The suddenness of the shift was apparent in two conflicting resolutions, passed within days of each other by the pro-Communist Plymouth Local no. 51 of the United Auto Workers (UAW). Just before the German invasion of the Soviet Union, Local 51 denounced interventionists as "war-mongers" and called upon the CIO to convene a national anti-war congress to defend neutrality. Immediately after the invasion, Local 51 passed a resolution attesting to its "uncompromising and militant opposition to Fascism" and declaring that providing aid to the countries fighting the Axis was "the real American interest." National UAW leaders, who were anti-Communist and who had supported intervention all along, christened Local 51 President C.G. "Pop" Edelen with a new nickname: "Flop" Edelen.[4]

Further weakening the resolve of the labor isolationists may have been the realization that the economic disasters they had expected from Roosevelt's programs did not seem to be materializing. On the contrary, evidence of returning prosperity was irresistible and labor isolationists wanted their share of the bounty. Labor groups that had discounted the prospect of a job boom early in the war started clamoring for defense contracts. Munitions factories, construction of army camps, and ancillary endeavors from highways to housing to mining for strategic minerals offered employment. Moreover, job-creating civil projects, such as airport improvements, suddenly could be justified and funded in the name of national defense.[5]

Montana unionists typified the changing mood of labor isolationists. Initially opposed to the war and to defense spending, they turned to berating isolationist United States Senator Burton Wheeler—a longtime ally—for failing to secure defense contracts for the state. Even the strongly anti-interventionist Chicago Federation of Labor saw economic benefits to be derived from Roosevelt's defense policies.[6]

All manner of unions envisioned the prospect of more paydays because of the defense program. The American Federation of Teachers (AFT) did not resolve to support intervention until 1941 and in August 1940 more than 200 of its locals expressed overwhelming opposition to getting involved in the war. Yet in that same month the AFT's Executive Council sought to tie greater spending in education to the defense effort. "Whereas public education is the front line of defense of the American democracy," the Executive Council proclaimed, expanded education programs were needed to teach democratic values, promote good citizenship, and bolster the morale of the country's youth during a time of great national peril.[7]

Pro-intervention pressure groups also influenced labor. The Committee to Defend America by Aiding the Allies (or White Committee) and Fight For Freedom, Incorporated, put their case to labor in a sophisticated and effective manner, and enjoyed considerable success. Meanwhile, the chief isolationist pressure group, America First, failed in its campaign to attract labor support.

The White Committee established contacts with national and international unions, state and city labor organizations, and individual union leaders. Concentrated in the Northeast and in heavy industry, White Committee influence was strongest in the New Jersey Federation of Labor, the Pennsylvania Federation of Labor, the Industrial Union Councils of New Jersey, Pennsylvania, and New York State, the Eastern Region of the Steel Workers' Organizing Committee, and the Industrial Union of Marine and Shipbuilding Workers. The International Ladies' Garment Workers' Union (ILGWU) championed the White Committee from its inception, made frequent donations, and was represented on the committee's national board by Vice President Samuel Shore. The Amalgamated Clothing Workers (ACW) also supported the White Committee. Union leaders who were conspicuous in their support of the White Committee included Frank Grillo (secretary-treasurer of the United Rubber Workers), Irving Abramson (president of the New Jersey Industrial Union Council), David Dubinsky and Luigi Antonini (president and vice president, respectively, of the ILGWU), George S. Counts (president, AFT), A. Phillip Randolph (president, Sleeping Car Porters), Thomas J. Lyons (president, New York State Federation of Labor), Walter Reuther (vice president, UAW), Arthur Huggins (president, International Brotherhood of Paperhangers), Dave Beck (president, Teamsters' Union), Gustav Strebel (chairman, New York State Industrial Union Council), and John Brophy (who held several important CIO posts). In addition, Philip Murray, who succeeded John L. Lewis as president of the CIO in 1940, AFL President William Green, and AFL Vice President Matthew Woll were sympathetic towards the White Committee. The Committee's labor contacts supplied mailing lists, endorsed White Committee statements, distributed tickets and provided speakers for the organization's rallies and called for union adoption of resolutions drafted by the White Committee. National and international unions sometimes even pressured their locals to cooperate with White Committee chapters.[8]

To coordinate its efforts to appeal to labor, the White Committee established a Trade Union Division (which later changed its name to the National Labor Division). Lyons, Beck, Reuther, Dubinsky, and dozens of other labor executives signed up to serve on the Division's Administrative Committee or its National Advisory Board.

The division ensured that the White Committee and its local chapters displayed the union label on its stationery and undertook an energetic publicity campaign. It retained well-known journalist Victor Riesel to give advice on press relations, establish contacts with reporters, and plant articles generated by the White Committee into matte services and clip sheets utilized by labor newspapers. The division issued press releases, distributed draft resolutions and petitions to labor groups, held inter-union conferences, and published pamphlets such as "Labor and the Totalitarian Threat" and "Organized Labor's Stake in the War." On August 1, 1941, it inaugurated a twice-monthly newsletter, the *Labor and Defense Press Service,* that was issued up until the attack on Pearl Harbor. Also, the White Committee's regular national newsletter, the *Progress Bulletin*, published occasional articles on labor matters.[9]

One of the division's primary messages was that organized labor was one of the groups that had the most to fear from the growing power of Adolf Hitler. It even adopted a slogan: "Dictatorship and Free Trade-Unionism cannot exist together on this earth." At the same time, it stressed that organized labor in Great Britain was strong and healthy, and that therefore American workers should share Britain's goals. The division also claimed that the expanding war economy was good for labor and that there was a rising tide of pro-intervention sentiment within the labor movement. It was even willing to adopt pro-union positions on issues such as excess profits taxes that were not, strictly speaking, part of the debate over intervention.[10]

The National Labor Division enjoyed only middling success at encouraging the White Committee's various chapters to establish labor divisions at the local level. About a dozen chapters in the Northeast—most notably, the Philadelphia chapter—set up labor divisions. Elsewhere around the country, there was apathy or outright resistance. Some White Committee chapters in the West and South did not care to establish labor divisions because they harbored anti-union sentiments. Worse still, in the Midwest, the job of organizing labor divisions was entrusted to O.L. Sprague.[11]

Another problem the National Labor Division faced was competition from the AFL's American Labor Committee to Aid British Labor. AFL leaders such as Matthew Woll preferred to concentrate on that body because it was essentially a relief organization that was not overtly political. The AFL traditionally had shunned political involvement. Yet even that competition did not really impede the White Committee in its quest to win labor's support. In the view of the director of the National Labor Division, there was no "psychological conflict" between the White Committee and the American Labor Committee to Aid British Labor. The American Labor Committee to Aid British Labor adhered to the same basic principles as the White Committee, and the two groups actually reinforced each other.[12]

The White Committee pursued an effective plan to sway labor's votes. The well-defined labor division orchestrated a publicity blitz, endeavored to build a network of chapters, and enlisted the support of a galaxy of labor's foremost executives. The committee's strong ties to those leaders assured it of a sympathetic hearing for its ideas in labor circles.[13]

If anything, Fight for Freedom, Incorporated, was even more aggressive than the White Committee in its courtship of labor. During the summer and fall of 1941, it secured the endorsement of many of the same national labor leaders who also supported the White Committee, including Reuther, Tobin, Counts, Brophy, and Randolph, as well as Woll and ACW President Sidney Hillman.

Those leaders in turn tried to recruit the rank-and-file. CIO Rubber Workers' Secretary-Treasurer Frank Grillo was one of Fight for Freedom's most avid boosters, and he urged other union members to join him. "I have investigated this Fight for Freedom Committee and I endorse them without reservation," he told unionists, after warning that peace groups were fronts for Communists and Nazis. The Fight for Freedom Committee, he added, "aims to fight for the preservation of political, social, and economic democracy." American labor, Grillo concluded, should help to stop Hitler "before he gets to our shores."[14]

Fight for Freedom appealed for support directly at the work place and the union hall. It claimed the support of 1,600 shop stewards and obtained thousands of workers' signatures on anti-neutrality petitions. The organization developed a special newsletter, the *Labor News Service,* which it sent to shop stewards and editors of labor newspapers. Its stories were reprinted in labor newspapers in all regions of the country. Of course, the message it presented was the same as the White Committee's. First: Hitler had to be stopped in Europe if the United States were to remain secure. Second: British labor thrived in a pro-union environment whereas German labor suffered terrible oppression. Third: American isolationists were anti-union. Fourth: more and more unionists were advocating intervention and contributing to the defense effort. Fifth: the Administration's defense buildup was an economic boon for organized labor.[15]

In June 1941, 99 AFL and CIO executives signed a letter to President Roosevelt that Fight for Freedom had circulated; it commended the chief executive for his foreign policies and called for repeal of the Neutrality Act. In July, Woll, Grillo, Hillman and ILGWU Secretary Frederick Umhey were featured speakers at a "Stop Hitler" unity rally for labor co-sponsored in New York City by Fight for Freedom and the Committee to Defend America by Aiding the Allies. One-time presidential hopeful Wendell Willkie and entertainers Burgess Meredith and Danny Kaye also appeared at that event. On October 3, celebrated labor figures joined delegates from various groups in an anti-neutrality "Continental Congress for Freedom" that Fight for Freedom convened in

Washington, D.C. Two days later, Fight for Freedom and the AFL's American Labor Committee to Aid British Labor co-sponsored a mass meeting at New York's Madison Square Garden.[16]

At the same time, Fight for Freedom undermined pro-neutrality meetings by trying to limit union participation in them. In May 1941 it persuaded 13 AFL and CIO leaders in New York City, including Antonini, Randolph, Strebel, and Umhey, to sign a statement encouraging unionists to boycott a "Labor Conference Against War" that was sponsored by an anti-interventionist group that allegedly had ties to the Communists.[17]

Fight for Freedom bartered for labor's sympathy by showing sympathy of its own. It demanded that union rights—particularly the right to strike—be safeguarded. The Committee announced its opposition to the Smith Bill, which would have prohibited strikes in defense plants. In May 1941, when United States Maritime Commission Chairman Emory S. Land characterized an illegal strike by machinists in San Francisco shipyards as "selfish and subversive," Fight for Freedom's Executive Committee Chairman Ulric Bell publicly rebuked Land and defended the right to strike. About the same time, Fight for Freedom expressed support for the UAW's organizing campaign at Ford Motors—simultaneously sending the organizing committee a request to sign Fight for Freedom's Statement of Principles.[18]

While establishing a reputation as labor's friend, Fight for Freedom portrayed isolationists as labor's enemies. When the Committee discovered an America First publication that did not bear the union label, it sent the offending document to the Typographical Workers Union, along with a note indicating its distress over its rival's apparent insensitivity to organized labor. In August 1941, members of America First crossed a picket line in Seattle to attend an anti-war rally at a non-union theater. Fight for Freedom had a field day, accusing America First of having "revealed its genuine anti-labor bias."[19]

In contrast with the Committee to Defend America by Aiding the Allies and Fight for Freedom, the America First Committee's appeal to labor brought results that were positively dismal. Certainly before 1941, there was considerable anti-interventionist feeling within the labor movement. That feeling went beyond the simple desire to stay out of war and demonstrated concurrence with many of the America First Committee's basic arguments. Yet America First was unable to exploit it.

It was not for lack of trying. America First clearly was aware of the value of labor support. The outcome was a disaster, but the campaign of O.L. Sprague represented a sincere if short-lived effort on the part of the Committee to organize labor support.[20]

The America First Committee's Director of Organization requested chapters to display the union label on all printed materials. The committee labored diligently to win influence among the teamsters, according to pro-intervention Teamsters union President Dan Tobin. A few America First chapters maintained active labor divisions—including, not surprisingly, the Chicago chapter, which claimed the support of 19 local unions representing 300,000 workers. John T. Flynn, chairman of the New York chapter, insisted that all paid work for the chapter be performed by union labor. The Detroit and Lansing chapters made a point of reaching out to labor, by corresponding with local union officials, inviting union members to meetings, and distributing America First buttons and pins. Rather than seek the endorsement of union executives, the secretary of the Detroit chapter appealed directly to the rank-and-file in the auto plants, and purported to "bring out thousands of workers" who professed adherence to America First's principles.[21]

In press releases, speeches, and articles in national and chapter newsletters, America First argued that Roosevelt's defense policies would be harmful to labor. It argued that workers in states whose senators opposed Roosevelt's programs would be frozen out of defense contracts. With Lend-Lease in force, the burden of producing goods for British defense, American defense, and American consumers would exceed both industrial capacity and raw material supplies, causing economic dislocations. America First predicted rationing of consumer goods and retrenchment in consumer industries—thereby throwing thousands out of work. Rapid expansion of defense industries, meanwhile, would necessitate over-simplification of industrial processes, permanently undermining the position of skilled labor. Labor would experience "incalculable suffering" when the defense emergency ended, because defense industries would close their doors, and consumer industries—having been ruined by the defense economy—would not be in a position to employ the former defense workers.[22]

Further, regimentation under the Administration's defense program would threaten organized labor. John T. Flynn, in a nationwide radio broadcast, warned that "the gains of labor, the long, painfully acquired rights of the worker in his job and his union, will be swept away. His labor problems will be settled by a man in uniform." And, as the Lansing chapter of America First told local unions, if the United States went to war, "most of the casualties will be the sons of laboring men, and labor, as always, will directly and indirectly pay the bill" through burdensome taxes.[23]

The committee stressed the pro-labor credentials of non-interventionists. A favorite tactic was to publicize the pro-labor voting records of United States congressmen who opposed intervention and the anti-labor records of those who supported it.[24]

It was an uphill battle, however, for America First to combat its negative image in the labor community. By 1940, labor groups that had formerly praised America First spokesmen such as Senator Burton Wheeler as allies were condemning them as Nazi sympathizers. The AFL announced that Wheeler was "dangerously close to forfeiting labor's good-will and respect" because of his position on foreign policy. The *St. Louis Union Labor Advocate*, which spoke for several AFL locals, associated Wheeler and his fellow isolationist spokesman Charles A. Lindbergh with the Nazis and called Lindbergh an "ultra reactionary" who "never once has spoken for Labor or the plain people." According to the *Labor News* of South Bend and Fort Wayne, Indiana, "The financial backers of the America First Committee . . . are notorious labor baiters." As American entry into the war drew near, the rhetoric became even more acrimonious. Two weeks before Pearl Harbor, a CIO group in Minnesota called for an "immediate" congressional investigation of "the America First Committee and other pro-fascist and appeasement groups who are trying to organize a fifth column in America."[25]

Whereas the Committee to Defend America by Aiding the Allies and Fight for Freedom could count on impressive rosters of top labor leaders to present their case to the rank-and-file, America First had ties with only three labor executives of national stature: John L. Lewis, Lewis' daughter Kathryn (who was secretary-treasurer of United Mine Workers' District 50), and Carpenters' union President William Hutcheson.

In November 1940, John L. Lewis resigned the presidency of the CIO. While still one of the labor movement's most charismatic figures, by 1941 Lewis was increasingly isolated and discredited within the CIO. He was an outspoken isolationist, but he held back from joining America First. America First officials desperately wanted Lewis on their side, but were never able to land him. America First Chairman Robert E. Wood wrote to Lewis: "I know of no one in the country whose voice will have such a powerful influence as yours at the present time, and I believe as a labor leader and an American Citizen you owe it to your country to speak." Lewis could only reply that he was "giving the subject continuous consideration. There are certain factors which I cannot overlook."[26]

One of those factors may have been the drubbing that Lewis was taking over even his implied connections with America First. In December 1940, the New York tabloid *PM* suggested that Lewis was an appeaser, said that his friendliness towards America First brought him into contact with several of organized labor's bitterest malefactors, and implied that Lewis was an anti-Semite who resented what he termed "Jewish unions" such as the ILGWU that happened to advocate aid to Britain.[27]

Kathryn Lewis joined the National Committee of America First early, and America First made the most of her family ties. When she and 57 other noted Americans signed an America First statement opposing Roosevelt's foreign policies in September 1941, she was identified as "Kathryn Lewis, labor executive, daughter of John L. Lewis." With interventionist sentiment gaining momentum in the labor movement by late 1941, however, she was quick to seize upon the controversy generated by a Lindbergh speech as an excuse to withdraw from the National Committee.[28]

Two weeks later, on October 13, 1941, Hutcheson replaced Lewis on the National Committee. America First was fortunate to have at least one first echelon labor executive remain in its camp, but even in his own union Hutcheson's influence on foreign policy matters was shaky. Some Carpenters locals publicly repudiated Hutcheson for his political views.[29]

Perhaps the America First Committee's biggest problem with labor was that it was aligned against a president who was very popular with union members. At a meeting of the national chapter chairmen in Chicago on July 12, 1941, a delegate from Oklahoma said that there was a strong union in her town. How could she respond, she wanted to know, when union members said, "'Well, Roosevelt has given us everything that we have gotten and now let him handle this war situation.'"[30]

The fact that so many union leaders endorsed the Committee to Defend America by Aiding the Allies and Fight for Freedom and so few lined up with America First underscored a fourth factor that contributed to the pro-intervention consensus. By mid-1941, everywhere the rank-and-file looked, they saw their leaders supporting intervention. The CIO and the AFL threw their weight behind the Administration's policies. Green, Woll, Murray, Hillman, and Reuther were among scores of union executives giving pro-intervention speeches. Countless pro-intervention articles circulated by the AFL and the CIO found their way into the pages of local labor newspapers. Labor connections smoothed the way for pro-intervention pressure groups to reach the rank-and-file. When Fight for Freedom decided to launch a "Stop Hitler" campaign in Texas, for example, all it had to do to kick things off was request UAW headquarters in Detroit to cable its Dallas local to cooperate in the undertaking.[31]

In September 1941, the Central Labor Council of Greater Cincinnati helped publicize a local America First rally. Senator Gerald P. Nye was the headline speaker, and "an invitation [was] extended especially to organized labor to attend."[32] The Cincinnati group, however, was one of the last isolationist holdouts in the labor movement. In the weeks before the Japanese attack on Pearl Harbor propelled the United States into the war, organized labor, for the most part, had coalesced in support of the Roosevelt Administration's foreign policies.

Labor support for intervention may have been inevitable, given its virtually unanimous view that Hitler was labor's greatest enemy. But for the first few months after Europe was plunged into war, the labor movement reacted as a microcosm of American society. While it edged toward intervention—as did the rest of the country—many segments resisted the drift toward involvement in the European hostilities. There was depth to their anti-interventionism, as they were skeptical of the British and the Russians, suspicious of American industrialists and financiers, wary of political dictatorship, and fearful of economic collapse as a result of the defense program. They spoke out against Lend-Lease, conversion to a war economy, and other aspects of Franklin Roosevelt's defense and foreign policies.

When the pro-intervention consensus finally was attained, it gave the AFL and the CIO the internal unity they needed to continue their fight against each other, to demand a role in wartime decisionmaking, and to jockey for position in postwar America.

Notes

1. George H. Gallup, *The Gallup Poll: Public Opinion, 1935-1971* (New York: Random House, 1972), I: 154, 178, 180-81, 183-85, 187-88, 211-12, 222, 225, 230-31, 233, 237-38, 243, 245, 251-54, 259-62, 273, 276, 279, 286, 298-301, 307; Wayne S. Cole, *Roosevelt and the Isolationists, 1932-45* (Lincoln: University of Nebraska Press, 1983), pp. 11-12, 364-65.

2. "American Labor Can Do It!," *Lansing Industrial News*, June 28, 1940, p. 2; "Preparedness," *Lansing Industrial News*, July 19, 1940, p. 2; "Labor's Prophecies Come True," Kalispell (Mont.) *Treasure State Labor Journal*, February 25, 1941, p. 2; "Kalispell, Missoula Councils Endorse Aid to British Labor," Kalispell *Treasure State Labor Journal*, May 27, 1941, p. 1; "Missoula Union News," Kalispell *Treasure State Labor Journal*, May 27, 1941, P. 4; "'American Peace Mobilization' Newest of Communist Propaganda Belts," Duluth *Labor World*, September 19, 1940, p. 4; "This and That," Duluth *Labor World*, September 19, 1940, p. 4; "This and That," Duluth *Labor World*, October 17, 1940, p. 3; "Flays Big Enemies of Democracy," Duluth *Labor World*, October 31, 1940, p.

12; "For America's Safety," Duluth *Labor World*, November 7, 1940, p. 2; "The Hour of Decision," Cheyenne *Wyoming Labor Journal*, June 21, 1940, p. 4; "He Said the Right Thing," Cheyenne *Wyoming Labor Journal*, January 3, 1941, p. 2; "Cheyenne Central Body News," Cheyenne *Wyoming Labor Journal*, June 13, 1941, p. 3; "It's Better to be Good than Sorry," *Denver Labor Bulletin*, May 1941; "Willkie, Patriot," *St. Louis Union Labor Advocate*, February 1, 1941, p. 2; "Central Trades Appeals for Prompt Passage of Aid-to-Britain Measure," *St. Louis Union Labor Advocate*, February 15, 1941, p. 1; "What's Back of Fight on British Aid," *St. Louis Union Labor Advocate*, May 1, 1941, p. 3; "Building Trades . . . Approve Roosevelt's Ship Deal," *St. Louis Labor Tribune*, September 7, 1940, p. 1; "So Labor May Know," *St. Louis Labor Tribune*, September 14, 1940, p. 1; "Implications of Lease-Lend Bill," *St. Louis Labor Tribune*, March 1, 1941, p. 4; "Washington Digest," *St. Louis Labor Tribune*, May 31, 1941, p. 4; "We Will Do Our Part," *St. Louis Labor Tribune*, May 31, 1941, p. 4; "Labor News from Britain," *St. Louis Labor Tribune*, September 21, 1940, p. 5; "Students Warned Against Fascist Menace in Nation," Peoria *Labor Temple News*, October 4, 1940, p. 2; "Tells Democracy Foes," Peoria *Labor Temple News*, October 25, 1940, p. 1; cartoon, Peoria *Labor Temple News*, October 24, 1941 p. 9; cartoon, Peoria *Labor Temple News*, October 31, 1941, p. 3. Also see LeRoy James Lenburg, *The CIO and American Foreign Policy, 1935-1955*, doctoral dissertation, Pennsylvania State University, 1973 (Ann Arbor, Mich.: University Microfilms 1974), pp. 50-1 and Timothy R.Dzierba, *Organized Labor and the Coming of World War II, 1937-1941*, doctoral dissertation, State University of New York, Buffalo, 1983 (Ann Arbor, Mich.: University Microfilms International, 1984) p. 106.

3. Dzierba, *Organized Labor and the Coming of World War II*, p. 107.

4. "Plymouth Local Throws Itself in Pro and Con Resolutions," *Michigan Labor Leader*, July 4, 1941; "The Line Has Changed Again," n.d. (ca. July 1941), file 9-19, box 9, Walter Reuther Papers, Reuther Library, Wayne State University, Detroit, Mich.

5. "St. Charles TNT Plant Will Be Constructed by the AFofL," *St. Louis Labor Tribune*, December 21, 1940, p. 1; "Government Armament Program Presages Huge Business Boom," *St. Louis Labor Tribune*, October 19, 1940, p. 4; "St. Louis Area Headed for Boom," *St. Louis Labor Tribune*, August 27, 1941, p. 3; "Shipbuilding Prospects Pick Up," Duluth *Labor World*, November 7, 1940, p. 6; "Improvement of Airport Considered," Duluth *Labor World*, November 7, 1940, p. 6; "Cantonment Construction Work on Fort Will Be Done by Union Workers," Cheyenne *Wyoming Labor Journal*, November 22, 1940, p. 1; "Over 1,500 Men Working at Fort," Cheyenne *Wyoming Labor Journal*, December 20, 1940, p. 1; "Army Housing to be Speeded Up," Cheyenne *Wyoming Labor Journal*, December 20, 1940, p. 5; "Building Projects Bring 5,000 People to Cheyenne," Cheyenne *Wyoming Labor Journal*, January 10, 1941, p. 1; "Fort Warren Cantonment to Have $311,500 Hospital," Cheyenne *Wyoming Labor Journal*, January 10, 1941, p. 1; "Seek New Projects From Government," Butte *Montana Labor News*, April 24, 1941, p. 1; "Strategic Mineral Act Will Assist Development

Here," Butte *Montana Labor News*, July 6, 1939, p. 1; "News of Cascade Trades Assembly," Butte *Montana Labor News*, March 13, 1941, p. 2; "News of Silver Bow Trades Council," Butte *Montana Labor Journal*, August 7, 1941, p. 4; "News of Silver Bow Trades Council," Butte *Montana Labor Journal*, September 26, 1940, p. 4; "Arms Plant for Bluffs," Council Bluffs *Farmer-Labor Press*, April 17, 1941, p. 1; "Inside the State," Sioux Falls *South Dakota Union News*, May 1, 1941, p. 1.

6. "News of the Cascade Trades Assembly," Butte *Montana Labor News*, February 13, 1941, p. 2; "News of Silver Bow Trades and Labor Council," Butte *Montana Labor News*, August 7, 1941, p. 1; "Defense Work Drive Gaining," Chicago *Federation News*, October 14, 1941, p. 10; "Defense Aids Good Housing," Chicago *Federation News*, September 6, 1941, p. 4.

7. "Executive Council Meetings," August 17-26, 1940, file 23-8, box 23, series III, Records of the American Federation of Teachers, Reuther Library, Detroit, Mich.; "Proceedings, Pre- and Post-Convention Meetings," August 19-28, 1941, file 25-2, box 25, series III, Ibid.; memo, "Report on Poll of Officers of Locals," August 8, 1940, file: "Convention, 1940," box 11, series III, Ibid.

8. Alfred Lewis to Clark Eichelberger, May 16, 1941, Huggins to Jaffe, December 27, 1940, Jaffe to Greene, June 9, 1941, Green to Watt, January 16, 1941, Green to White, September 27, 1940, Antonini to White, May 23, 1940, Green to Lewis, December 27, 1940 (plus attachment), file: "Admin. Mgmt.-Labor Div.," box 4, Committee to Defend America by Aiding the Allies Archives, Princeton University Library, Princeton, N.J.; Jaffe to Reuther, December 13, 1940, Abramson to Lewis, May 27, 1941, Randolph to Lewis, December 11, 1940, untitled folder, box 4, Ibid.; White to David Dubinsky, July 6, 1940, Dubinsky to White, June 13, 1940, White to Luigi Antonini, June 7, 1940, George Field to Dubinsky, May 22, 1940, file 3B, box 174, David Dubinsky Papers, ILGWU Archives, Labor-Management Documentation Center, Cornell University, Ithaca, NY; Dubinsky to Samuel Shore, February 27, 1941, Dubinsky to Gibson, February 18, 1941, Address of Frederick F. Umhey, July 17, 1941, Jay Lovestone to Umhey, August 8, 1941, Alfred Lewis to Shore, March 5, 1941, Alfred Lewis to Dubinsky, February 1, 1941, Dubinsky to Samuel Otto, February 4, 1941, file 3A, box 174, Ibid.

9. Notebook, "Press Service: Labor Division," box 12, Committee to Defend America by Aiding the Allies Archives; Banta to Umhey, September 3, 1940, Lewis to Eichelberger, May 16, 1941, Lewis to Editors of Labor Papers (plus attachment), March 7, 1941, Lewis to Chapter Representatives, February 10, 1941, file: "Admin. Mgmt.-Labor Div.," box 4, Ibid.; pamphlet, "Labor and the Totalitarian Threat," file: "Printed Matter," box 8, Ibid.; *Progress Bulletin*, March 3, 1941, "Organization Book #12," box 8, Ibid.; *Progress Bulletin*, June 4, 1941, file: "1941 Progress Bulletins," box 8, Ibid.; Jaffe to ILGWU, July 29, 1940, White Committee Pamphlet: "Organized Labor's Stake in the War," Eichelberger to Dubinsky, plus attachment, July 11, 1940, file 3B, box 174, Dubinsky Papers.

10. Lewis to Editors of Labor Papers, March 7, 1941 (plus attachment), White Committee press release, n.d. ("The rank and file . . . . "), White Committee press release, March 29, 1941, White Committee press release, n.d. ("Labor in the

United States is achieving . . . ."), Alfred Baker Lewis, "Do We Have a Stake in this War?," (White Committee booklet), "Organized Labor's Stake in this War," (White Committee pamphlet), file: "Admin. Mgmt.-Labor Div.," box 4, Committee to Defend America by Aiding the Allies Archives; "Labor and the Totalitarian Threat" (White Committee pamphlet), file: "Printed Matter," box 8, Ibid.; Alfred Lewis to Dubinsky, plus attachments, September 5, 1940, file 3A, box 174, Dubinsky Papers.

11. Lewis to Eichelberger, May 16, 1941, Lewis to Chapter Representatives, February 10, 1941, file: "Admin. Mgmt.-Labor Div.," box 4, Committee to Defend America by Aiding the Allies Archives.

12. Lewis to Eichelberger, file: "Admin. Mgmt.-Labor. Div.," box 4, Committee to Defend America by Aiding the Allies Archives.

13. Lewis to Chapter Representatives, February 10, 1941, file: "Admin. Mgmt.-Labor Div.," box 4, Committee to Defend America by Aiding the Allies Archives.

The White Committee also was assiduous about smoothing over differences or misunderstandings that arose between itself and labor. When its Dallas chapter placed a newspaper advertisement that was critical of labor, William Allen White himself immediately sent letters to labor leaders disavowing the advertisement and reiterating his life-long support of labor. And the Trade Union Division moved lightening fast to mollify ILGWU Vice President Samuel Shore when he interpreted White Committee involvement in a Painters' Union rally as interference in internal union politics. See Alfred Lewis to Dubinsky, February 28, 1941, Irwin Jaffe to Shore, February 21, 1941, Shore to Jaffe, March 4, 1941, Jaffe to Shore, March 5, 1941, file 3A, box 174, Dubinsky Papers; White to Dubinsky, July 13, 1940, box 3B, box 174, Ibid.

14. Press release, n.d. ("More than 1,600 local labor leaders"), press release, May 19, 1941, file: "Labor," box 45, Fight for Freedom Archives, Princeton University, Princeton, N.J.; Rosonfield to Ulric Bell, October 18, 1941, Rosonfield to Spivack, October 24, 1941, file: "Labor Statement," box 45, Ibid.

15. Mark Lincoln Chadwin, *The Hawks of World War II*, (Chapel Hill: University of North Carolina Press, 1968) p. 183; Press release, n.d. ("More than 1,600 local labor leaders"), Spivack to Editors, September 12, 1941, *Labor News Service* for May 29, 1941, June 6, 1941, and August 15, 1941, file: "Labor," box 45, Fight For Freedom Archives; Table, "Labor News Service," n.d. (ca. November 1941), *Labor News Service* for October 10, 1941 and September 26, 1941, file: "Labor News Service," box 45, Ibid.

16. McDevitt, *et al* to Roosevelt, June 11, 1941, Bluestein to Rosenfield, August 21, 1941 (plus attachment), "Program of 'Beat Hitler' Rally," July 17, 1941 (plus attached speeches), file: "Labor," box 45, Fight for Freedom Archives; *Labor News Service* for October 3, 1941 and June 13, 1941, file: "Labor News Service," box 45, Ibid.

17. Press release, May 26, 1941 ("Thirteen prominent"), file: "Labor," box 45, Fight for Freedom Archives.

18. Chadwin, *Hawks of World War II*, pp- 181-82; Press release, n.d. (ca.

May 24, 1941; "Sharp disagreement . . ."), *Labor News Service*, May 29, 1941, press release, n.d. ("The executive committee . . . ."), Widman to Bell, April 28, 1941, Bell to Widman, May 3, 1941, file: "Labor," box 45, Fight for Freedom Archives.

19. Miller to Wright, September 13, 1941, *Labor News Service*, August 15, 1941, file: "Labor," Fight for Freedom Archives.

20. See Bulletin no. 12, January 18, 1941 and Bulletin no. 29, January 28, 1941, white scrapbook, box 340, America First Papers, Hoover Institution Archives, Stanford University, Palo Alto, Calif.

21. Wayne S. Cole, *America First: The Battle Against Intervention, 1940-1941* (Madison: University of Wisconsin Press, 1953), p. 77; Hunt to Reasoner, July 18, 1941, Reasoner to Vietig, July 25, 1941, Hunt to Virtue et al, July 17, 1941, unidentified typescript ("Robert Vietig who spoke . . "), ca. July 29, 1941, file: "Lansing, Mich.-General Files," box 254, America First Papers; "Transcript of Remarks," National America First Committee Meeting, Chicago, July 12, 1941, pp. 8-9, file: "Nye Materials," box 88, Ibid.; Flynn to Chapter Chairman, August 8, 1941, "Notes of Meeting of Chapter Officers," July 31, 1941, file: "Women's Division-Meetings and Letters," box 178, Ibid.; Bulletin no. 12, January 18, 1941, white scrapbook, box 340, Ibid.; Wayne (Johnson) to Bell, May 29, 1941, file: "Labor," box 45, Fight for Freedom Papers.

22. *Did You Know?* (newsletter of America First Committee Research Bureau), September 30, 1941, file: "America First Research Bureau," box 297, America First Committee Papers; "The Economic Consequences of the Lease-Lend Program," n.d., pp. 10-15, green scrapbook, box 340, Ibid.,; "Montana, N. Dakota Out," Los Angeles *America First News*, October 2, 1941, p. 1, "Clipping File," box 293, Ibid.; "Talk by John Flynn," March 8, 1941, file: "Clippings-March 1941," box 52, Ibid.

23. "Talk by John T. Flynn," March 8, 1941, file: "Clippings-March 1941," box 52, America First Papers; Hunt to Virtue, *et al*, July 17, 1941, file: "Lansing, Mich.-General Files," box 254, Ibid.; "War Costs Hit New Altitude," New York *America First Bulletin*, October 25, 1941, p. 1, "Clipping File," box 293, Ibid.

24. "90% For Labor . . . 80% Against Labor," *Minnesota Beacon*, August 14, 1941, p. 4, "Clipping File," box 293, America First Papers; unidentified typescript, ("Robert Vietig who spoke . . . ."), ca. July 29, 1941, file: "Lansing, Mich.-General Files," box 254, Ibid.

25. "Facing the Facts," AFL *Weekly News Service*, July 2, 1940; "For Peace," *St. Louis Union Labor Advocate*, February 1, 1939, p. 4; "Wheeler Hits Back at Iowa Paper Editor," *St. Louis Union Labor Advocate*, September 15, 1939, p. 3; "Nazi Venom!," *St. Louis Union Labor Advocate*, August 1, 1941, p. 2; "Wrong Way Lindbergh," *St. Louis Union Labor Advocate*, October 15, 1941, p. 2; "Father Coughlin Pets Lewis," *St. Louis Union Labor Advocate*, November 15, 1941, p. 2; "Lindbergh is Anti-Labor," South Bend/Fort Wayne *Labor News*, October 31, 1941. Also see, "John L. Lewis Linked Through Daughter to Hitler Appeasers," New York *PM*, December 2, 1940, p. 10; Hennepin County Industrial Union Council Resolution, November 26, 1941, item 815, reel 11, *CIO Files of*

John L. Lewis, Part II.

26. Robert Wood to J.L. Lewis, May 21, 1941, Wood to K. Lewis, May 26, 1941, Wood to J.J. Lewis, May 26, 1941, J.L. Lewis to Wood, May 29, 1941, file: "R.E. Wood Letters," box 286, America First Papers.

Others besides General Wood attempted to lure John L. Lewis into a more conspicuous position in the anti-interventionist movement. Prominent Yale Professor A. Whitney Griswold praised Lewis for his opposition to aiding Britain, and in 1940 wrote Lewis that "Many people outside the ranks of organized labor must look to you for leadership in this matter." See A. Whitney Griswold to Lewis, July 1, 1940, file: "Lewis-1940 Election," box 5B, John Brophy Papers, Catholic University, Washington, DC.

27. "John L. Lewis Linked Through Daughter to Hitler Appeasers," New York *PM*, December 2, 1940, p. 10.

28. "America First," San Francisco *Herald*, October 2, 1941, p. 1, "Clipping File," box 293, America First Papers; K. Lewis to Wood, September 29, 1941, "Miscellaneous" file, box 56, Ibid.; K. Lewis to R. Douglas Stuart, October 10, 1941, file: "Miscellaneous Correspondence Before Dissolution," box 163, Ibid.

29. Press release, October 13, 1941, file: "Lansing, Mich.-General Files," box 254, America First Papers; "Duluth Carpenters Repudiate Willkie Okay by Hutcheson," Duluth *Labor World*, October 10, 1940, p. 1; "Waco Carpenters Oppose Action of Their Nat'l Pres.," *Waco Farm and Labor Journal*, October 25, 1940, p. 1. Also see, "It Looks Like This," *Madison Union Label News*, November 1940, p. 1.

30. "Transcript of Remarks," National America First Committee Meeting, July 12, 1941, file: "Nye Materials," box 88, America First Committee Papers.

31. Rosenfield to George Addes, October 29, 1941, file: "Labor," box 45, Fight for Freedom Archives; Dzierba, *Organized Labor and the Coming of World War II*, p. 113; Gerald R. Gordon, *The AFL, the CIO, and the Quest for a Peaceful World Order*, doctoral dissertation, University of Maine, Orono, 1967 (Ann Arbor, Mich: University Microfilms, 1968) p. 163. Many of the pro-intervention articles in local newspapers cited above were originally published in the AFL's *Weekly News Service*.

32. "Slate Another Senator Nye Talk Here," Cincinnati *Chronicle*, September 12, 1941, p. 4.

THE FIRST LINE OF DEFENSE: THE NATIONAL LABOR CENTERS BUILD FOR WAR AND PLAN FOR PEACE, 1939-1941

PART IV

AFL Attitudes Toward Intervention

CHAPTER 11

"You used to write an awful lot about the workingman," growled Jedidiah Leland to Charles Foster Kane. "He's turning into something called organized labor. You're not going to like that one little bit when you find out it means your workingman expects something as his right and not your gift."[1] That scene, set in 1916, appeared in the most controversial motion picture of 1941: *Citizen Kane,* by Orson Welles.

Leland's prediction was coming true at the same time *Citizen Kane* was released by RKO Studios. Emboldened by several years of growth, political victories (such as the Wagner Act), and organizational successes, the labor movement was demanding as its right a greater and more independent role to play in the industrial process. The American Federation of Labor (AFL) and the Congress of Industrial Organizations (CIO) both used the deteriorating international situation as a prod to achieve fuller acceptance of such essential union goals as collective bargaining and to exact recognition as a partner with government and management in the policy and decision-making process.

At the core of organized labor's argument was the contention that labor was America's "first line of defense." Leaders of both the AFL and the CIO harked back to that theme often during the two years leading up to the entrance of the United States into World War II. What it meant was that the working classes, in addition to furnishing the majority of soldiers and sailors who would go to war, also did the back-breaking toil in factories that produced the goods that made modern war possible. In the words of United Auto Workers Vice President Walter Reuther, America's battles would "be won on the assembly lines of Detroit." The first line of defense, then, was actually the home front. Without good wages, decent working conditions, adequate housing, the right to organize and bargain, and a voice in policymaking, labor could not produce the tanks, guns, battleships, uniforms, airplanes, or other materials at maximum efficiency. And without maximum efficiency in production, no war could be won.[2]

When the war in Europe began on September 3, 1939, both of the national labor centers quickly announced their firm opposition to any kind of American intervention. They opposed loans and all other forms of assistance to the Allied powers fighting the Axis, ruled out military activities beyond the Western Hemisphere, and urged Americans to resist pro-war propaganda and to remain neutral.

For years, however, the AFL had demonstrated its concern for the victims of fascism and its antipathy towards Nazi Germany and the other Axis powers. It had applauded the pro-labor climate in democratic Britain and protested against the anti-labor crusade in totalitarian Germany. It had supported fundraising appeals to help victims of Nazi persecution and instituted economic boycotts against Germany and Japan. The AFL's pro-British predilections were clear, and by October 1939 it had edged away from anti-interventionism to the extent that it offered to endorse revision of the neutrality law. Further, in early 1940, its opposition to military conscription—an important step toward intervention—was lukewarm and short lived. Nonetheless, it maintained an official posture of opposing American intervention.

For the first several months after World War II began, during the winter of 1939-40, a period of military inactivity called the "Phony War" or the "Sitzkrieg" occurred. Military action resumed in the spring of 1940, and most of Western Europe quickly fell under Nazi domination. The AFL was alarmed by the German advance and became convinced of the imminent danger to the United States if Britain were to be conquered. Thus, it abandoned its anti-interventionism. For the remainder of 1940 and throughout 1941 the AFL advocated intervention and lent its support to the foreign and military policies of the Franklin D. Roosevelt Administration.

In contrast, the CIO was fervently anti-interventionist almost until 1941. Ironically, much of the CIO's leadership supported Roosevelt and intervention, but for most of 1939 and 1940 CIO President John L. Lewis firmly held the reins. Lewis was an isolationist. With the backing of the CIO Communists, Lewis kept the CIO in the anti-interventionist camp. The official policy of the CIO was that the United States should remain aloof from the European conflict, build a defensive wall around the Western Hemisphere, and concentrate on domestic spending and the expansion of New Deal initiatives.

Lewis resigned the presidency of the CIO in November 1940, and interventionists took control of the CIO. They quickly reversed Lewis' isolationist policies. After Germany invaded the Soviet Union in June 1941, the CIO's sizeable Communist faction likewise turned to interventionism, putting virtually the whole of the CIO—like the AFL—in support of Roosevelt's policies.

The positions of both of the national labor centers on foreign and domestic matters were related to their positions on domestic matters. Participation in the defense program became leverage with which to achieve domestic objectives. As jobs became more plentiful because of the war boom, and defense production became more critical, the AFL de-emphasized its support for the 30-hour week as a tool to expand employment. Low-cost housing programs had been a vital AFL objective for years; with the defense program in full swing, the AFL altered its strategy slightly in order to tie its old low-cost housing program to the preparedness program by making new calls for defense housing. The AFL offered a no-strike pledge that would maintain high levels of defense production in exchange for acceptance of its traditional goals of a union shop and a greater voice for labor in policymaking. With the defense emergency in effect, it demanded stringent economic planning that would produce at war's end the sort of consumer purchasing power-based economy the AFL had championed throughout the 1930s.

During the Lewis era, when the CIO supported non-intervention and arguably was less convinced of the urgency of defense production, the CIO was more militant in labor relations matters and more prone to strike in order to share in the rewards of the expanding defense economy. Lewis also used isolationist rhetoric to win converts and political allies. After the CIO adopted a more interventionist position, it devised a series of defense production and housing plans aimed not only at enhancing preparedness but also at saving jobs in consumer industries, preventing dislocations in the conversion to a war economy that would have hurt union members, giving labor an equal voice with management in industrial policymaking, and increasing workers' independence both on and off the job. Patriotism and concern for American security in light of Axis aggrandizement animated the AFL and the CIO in adopting foreign policy positions, but so did a strong sense of self-interest.

Going to a war footing meant opportunities for organized labor at home as well as threats. On the one hand, the CIO and the AFL both made great organizational strides, particularly in the defense industries. On the other, they had to fend off attempts to impose severe restrictions upon organized labor as defense measures. Most CIO and AFL leaders were determined to aid the anti-Axis coalition, committed to military preparedness, and wary of attacks upon union prerogatives. Therefore, they worked hard to persuade the rank-and-file to support intervention and to avoid unnecessary job actions that would delay defense production and play into the hands of the anti-labor forces.

The national labor centers moved from initial insistence upon American neutrality to strong support for American intervention in World War II. They coupled their support for intervention, however, with a package of proposals and quid pro quos intended to enhance the domestic position of organized labor.

⊕ ⊕ ⊕

In the weeks and months before the war in Europe began, the AFL urged the United States to remain as isolated as possible from the approaching conflict. Not only did it warn against American entry into a European war, it also opposed measures that would permit the United States to provide aid short of war to the European democracies.

Isolationists in Congress won a major battle in the spring of 1939 when they blocked an Administration-supported effort to revise the Neutrality Act. The proposed revision would have repealed the arms embargo and enabled American firms to sell munitions to belligerent on a cash-and-carry basis.[3]

The AFL joined the isolationists in opposition to neutrality revision. In a statement prepared for the *New Haven Labor Digest*, AFL President William Green warned that amending the Neutrality Act would reduce democratic control over foreign policy and vest too much power in the Executive Branch. In testimony before the Senate Foreign Relations Committee in April, AFL Legislative Representative Paul Scharrenberg implied that the proposed amendment to the Neutrality Act was an effort "to promote war hysteria," asserted that activities of the munitions industry were "a matter of public concern," and urged that America not repeat its mistake of 1917 and risk sending "another generation into the trenches" by becoming entangled in European affairs. There should be no change in American foreign policy, he said, and the Neutrality Act of 1937 should remain in force without amendment. "This is no time for experimentation," Scharrenberg told the committee. "Labor therefore urges continuance of a measure that has been helpful in the hope that peace may be served."[4]

Throughout the summer of 1939, Green issued statements blasting "sinister influences" that were working "to cultivate a war consciousness among our people." He and the Federation championed "a policy of strictest neutrality" in event of war and called upon organized labor to use its political muscle to thwart any move to embroil the United States in future hostilities. In August, the AFL Executive Council asserted that the United States should resist involvement in a European war "at any cost." In his Labor Day message—issued just hours before World War II began—Green reiterated the AFL position that the United States should not take sides in any European conflict and that it do no more than serve as a disinterested mediator between the potential combatants.[5]

World War II began on September 3, 1939, when Great Britain and France declared war on Germany in response to that country's invasion of Poland. For the first months of the war, the AFL held its anti-interventionist position. In a nationwide radio broadcast on September 4, President Green declared "There must be no European entanglement and no involvement in European wars. We call upon our Government to scrupulously avoid the commission of any overt act, to maintain a strictly neutral attitude and thus avoid the tragic and unhappy experiences through which our people passed during the [First] World War."[6]

With the war a week old, the AFL *Weekly News Service* ran a major statement that anticipated many of the arguments that would be made later by America First and leading isolationist spokesmen. Praising the Nye Committee for having "exposed the machinations of munitions makers who foment war to make fat profits," it dismissed war as the product of greed and propaganda. To stay at peace, the article implied, America need only squelch the businessmen who would push the country toward war for personal gain. It indicated continued AFL resistance to neutrality revision along the cash-and-carry lines proposed by the Roosevelt administration in the spring, arguing that if the United States sold arms to belligerent it would be unable "to stay neutral and see [its] customers get licked." Conceding that Americans hated Hitler and sympathized with the democracies, the statement nonetheless placed partial blame for Hitler's rise on the "short-sighted 'settlement' of the last war engineered by England and France." Finally, it stated that the Soviet Union, not Germany, was the real enemy. Soviet dictator Josef Stalin, opined the *Weekly News Service*, would watch from the sidelines until Hitler and the democracies had battled each other to a standstill. Then he would "march in and take over the whole works."[7]

In October, the annual convention of the AFL convened in Cincinnati. Ohio Governor John W. Bricker, an isolationist, welcomed the delegates to his state with the recommendation that "here in America, let us look to our own problems." By remaining aloof and at peace, according to the governor, the United States could lead the European powers out of war by the sheer power of example.[8]

The convention echoed Bricker's sentiments. The report of the Executive Council, which demanded that the United States remain neutral "in spirit and in act," was adopted by the convention. The Executive Council report and President Green's keynote address alike warned against the influence of pro-war propaganda, predicted that United States intervention would result in the regimentation of labor and the elimination of labor's social gains, painted grim pictures of American battlefield losses should the country be drawn into the war, reminded delegates of the disillusionment that followed World War I, and argued that America's role in the war should be limited to that of mediator.[9]

At its spring meeting in May 1940, the Executive Council confirmed its anti-war stance, ruling out any kind of assistance to the beleaguered European democracies. It opposed assistance partly on the grounds that it would be useless inasmuch as the European war was expected to be over in a few weeks. The Executive Council said that it would be disastrous for the United States to permit its "national sympathy" for the democracies to encourage a "war psychology." It repeated its prediction that involvement in the war would jeopardize democracy at home. It demanded that the country concentrate its military efforts on building up its defenses and ensuring the safety of the Western Hemisphere. Summing up the Executive Council's position in a speech on May 25, Green said "The United States is not prepared for a defensive war, let alone participation in a foreign conflict. Furthermore, it would be impossible for us to render any considerable aid to our friends in Europe in time to help them."[10]

While always pledging support to the government on military defense matters—provided labor standards were not sacrificed—the AFL issued few official statements on preparedness during late 1939 and early 1940. During that period, however, support for preparedness seemed limited to the establishment of military forces adequate to repel invaders; little was said about collective security and extension of military capability to the Eastern Hemisphere.[11]

The AFL may have promoted a spirit of cooperation for national defense production, but it aggressively resisted efforts to mandate labor compliance. An "Industrial Mobilization Plan" developed in 1939 by the Navy and War Departments seemed to threaten collective bargaining during national emergencies. The AFL fought the proposal, popularly called the M-Plan, which was never actually put into operation. According to the AFL *Weekly News Service,* "the retrogressive provisions of the [M-Plan] regimentation scheme" reflected "the anti-labor orientation of the European dictatorships dominated by Hitler, Mussolini, and Stalin."[12]

Likewise, the AFL expressed wariness over proposals for a peacetime draft. In a book published at the start of the European war, Green called for a ban on conscription for overseas military service. In January 1940, the AFL was critical of a suggestion by United States Army Chief of Staff General George C. Marshall that the Civilian Conservation Corps be militarized in event of war. One objection was that Marshall's proposal, if implemented, would have the effect of forcing the jobless into the Army.[13]

In May 1940, prominent New York attorney Grenville Clark formed a committee to campaign for passage of a conscription bill. The following month, the Burke-Wadsworth Bill, calling for a draft, was introduced in Congress. The bill won the endorsement of the Roosevelt administration. Despite vigorous opposition by Senators Burton Wheeler, George Norris, Gerald Nye, and Hiram Johnson, as well as other key isolationists, the bill was passed by Congress and signed into law in September 1940.[14]

Carpenters' Union President William Hutcheson was the most dedicated anti-interventionist on the AFL's Executive Council. Partly at his instigation, the Federation came out against the Burke-Wadsworth Bill. During the first week of August, Green officially announced the AFL's opposition to a draft and urged the Army to try to rely on voluntary enlistments to raise a force of 1,500,000 troops. Green repeated the AFL's anti-Burke-Wadsworth message several times in the ensuing weeks.[15]

The CIO, which considered itself the leader of the anti-draft forces, expressed pleasure that the AFL had come out against Burke-Wadsworth. Still, the CIO suggested that the AFL's position was an overly cautious one, "with room enough for retreat if the going got tough." The CIO's assessment of the AFL's position was not without merit. Indeed, Green's initial statement against the Burke-Wadsworth Bill was hardly trenchant. It even promised AFL support for conscription if a program of voluntary enlistments failed, and then listed a handful of safeguards that a draft law would have to include in order to secure AFL endorsement. Among the safeguards were job protection, reasonable compensation, an assurance that draftees would be deployed for home defense only and not be sent overseas, and government payment of transportation costs to and from military assignments.[16]

Mild as its anti-draft statement was, the AFL began backing away from it within weeks. On September 3, the AFL *Weekly News Service* predicted that conscription, in concert with other defense initiatives, would cut unemployment by 4.5 million. Days later, with the vote on the Burke-Wadsworth Bill still in doubt, Green effectively withdrew the AFL's objections to the bill. "We are not opposed to conscription," he told the Teamsters' convention, "if the country needs the manpower. When the legislation is passed by Congress and approved by the President, we'll support it and we will carry it out." As soon as the Burke-Wadsworth Bill became law on September 16, Green emphasized the measure's positive aspects, pledged AFL cooperation, and urged the rank-and-file to comply. From then on, the AFL's principal activities regarding conscription revolved around draftees' welfare (protecting job seniority while they were in the military, exempting them from union dues, and so forth). Conceivably, that attitude could have aided the draft program by ameliorating the concerns of potential conscripts.[17]

The Federation's wavering on the draft issue mirrored its general ambivalence concerning America's response to the war in Europe. Until the "Phony War" came to an end in spring 1940, the AFL tried to steer a middle course between anti-interventionist affiliates (such as the Central Labor Council of Greater Cincinnati) and pro-interventionist affiliates (such as the Atlanta Federation of Trades and Allied Unions). It engaged in anti-foreign war and pro-neutrality rhetoric, warning against entangling alliances, suggesting that the European democracies were threatening to draw the United States into the hostilities, and predicting dire domestic consequences if they were successful. Yet at the same time the logic of its position seemed pro-interventionist. It intensified its praise of the democracies and its condemnation of the Axis powers; it lent moral and tangible support to the Allies through its continued commitment to the Chest for the Liberation of Europe and to the economic boycotts of Germany and Japan.[18]

The dichotomy did not really last very long. Events gradually pushed the AFL into an openly interventionist stance.

The first position that the AFL abandoned was its rigid opposition to neutrality revision. In October 1939, with the war in Europe only a month old, the AFL endorsed a Roosevelt administration proposal to substitute the "cash and carry" plan for the arms embargo provision of the Neutrality Act. The repeal would have permitted belligerents to purchase arms in American markets, provided they paid cash—no loans, as in World War I—and transport the arms on their own vessels. Realistically, because they controlled North Atlantic sea lanes, only the Allies could take advantage of "cash and carry." Thus, only six months after having rejected "cash and carry" in the spring of 1939, the AFL announced that it favored the plan. It professed to accept President Roosevelt's argument that "cash and carry" would help preserve American neutrality.[19]

The key variable accounting for the reversal was the war. In April, when the AFL opposed neutrality revision, an uneasy peace continued to prevail in Europe. In October, when it supported neutrality revision, World War II was already underway. Yet another factor, however, may have been economic self-interest.

The AFL component that was possibly the strongest advocate of neutrality revision was the Metal Trades Department. The rank-and-file of the unions that made up the Metal Trades Department stood to gain the most immediate benefits from increased arms sales.[20] The next big move for the AFL was to go from support for theoretically neutral "cash and carry" arms sales to an outright abandonment of neutrality and support for full-fledged aid to the European democracies. As late as May 1940, the AFL Executive Council had reasserted its endorsement of neutrality and its opposition to aid, claiming that resources would be better spent on America's own military machine and that aid would not be effective in the European war. It even urged Americans to apply "mental brakes," lest sympathy for the victims of fascism blind the country to "the paramount importance of maintaining . . . neutrality." Also in May, however, the "Phony War" in Europe came to an end, combat resumed, and by early June Britain and France were in imminent danger of being overwhelmed. The deteriorating conditions in Europe gave new urgency to the American response, and the AFL changed its position.[21]

In a speech to the pro-intervention International Ladies' Garment Workers' Union (ILGWU) on June 6, Green not only announced that the AFL supported giving as much aid as possible to the beleaguered Allies, but he also said that credit should be extended to the Allies, if necessary. Five days later, he told the American Federation of Musicians, meeting in Indianapolis, that the United States government should give to the Allies "all the supplies they need—even on credit—[and] even though those supplies must be shipped abroad without compensation for the moment . . . because the cause of democracy has reached desperation."[22]

In September 1940, after the fall of France and during the Battle of Britain, the AFL came out "wholeheartedly" in favor of Roosevelt's "fine deal" to give naval destroyers to Great Britain in exchange for leases on military bases in the Western Hemisphere. In addition, the Federation hinted throughout the summer and autumn that it would support going to war to defend Canada. Such a position was not inconsistent with the isolationist doctrine of continental defense, of course, but it nonetheless indicated solidarity with the British Commonwealth and concern over Nazi Germany's successes and its threat to the Americas.[23]

The AFL coupled its support for programs to help the British with opposition to programs that might aid—even inadvertently—the Axis powers. Former President Herbert Hoover, who won international acclaim for masterminding the extensive relief effort in Russia after the First World War, sought to mount a similar campaign to feed residents of the European countries that Germany had conquered. The AFL rejected the Hoover invitation to participate in the relief movement. Pointing out that the misery in occupied Europe was the creation of Hitler and Italian dictator Benito Mussolini, the AFL argued that sending food to those areas under any guise would benefit the Axis. No matter how "humane and praiseworthy" the plan was in principle, in reality it would simply increase the overall supply of foodstuffs in Axis-controlled areas, thereby making it possible to increase allocations of resources to the German and Italian military machines. In a telegram to the former president, Green declared that it would be "asking too much of Great Britain in her hour of distress . . . to lift her blockade" of continental Europe for such a purpose.[24]

Possibly the most heated skirmish between interventionists and non-interventionists was the battle over the Lend-Lease Bill. Fully within the interventionist camp by early 1941, the AFL endorsed the bill enthusiastically.

The AFL fired its opening salvo in favor of Lend-Lease on January 17 with a stinging rejection of isolationist Congressman Hamilton Fish's invitation to speak out against it. A week later, Green testified in support of the measure before the Foreign Affairs Committee of the United States House of Representatives. Aid to Britain had to "be placed upon a firm foundation of a specific grant of statutory authority," Green told the committee. Although he suggested several amendments "to clarify and perfect" the proposed law, Green testified that the AFL and the "vast majority of the wage earners of America" considered the basic provisions of Lend-Lease to be "a necessary and indispensable instrumentality of the national defense effort of the United States."[25]

For the balance of 1941, the AFL was a vigorous exponent of the Roosevelt administration's policy of assisting the European democracies. In May, Green suggested that convoys be considered as a way of ensuring that war materials reached England. In June, the Executive Council recommended that aid to Great Britain "be redoubled in quantity and speed." In August, the Executive Council endorsed the recent United States occupation of Iceland in order to protect North Atlantic shipping lanes. Also in August, the AFL praised the Atlantic Charter, that had been concluded by Roosevelt and British Prime Minister Winston Churchill. The AFL said the Atlantic Charter promised a "square deal" after the war.[26]

When Germany invaded the Soviet Union in June, the AFL initially crowed that having "Stalin and Hitler fight each other groggy" would give the United States more "breathing space" to continue building up its own defenses and those of Britain. In August it changed its tune somewhat, as the Executive Council expressed approval of the administration's decision to extend aid to the Soviet Union. The AFL retained its fervent anti-communism, denied that the United States and the Soviet Union could ever be friends or allies, and remained convinced that the Soviet Union was an enemy of democracy. But the Executive Council admitted that Germany was the chief enemy of democracy, and that therefore it was wise to help Russia defeat or at least impede the Nazis. Meanwhile, the AFL ridiculed pro-communist labor groups—mainly in the CIO—for reversing themselves and suddenly calling for interventionist policies once Germany had attacked Russia.[27]

In addition to supporting Roosevelt's foreign policies, the AFL also supported his administration's military policies. On numerous occasions, the AFL expressed complete confidence in Roosevelt's preparedness programs, acceptance of the notion of collective security implicit in America's role as the "arsenal of democracy" that would furnish military supplies to the Allies, and even a willingness to accept cuts in domestic programs. It denied the assertions of some anti-interventionists that Roosevelt's defense policies were propelling the United States toward war and countered that only by adopting Roosevelt's policies of building "an invincible national defense" and extending aid to the allies could the country hope to avoid war. The AFL and its affiliated unions bought hundreds of thousands of dollars' worth of defense bonds and encouraged the rank-and-file to do likewise.[28]

In July, the AFL established a 7-member Defense Committee, headed by Matthew Woll, to coordinate the Federation's defense-related activities, ensure the availability of manpower for defense production, assist with issues related to the allocation of raw materials and the awarding of defense contracts, promote defense training, and generally contribute to efficient defense production. The committee also pushed for greater involvement of AFL representatives in governmental bodies handling defense contracts. Central labor bodies, meanwhile, formed similar defense committees at the local level.[29]

Formation of the committee and its local counterparts coincided with the opening of field branches by the Office of Production Management (OPM). The timing was not accidental. The AFL's National Defense Committee expressly intended to develop policies of cooperation with OPM and set up the local committees to carry out those policies by working with the OPM's new field branches. The rationale for designing such an apparatus to facilitate cooperation with OPM was simple. Proposals for greater controls were in the air; "If voluntary cooperation brings effective results," reasoned the committee, "it will forestall support for the compulsory program."[30]

Centerpiece of the AFL's defense program was a no-strike pledge. While firmly reserving in principle the right to strike, the AFL importuned its affiliates to abjure strikes voluntarily on defense-related jobs and to submit disputes to the Labor Department's Conciliation Service or the federal government's brand new National Defense Mediation Board. The Metal Trades Department and the Building and Construction Trades Department were two AFL components whose member unions were most heavily engaged in defense work, and in January 1941 those departments were the first to declare a no-strike policy. In April, Green wrote to all national and international unions, state federations of labor, city central bodies, and directly-affiliated federal labor unions, urging them to follow the lead of the Metal Trades and the Building and Constructions Trades Departments. When Roosevelt proclaimed an unlimited national emergency in May, the AFL showed solidarity with the president by "putting teeth into the no-strike policy." It made the policy mandatory for the federal labor unions directly under its control and called upon national and international unions to discipline locals that ignored the policy. The AFL claimed that its no-strike pledge was 99 percent effective.[31]

The AFL based its support for Roosevelt's foreign and military policies on three premises. First was the conviction that American security was imperiled by Germany. For years the AFL had condemned the expansionism, the anti-Semitism, and especially the anti-union initiatives of the Nazi government, but when World War II began the Federation claimed that the United States had no interests at stake in the hostilities and that it should remain aloof. By 1940, however, after the Blitzkrieg had begun, the German threat seemed imminent. The AFL was once isolationist, wrote AFL Publicity Director Philip Pearl, but that changed when "the impact of this war shattered our comfortable feeling that America is and always will be secure against any outside foe." Pearl concluded: "The isolationists may close their eyes . . . but the truth is that Hitler will get us if we don't watch out!"[32]

The second belief was that a British victory over Germany was essential if the United States were to avoid going to war itself. In July 1941, the AFL's Secretary-Treasurer, George Meany, called Britain "the bulwark that stands between us and Hitler's legions of destruction." If Hitler were not stopped in Europe, in other words, he would move into the Western Hemisphere—or, at the very least, control a vast totalitarian empire whose slave labor would undercut American markets and harm the United States economically. Therefore, it seemed to make good sense for America to serve as the "Arsenal of Democracy." Strengthening Britain through Lend-Lease and other assistance would improve chances for a German defeat and thereby protect the United States.[33]

Finally, there was the related notion that Britain was fighting for democracy and free trade unionism everywhere. If the United States was the "Arsenal of Democracy," then Britain was the "Army of Democracy." "We stand in the same relationship to Great Britain in 1941," said an editorial in the AFL *Weekly News Service*, "as our civilians at home to our army fighting in Europe in 1917." More succinct was a statement made by an AFL official in New York City, which was publicized nationally by the AFL: "The trade unionists of Great Britain are fighting our fight and we would be traitors to the trade union movement if we let them down now."[34]

Not only did the AFL call for the United States government to assist Great Britain, it also established an organization through which it could aid Britain directly. In December 1940, AFL Vice President Matthew Woll announced the formation of American Labor's Committee to Aid British Labor as a division of the League for Human Rights, Freedom and Democracy. Local chapters soon appeared throughout the country. When the committee was announced, British Trades Union Congress President Sir Walter Citrine was on a mission to the United States to drum up American support for Britain. Woll billed the Committee as the AFL's official response to Citrine's mission.[35]

American Labor's Committee to Aid British Labor intended to support the British war effort by contributing to the welfare of British workers and their families. During 1941, it raised approximately $1,000,000 for that purpose, and received donations of blankets, clothes, and other goods as well. When it inaugurated a major fundraising campaign in May 1941, former Republican presidential nominee Wendell Willkie purchased the first subscription book. The committee won the applause of President Roosevelt and Prime Minister Churchill. In addition to furnishing assistance the British labor, the group was also a vital propaganda tool for the AFL among its own ranks, helping to generate sympathy for Britain and support for intervention.[36]

The AFL made a fairly expeditious conversion from anti-interventionism in 1939 to pro-interventionism by mid-1940. For the CIO, the transition was more difficult, and it required the resignation of its founder.

Notes

1. Orson Welles and Herman J. Mankiewicz, "The Shooting Script," *The Citizen Kane Book* (Boston: Little Brown, 1971), p. 387.

2. "First Line of Defense," *CIO News*, February 12, 1940, p. 4; "The CIO Position on Natl. Defense," *CIO News*, June 10, 1940, p. 3; "Labor is Bulwark of Democracy, Rubber Union Told," *CIO News*, September 23, 1940, p. 2; "Thomas Defends '500 Planes' Plan," *CIO News*, January 6, 1941; "Labor is Nation's 'First Defense Line,'—Murray," *CIO News*, December 2, 1940, p. 1; "Facing the Facts," AFL *Weekly News Service*, December 10, 1940; "AFL for National Defense First, Green Replies to Labor Critics," AFL *Weekly News Service*, December 17, 1940; Henry M. Christman, ed., *Walter P. Reuther: Selected Papers* (New York: MacMillan Co., 1961), p. 1.

3. Wayne S. Cole, *Roosevelt and the Isolationists* (Lincoln: University of Nebraska Press, 1983), pp. 311-18.

4. "Amendments to Neutrality Act Opposed by A.F.L.," AFL *Weekly News Service*, April 29, 1939; Document G-614, William Green typescript for *New Haven County Labor Digest*, April 26, 1939, file: "Magazine Articles," series 11E, box 13, William Green Papers, American Federation of Labor Collection, Wisconsin State Historical Society, Madison, Wis.

5. "Peace in Labor Movement," AFL *Weekly News Service*, August 12, 1939; "Green Declares Workers Are Vitally Concerned in Maintaining Democracy," AFL *Weekly News Service*, September 2, 1939; Document G-618, Green typescript for *Wisconsin Labor*, May 16, 1939, file: "Magazine Articles," series 11E, box 13, Green Papers; Document G-616, Green typescript for *Knoxville Labor News*, May 3, 1939, Ibid.; Document G-622, Green typescript for Indiana State Federation of Labor, June 28, 1939, Ibid.; Document G-623, Green typescript for Cortland (N.Y.) Central Trades and Labor Assembly, July 14, 1939, Ibid.

6. AFL Press Release B-389 (also identified as B-387), September 4, 1939, file: "Labor Speeches," series 11E, box 3, Green Papers. The September 4 speech apparently was a re-written version of the Labor Day message cited in note 3, above (AFL *Weekly News Service*, September 2, 1939).

7. "Facing the Facts," AFL *Weekly News Service*, September 9, 1939.

8. "59th American Federation of Labor Convention Opens With 512 Delegates," AFL *Weekly News Service*, October 7, 1939.

9. "Green Declares United States Must Not Become Involved in European War," AFL *Weekly News Service*, October 7, 1939; "United States Must Not Enter War in Europe, A.F. of L. Declares," AFL *Weekly News Service*, October 21, 1939; "Keep America Out of European War Demands the A.F. of L. Convention," AFL *Weekly News Service*, October 21, 1939.

10. Green speech no. B-403 (attached to 400-402), Hartford, Conn., May 25, 1940, file: "Labor Speeches," series 11E, box 3, Green Papers.

11. "Green Presents Program to Preserve American Neutrality and Avoid War," AFL *Weekly News Service*, October 7, 1939; "AFL Pledges Aid in National

Defense Program," AFL *Weekly News Service*, May 21, 1940; "A.F. of L. 1940 Legislative Program Visions Benefits for Toiling Millions," AFL *Weekly News Service*, January 13, 1940.

12. "War Dictatorship Over American Workers Denounced by the A.F. of L.," AFL *Weekly News Service*, December 2, 1939; "Woll Hits Anti-Labor Provision of Industrial Mobilization Plan," AFL *Weekly News Service*, December 9, 1939. Contingency plans for wartime industrial mobilization were formulated at various points during the interwar era. The particular plan put together in 1939 was rejected by President Franklin D. Roosevelt, partly out of his sensitivity to the reactions of organized labor. See Albert Blum, "Roosevelt, the M-Day Plans, and the Military Industrial Complex," *Military Affairs*, 36 (April 1972): 44-6.

13. William Green, *Labor and Democracy* (Princeton, N.J.: Princeton University Press, 1939), p. 190; "General Marshall Plans Army Service for C.C.C.," AFL *Weekly News Service*, January 6, 1940; "Military Training Demanded for C.C.C.," AFL *Weekly News Service*, June 4, 1940.

14. Cole, *Roosevelt and the Isolationists*, pp. 375-79.

15. William Hutcheson to William Green, June 20, 1940 and Green to Hutcheson, June 20, 1940, file: "Miscellaneous Correspondence," series 11C, box 44, Green Papers; "Green Against Draft Unless President Shows it is Necessary for Defense," AFL *Weekly News Service*, August 6, 1940; "All Aid for Britain Short of War Urged by Green as Defense Step," AFL *Weekly News Service*, August 27, 1940; "N.Y. Federation Endorses Roosevelt," AFL *Weekly News Service*, August 27, 1940.

16. "Protest Plans for Conscription," *CIO News*, August 12, 1940, p. 5; "Green Against Draft Unless President Shows it is Necessary for Defense," AFL *Weekly News Service*, August 6, 1940.

17. "Predict New Jobs for 4,500,000 Idle Workers," AFL *Weekly News Service*, September 3, 1940; "Labor Must Have Work and Stand Together for Defense of Democracy, Says Green," AFL *Weekly News Service*, September 10, 1940; "Green Urges Labor to Aid Draft Act," AFL *Weekly News Service*, September 17, 1940; "Labor and Legion Take Joint Stand for Defense and Against Dictators," AFL *Weekly News Service*, September 24, 1940; "AFL Exempts Draftees From Union Dues," AFL *Weekly News Service*, October 8, 1940; "Job Rights During Training or War Are Protected by AFL Agreements," AFL *Weekly News Service*, October 15, 1940. Also see, "Relief Rolls Slash Visioned from Draft," AFL *Weekly News Service*, September 10, 1940.

18. "United States Must Not Enter War in Europe, A.F. of L. Declares," AFL *Weekly News Service*, October 21, 1939; Philip Taft, *The A. F. of L. From the Death of Gompers to the Merger* (New York: Harper and Brothers, 1959), p. 248; American Federation of Labor, *Report of Proceedings of the Fifty-Ninth Annual Convention of the American Federation of Labor* (Washington: Judd and Detweiler, 1939), p. 29.

19. "Green Declares United States Must Not Become Involved in European War," AFL *Weekly News Service*, October 7, 1939; "Green Presents Program to

Preserve American Neutrality and a Avoid War," AFL *Weekly News Service*, October 7, 1939; Green, *Labor and Democracy*, p. 189.

20. "Repeal of Arms Embargo Favored by AFL Metal Trades Department," AFL *Weekly News Service*, October 7, 1939.

21. Document G-663-1/2, Green typescript, for Labor Service Bureau, May 28, 1940, file: "Magazine Articles," series 11E, box 13, Green Papers; "Executive Council Drafts Plank," AFL *Weekly News Service*, May 14, 1940.

22. Green speech no. 405, June 6, 1940, file; "Labor Speeches," series 11E, box 3, Green Papers; Green speech no. 406, June 11, 1940, Ibid.

23. "AFL Will Follow Non-Partisan Policy in Presidential Campaign, Says Green," AFL *Weekly News Service*, July 23, 1940; "Labor Must Work and Stand Together for Defense of Democracy, Says Green," AFL *Weekly News Service*, September 10, 1940; "Green Addresses Two Conventions," AFL *Weekly News Service*, September 17, 1940; "Green Pledges President Roosevelt Labor Will Help National Defense," AFL *Weekly News Service*, June 4, 1940.

24. "Green Opposes Hoover Program," AFL *Weekly News Service*, October 22, 1940.

25. Press Release no. F-867 (Green to Hamilton Fish), January 17, 1941, file: "News Releases," series 11E, box 10, Green Papers; Press Release no. F-868, ("Statement of William Green . . . in Support of the 'Lend-Lease' Bill Before the Committee on Foreign Affairs of the House of Representatives,"), January 25, 1941, Ibid.

Many individual unions also came out in favor of Lend-Lease. The ILGWU, for example, worked with the White Committee on a pro-Lend-Lease campaign. See David Dubinsky to Robert Jager, January 29, 1941, Luigi Antonini to Dubinsky, March 5, 1941, circular letter from Executive Secretary (Frederick Umhey), February 13, 1941, file 3A, box 174, David Dubinsky Papers, Labor-Management Documentation Center, Cornell University, Ithaca, NY.

26. "Anti-Labor Measures Facing Defeat," AFL *Weekly News Service*, May 20, 1941; "Aid to Britain Must Be Redoubled," AFL *Weekly News Service*, June 3, 1941; "AFL Executive Council Sees No Need for Sending U.S. Troops to Europe," AFL *Weekly News Service*, August 12, 1941; "Facing the Facts," AFL *Weekly News Service*, August 19, 1941.

27. "Facing the Facts," AFL *Weekly News Service*, June 24, 1941; "Green Greets British Labor Head and Pledges Aid in Two-Way Talk," AFL *Weekly News Service*, July 15, 1941; "Facing the Facts," AFL *Weekly News Service*, July 22, 1941; "AFL Executive Council Sees No Need for Sending U.S. Troops to Europe," AFL *Weekly News Service*, August 8, 1941; "Facing the Facts," AFL *Weekly News Service*, August 19, 1941.

28. "AFL Will Give 'Capacity Service' to Nation in Defense Emergency," AFL *Weekly News Service*, June 3, 1941; "Green Names AFL Defense Committee," AFL *Weekly News Service*, July 8, 1941; "Facing the Facts," AFL *Weekly News Service*, July 8, 1941; "AFL Supports Total Defense Program," AFL *Weekly News Service*, January 14, 1941; "Legislative Program for 1941," AFL *Weekly News*

Service, January 14, 1941; "Green Raps Critics of Roosevelt," AFL *Weekly News Service*, January 21, 1941; "All Legislation Outlawing Strikes Attacked by AFL Executive Council," AFL *Weekly News Service*, February 18, 1941; "7,000,000 Jobless, AFL Council Says," AFL *Weekly News Service*, May 29, 1941; "Musicians Union Buys Defense Bonds," AFL *Weekly News Service*, June 3, 1941; "How We Stand," AFL *Weekly News Service*, May 29, 1941.

29. "Green Names AFL Defense Committee," AFL *Weekly News Service*, July 8, 1941; "Facing the Facts," AFL *Weekly News Service*, July 8, 1941; Green to Central Labor Unions and State Branches, July 15, 1941, Florence Thorne to Matthew Woll, July 17, 1941, Minutes of Fourth Meeting of AFL National Defense Committee, July 30, 1941, file 12, box 14, Philip Taft Papers, Labor-Management Documentation Center, Cornell University, Ithaca, NY.

30. Green to Robert Watt, plus attachment, July 30, 1941, file 12, box 14, Taft Papers.

31. "Metal Trades Unions Adopt 'No Strike' Plan," AFL *Weekly News Service*, January 7, 1941; "19 Building Unions Limit Defense Fees and Banish Strikes," AFL *Weekly News Service*, January 14, 1941; "Painters Sign National Agreement Barring Defense Projects Strikes," AFL *Weekly News Service*, March 25, 1941; "Building Trades Ban Jurisdictional Work Stoppages on Defense Projects," AFL *Weekly News Service*, April 1, 1941; "Green Urges AFL Unions Ban Strikes During National Defense Emergency," AFL *Weekly News Service*, April 22, 1941; "Green Gets Medal for Defense Aid," AFL *Weekly News Service*, May 13, 1941; "AFL Executive Council Puts Teeth into No-Strike Policy for Defense," AFL *Weekly News Service*, May 29, 1941; "Building Trades Sign Epochal Pact With Government Banning Strikes," AFL *Weekly News Service*, July 29, 1941. Also see "Canal Defense Plans Not Halted by Strikes," AFL *Weekly News Service*, January 7, 1941.

32. "Facing the Facts," AFL *Weekly News Service*, July 8, 1941.

33. "Preserve Peace and Democracy, Build Strong National Defense, and Maintain Social Gains, Report Urges," AFL *Weekly News Service*, November 20, 1940; "Green Raps Critics of Roosevelt," AFL *Weekly News Service*, January 21, 1941; "Facing the Facts," AFL *Weekly News Service*, July 8, 1941; "AFL Executive Council Puts Teeth into No-Strike Policy for Defense," AFL *Weekly News Service*, May 29, 1941; "All Legislation Outlawing Strikes Attacked by AFL Executive Council," AFL *Weekly News Service*, February 18, 1941; "Meany Pledges Workers will Make Great Arsenal of Democracy Here," AFL *Weekly News Service*, July 22, 1941; "Harrison Warns Hitler Will Attack U.S. Trade," *Hannibal Labor Press*, July 12, 1940.

34. "750,000 New York AFL Unionists Pledge Full Aid to British Labor," AFL *Weekly News Service*, May 6, 1941; "Editorial," AFL *Weekly News Service*, June 3, 1941. Also see "Lyons Urges United Union Support of Movement to Aid British Labor," AFL *Weekly News Service*, March 4, 1941.

35. "U.S. Labor Group Established to Assist Workers in Britain," AFL *Weekly News Service*, December 31, 1940.

36. "Roosevelt, Willkie, and Lord Marley Support Aid British Labor Campaign," AFL *Weekly News Service*, May 20, 1941; "Green Lauds Subscription Books to Aid Labor in Great Britain," AFL *Weekly News Service*, May 29, 1941; "O'Connor Declares Aid Britain Week," AFL *Weekly News Service*, June 17, 1941; "Woll Group Aiding British Labor Reports Great Progress in Drive," AFL *Weekly News Service*, July 1, 1941; "Roosevelt Urges Full Support of 'Aid British Labor Week,'" AFL *Weekly News Service*, July 15, 1941; "Campaign to Aid British Labor Stimulated by National Week," AFL *Weekly News Service*, July 29, 1941; "Three Units Cooperate to Provide Dresses for 2400 British Girls," AFL *Weekly News Service*, August 19, 1941; "New York Unit to Make Clothing for British Refugee Children," AFL *Weekly News Service*, September 23, 1941; "Green, Woll, Urge All Local Unions to Raise Funds to Aid British Labor," AFL *Weekly News Service*, April 29, 1941; "AFL Chiefs Join Unit to Aid British Labor," AFL *Weekly News Service*, April 22, 1941; "Kansas City Pledges 5,000 Blankets in Campaign to Aid British Labor," AFL *Weekly News Service*, April 1, 1941; "Unions Back Campaign to Aid British Labor," AFL *Weekly News Service*, February 11, 1941.

CIO Attitudes Toward Intervention

CHAPTER 12

Like the AFL, the CIO called for the United States to remain neutral when the war began in Europe. In a nationwide radio broadcast on September 4, 1939—the day after World War II commenced—CIO President John L. Lewis declared that "Labor in America wants no war nor any part of war." He denounced the "war-lusting rulers of Europe" and warned against propaganda designed to draw the United States into the fray. Other CIO leaders and various CIO unions quickly echoed Lewis' sentiments. In October, at the CIO's annual convention, Lewis gave a stirring speech in favor of non-interventionism and the delegates resolved to support "President Roosevelt's neutrality policy based on the cardinal principle of keeping America out of war."[1]

Unlike the AFL, the CIO held to anti-interventionism as its official position until late 1940. It frequently criticized defense spending, vehemently opposed the draft, promulgated many isolationist arguments, and resorted to inflammatory, class-based rhetoric against the war. For well over a year into the war it remained highly militant in labor relations matters, in contrast with the AFL, and even launched a series of controversial strikes in defense plants.

Although it was anti-interventionist, the CIO frequently alluded to its acceptance of "the necessity for national defense." "We will defend our country," intoned Lewis in April 1940. "Let no one doubt that the sons of American working men and women will be the first in line should the integrity of our nation be attacked." The CIO used its supposedly pro-defense posture to score points in labor relations matters. As its organizational activities accelerated in the expanding defense industries, such as aviation, the CIO argued that union contracts would facilitate defense production. The CIO also accused anti-union employers of sabotaging national defense by causing production slowdowns in order to maximize profits or exact concessions from the government.[2]

The type of defense that the CIO advocated, however, was strictly confined to the Western Hemisphere and the repulse of an invasion. There was no sense of collective security. By mid-1940 the AFL saw a direct relationship between British security and American security, and supported the use of American plants to produce war materials for the defense of both countries. The CIO, on the other hand, criticized manufacturers who produced articles of war for Great Britain, saying that they caused production for America's own defense to lag. And, of course, the CIO rejected any kind of overseas military action or attempts, in the words of a CIO publication, to be "saviors of the world."[3]

The CIO's principal argument throughout 1939 and 1940 was that the greatest threats to American security were not foreign foes such as Germany or Japan but instead were domestic problems such as unemployment, low wages, hunger, poor health care, and inadequate housing. "Our war," said CIO Vice President Reid Robinson, was "the fight for jobs and an American way of living for all Americans." The CIO emphasized that domestic spending was more important to American defense than military spending. It opposed budget cuts in the Works Progress Administration (WPA), the Public Works Administration (PWA), the Civilian Conservation Corps (CCC), and other relief programs, especially when those cuts were necessitated by the increasing budget for preparedness. According to Lewis, "The best way to stay out of war, and the best defense against internal or external attack, is to create within our borders a prosperous, happy nation." And to do that required increased domestic spending. There should be no "retreat," said a *CIO News* editorial, from "responsibility and effectiveness in promoting the public welfare."[4]

Long after the AFL had come to appreciate the domestic economic activity generated by the war in Europe, the CIO was still belittling the concept of a war boom. Even as it was preparing to organize workers in the expanding defense industries, the CIO was insisting that the defense program would make scarcely a dent in unemployment. It maintained that defense spending actually hurt the economy by depleting consumer purchasing power, claimed in March 1940 that whatever benefits may have accrued from defense spending were already dissipating, and predicted business contraction in 1940 and a revival of the Depression.[5]

CIO leaders even intimated that relief and other domestic programs were a prerequisite for worker support of defense. "An army of four million conscripts cannot save our nation if the people doubt it is worth saving," said Lewis. In September 1940, Lewis called citizen loyalty America's "best defense," argued that such loyalty had to be grounded in the conviction that democracy was "the best way of life," and suggested that only the sort of domestic programs advanced by the CIO could guarantee that conviction. A few weeks later, CIO Secretary-Treasurer James Carey restated the point when he said that "the only way we're going to protect the American way of life is to give everyone a stake in democracy," and that the CIO's "crusade against poverty and misery" could do that.[6]

Further, the CIO took the position that interventionist talk was merely a smokescreen to obscure domestic economic problems. CIO leaders and CIO publications held that the attention being paid to events in Europe was the latest manifestation of a centuries' old tradition whereby politicians who were unable to solve difficulties at home cynically diverted attention from those problems with "the excitement of a foreign war."[7]

That line of reasoning dovetailed smoothly with the class-oriented, anti-war rhetoric adopted by the CIO. Lewis and other members of the Executive Board stumped the country repeating the standard charge that had emerged from the post-World War I disillusionment: in 1940, as in 1917, businessmen sought quick profits by using workers as cannon fodder in an imperialistic war.

In September 1940, at a Labor Day rally of the Emergency Peace Mobilization held in Chicago, Reid Robinson suggested that "corporate interests must have Government armament orders to make huge profits," and declared "we hate war because the workers do the fighting, the bleeding, and the dying, while others reap the harvest of blood-soaked profits." CIO Publicity Director Len DeCaux wrote that "the plain people" were "misrepresented by the war-mongers of Washington and Wall Street." He sneered at the "fat clubmen, bad-tempered ex-brass hats, Wall Street financiers, and [the] flock of gentry who specialize in clipping coupons and having other people work and fight for them." It was "easier to interest the rich and powerful in sending other people's sons" to war, concluded Lewis, than it was to "get them to concern themselves about providing jobs and education." The war, said Robinson, was the doing of "the same people [who] believe in keeping us unemployed in this country and depriving us of our rights as American citizens."[8]

The CIO did not conceive of the war as an attack by totalitarian states upon democratic ones but rather as a power struggle between imperialistic governments. The Steel Workers Organizing Committee (SWOC) proclaimed that "the moral issues in the current conflicts are over-shadowed by considerations of power politics that have dominated the actions of the belligerent for several centuries." Transport Workers Union President Michael Quill—who was part of the Lewis camp and whose speeches were covered by the *CIO News*—called Hitler a "madman," but blamed his rise on the machinations of businessmen in the United States and Britain and dismissed the European struggle as a "bankers' war."[9]

On rare occasions, the CIO took a position on some specific issue related to the war in Europe. In April 1940, for example, Lewis implied the CIO's opposition to providing financial assistance to the Allies when he spoke disparagingly of loans made to Britain and France during the First World War. Those loans, he said, created fortunes for American businessmen, were never repaid, and continued to "lie against the account of the United States as a bar to expenditures for our unemployed, our ill, and our aged."[10] Usually, however, the CIO avoided focusing on particular proposals of the interventionists and the Roosevelt administration, preferring to rely on frequently repeated and fairly general anti-intervention diatribes.

Yet on at least one specific issue the CIO made its position abundantly clear: the prospect of a military draft in peacetime. During the summer and fall of 1940, it battled relentlessly against the Burke-Wadsworth Conscription Bill.

When Lewis met with the Resolutions Committee at the 1940 Republican Convention in June, the 1936 Republican presidential nominee, Alf Landon, asked Lewis' opinion of President Roosevelt's proposal for compulsory military training for young men. With characteristic puffiness, the CIO executive responded: "I think it is a fantastic suggestion from a mind in full intellectual retreat."[11]

In July, Congress held hearings on the conscription bill introduced by Democratic Senator Edward Burke and Republican Representative James Wadsworth. The bill enjoyed the support of President Roosevelt as well as Roosevelt's Republican challenger in the 1940 election campaign, Wendell Willkie. Opinion polls indicated a large majority of voters also favored the proposed legislation.[12]

The CIO came out as an adamant opponent of the Burke-Wadsworth Bill. On August 2, Lewis dispatched a letter of protest to the House and Senate Military Affairs Committees. In the ensuing weeks, Lewis spoke out against "the fascist nature of the bill," argued that the draft violated individuals' civil liberties in a manner reminiscent of Nazi Germany, warned that the conscription bill would rend the social fabric of the country and cause economic dislocations, and urged reliance on voluntary enlistments. Drawing attention to what he considered inadequate taxes on wartime profits, Lewis said that "conscription would establish the principle in this nation that the lives of our young men are less privileged than the profit rights of dollars." Lewis commented with horror—and with justification—that the bill had been drafted by prominent New York attorneys, and claimed that the bill was one more attempt to control American workers.[13]

The CIO pressed its campaign against the Burke-Wadsworth

Bill with anti-draft speeches by its leaders, editorials in its publications, letters of protest, and delegations to Capitol Hill. It cited examples of employers who had used the threat of the prospective draft explicitly to intimidate employees and argued that supporters of the draft included "the worst enemies of the labor movement." The *CIO News* claimed for Lewis the mantle of instigator of a nationwide movement against the draft and crowed that other labor organizations had fallen into line behind the CIO—although it correctly interpreted William Green's position to be cautious enough to permit him to back his way into supporting the legislation.[14]

It was all to no avail. With a few modifications—reducing the age period for draft eligibility, for instance—the Burke-Wadsworth Bill became law in September 1940. From then on, the CIO worked to protect the civilian jobs of draftees, sought better pay and conditions in the military for draftees, clamored for labor representation on local draft boards, and complained when supposedly anti-union members were seated on draft boards.[15]

One of the CIO's closest political allies during the conscription debate was Democratic United States Senator Burton Wheeler of Montana. Wheeler was one of the Senate's most vociferous isolationists, and throughout 1940 the *CIO News* gave ample coverage to his anti-interventionist speeches. In July 1940, Wheeler and John L. Lewis shared the microphone at the annual convention of Townsend Clubs, where they both spoke out against American involvement in World War II. Lewis also used the occasion to urge the Democratic Party to nominate Wheeler for president. Later, the senator returned the compliment by praising Lewis' mastery of foreign affairs. In the fall, the CIO endorsed Wheeler's call for a Nye Committee-like investigation of American defense industries and their ties to European companies.[16]

In truth, the enunciated policies of the CIO on foreign policy matters were little more than the enunciated policies of John L. Lewis and his allies in the CIO's left wing. Lewis dominated the CIO and he and the Communists controlled its publications. Both opposed Roosevelt's foreign and military policies, and were able to convey the impression that the CIO was weighing in with the isolationists.[17]

Despite the CIO's official position, much of the CIO's hierarchy made common cause with their counterparts in the AFL in favor of Roosevelt's interventionist policies. CIO Secretary-Treasurer James Carey, R.J. Thomas and Walter Reuther of the United Auto Workers, Frank Grillo of the Rubber Workers, Emil Rieve of the Textile Workers, and Van Bittner of the Steel Workers Organizing Committee, the Packinghouse Workers Organizing Committee, and the United Mine Workers, along with the presidents of the Industrial Union Councils of New Jersey, Pennsylvania, Ohio, Maryland, and St. Louis, were among the CIO leaders who defied Lewis and supported Roosevelt and intervention. Another CIO leader, David Dubinsky, had broken with Lewis in 1938 and in June 1940 returned his International Ladies' Garment Workers Union' to the AFL. He had also opposed Lewis' isolationism, although his reasons for leaving the CIO were internal in nature and based on Lewis' heavy-handed leadership. The CIO interventionists took their case to the rank-and-file, condemning the brutality of the European dictators, warning of the threat Hitler posed to the United States, endorsing aid for Britain, and urging workers to move forward with defense production. Within their CIO unions, they resisted militance and tried to prevent strikes in defense industries. Appealing to audiences beyond the CIO, they gave pro-intervention radio addresses and frequently lent their support to the activities of the Committee to Defend America by Aiding the Allies and the Fight for Freedom Committee.[18]

Walter Reuther, the young and ambitious vice president of the United Auto Workers, was one of the CIO's most eloquent interventionists. He and his brothers had visited Germany in 1933, where they witnessed firsthand the terrors of Nazism and made friends with labor leaders who later were executed by the Nazis. Also, Reuther headed the anti-communist forces within the UAW, and he used the issue of intervention to discredit the anti-intervention, anti-Roosevelt Communists.[19]

Over the vehement opposition of the Communist faction—

which called Reuther and his supporters "imperialist warmonger lackeys"—Reuther persuaded the 1940 UAW convention to pass resolutions supporting President Roosevelt and condemning the dictatorships and military aggression of the Axis powers and the Soviet Union alike. In his speeches and radio broadcasts, Reuther echoed the standard themes of interventionism: that Hitler was bent on world domination and that free workers were turned into slaves wherever Nazism was triumphant; that Nazi aggression was edging ever closer to the Western Hemisphere; that Britain was all that stood between the United States and Nazi invasion; and that the more war materials the United States could produce and ship to Britain the stronger the guarantee that the war would not reach American shores. Maximum, high-quality production of war materials for Great Britain and for the bolstering of America's own defenses was, in Reuther's words, "labor's answer to Hitler aggression, American labor's reply to the cries of its enslaved brothers under the Nazi yoke in Europe."[20]

John Brophy, Director of Industrial Union Councils, also broke with Lewis over the intervention issue. In a series of speeches around the country in 1941, Brophy called for "aid without stint to the British cause." Speaking in Birmingham, Alabama, in June, Brophy stated that "It would be folly of the most fatal kind for us to suppose that the free labor movement could long endure in this country if Hitler's armies were to make permanent their grip upon the conquered peoples of Europe."[21]

The CIO's most influential interventionist, however, was Sidney Hillman. President of the Amalgamated Clothing Workers (ACW) and a vice president of the CIO, Hillman spoke out fervently against Nazism and supported massive assistance to the countries fighting the Axis forces. His opinions reflected those of his rank-and-file in the Amalgamated, in which two groups were heavily represented: refugees from Fascist Italy, and immigrants and first-generation Americans from Eastern Europe, whose relatives and former homelands were being crushed by the Axis. Hillman was largely responsible for moderating the CIO's anti-war pronouncements with assertions of support for national defense.[22]

President Roosevelt considered Hillman his most trusted

ally in the labor movement—a fact that irked Lewis. On May 29, 1940, Roosevelt appointed a National Defense Advisory Commission (NDAC) to study and make recommendations on an array of issues related to defense production and the wartime economy. He named Hillman to that commission, with responsibilities in the area of labor relations and labor supply. Within three weeks, Hillman put together a Labor Policy Advisory Committee, with equal representation for the AFL and the CIO, which drafted a statement of labor policy that the commission adopted unanimously. On January 21, 1941, Roosevelt replaced the commission with a more powerful Office of Production Management (OPM), with General Motors President William S. Knudsen as Director-General and Hillman as Associate Director-General. Knudsen and Hillman were joined on the OPM's governing council by Secretary of War Henry Stimson and Secretary of the Navy Frank Knox.[23]

Hillman thus was organized labor's chief representative in an administration gearing for war, but, in a sense, he was also that same administration's chief representative in the labor movement. In his capacity as NDAC commissioner and later as OPM associate director-general, Hillman exhorted labor and management alike to remember the Axis threat and to speed the production of articles of defense. He warned delegates to the 1940 ACW convention not "to be lulled into a false sense of security, which, unfortunately, democratic countries abroad allowed themselves to do," and recommended that Americans put themselves in a position where they would "not even be challenged" because the Axis would know how well prepared they were. Taking the same message to businessmen, he told the Detroit Chamber of Commerce in 1941: "We are ahead of schedule in many things, but we must be ahead of schedule in the production of every item that will contribute to our final goal—the defeat of Hitlerism." "Business as usual" and "strikes as usual," he said on another occasion prior to United States entry into the war, should be put aside pending defeat of the Axis powers. And, he defended the administration's defense policy from attacks in the press, denying journalist Walter Lippman's allegations in July 1940 that Roosevelt was failing to utilize existing plant capacity sufficiently in the defense build-up and asserting that Roosevelt's "underlying program has been definitely and unequivocally to obtain maximum production as expeditiously as possible."[24]

Hillman's appointments to NDAC and OPM exacerbated the strains in his relationship with John L. Lewis and further alienated Lewis from the Roosevelt Administration. Lewis criticized Hillman over appointments he made to the Labor Policy Advisory Committee, and there was a heated wrangle over Lewis' demand that Roosevelt issue an Executive Order requiring that defense contractors abide by the National Labor Relations Act—a demand that the administration had rejected a year earlier on legal grounds. Hillman rebuffed Lewis on both counts, and in exasperation told Lewis in November 1940 that NDAC had enjoyed considerable achievements on behalf of labor in only five months of operation. "I challenge anyone to cite comparable accomplishments for the welfare of American labor in so brief a period," he wrote, adding, "May I point out that all this has been accomplished despite the tragic split in the ranks of labor."[25]

The showdown between Lewis and the CIO interventionists came during the 1940 presidential campaign. In October, Lewis came out in support of Roosevelt's Republican opponent, Wall Street attorney Wendell Willkie. Roosevelt enjoyed immense popularity in the labor movement, and unionists were shocked by Lewis' endorsement of Willkie. Even Lewis' friends of convenience in the communist faction of the CIO were disappointed—not because they liked Roosevelt, of course, but because they could not stomach a Republican candidate. Even more stunning, Lewis declared that a vote for Roosevelt would be tantamount to a vote of no-confidence in himself, and he vowed to resign as CIO president if the votes of CIO members did not put Willkie into the White House.[26]

Lewis, a Republican, had been distancing himself from Roosevelt throughout the president's second term. He believed that Roosevelt had not reciprocated labor's support in the 1936 election and had not done enough to strengthen the CIO. Lewis may also have envisioned a political career of his own, which he feared would be thwarted by Roosevelt. Lewis endorsed Willkie mainly because he believed Roosevelt's New Deal was spent and because he disagreed with Roosevelt's foreign policies. In his initial statement of support for Willkie, Lewis claimed that Roosevelt was leading the country into war and that Willkie would guarantee peace. Conceivably, Lewis was also piqued at Hillman's growing influence with the country's chief executive. His threat to resign as CIO president if Roosevelt were reelected was a calculated gamble. If Willkie were elected—which Lewis probably did not expect—then Lewis would not have to compete with Roosevelt for the loyalty of the CIO's rank-and-file. If Roosevelt won, then Lewis would have an ideal excuse to resign his CIO leadership, which was increasingly problematic for him anyway, and concentrate on his real base of support in the United Mine Workers union (UMW).[27]

Hillman, Reuther, Thomas, Rieve, Carey, and even Philip Murray, Lewis' second-in-command at the UMW, were partisans of Franklin Roosevelt and were delighted at the opportunity to oust the CIO president. Unhappy with Lewis' dictatorial management style within the CIO, they also believed in Roosevelt's domestic programs and were interventionists. They campaigned hard to deliver the votes of organized labor to Roosevelt in 1940, just as in previous elections.[28]

In a radio broadcast less than one week before the election, Walter Reuther declared that "Labor is as strongly for President Roosevelt today as it was in 1932 and in 1936." He pointed to the great strides made by organized labor during the first two Roosevelt administrations, and also emphasized labor's support for Roosevelt's stand against Hitler and Mussolini. According to Reuther, "American labor counts as one of the greatest contributions of President Roosevelt the fact that he has opened for British labor and the British people the avenues for obtaining the materials of defensive war." Calling Lewis an advocate of appeasement, he took pleasure in quoting a year-old statement Lewis had made that praised Roosevelt's foreign policy acumen. "I believe Mr. Lewis was right in 1939," said Reuther, "and that he is wrong today."[29]

Roosevelt was easily elected to a third term. At the CIO convention that took place just two weeks later, Hillman and Murray maneuvered stealthily to ensure that Lewis would not back out of his pledge to step down. Murray, who in addition to being vice president of the UMW was also chairman of the SWOC, won election as Lewis' successor.[30]

Lewis' departure meant that the CIO, like the AFL, would be controlled by interventionists. The difference was apparent immediately. The impassioned anti-war rhetoric vanished from the *CIO News* overnight. On November 25, it featured a full-page reprint of Hillman's speech to the convention, in which he called for the United States to assist Great Britain. Subsequent issues carried additional articles on Hillman and his work on the NDAC, and quoted the ACW president encouraging continuous defense production. Although the convention continued to emphasize domestic economic threats to national defense and passed a resolution saying that the United States should stay out of war, it also approved a resolution condemning totalitarianism. And in his first national radio address after becoming CIO president, Philip Murray stressed his organization's support for "all measures necessary for the true defense of America."[31]

During the first two months of Murray's presidency, the CIO proposed four programs to facilitate defense production. The Murray Defense Plan proposed tripartite councils of labor, management, and government representatives in all defense industries to expand and coordinate production and reduce unemployment caused by conversion to a war economy. The Murray Steel Plan sought to treat the steel industry as a single production unit for purposes of placing orders and utilizing plant capacity, thereby improving efficiency. The CIO Housing Plan envisioned 10,000 housing starts per month to shelter defense workers and their families. The Reuther Plan promised to build up to 500 war planes every day through conversion of automobile factories to airplane factories and the more efficient utilization of plant capacity and the labor supply.[32]

Clearly, the various defense plans were self-serving for the CIO. They were aimed at increasing union control in the workplace through greater rationalization of the industrial process, giving labor a voice in policy matters commensurate to its importance, and improving the working and living conditions of the rank-and-file. As an editorial in the *CIO News* put it, the Murray Defense Plan "is fully as much concerned with the domestic welfare of the American people as it is with armaments."[33]

Nevertheless, the Murray Defense Plan, the Murray Steel Plan, the Reuther Plan, and the CIO Housing Plan were serious and constructive proposals to eliminate bottlenecks, improve efficiency, galvanize defense production, and contribute to an Axis defeat. "The problems of national defense center about planning the utilization of our productive capacity," James Carey told a group of Chicago businessmen in April 1941. The CIO plans sought to accomplish proper utilization. Without it, and without sufficient production, Carey predicted "we shall leave ourselves defenseless, subject our allies to a Hitler victory, and destroy the American standard of living."[34]

When the Murray Defense Plan was announced in December 1940, the CIO claimed that Murray and Lewis had visited the White House three months earlier to discuss the concept with President Roosevelt. To be sure, the CIO Executive Board had discussed and approved proposals to speed defense production as early as June, well before Lewis resigned. Yet the various defense proposals put forth by the CIO at the end of 1940 and the beginning of 1941 really represented the ideas of the new breed of unionists, such as Reuther, who saw defense cooperation not merely as accommodation but instead as an opportunity to precipitate structural changes that would enhance the power of organized labor. Being announced, as they were, in the first months after Lewis resigned, the very positive suggestions the CIO made to stimulate the defense buildup appeared to symbolize a significant departure from the unleavened gainsaying of the Lewis era.[35]

In February 1941, Murray appeared before the Senate Foreign Relations Committee to testify in favor of the Lend-Lease Bill. Murray was markedly cautious in his endorsement of the measure, and he seemed to be more concerned with securing guarantees that the National Labor Relations Act, the Wage-Hour Act, and other laws protecting labor would not be compromised by the proposed legislation. He also rejected the notion of convoys and reiterated CIO opposition to direct American involvement in the war. Still, he threw the weight of the CIO behind the most important single piece of pro-intervention legislation, and told the senators that the CIO "supports the policy of giving full aid to Great Britain."[36]

A month later, Murray showed support for Roosevelt's defense program by joining a new, eleven-member National Defense Mediation Board. He accepted the appointment against his better judgment, however, because he feared the body would be an entering wedge for compulsory arbitration. While fully in accord with national defense policies, Murray and the other CIO representative—UMW Secretary-Treasurer Thomas Kennedy—resigned from the board less than a month before Pearl Harbor, following a board decision in a coal mining dispute that was unfavorable to the CIO.[37]

The left wing of the CIO resisted interventionism and pleas for continuous defense production, and hewed to the virtually obstructionist example set by Lewis. Pro-communist CIO Vice Presidents Joseph Curran and Reid Robinson—who were also presidents of the National Maritime Union and the Mine, Mill, and Smelter Workers Union, respectively—opposed Lend-Lease. Mike Quill's Industrial Union Council of New York City staged a rally against Lend-Lease. In late 1940 and the first part of 1941, Communist-dominated UAW locals led several strikes at important defense plants. At least one of them, at North American Aviation near Los Angeles, was bitterly opposed by UAW and CIO leaders. Sidney Hillman himself, as associate director-general of OPM, gave Roosevelt his concurrence to use troops to break the strike.[38]

Everything changed after the German invasion of the Soviet Union in June. The Communists immediately proclaimed their anti-fascist militancy and their strong endorsement of American aid to Britain and the Soviet Union. Almost the entire CIO, excluding Lewis and his exponents, fell into line behind Roosevelt's foreign and defense policies. Long-time anti-interventionist Curran found himself trying to boost British morale with a shortwave broadcast on a program called the "Friendship Bridge," under the auspices of the British-American Ambulance Corps. Quill's Greater New York Industrial Union Council, meanwhile, pledged to raise $400,000 for British war relief.[39]

Belatedly following the lead of the AFL, the CIO established a national committee to coordinate war relief fundraising. At the behest of Irving Abramson, president of the New Jersey Industrial Union Council and one of the CIO's earliest proponents of intervention, the CIO sponsored the CIO Children's Village in Great Britain. The Children's Village served as a refuge for British children whose neighborhoods had been attacked by German bombers during the Blitzkrieg. And, as Abramson pointed out, it demonstrated to British workers that "there is another labor organization in this country besides the A.F. of L."[40]

The final skirmish between the interventionists and anti-interventionists occurred in October and November of 1941, over an amendment to the Neutrality Act that would have permitted American merchant ships to be armed and to carry cargo in war zones. The amendment was adopted, thereby completing the evisceration of the Neutrality Act. The CIO aligned with the interventionists in the debate over the amendment. CIO Secretary James Carey wired each member of Congress, urging them to support the amendment and stating that "American workers are united in demanding freedom of the seas and the right of American ships to protect themselves from Nazi pirates." Characteristically, the balance of the telegram consisted of a defense of collective bargaining.[41]

At its 1941 Convention in November, the CIO clearly stated its adherence to intervention and preparedness. While not going as far as to take a no-strike pledge, the delegates did promise to rely on peaceful means whenever possible to resolve disputes in defense industries and stated that "business as usual" was impossible while the United States was engaged in a battle against Hitler. The convention recognized the sacrifices of the British people, noted that the first target of Nazism was organized labor, and denounced "Hitler's aim of world conquest." In his report to the convention, President Murray stated that the United States "could not remain oblivious to foreign affairs," and offered the CIO's "complete support to President Roosevelt's policy of furnishing through our Government all possible economic and material aid to Great Britain, the Soviet Union, and China, which are the nations now carrying on the struggle to rid the world of Nazism, the enemy of mankind."[42]

The AFL and the CIO, which had initially opposed intervention in World War II, evolved into strong supporters of President Roosevelt's programs of aiding the Allies and building a strong military. As they adopted interventionism, the national labor centers also modified their domestic programs in order to facilitate the military buildup, protect labor from restrictive legislation, and take advantage of the domestic opportunities offered by the defense effort.

Notes

1. "Labor and the European War," *CIO News*, September 11, 1939, p. 4; "Two CIO Unions Warn Tory Foes of Labor," *CIO News*, September 25, 1939, p. 1; "Transit Union Asks Support of Civil Rights," *CIO News*, September 25, 1939, p. 1; "Advises New Deal Against 'Appeasement,'" *CIO News*, September 25, 1939, p. 2; "Labor and the War," *CIO News*, October 16, 1939, p. 4; "The CIO's Stand on the War," *CIO News*, October 16, 1939, p. 4; "CIO Progress and Problems Discussed by Lewis in Report," *CIO News*, October, 16, 1939, p. 5.

2. "Pres. Lewis Discusses Major U.S. Issues at Natl. Negro Congress," *CIO News*, April 29, 1940, p. 6; "Lewis' Speech to Youth Congress," *CIO News*, February 19, 1940, p. 5; "Lewis Explains Stand on Labor Unity, War," *CIO News*, May 20, 1940, p. 3; "National Defense," *CIO News*, May 27, 1940, p. 4; "Probe Ford's Nazi Ties, Auto Union Asks U.S.," *CIO News*, June 3, 1940, p. 2; "Auto Union Head Raps Ford Stall on Making Planes," *CIO News*, July 8, 1940, p. 1; "Launch Aircraft Drive," *CIO News*, July 15, 1940, p. 1; "Launch Drive in Aircraft," *CIO News*, July 15, 1940, p. 3; "American," *CIO News*, July 22, 1940, p. 4; "Congress Urged to OK Taxes on Big Defense Profits," *CIO News*, August 19, 1940, p. 3; "Defense Sabotage," *CIO News*, August 26, 1940, p. 4.

3. "Lewis Calls Democracy, Jobs, Best Defense," *CIO News*, September 2, 1940, p. 3, p. 3; "Lewis' Speech to Youth Congress," *CIO News*, February 19, 1940, p. 5; "Pres. Lewis Discusses Major U.S. Issues at Natl. Negro Congress," *CIO News*, April 29, 1940, p. 6.

4. "CIO Unions Show Strength in Big Labor Day Parades," *CIO News*, September 9, 1940, p. 1; "Pres. Lewis Discusses Major U.S. Issues at Natl. Negro Congress," *CIO News*, April 29, 1940, p. 6; "Lewis Invites Natl. Negro Congress to

Join Labor League," *CIO News*, April 29, 1940, p. 5; "U.S. Must Solve Key Problems in '40—Lewis," *CIO News*, January 1, 1940, p. 3; "U.S. Budget Slashes WPA, Ups Arms Costs," *CIO News*, January 8, 1940, p. 1; "No Time to Slash Relief," *CIO News*, January 8, 1940, p. 4; "Lewis Urges Congress Tackle Major Problems," *CIO News*, January 15, 1940, p. 1; "Program for National Defense: U.S. Must Take Care of 10,000,000 Jobless, Murray Demands," *CIO News*, January 22, 1940, p. 5; "First Line of Defense," *CIO News*, February 12, 1940, p. 4; "Looking Ahead," *CIO News*, February 19, 1940, p. 4; "Looking Ahead," *CIO News*, March 4, 1940, p. 4; "'Keep Eyes on Home Problems'—Robinson," *CIO News*, March 11, 1940, p. 6; "Little Steel Contracts Seen Near," *CIO News*, March 20, 1940, pp. 3, 6; "U.S. Must Avoid War, Solve Own Problems," *CIO News*, June 24, 1940, p. 6; "Save Social Legislation, Avoid War, Murray Tells Democrats at Chicago," *CIO News*, July 22, 1940, p. 3; "Lewis Urges 'Re-Dedication' to Peace, Security," *CIO News*, September 2, 1940, p. 1; "Menace to Nation is Unemployment, Lewis Tells GOP," Philadelphia *Evening Bulletin*, June 19, 1940, clipping "1940-Lewis" file, box 5B, John Brophy Papers, Catholic University, Washington, DC.

5. "Budget Proposals Slash WPA Program, Lift Funds for Arms," *CIO News*, January 8, 1940, p. 3; "Fall in Business Index Predicted in CIO Report," *CIO News*, January 8, 1940, p. 7; "No Time to Slash Relief," *CIO News*, January 8, 1940, p. 4; "Explains CIO Stand on Politics," *CIO News*, March 18, 1940, p. 2; "U.S. Facing Depression, 11,939,000 Are Jobless," *CIO News*, March 18, 1940, p. 5; "Looking Ahead," *CIO News*, September 16, 1940, p. 5; Minutes of June 3-5, 1940, pp. 23, 25, 322, 329, reel no. 1, Proceedings of International Executive Board, CIO, Walter Reuther Library, Wayne State University, Detroit, Michigan.

6. "U.S. Drift to War Growing, Lewis Warns," *CIO News*, September 9, 1940, p. 3; "Lewis Calls Democracy, Jobs, Best Defense," *CIO News*, September 2, 1940, p. 3; "Labor is Bulwark of Democracy, Rubber Union Told," *CIO News*, September 23, 1940, p. 2.

7. "President Lewis Discusses Major U.S. Issues at Natl. Negro Congress," *CIO News*, April 29, 1940, p. 6; "'Keep Eyes on Home Problems,'—Robinson," *CIO News*, March 11, 1940, p. 6; "Defense and Jobs," *CIO News*, July 1, 1940, p. 4; "U.S. Drift to War Growing, Lewis Warns," *CIO News*, September 9, 1940; "Murray Scores 'Dollar Patriotism,' of Business," *CIO News*, September 9, 1940, p. 3.

8. "Looking Ahead," *CIO News*, Mary 6, 1940, p. 4; "Pres. Lewis Discusses Major U.S. Issues at Natl. Negro Congress," *CIO News*, April 29, 1940, p. 6; "Fifth Column: Robinson Urges: Keep An Eye on Democracy's Tory Foes," *CIO News*, June 3, 1940, p. 6; "Weak-Kneed Mothers Cut War Profits," *CIO News*, April 15, 1940, p. 7; "Lewis' Speech to Youth Congress," *CIO News*, February 19, 1940, p. 5; "Peace—It's Terrible!," *CIO News*, April 8, 1940, p. 2; "Union Heads Voice Plea: 'Avoid War,'" *CIO News*, September 9, 1940, p. 8.

9. "Lewis' Speech to Youth Congress," *CIO News*, February 19, 1940, p. 5; "Little Steel Contracts Seen Near," *CIO News*, March 20, 1940, p. 3; "Electrical Union Reports 50,000 New Members," *CIO News*, September 9, 1940, p. 3.

10. "Pres. Lewis Discusses Major U.S. Issues at Natl. Negro Congress," *CIO*

News, April 29, 1940, p. 6.

11. "Lewis Gives GOP List of Labor Demands," *CIO News*, June 24, 1940, p. 5.

12. Wayne Cole, *Roosevelt and the Isolationists 1932-45*, (Lincoln: University of Nebraska Press, 1983), pp. 376-77.

13. "Conscription Bill Viewed as Threat to Basic Rights," *CIO News*, August 5, 1940, p. 3; "Against Conscription," *CIO News*, August 5, 1940, p. 4; "Lewis Hits War, Militarism, in Talk at Mill Parley," *CIO News*, August 12, 1940, p. 3; "Protest Plans for Conscription," *CIO News*, August 12, 1940, p. 5; "Lewis Blasts Draft Bill, Asks Limit on War Profits," *CIO News*, August 19, 1940, p. 1; "Lewis Renews Attack on Draft Bill," *CIO News*, August 19, 1940, p. 3; "Text of Lewis' Draft Message," *CIO News*, August 19, 1940, p. 4; "U.S. Drift to War Growing, Lewis Warns," *CIO News*, September 9, 1940, p. 3.

14. "Conscription Bill Viewed as Threat to Basic Rights," *CIO News*, August 5, 1940, p. 3; "Against Conscription," *CIO News*, August 5, 1940, p. 4; "Unions Condemn Draft," *CIO News*, August 12, 1940, p. 1; "Unanimous," *CIO News*, August 12, 1940, p. 4; "Protest Plans for Conscription," *CIO News*, August 12, 1940, p. 5; "Boatmen Hear Murray Assail Profit Hogs," *CIO News*, August 12, 1940, p. 7; "Oppose Conscription Bill," *CIO News*, August 19, 1940, p. 1; "CIO Delegations See Congress on Draft," *CIO News*, August 19, 1940, p. 5; "Oppose Draft," *CIO News*, August 26, 1940, p. 1; "Protest Anti-CIO Use of Draft Threat," *CIO News*, September 2, 1940, p. 1; "White Collar Workers Report Gains for Union," *CIO News*, September 9, 1940, p. 2.

15. "See Need for Labor Voice on Draft Boards," *CIO News*, September 9, 1940, p. 3; "Ask Draft Boards Seat Unionists," *CIO News*, October 7, 1940, p. 5; "Rap Draft Appointees in Michigan," *CIO News*, October 7, 1940, p. 5; "Hit Draft Appointees," *CIO News*, October 21, 1940, p. 2; "Seek CIO Voice on Draft Boards," *CIO News*, October 21, 1940, p. 3; "Stacked Against Labor," *CIO News*, October 21, 1940, p. 4; "The Draft Act—What It Means," *CIO News*, September 23, 1940, p. 5; "Anti-Labor Boards," *CIO News*, November 4, 1940, p. 1; "Plaything Workers Ready if Draft Bill Passes," *CIO News*, August 12, 1940, p. 3; "Offer 6-Point Plan to Insure Democratic Spirit in Army," *CIO News*, January 13, 1941, p. 2.

16. "Wheeler Addresses Miners," *CIO News*, January 29, 1940, p. 1; "People Don't Want War, Wheeler Tells Congress," *CIO News*, June 17, 1940, p. 6; "Wheeler Renews Plea That U.S. Avoid War," *CIO News*, June 24, 1940, p. 2; "Adopt Anti-War Platform, Lewis Advises Democrats," *CIO News*, July 8, 1940, p. 1; "Lewis Boosts Wheeler, Asks Peace Stand," *CIO News*, July 8, 1940, p. 3; "At Old Age Meeting," *CIO News*, July 15, 1940, p. 6; "Protest Plans for Conscription," *CIO News*, August 12, 1940, p. 5; "Lewis Renews Attack on Draft Bill," *CIO News*, August 19, 1940, p. 3; "War Means End of Generation's Liberty, Wheeler Declares," *CIO News*, August 26, 1940, p. 6; "Wheeler Asks Arms Trust Be Probed," *CIO News*, September 16, 1940, p. 3; "Final Voting Due on Conscription," *CIO News*, September 16, 1940, p. 5; "Wheeler Gets Probe of Arms Tie-Ups," *CIO News*, September 30, 1940, p. 8; "To Probe Foreign Ties of Industry," *CIO News*, October 14, 1940, p. 1; "Wheeler Praises Lewis' Knowledge of U.S. Affairs," *CIO News*,

November 4, 1940, p. 5; "Labor Wins Many Seats in Congress," *CIO News*, November 11, 1940, p. 3.

17. LeRoy James Lenburg, *The CIO and American Foreign Policy, 1935-1955*, doctoral dissertation, University of Pennsylvania, 1973 (Ann Arbor, Mich: University Microfilms, 1974), pp. 40, 46, 49, 66-7; Melvin Dubofsky and Warren Van Tine, *John L. Lewis: A Biography* (New York: Quadrangle, 1977), p. 367; Matthew Josephson, *Sidney Hillman: Statesman of American Labor* (Garden City, N.Y.: Doubleday and Co., 1952), pp. 468-73; Saul Alinsky, *John L. Lewis: An Unauthorized Biography* (New York: G.P. Putnam's Sons, 1949), p. 206.

18. Victor Reuther, *The Brothers Reuther and the Story of the UAW* (Boston: Houghton-Mifflin Co., 1976), pp. 220-24; David Dubinsky and A.H. Raskin, *David Dubinsky: A Life With Labor* (New York: Simon and Shuster, 1977), pp. 271-72; Herbert Harris, *Labor's Civil War*, (New York: Alfred A. Knopf, 1940), pp. 230, 240; Nelson Lichtenstein, "Defending the No-Strike Pledge: CIO Politics During World War II," *Radical America* 9 (July-August 1975): 52; Roger Keeran, *The Communist Party and the Auto Workers Union* (Bloomington: Indiana University Press, 1980), pp. 210-25; Press Release, May 19, 1941, file: "Labor," box 45, Fight for Freedom Archives, Princeton University Library, Princeton, N.J.; "U.S. Labor Gives President Strong Support on 'Stop Hitler' Moves," *Labor News Service*, May 29, 1941, "Emil Rieve Says Lindbergh is Flying in Fog," *Labor News Service*, May 28, 1941, "99 AFL and CIO Leaders Urge Full Measures to Defeat Axis Menace," *Labor News Service*, June 13, 1941, file: "Labor," box 45, Fight for Freedom Archives; Alfred Lewis to Chapter Representatives, February 10, 1941, file: "Admin. Mgmt.—Labor Div.," box 4, Committee to Defend America by Aiding the Allies Archives, Princeton University Library, Princeton, N.J.; Lenburg, *CIO and American Foreign Policy*, p. 52; Timothy R. Dzierba, *Organized Labor and the Coming of World War II, 1937-1941*, doctoral dissertation, State University of New York at Buffalo, 1983 (Ann Arbor, Mich.: University Microfilms International, 1984), p. 106.

19. Reuther, *Brothers Reuther*, pp. 221-22; Keeran, *Communist Party and the Auto Workers*, pp. 206-7.

20. Reuther, *Brothers Reuther*, pp. 221-23; Keeran, *Communist Party and the Auto Workers*, pp. 210-11; Walter Reuther radio address, October 31, 1940, file 539-13, box 539, Walter Reuther Papers, Walter Reuther Library, Wayne State University, Detroit, Mich.; Reuther radio address, "More Airplanes for Defense," December 28, 1940, file 539-14, box 539, Ibid.

21. "War Aims of Democracy," typescript, June 28, 1941, file: "1941—Speeches," box 5B, Brophy Papers; Typescripts of speeches in Chattanooga, Tennessee, May 31, 1941, and New York City, July 2, 1941, Ibid.; Diary entries, April 29, 1941, April 30, 1941, June 21, 1941, June 28, 1941, and July 28, 1941, box 3B, Ibid.

22. Josephson, *Hillman*, pp. 462, 471; Sidney Hillman speech, New York City, November 9, 1941, file: "Sidney Hillman," box 16, series 5C, Boris Shishkin Papers (Files of the Economist), American Federation of Labor Collection,

Wisconsin State Historical Society, Madison, Wis.

23. James MacGregor Burns, *Roosevelt: The Lion and the Fox* (New York City: Harcourt Brace and World, 1956), p. 351; Dubofsky, et al., *Lewis*, pp. 357-64; Josephson, *Hillman*, pp. 469-72, 483; Bruno Stein, "Labor's Role in Government Agencies During World War II," *Journal of Economic History* XVII (1957): 390-394; "Office of Production Management," August 12, 1941, file: "OPM: Personnel," box 23, series 5C, Shishkin Papers; "Chronology of Record of Activities on Labor Policies," n.d., typescript, folder 5, box 78, Sidney Hillman Papers, ACW Archives, Labor-Management Documentation Center, Cornell University, Ithaca, NY; Hillman to Lewis, November 19, 1940, Ibid.

24. "Defense Program Must Not Be a Cloak for Anti-Labor Drive—Hillman," *CIO News*, June 3, 1940, p. 6; Hillman speech, Detroit, November 13, 1941, file: "Sidney Hillman," box 16, series 5C, Shishkin Papers.; Hillman speech, New York City, November 9, 1941, file: "Sidney Hillman," box 16, series 5C, Ibid.; Hillman to Walter Lippman, July 18, 1940, folder 13, box 78, Hillman Papers.

25. "Lewis Backs Willkie," *CIO News*, October 28, 1940, p. 1; Dubofsky, et al., *Lewis*, pp. 357-64; Reuther, *Brothers Reuther*, pp. 222-23; Hillman to Lewis, July 30, 1940, Hillman to Lewis, September 13, 1940, Maxwell Brandwen to Hillman, July 18, 1940, Lewis to Hillman, July 15, 1940, Lewis to Hillman, July 29, 1940, Hillman to Lewis, August 7, 1940, folder 3, box 78, Hillman Papers; editorial, "Lewis Meets His Match," *New York Herald-Tribune*, December 8, 1940, clipping in folder 5, box 78, Ibid.; Hillman to Lewis, November 19, 1940, folder 5, box 78, Ibid; Lewis to Roosevelt, January 18, 1939, Roosevelt to Lewis, January 30, 1939, folder 2, box 78, Ibid. Also see Robert H. Zieger, *John L. Lewis, Labor Leader* (Boston: Twayne Publishers, 1988), p. 341.

26. Dubofsky, et al., *Lewis*, pp. 357-64; Lenburg, *CIO and American Foreign Policy*, pp. 34-6; "Lewis Backs Willkie," *CIO News*, October 28, 1940, p. 1; Josephson, *Hillman*, pp. 474-75, 483.

27. Reuther radio address, October 31, 1940, folder 539-13, box 539, Reuther Papers; Dubofsky, et al., *Lewis*, pp. 367-69; Lichtenstein, "No Strike Pledge," p. 52; Josephson, *Hillman*, pp. 476-79; Lenburg, *CIO and American Foreign Policy*, pp. 55-7.

28. Reuther radio address, October 30, 1940, file 539-13, box 539, Reuther Papers.

29. Dubofsky, et al., *Lewis*, pp. 367-69; "Elect Murray CIO Head as John L. Lewis Retires," *CIO News*, November 25, 1940, p. 1.

30. "Hillman Tells Views on Unity, National Defense Production," *CIO News*, November 25, 1940, p. 11; "Hillman Picks Shipyard Committee," *CIO News*, December 2, 1940, p. 5; "National Defense," *CIO News*, December 9, 1940, p. 4; "Re-Affirm Defense Support," *CIO News*, December 16, 1940, p. 6; "Keep U.S. Out of World War," *CIO News*, November 25, 1940, p. 9; "Convention Resolutions," *CIO News*, November 25, 1940, p. 10; "Labor Is Nation's 'First Defense Line,'—Murray," *CIO News*, December 2, 1940, p. 1; "Hillman on Defense Super Council," *CIO News*, December 30, 1940, p. 3.

31. Henry M. Christman, ed., *Walter Reuther: Selected Papers* (New York: MacMillan Co., 1961), pp. 1-12; "President Murray Proposes New Defense Structure," *CIO News*, December 23, 1940, p.1; "Fourth CIO Plan," *CIO News*, December 3, 1941, p. 3.

32. "The CIO Plan," *CIO News*, January 20, 1941, p. 4; "Brophy Urges Labor Plan for Future," *CIO News*, February 17, 1941, p. 5. Also see James Carey speech to Executives Club, Chicago, April 4, 1941, CIO Press Releases, AFL-CIO Archives, George Meany Center, Silver Spring, Md.

33. "The CIO Steel Plan," *CIO News*, February 3, 1941, p. 4; Carey speech to Executives Club, Chicago, April 4, 1941, CIO Press Releases.

34. Pres. Murray Proposes New Defense Structure," *CIO News*, December 23, 1940, p. 1; Irving Howe and B.J. Widick, *The UAW and Walter Reuther* (New York: Random House, 1949), pp. 108-10; Meeting Minutes, June 3-5, 1940, pp. 218-22, reel 1, Proceedings of International Executive Board, CIO.

35. "Murray Defends Labor Rights in Arms Bill Testimony," *CIO News*, February 10, 1941, p. 1; "Murray Statement on 'Lend-Lease' Bill Urges Protection for Labor," *CIO News*, February 10, 1941, p. 3; "Text of Pres. Murray's Statement to Senate of 'Lease-Lend' Proposal," *CIO News*, February 10, 1941, p. 6; Congress of Industrial Organizations, *Daily Proceedings of the Fourth Constitutional Convention of the Congress of Industrial Organizations* (Detroit: Congress of Industrial Organizations, 1941), p. 40.

36. Nelson Lichtenstein, *Labor's War at Home: The CIO in World War II* (Cambridge: Cambridge University Press, 1982), pp. 50-1; Philip Murray and Thomas Kennedy to Franklin Roosevelt, November 11, 1941, CIO Press Releases.

37. Keeran, *Communist Party and the Auto Workers*, pp. 212-18, 222-25; Lichtenstein, *Labor's War at Home*, pp. 49-50, 56-63; Lenburg, *CIO and American Foreign Policy*, pp. 76-8. Also see Dzierba, *Organized Labor and the Coming of World War II*, p. 125.

38. "Curran to Talk to British," *CIO News*, October 27, 1941, p. 5; Dzierba, *Organized Labor and the Coming of World War II*, p. 107; Lenburg, *CIO and American Foreign Policy*, p. 90; Keeran, *Communist Party and the Auto Workers*, pp. 220-21; Dubinsky, et al., *Dubinsky*, p. 272. Also see "'Labor Must Fight for All-Out Production," *CIO News*, November 3, 1941, p. 2; "Ask Change in Neutrality Act," *CIO News*, October 20, 1941, p. 8; "Back Anti-Nazis," *CIO News*, September 1, 1941, p. 8; "200 Attend Minnesota CIO Parley," *CIO News*, September 8, 1941, p. 8; "Metal Workers Urge Fascism's Defeat in U.S., Abroad," *CIO News*, August 18, 1941, p. 8; "Murray Hits CIO Gains, Asks Aid to Hitler's Foes," *CIO News*, November 17, 1941, p. 1.

39. Announcement concerning British Children's Village, November 13, 1941, CIO Press Releases; Meeting Minutes, June 5, 1942, pp. 399-402, reel 1, Proceedings of International Executive Board, CIO; CIO, *1941 Proceedings*, pp. 206-9.

40. Robert A. Divine, *The Reluctant Belligerent: American Entry into World War II* (New York: John Wiley and Sons, 1965), pp. 146-47; Wayne S. Cole,

Charles A. Lindbergh and the Battle Against American Intervention in World War II (New York: Harcourt, Brace, Jovanovich, 1974), p. 196; Carey to Members of the House of Representatives, n.d. (ca. November 1941), folder 1, box 80, Hillman Papers.

41. CIO, *1941 Proceedings*, pp. 40-1, 57, 204, 206, 330.

The Primacy of Domestic Objectives

CHAPTER 13

Almost as soon as World War II began, and well before the United States became a belligerent, the American labor movement began to sense the domestic social, political, and economic implications of the hostilities. Labor knew that many industries might be ruined during the transition to a war footing. It also realized that even if rearmament generated wartime prosperity, reconversion to a peacetime economy threatened to kick off a severe depression. In a nationally broadcast address in September 1940, AFL President William Green warned of grave economic and social problems for the entire world following the war.[1]

Further, labor faced an array of political threats as war approached. Ostensibly to speed the defense buildup, anti-labor members of Congress sponsored legislation to restrict union rights to organize and strike and to roll back labor's hard-won social gains. The prospect of political retrenchment terrified organized labor. During wartime, stated the AFL Executive Council, "Nothing is easier than to shift from a democratic organization and control to bureaucratic domination and absolutism." At the same time, "dollar-a-year men"—top level corporate officials who donated their time—flooded into Washington to take charge of government defense councils and industrial boards. Having employers increasing their influence during a period of national emergency could have dire consequences for labor. According to the CIO Executive Board, the corporate executives formed "a super-government, not responsible or responsive to the needs or demands of the people of this country."[2]

By coordinating their foreign and military positions with their domestic programs, the national labor centers not only could protect labor, but also could take positive action to build for the future. Shortly after the United States actually entered the war, the CIO Executive Board spelled out the strategy. The war effort needed labor's support. In return for that support, and to make that support effective, labor needed morale-building guarantees: that living standards would be protected; that unions would be able to grow; that an equitable tax system would be developed; that profiteering would be checked; that social security would be broadened; that unemployment would be cushioned; and, above all, that labor would take its rightful place in policymaking bodies.[3]

The AFL and CIO revised their domestic programs in light of the international crisis. With a growing consensus favoring interventionism within the labor movement, the national labor centers devised domestic plans that encouraged interventionism and facilitated rearmament and at the same time protected labor from restrictive governmental policies and economic dislocations. More than that, the domestic programs sought to attain for organized labor a greater degree of power and independence—not just for the period of the defense emergency, but for the postwar era as well.

⊕ ⊕ ⊕

The AFL integrated its support for intervention and preparedness with its larger domestic program. The Federation adopted foreign policy positions that could help it achieve domestic goals, abandoned some domestic programs that conflicted with interventionism, and altered other domestic programs to bring them into line with interventionism. While the AFL was prepared to use interventionism as a way of advancing the domestic interests of organized labor, it also recognized that failure to support intervention and preparedness ran the risk of damaging labor's position at home. To realize its objective of achieving domestic gains by supporting intervention, the AFL leadership had to launch an aggressive campaign to arouse rank-and-file sympathy for Great Britain and for the Franklin D. Roosevelt administration's foreign and military policies.

When war was declared in Europe, the AFL—which was still straddling the fence between interventionism and isolationism anyway—tended to deny that a war boom would create prosperity. It expressed doubts that war-related employment would make much of a dent in the "jobless army." Further, it predicted that war business would lead to new problems and dangers, and suggested that such federal programs as the Works Progress Administration (WPA) remained necessary.[4]

Because of the war, the AFL soon changed its position. By the third quarter of 1940, it was becoming increasingly evident that production of war materials for the United States and Britain was indeed stimulating the American economy. Not only were more workers employed in defense industries, but the increased purchasing power that those jobs created led to expanded sales and higher employment in consumer industries as well. Official pronouncements of the Federation cheered the steadily decreasing unemployment rate. As employment rose, so did membership in AFL unions and so did wages. The AFL had long called for increased spending on unemployment relief and federal jobs programs, but economic prospects in early 1941 looked so rosy that the AFL actually reversed course and supported budget cuts in those areas so as to increase the availability of resources for lucrative defense production.[5]

The 30-hour week was another casualty of the burgeoning war economy. Throughout the 1930s, the AFL repeatedly had insisted that the 30-hour work week was its most important goal. Reducing the work week, it claimed, would spread employment, generate purchasing power, and end the Depression. There was an isolationist tinge to the proposal, as it was presented as a way of achieving economic health through purely domestic activities, without recourse to overseas markets that could embroil the United States in war. At the 1939 AFL Convention, the Executive

Council "re-emphasize[d] the need of continually striving toward the shorter work week on the part of all unions with the 30-hour week as our goal."[6]

At the same time that it became clear that defense production was accomplishing the same economic goals as the 30-hour week—by the 3rd quarter of 1940—the AFL started backing away from the concept. Jobs were being created without the 30-hour week, and shortening the work week might impede the preparedness effort. The AFL's *Weekly News* Service even announced in August 1940 that the Federation officially had renounced the 30-hour week. A retraction followed immediately, but for all intents and purposes the 30-hour week was a dead issue. At the 1940 convention, the Executive Council and a Committee on the Shorter Work Day recommended union compliance with a new national law establishing the basic work week at 40 hours, and shelved several resolutions calling for the 30-hour week in defense industries. The 1941 convention endorsed the 30-hour week in principle, but explicitly rejected it in cases where it interfered with defense.[7]

If the AFL's interventionist stance caused it to abandon the cherished 30-hour week, it may have also encouraged the AFL to move away from its reliance on the domestic market. Reciprocity treaties and the lure of foreign markets once frightened the AFL as a distraction from the related goals of increased purchasing power and an expanded domestic market. When he testified for the AFL in favor of Lend-Lease before the House Foreign Affairs Committee in January 1941, however, AFL President William Green argued that overseas markets would be indispensable for the United States if it were to maintain high levels of employment. Accordingly, he called for a "reciprocity-for-aid" amendment to the Lend-Lease Bill. Countries receiving American largess via Lend-Lease, he said, should be required to open their markets to American goods after the war.[8]

In addition to dropping domestic programs that were no longer consistent with its foreign policy positions, the AFL adapted other programs to fit more comfortably with interventionism and preparedness. For example, for years the AFL had urged the federal government to fund low-cost housing. The Federation saw low-cost housing not simply as shelter for working class families, of course, but also as a powerful stimulus to the economy and an important source of jobs. It even tended to see defense spending as being in conflict with housing appropriations. By 1940, the conflict was resolved. The AFL gave a new name to an old program, as it championed increased federal spending for defense housing. With more and more people working in defense plants—many of whom had to move to new localities to do so—existing housing was being stretched to the limit and new housing became necessary. Providing low-cost housing for those workers, as well as paying them good wages, providing healthful working conditions, and otherwise maintaining the high labor standards for which the AFL had always fought, could suddenly be justified in the name of national defense. Without adequate housing, the argument went, workers' efficiency would be impaired and defense production would suffer.[9]

Finally, the AFL tried to use the defense buildup as leverage to achieve a wide array of traditional union goals. Cooperation with the preparedness program could be a way of enhancing the power of organized labor relative to management and government. The AFL sought recognition for organized labor as a full partner with government and employers in the planning of preparedness and the economy, and was ready to use that position to defend jobs and collective bargaining alike.[10]

In return for observing its no-strike pledge, the AFL made it clear that it expected federal protection for the union shop. Laws ensuring labor's right to organize and bargain collectively, as well as other pieces of social legislation that the AFL valued, were prerequisites for labor's cooperation in the defense effort. Emphasizing the positive, AFL leaders argued that collective bargaining enhanced industrial efficiency and would thereby contribute to maximum defense production.[11]

Throughout the Depression, the AFL had decried profiteering and had blamed the failure of wages to keep pace with prices for inadequate purchasing power and declining living standards. As early as 1937, the Federation had called for establishment of a government commission to control prices. The defense emergency enabled the AFL to renew its calls for price controls. The AFL also called for excess profits taxes. Together, price controls and excess profits taxes would dampen inflation and spread the wealth "as insurance against strikes."[12]

The AFL maintained that the defense emergency warranted other forms of economic planning. To protect consumer industries, the AFL advocated central coordination of raw material allocation. Planned allocation would ensure that strategic goods would not be absorbed entirely by defense industries. Consumer industries could continue to operate and employees in consumer industries could keep their jobs. Further, to make the most of defense spending and to curb the power of corporate giants, the AFL called for defense contracts to be spread out equitably among many companies in all geographic regions and tried to steer defense contracts to union shops. It further called for surplus labor to be hired in lieu of lengthening the work week to meet production quotas. That kind of planning, the AFL asserted, would not only be fair but it would also be efficient. Thus it could be justified strictly as a defense measure. Moreover, the AFL hoped that such planning would maximize employment opportunities for its rank-and-file.[13]

The most important goal that the AFL wanted to achieve through economic planning during the defense emergency was to ensure a stronger position for organized labor after the defense emergency. More than a year before the United States would enter the war, and only a few months into the defense buildup, AFL publications and reports began to express anxiety over a postwar economic depression. The Federation's *Monthly Survey of Business* warned that without proper guidance the preparedness program would "disrupt our economic life . . . destroy labor standards, [and] leave mills and men stranded after the first years of intense activity are over." According to the *American Federationist,* planning was necessary to avert "mass unemployment and economic collapse" after the defense emergency, the return of peace, and the homecoming of job-seeking veterans.[14]

Thus, the AFL's Executive Council predicted in August 1941

that a new depression "is the inevitable prospect for America unless we begin to prepare for peace as we are strengthening our defenses against the threat of war." The Executive Council recommended that a planning council composed of representatives from government, labor, industry, and agriculture implement a multi-faceted program to ease economic reconversion after the war. The program would include a reduction in consumption taxes in order to boost consumer spending; development of new consumer industries, such as television and air conditioning; appropriations for peacetime public works and low-cost housing; and taxation of business profits during the defense boom in order to accumulate reserves that would permit unemployment benefits adequate to sustain purchasing power. In short, the AFL proposed to use emergency economic planning to create a postwar economy very similar to the sort of economy it had championed for years: one based on expanded purchasing power, government pump-priming, and unemployment relief.[15]

An essential component of planning was organized labor's participation. The AFL demanded representation on all government boards involved in planning defense measures in order to facilitate production, achieve such economic goals as postwar employment, and guard against a diminution of labor's power. According to an Executive Council report when the European war was only one month old, organized labor deserved status as a full partner in emergency planning with government and management because of labor's numbers, because labor was one of the "essential factors of defense," and because labor bore the greatest burden during wartime. "Failure to give labor such representation," declared the Executive Council, "would be sufficient to cause the greatest doubts in labor's mind." For many reasons, the AFL was prepared to support Roosevelt's defense effort, but that support was contingent upon having a voice in defense councils. And in making the case for labor representation, the AFL frequently pointed to the salutary effect labor representation had had on Great Britain's war effort.[16]

While seeking partnership with government and management through tripartite planning agencies, the AFL also worked to increase its influence through independent means. In July 1941 the AFL established a national defense committee and called upon its more than 700 city central bodies to establish local committees. The purpose of the committees was to nudge the defense effort and the economy along lines beneficial to organized labor. They would help furnish workers for defense production, disseminate information regarding the availability of plant capacity and raw materials, make sure that smaller factories were aware of potential defense contracts, plan for postwar employment programs, and engage in other activities designed to prevent bottlenecks, spread jobs, and protect labor's position.[17]

Similarly, CIO President John L. Lewis always insisted that the CIO have a role in wartime policymaking. In his report to the 1939 CIO convention, Lewis presented his organization's five key demands with respect to the month-old war in Europe. One of them was that labor enjoy "adequate representation in all governmental boards and agencies set up to cope with the war situation and to mobilize national defense."[18]

National CIO policy during the Lewis administration tended to resist compromising domestic programs in order to accommodate defense programs. "America's problems must and will be solved in this country by American methods," stormed Lewis in his New Year's Day Message for 1940. The United States, he continued, "must steadfastly turn aside from giddy dreams of foreign adventures." Rather than abandon or moderate programs as the AFL was doing in order to take advantage of the opportunities offered by the defense buildup and the prospect of intervention, Lewis intended to press forward with his domestic agenda without consideration for the war in Europe and its effects upon the United States. The CIO would continue to be militant, to concentrate on the organization of basic industries, and to stress the need for domestic jobs programs and relief spending.[19]

The CIO position throughout the Lewis years was always that rearmament was not economically beneficial, that unemployment was continuing to run at very high levels, and that funding for such federal programs as the WPA and the Civilian Conservation Corps (CCC) should be maintained. In contrast, the

AFL showed a willingness to countenance budget reductions for WPA as the defense economy began heating up. Even in 1941, after Lewis had departed and the CIO had moved into the interventionist camp, the CIO continued to oppose cuts in WPA funding. On May 27, 1941, Secretary-Treasurer James Carey announced that he was "profoundly shocked" by President Roosevelt's appropriation request for WPA for fiscal year 1942, and he urged a three-fold increase.[20]

If anything, the CIO during the Lewis years seemed to respond to the national defense emergency by reasserting its confrontational attitude on domestic issues. Many interventionists in the labor movement supported a no-strike pledge, and a significant portion of the AFL had committed to that pledge by early 1941. With major defense contractors such as Bethlehem Steel and the Ford Motor Company stingy about sharing defense profits with employees in the form of increased wages, and even unwilling to obey the National Labor Relations Act, Lewis and militants on the local level felt no compunction about resorting to the strike mechanism. They saw it as the only effective way to enjoy any of the proceeds of the defense bonanza, and, in some cases, the only way to organize non-union shops. In 1940 and 1941, such CIO unions as the Industrial Union of Marine and Shipbuilding Workers, the United Auto Workers, and the Steel Workers Organizing Committee struck defense contractors such as Allis-Chalmers, Ford, Bethlehem Steel (and its shipbuilding subsidiaries), North American Aviation, Vultee Aircraft, and International Harvester. They threatened strikes at such giants as General Motors and U.S. Steel. In April 1941, five months after resigning as CIO president, Lewis took his coal miners out against the southern mine operators. The strikes created a national uproar, but on the whole the tactic was successful. National CIO leaders who supported intervention were not always in favor of the defense strikes, but they defended them in public. In many cases—but not all—the argument that employers had caused the strikes through their unwillingness to negotiate was accurate.[21]

The primary objectives of John L. Lewis as president of the CIO were to build up the rank-and-file membership of the CIO and to augment the CIO's political clout. His strategy for achieving those objects included championing non-interventionism and refusing to accommodate the defense effort.

Non-interventionism helped Lewis court the black community. The National Negro Congress had ties to the Communists, and thus would have opposed intervention up until the time of Adolph Hitler's invasion of the Soviet Union. In April 1940, Lewis appealed for the group's support. Speaking to a large gathering of the National Negro Congress, he railed against "war mongers" who were unable to solve domestic problems and turned instead to "the dishonorable formula of foreign war." He explicitly put "the threat of war" in the same category with "the injustices of the poll tax and lynch law," thus attempting to link anti-war concerns with civil rights concerns. The National Negro Congress responded with a similar argument, publicized by the CIO, to the effect that "the Negro people have everything to lose and nothing to gain by American involvement" in what it called "an imperialistic war." The only war Americans should fight, it maintained, was against hunger, lynching, peonage, and Jim Crowism. Subsequently, the National Negro Congress affiliated with the CIO's political wing, Labor's Non-Partisan League, and encouraged blacks to join CIO unions. It was particularly helpful in recruiting black workers into the United Auto Workers (UAW) during the difficult struggle to organize Ford Motors.[22]

Lewis and the CIO took a similar tack with the American Youth Congress. As potential "cannon fodder," according to Lewis, young men had a greater right than anyone to protest against war. He showed sympathy for the anti-war stance of the American Youth Congress and pointed out that the CIO also opposed intervention. He criticized President Roosevelt for not taking the group's positions seriously, and protested cuts in federal programs such as the CCC that were aimed at youth.[23]

Even during the Lewis presidency, however, the CIO occasionally would affect a pro-preparedness posture as a way of achieving domestic goals. In particular, the CIO used the issue of preparedness as a weapon against management. Excess profits taxes (as part of a general tax restructuring), collective bargaining, and industrial unionism could all be justified in terms of the defense effort. Non-union corporations that violated labor laws and companies that slowed production in order to block excess profits taxes or to compel favorable government action were condemned by CIO spokesmen for their apparent Nazi sympathies and "un-American brazenness," and accused of carrying out "bold sabotage." Anti-union corporate interests were "dollar patriots" and "profit hogs" who callously manipulated the defense program for their own gain and actually hampered preparedness. Collective bargaining, enhanced job training, better working conditions, and high wages, meanwhile, translated into industrial peace, high worker morale, and increased defense production, according to the CIO. Starting when Lewis was president and continuing after Philip Murray succeeded him, the CIO put forth as defense measures the excess profits tax and the proposal that companies that flouted federal labor laws should be denied defense contracts.[24]

The labor executives who took control of the CIO after John L. Lewis resigned—including Murray, Sidney Hillman, R.J. Thomas, Walter Reuther, Emil Rieve, and James Carey—were interventionists. In short order following Lewis' decision to step down in November 1940, the CIO developed four plans that reversed Lewis' policies and responded in a constructive manner to the defense emergency: the Murray Defense Plan (or Industry Council Plan), the Murray Steel Plan, the Reuther Aircraft Production Plan, and the CIO Housing Plan. The plans promised to increase defense production, but they were also aimed at achieving important domestic goals.[25]

The two Murray Plans and the Reuther Plan incorporated a range of mechanisms to rationalize defense industries, reduce waste and duplication of effort, convert plants that produced consumer goods to plants that produced military goods, facilitate the efficient distribution of raw materials, and allocate contracts broadly enough to avert bottlenecks. Patriotism and a sense of duty helped prompt the CIO to offer the plans. Said Walter Reuther of his airplane production proposal: "This plan is put forward in the belief that the need for planes is immediate and terrifying . . . . We dare not invite the disaster that may come with further delay." Reuther and other CIO executives complained about industrialists who appeared to be dragging their feet in order to maximize profits and who resisted conversion to a wartime mode that was not on their own terms.[26]

The plans, however, were also geared to the specific advantage of labor. Under the Murray Plans, organized labor would have a voice equal to that of management in councils that would make policy for entire industries. Under all the plans, the utilization of existing factory space and the management of resources would facilitate conversion to defense production in such a way as to cause the least disruption to workers. The plans for speeding defense production, then, would also bring about enhanced job security and a larger measure of control in the workplace.[27]

If the Murray Defense Plan, the Murray Steel Plan, and the Reuther Aircraft Plan sought to increase workers' control in the workplace, then the CIO Housing Plan sought to increase workers' control over their private lives. As workers and their families moved to industrial centers to take jobs in defense plants, the problem of finding shelter for them became critical. Improved housing was necessary if there were to be a large and effective workforce to produce goods for defense. The CIO Housing Plan, successfully piloted in a project for shipyard workers in Camden, New Jersey, would contribute to defense production by expanding the availability of housing. But the plan also called for a significant role for residents of the defense housing in neighborhood policymaking, and included options for them to buy their homes. The CIO's Housing Committee likened the plan to a mutual insurance company, with the residents of the homes as stockholders, rather than as mere tenants in a company town.[28]

At the same time that the AFL and the CIO were proposing to increase their power and planning for the postwar era, they also were battling to preserve labor's existing social gains and to defeat anti-labor legislation. Both at the state and federal level, bills to restrict the rights of labor to organize and strike were proposed, supposedly to maintain production during the defense emergency. In 1941, for example, the United States Congress considered the Vinson Bill, the Smith Bill, the Ball Bill, amendments to the Selective Service Act, and the May and Connally Amendments (to the Burke-Wadsworth Act). Those bills would have frozen the open shop, jailed workers who staged walkouts in defense industries, imposed compulsory arbitration, broadened provisions empowering the president to seize and operate defense plants, mandated "cooling-off" periods in labor disputes, and imposed other provisions distasteful to unions. According to the CIO, the bills threatened to "emasculate the Wagner Act."[29]

The AFL and the CIO fought back with intensive lobbying, letter-writing campaigns, and angry speeches. AFL Secretary-Treasurer George Meany debated a proponent of the Vinson Bill over the Mutual Broadcasting System. Phil Murray convened an emergency conference of delegates from all CIO affiliates to pass a strongly-worded resolution against laws aimed at curtailing labor's rights. The *CIO News* called the Vinson Bill "an attack on democracy," and both national labor centers explicitly likened the anti-labor legislation to the methods of Adolph Hitler. The proposed laws typically were characterized as efforts by conservatives to defend corporate profits and reverse the New Deal. The national labor centers insisted that laws to regiment labor were unnecessary because there were no labor shortages and because defense production was at record-breaking levels. Regimentation, in fact, would hurt production by lowering worker morale and undermining healthy labor relations. Further, the AFL and the CIO argued, recognition of collective bargaining and labor's right to organize and strike would increase efficiency and raise production.[30]

The best card for organized labor to play was the no-strike pledge, partly on the theory that voluntary restraint would preclude the need for compulsory restraint. The AFL largely supported a voluntary no-strike pledge by early 1941. Even CIO interventionists such as Phil Murray, however, were reluctant to support a no-strike pledge, although they did urge CIO unions to use the strike weapon sparingly. As soon as the United States declared war, though, the CIO joined the AFL in pledging not to strike. By keeping work stoppages to a minimum, AFL and CIO leaders hoped to defuse arguments in favor of restrictive legislation. To substantiate their case, they pointed to production increases and to testimonials to labor's defense contributions made by Secretary of War Henry Stimson, Under-Secretary of War Robert Patterson, Navy Secretary Frank Knox, federal Wage-Hour Administrator Philip Fleming, and Federal Security Administrator Paul McNutt.[31]

If the strategy were to be effective, however, it had to command the allegiance of the rank-and-file. The AFL and CIO hierarchies took a three-part message to their memberships: avoid strikes, increase production, and support intervention. Without the rank-and-file on their side, the interventionists who led the AFL and, by 1941, the CIO, could not give tangible support to Roosevelt's policies of aiding the allies and building up the military. Unless they could deliver that support, the AFL and CIO leaders could not hope to have a meaningful role in policymaking and would be weakened in their fight against anti-labor legislation.

The AFL made a concerted appeal to its rank-and-file. The key objective was to generate sympathy for Britain and to reinforce the perception that the survival of Britain was essential to the survival of democracy. On a regular basis, the AFL *Weekly News Service* depicted the plight of Great Britain, arguing that even in wartime organized labor thrived in Great Britain and stressing that the British labor movement was giving its full support to the war effort. It frequently pointed out that the British labor movement even held a seat on Britain's war cabinet: the Minister of Labor was veteran union official Ernest Bevan. The pro-British references contained in AFL publications and in the speeches of AFL leaders actually served a dual purpose. In addition to encouraging interventionist sentiment, they also validated the AFL's position on domestic issues. Britain furnished a splendid example that the AFL could use to demonstrate that a democratic country could fight a war without having to scale back union prerogatives or guarantees of social security.[32]

In October 1940, British Trades Union Congress President Sir Walter Citrine accepted an AFL invitation to visit the United States in order to plead the British case in person. An address to the AFL's annual convention highlighted a cross-country speaking tour that lasted several weeks. Citrine poignantly described for

American unionists his country's desperate struggle—the dreadful bombing raids, with worse yet to come; thousands dead, many more crippled. Yet in spite of it, he said, British morale remained high and Britons continued to fight for the cause of democracy. He assured the AFL convention that the British government was respecting the rights of organized labor, that it consulted labor on all war matters, and that it had imposed a 100 percent excess profits tax to prevent the creation of wartime millionaires. He reminded his audience that Hitler and the Nazis were out to crush labor and that British labor was fighting to preserve the labor movement everywhere in the world. He finished with a cry for "planes, planes, and more planes." The British Navy was the first line of defense for American democracy, he said, but he urged the AFL members "to make the first line of defense for all democracy the American work shop." The AFL feted Citrine in December with a testimonial dinner in Washington, at which the British labor leader repeated his message for members of Congress, Supreme Court justices, and Cabinet secretaries.[33]

The AFL complemented its campaign in support of Britain with harsh reminders of the anti-democratic, anti-labor terrorism of the Nazis and with encouragement to workers to keep producing for the defense drive. It attempted to quiet the fears of the rank-and-file, saying that "the War Department will follow a progressive, sympathetic, and cooperative policy toward labor in the defense program," and that key figures in the Roosevelt administration opposed anti-strike laws. It called upon the rank-and-file to make full use of the government's mediation services to settle industrial disputes. The AFL further put the case for interventionism by identifying anti-labor forces with non-interventionism. AFL Publicity Director Philip Pearl described newspaper publisher Roy Howard both as an "enemy" of the AFL and as the "chief of appeasers." Pearl suggested that Howard's non-interventionism stemmed from a fear that labor's influence would increase during a defense buildup. In addition, Pearl warned Senator Burton K. Wheeler—who could boast a strong record of support for the labor movement—that he was "coming dangerously close to forfeiting labor's goodwill and respect" by opposing intervention.[34]

The CIO's principal publication, the *CIO News*, occasionally ran stories favorable to Great Britain. On January 27, 1941, for instance, it carried a report about the success of collective bargaining in Britain as a method of resolving wartime industrial disputes. The following July, it reported that a British labor union had lent moral support to the UAW strike against North American Aviation. And, of course, favorable references to Britain were included in the statements of CIO leaders that were printed in the *CIO News,* such as Murray's testimony endorsing Lend-Lease. Yet for the most part, even after John L. Lewis' resignation, the *CIO News*—in contrast to the AFL *Weekly News Service*—hardly mentioned the suffering and heroism in Great Britain, nor even Britain's pro-labor record. Similarly, it seldom alluded to the anti-labor activities of the Nazis, except by metaphor—as when it likened its domestic enemies in the business community and elsewhere to Adolph Hitler or Fifth Columnists, or when it called the introduction of anti-labor bills a "blitzkrieg" or "putsch."[35]

Pro-intervention CIO leaders, however, made it plain to the rank-and-file just where they stood. Alan Fitzgerald of the United Electrical, Radio, and Machine Workers urged labor to step up production because "if we fail to defeat Hitler, then all our concerns about wages, hours, business, profits, taxes, and prices . . . will be meaningless." James Carey declared "We stand united . . . in our support for the defense program of the United States, and our national policy of aid without stint to Great Britain and all nations resisting the aggressions of Nazi tyranny." Steady defense production was essential, according to Sidney Hillman, because "the forces of Hitlerism are determined to tear down all that we have built." Therefore, "the less we use the right to strike now, the more effectively we safeguard it for the future." "American labor," stated Walter Reuther, "does not believe in appeasement." Besides giving speeches supporting intervention and calling for efficient defense production, CIO leaders joined AFL leaders on stage at rallies of the Committee to Defend America by Aiding the Allies and the Fight for Freedom Committee.[36]

The rank-and-file got the message. The influence of AFL and CIO leaders was one of the factors that brought about a pro-interventionist consensus within the labor movement. In April 1941, President Roosevelt acknowledged the strong support that organized labor was giving to his foreign and military policies.[37]

Partly because of Communist opposition to intervention until mid-1941, and partly because even the non-Communist CIO leaders were slow to endorse a no-strike pledge, a number of CIO strikes took place in defense plants in 1940 and 1941. Sensitive to potential criticism for halting defense production, the CIO argued that the strikes had been caused by employer intransigence. The AFL, meanwhile, was furious, because the strikes gave ammunition to those seeking enactment of anti-strike legislation.[38]

Yet the AFL was also able to use the CIO strikes to strengthen itself in its battle against its rival. Always eager to discredit the CIO, the AFL seized upon the strike issue as proof of the CIO's disloyalty at a time of national peril. That line of reasoning fit comfortably with AFL assertions that the CIO was dominated by Communists and that it was affiliated with appeasers. While the German-Soviet Non-Aggression Treaty was still in force, the AFL gleefully—and inaccurately—depicted the CIO as being silent about Stalinist tyranny and Nazi tyranny alike. By making such arguments, the AFL may have been trying to get an edge on the CIO in their vicious competition to organize defense plants.[39]

While the AFL used the issue of patriotism to inflame passions against the CIO during the tense period leading up to American entry into World War II, the CIO likewise tried to use its own preparedness plans to steal a march on the AFL. One of the clearest intentions of the Reuther "500 Planes-a-Day" Plan was to provide work for automobile workers, who were organized by the UAW. The AFL's International Association of Machinists (IAM), already battling the UAW to organize aircraft plants, did not want to see the battleground shifted to automobile factories. The IAM bitterly resisted Reuther's scheme. The CIO Defense Housing Plan, meanwhile, envisioned extensive use of pre-fabricated housing. The pre-fabricated home industry was organized by the CIO's United Construction Workers, and attempts to expand the use of pre-fabrication were opposed to the point of physical violence by the AFL's Brotherhood of Carpenters.[40]

The national labor centers achieved at least partial victories in their efforts to parlay their interventionism into domestic gains. Tripartitism—the equal representation of business, government, and labor—became the guiding principle underlying the numerous agencies that the federal government established to handle defense-related matters. Top level union officials were named to the National Defense Mediation Board during the period prior to American entrance into the war, as well as to the National War Labor Board that succeeded it in early 1942. Those agencies were responsible for mediating labor disputes and worked to obtain from labor and management voluntary agreements to refrain from strikes and lockouts. Sidney Hillman, of course, was labor's spokesman on the National Defense Advisory Commission (NDAC) and on the Office of Production Management (OPM) that superseded the NDAC. Labor was further represented in the NDAC by a Labor Policy Advisory Committee made of 12 delegates from the AFL, the CIO, and the Railroad Brotherhoods. Under the OPM, representatives of more than 40 unions served on 11 formal and 4 informal advisory committees in such industries as rubber, automobiles, farm machinery, nonferrous metals, construction, and die-casting. A Production Planning Board formulated long-range policies for OPM, with the CIO's James Carey and the AFL's William Green representing labor. Hillman was eased out when the War Production Board (WPB) replaced OPM in 1942, but labor continued to be represented by Joseph Keenan of the AFL and Phillip Clowes of the CIO. The OPM's industry advisory committees were carried over to the WPB. In addition, nearly 5,000 voluntary labor-management committees were established under WPB, which resembled the industry councils envisioned by the Murray Defense Plan. Another wartime agency that grew out of OPM, the War Manpower Commission, included equal representation for labor and management on its Management-Labor Policy Committee.[41]

Labor's influence in the industrial process grew in informal ways, too. For instance, small businessmen approached labor executives as supplicants, appealing for their support in obtaining defense contracts and raw materials.[42]

Organized labor realized other objectives. Long-sought price controls became a reality in 1941 with the establishment of the Office of Price Administration (OPA). Like other defense agencies, OPA adhered to tripartitism, and by 1943 more than 700 labor representatives served on OPA's 94 district advisory boards. Organizational victories were won at Bethlehem Steel, Republic Steel, Ford Motors, and other corporations that had shut unions out for years. At Hillman's instigation, a handful of defense contracts were withdrawn from companies that were in violation of the Wagner Act. And organized labor succeeded in keeping the Vinson Bill, the Smith Bill, the May Amendment, and other anti-labor/anti-strike proposals from becoming law.[43]

The union gains were not without drawbacks. The "dollar-a-year men" came to exert far more power than labor representatives on the supposedly tripartite committees, and the economic centralization necessary for defense production ultimately worked to the advantage of the large corporations. The WPB's voluntary labor-management committees were at best a watered-down version of the Murray Plan's industry councils; while organized labor supported them, they were never satisfied with them. Anti-strike legislation failed, but the effect of anti-strike legislation was achieved through the imposition of anti-strike edicts by the National Defense Mediation Board and the War Labor Board—to the considerable disquiet of the rank-and-file, who became increasingly prone to call wildcat strikes during the war. Auto factories were converted to airplane production, as the Reuther Plan had recommended, but the provisions of the Reuther Plan calling for an orderly transition and the continued production of cars for the consumer market were dropped. And price stabilization, which labor had wanted, was accompanied by wage stabilization, which it had opposed.[44]

Nonetheless, when World War II ended in 1945, organized labor held a far more secure and stable position in the United States than it had held before the war. One of the contributing factors was the wise adaptation of domestic programs undertaken by interventionists in the labor movement during the immediate pre-war period, 1939-1941.[45]

Notes

1. "Labor and Legion Take Joint Stand for Defense Against Dictators," AFL *Weekly News Service*, September 24, 1940; "Profits Nearing Peaks, Wages Lag, A.F. of L. Business Survey Warns," AFL *Weekly News Service*, August 13, 1940; "Plans to Prevent Economic Breakdown After Defense Emergency Urged by AFL," AFL *Weekly News Service*, March 4, 1941. Also see "Geneva Labor Office is Functioning Despite European War, Winant Says," AFL *Weekly News Service*, October 28, 1939 and "International Labor Office Functions Despite European War, Goodrich Says," AFL *Weekly News Service*, January 13, 1940.

2. "Preserve Peace and Democracy, Build Strong National Defense, and Maintain Social Gains, Report Urges," AFL *Weekly News Service*, November 20, 1940; *1941 CIO Proceedings*, p. 41.

3. Meeting Minutes, January 24-26, 1942, pp. 36-7, reel 1, Proceedings of the International Executive Board, Congress of Industrial Organizations, Walter Reuther Library, Wayne State University, Detroit, Mich.

4. "Labor is Warned Not To Expect Job Boom," AFL *Weekly News Service*, November 11, 1939; "Unemployment is America's Chief Unsolved Problem, Green Declares," AFL *Weekly News Service*, January 1, 1940; "9,377,000 Workers Still Unemployed," AFL *Weekly News Service*, January 6, 1940.

5. "National Defense Plan Boosts U.S. Payroll," AFL *Weekly News Service*, June 11, 1940; "Age Limit Raised to Sixty-Two," AFL *Weekly News Service*, July 30, 1940; "Jobs for Women Urged in Defense Industries," AFL *Weekly News Service*, July 23, 1940; "Arsenals Add 24,000 to Work Force," AFL *Weekly News Service*, August 13, 1940; "Predict New Jobs for 4,500,000 Idle Workers," AFL *Weekly News Service*, September 3, 1940; "Miss Perkins Reports Employment Gains," AFL *Weekly News Service*, September 3, 1940; "Facing the Facts," AFL *Weekly News Service*, December 24, 1940; "1,100,000 Jobless Get Work in Year," AFL *Weekly News Service*, December 31, 1940; "Miss Anderson Outlines Defense Work of Women," AFL *Weekly News Service*, March 4, 1941; "540,000 Job Rise During December," AFL *Weekly News Service*, January 28, 1941; "Large Wage Increases Gained by Machinists," AFL *Weekly News Service*, March 18, 1941; "Jobless Cut Fifty Percent," AFL *Weekly News Service*, March 18, 1941; "Skilled Labor Sought," AFL *Weekly News Service*, November 12, 1940; "Schools Train Thousands for Defense Employment," AFL *Weekly News Service*, September 10, 1940; "End of Jobless Problem Visioned," AFL *Weekly News Service*, December 31, 1940; "U.S. Plans 3,100 Miles of New Defense Highways," AFL *Weekly News Service*, September 10, 1940; "War, Navy Depts. Fill 90,000 Defense Jobs," AFL *Weekly News Service*, September 24, 1940; "430,000 Unemployed Get Jobs in August," AFL *Weekly News Service*, October 1, 1940; "New Jobs for Five Million Forecast as Defense Production Increases," AFL *Weekly News Service*, October 8, 1940; "AFL Union Drive in Aircraft Plants Nets 30,000 Members, Higher Pay," AFL *Weekly News Service*, December 10, 1940; "Boilermakers Organizing All Navy Yard Employees," AFL *Weekly News Service*, October 15, 1940; "Two Million New

Jobs Predicted in 1941 With Defense Expansion," AFL *Weekly News Service*, October 22, 1940; "Age Limits Raised for Naval Workers," AFL *Weekly News Service*, October 29, 1940; "Huge Unemployment Slash Recorded as Defense Production Expands," AFL *Weekly News Service*, November 7, 1940.

6. American Federation of Labor, *Report of Proceedings of the Fifty-Ninth Annual Convention of the American Federation of Labor* (Washington: Judd and Detweiler, 1939), p. 27; "Thirty Hour Week Urged by Meany," AFL *Weekly News Service*, May 14, 1940; "Green Offers Plan to Increase Jobs," AFL *Weekly News Service*, May 14, 1940.

7. American Federation of Labor, *Report of Proceedings of the Sixtieth Annual Convention of the American Federation of Labor* (Washington: Judd and Detweiler, 1940), pp. 29, 98, 650-58; American Federation of Labor, *Report of Proceedings of the Sixty-First Annual Convention of the American Federation of Labor* (Washington: Judd and Detweiler, 1941), pp. 29, 610-11; "Labor Will Sacrifice 30-Hour Week for National Defense, Green Says," AFL *Weekly News Service*, August 20, 1940; Mimeographed notice to labor editors, AFL *Weekly News Service*, August 21, 1940.

8. "Lease-Lend Bill is 'Indispensable' President Green Tells Lawmakers," AFL *Weekly News Service*, January 28, 1941.

9. "Bates Urges Congress to Provide 600 Millions for Defense Housing," AFL *Weekly News Service*, July 15, 1941; "Many Defense Workers to Live in Trailers," AFL *Weekly News Service*, February 25, 1941; "Low-Cost Housing Construction Scheduled for Big Boom Period," AFL *Weekly News Service*, January 7, 1941; "Defense Workers Hit by Housing Shortage," AFL *Weekly News Service*, December 31, 1940; "AFL for National Defense First," AFL *Weekly News Service*, December 17, 1940; "AFL Asks for 300 Million Dollar Fund to Build Homes for Defense Workers," AFL *Weekly News Service*, August 20, 1940; "House Approves AFL Housing Bill; Union to Work Two Shifts on USHA," AFL *Weekly News Service*, September 17, 1940; "Labor and the USHA," AFL *Weekly News Service*, September 24, 1940.

10. See "Full Cooperation with Government Promised," AFL *Weekly News Service*, May 21, 1940; "Anti-Labor 'Nonsense' Ridiculed by Fleming," AFL *Weekly News Service*, September 17, 1940; Meeting Minutes, May 13-21, 1940, pp. 111-12, American Federation of Labor Executive Council Minutes, volume 86, AFL-CIO Archives, George Meany Center, Silver Spring, Md.

11. "'Help National Defense, Oust Reds,' Green Tells Huge Americanism Rally," AFL *Weekly News Service*, June 11, 1940; "N.Y. Federation Endorses Roosevelt," AFL *Weekly News Service*, August 27, 1940; "AFL for National Defense First, Green Replies to Labor Critics," AFL *Weekly News Service*, December 17, 1940; "AFL Supports Total Defense Program But Will Fight for Labor's Rights," AFL *Weekly News Service*, January 14, 1941; "Lyons Urges Legislation to Punish Employers Who Evade Labor Laws," AFL *Weekly News Service*, May 13, 1941; "Green Denounces Anti-Strike Bill," AFL *Weekly News Service*, May 20, 1941; Meeting Minutes, September 13-21, 1940, pp. 111-12, AFL

Executive Council Minutes, vol. 86.

12. Meeting Minutes, August 4-13, 1941, p. 6, AFL Executive Council Minutes, vol. 87-A,; AFL, *1941 Proceedings*, pp. 473, 625; "Workers Must Get Pay Rise, AFL Says; Federation Claims Large Increase in Profits Make Pay Boost Necessary," AFL *Weekly News Service*, February 22, 1936; "Industrial Council Urges High Wage Scales and Lower Prices," AFL *Weekly News Service*, March 21, 1936; "Price Profiteering is Condemned by AFL as Injury to Workers," AFL *Weekly News Service*, May 15, 1937; "A.F. of L. Hits Price Increases," AFL *Weekly News Service*, November 11, 1939; "War on Profiteers Pledged by Green," AFL *Weekly News Service*, September 30, 1939; "Corporate Profits Soar; How About Wages?," AFL *Weekly News Service*, August 6, 1940; "Profits Nearing Peaks, Wages Lag," AFL *Weekly News Service*, August 13, 1940; "Preventing War," AFL *Weekly News Service*, June 4, 1938; "Facing the Facts," AFL *Weekly News Service*, June 3, 1941; "AFL Executive Council Sees No Need for Sending U.S. Troops to Europe," AFL *Weekly News Service*, August 12, 1941; AFL Press Release, November 15, 1941, file 12, box 14, Philip Taft Papers, Labor-Management Documentation Center, Cornell University, Ithaca, NY.

13. "Labor's Voice in Defense is Asked," AFL *Weekly News Service*, June 18, 1940; "AFL Endorses Lease-Lend Measure, AFL *Weekly News Service*, January 21, 1941; "OPM Acts to Prevent Job Losses Under Aluminum Priorities Order," AFL *Weekly News Service*, March 25, 1941; "Green Names AFL Defense Committee," AFL *Weekly News Service*, July 18, 1941; "Green Outlines Five-Point Program to Mitigate 'Defense Unemployment,'" AFL *Weekly News Service*, July 22, 1941; "Defense Unemployment Crisis Seen," AFL *Weekly News Service*, August 19, 1941; William Green to Donald Nelson, October 8, 1941, file: "Priorities Cases," box 27, series 8A, Florence Thorne Papers (Director of Research), AFL Collection, Wisconsin State Historical Society, Madison, Wis.; Green to I.M. Ornburn, plus attachment, June 30, 1941, file: "Priorities Cases," box 27, series 8A, Thorn Papers; Jennie Matyas to David Dubinsky, June 21, 1940, Green to Dubinsky, plus attachments, October 16, 1940, Henry Schwartz to Dubinsky, August 8, 1940, file 4B, box 174, David Dubinsky Papers, ILGWU Archives, Labor-Management Documentation Center, Cornell University, Ithaca, NY.

14. "Plans to Prevent Economic Breakdown After Defense Emergency Urged by AFL," AFL *Weekly News Service*, March 14, 1941; "Profits Nearing Peaks, Wages Lag," AFL *Weekly News Service*, August 13, 1940; "Facing the Facts," AFL *Weekly News Service*, August 12, 1941.

15. Meeting Minutes, August 4-13, 1941, AFL Executive Council Minutes, vol. 87-A, pp. 37-8; "Plans to Prevent Economic Breakdown After Defense Emergency Urged by AFL," AFL *Weekly News Service*, March 4, 1941.

16. "Green Urges Labor Participation in All Phases of Defense Program," AFL *Weekly News Service*, May 6, 1941; "Labor Representation in Defense Units Asked," AFL *Weekly News Service*, December 17, 1940; "United States Must Not Enter War in Europe, A.F. of L. Declares," AFL *Weekly News Service*, October 21, 1939; "Full Cooperation With Government Promises," AFL *Weekly News Service*,

May 21, 1940; "AFL Planks for Labor Protection Presented to G.O.P. Convention," AFL *Weekly News Service*, June 18, 1940.

17. "Green Names AFL Defense Committee," AFL *Weekly News Service*, July 8, 1941.

18. "CIO Progress and Problems Discussed by Lewis in Report," *CIO News*, October 16, 1939, p. 5. Also see "The War—Unions Must Have a Voice," *CIO News*, May 27, 1940, p. 6; "Lewis Explains Stand on Labor Unity, War," *CIO News*, May 20, 1940, p. 3; and "Looking Ahead," *CIO News*, March 4, 1940, p. 4.

19. "U.S. Must Solve Key Problems in '40—Lewis," *CIO News*, January 1, 1940, p. 3. For an indication of the CIO's trenchant attitude early in the war, see "Report of R.J. Thomas," December 4, 1939, file 1-34, box 1, George Addes Papers, Reuther Library, Wayne State University, Detroit, Mich.

By the same token, John L. Lewis was not averse to steering defense contracts the way of a CIO union when the opportunity arose. See Leonard Lageman to Lewis, August 11, 1941, item 840, and Lewis to John Jones, August 14, 1941, item 838, reel 11, *CIO Files of John L. Lewis*, part II.

20. "What's Behind the 'Labor Shortage' Talk?," *CIO News*, January 1, 1940, p. 4; "U.S. Budget Slashes WPA, Ups Arms Costs," *CIO News*, January 8, 1940, p. 1; "No Time to Slash Relief," *CIO News*, January 8, 1940, p. 4; "Fall in Business Index Predicted in CIO Report," *CIO News*, January 8, 1940, p. 7; "First Line of Defense," *CIO News*, February 12, 1940, p. 4; "Looking Ahead," *CIO News*, March 4, 1940, p. 4; James Carey statement concerning WPA, May 22, 1941, Congress of Industrial Organizations Press Releases, AFL-CIO Archives, George Meany Center, Silver Spring, Md.; Philip Murray statement concerning WPA, April 23, 1941, CIO Press Releases; Carey statement concerning unemployment, January 23, 1941, CIO Press Releases; CIO Executive Board statement, January 8, 1941, CIO Press Releases.

21. Nelson Lichtenstein, *Labor's War at Home: The CIO in World War II* (Cambridge: Cambridge University Press, 1982), pp. 44-51, 60-3; Roger Keeran, *The Communist Party and the Auto Workers Union* (Bloomington: Indiana University Press, 1980), pp. 212-25; "Metal Unions Adopt 'No-Strike' Plan," AFL *Weekly News Service*, January 7, 1941; "19 Building Unions Limit Defense Fees and Banish Strikes," AFL *Weekly News Service*, January 14, 1941; "Bethlehem Steel Forces Stoppages," *CIO News*, March 24, 1941, p. 3; "$1-Day Raise Demanded by Mine Union," *CIO News*, March 17, 1941, p. 3; "Two Outlaws," *CIO News*, March 3, 1941, p. 4; "CIO on the Job," *CIO News*, March 31, 1941, p. 4; "'Bethlehem is to Blame for Strike'—Bittner," *CIO News*, March 31, 1941, p. 5; "Placing the Blame," *CIO News*, April 7, 1941, p. 4; "CIO Wins Ford Strike," *CIO News*, April 14, 1941, p. 1; "CIO Wins 75-Day Allis Strike," *CIO News*, April 14, 1941, p. 5; "Coal Lockout Before U.S. Mediation Board," *CIO News*, April 28, 1941, p. 1; Carey radio address, April 2, 1941, CIO Press Releases.

22. "Lewis Invites Natl. Negro Congress to Join Labor League," *CIO News*, April 29, 1940, p. 5; "Negro Congress Accepts Lewis' Invitation," *CIO News*, May 6, 1940, p. 1; "Negro Group Accepts Bid, Joins League," May 6, 1940, p. 3; Keeran,

Communist Party and the Auto Workers, p. 219. Also see "U.S. Must Avoid War, Solve Own Problems," *CIO News*, June 24, 1940, p. 6.

23. "Lewis' Speech to Youth Congress," *CIO News*, February 19, 1940, p. 5; "Looking Ahead," *CIO News*, February 19, 1940, p. 4.

24. "Probe Fords Nazi Ties Auto Union Asks U.S.," *CIO News*, June 3, 1940, p. 2; "From Hitler to Ford," *CIO News*, June 3, 1940, p. 2; "Asks Uncle Sam, 'Don't Buy Fords,'" *CIO News*, June 3, 1940, p. 2; "The CIO Position on National Defense," *CIO News*, June 10, 1040, p. 3; "Smith Bill Sabotage," *CIO News*, July 1, 1940, p. 4; "Urge U.S. Adopt Program to Train Apprentices," *CIO News*, July 1, 1940, p. 5; "Auto Union Head Raps Ford Stall on Making Planes," *CIO News*, July 8, 1940, p. 1; "Launch Drive in Aircraft," *CIO News*, July 15, 1940, p. 3; "American," *CIO News*, July 22, 1940, p. 4; "Plan Defense Labor Training Program," *CIO News*, July 29, 1940, p. 1; "Stop U.S. Contracts to Law Violators, Lewis Demands," *CIO News*, July 29, 1940, p. 3; "Looking Ahead," *CIO News*, August 12, 1940, p. 4; "Boatmen Hear Murray Assail Profit-Hogs," *CIO News*, August 12, 1940, p. 7; "Bethlehem Accused of Flouting U.S.," *CIO News*, August 19, 1940, p. 1; "Congressmen Urged to OK Taxes on Big Defense Profits," *CIO News*, August 19, 1940, p. 3; "Defense Sabotage," *CIO News*, August 26, 1940, p. 4; "Profit Demands Block Defense, Officials State," *CIO News*, August 26, 1940, p. 6; "Murray Hits Bethlehem Record," *CIO News*, August 26, 1940, p. 8; "Flay Efforts to Ease Excess Profits Tax," *CIO News*, September 16, 1940, p. 3; "National Defense," *CIO News*, December 9, 1940, p. 4; "U.S. Heeds Ford Plea, Bards Order to Ford," *CIO News*, February 3, 1941, p. 3; Statement of CIO Executive Board concerning defense contractors, January 8, 1941, CIO Press Releases; Statement of CIO Executive Board concerning WPA and taxes, January 8, 1941, CIO Press Releases; Murray statement to House Ways and Means Committee, May 2, 1941, CIO Press Releases; Kathryn Lewis statement on federal taxation, May 28, 1941, CIO Press Releases.

25. "Fourth CIO Plan," *CIO News*, February 3, 1941, p. 3.

26. Victor Reuther, *The Brothers Reuther and the Story of the UAW* (Boston: Houghton-Mifflin Co., 1976), pp. 224-42; Henry M. Christman, ed., *Walter Reuther: Selected Papers* (New York: MacMillan Co., 1961), p. 12; Allan Haywood radio address, September 1, 1941, CIO Press Releases; Statement concerning labor shortages, July 18, 1941, CIO Press Releases; Carey speech, April 4, 1941, CIO Press Releases. Also see "More Aluminum Today," July 14, 1941, CIO Press Releases.

27. Carey speech, April 4, 1941, CIO Press Releases.

28. "Memorandum Submitted by the Housing Committee of the Congress of Industrial Organizations to the Office for Emergency Management," April 14, 1941, CIO Press Releases; Statement of Thomas Kennedy, January 24, 1941, CIO Press Releases.

29. Meeting Minutes, May 19-28, 1941, pp. 29-33, AFL Executive Council Minutes, vol. 87; Murray statement concerning Vinson Bill, April 28, 1941, CIO Press Releases; Julius Emspak statement concerning Ball Bill, May 21, 1941, CIO

Press Releases; Murray statement concerning Vinson Bill and Connally Amendment, June 23, 1941, CIO Press Releases; "Vigilance Called For," *CIO News*, January 6, 1941, p. 4; "Text of Statement on Anti-Labor Bills," *CIO News*, February 17, 1941, p. 3; "CIO Leaders Blast Bills Against Labor," *CIO News*, February 17, 1941, p. 3; "Vinson Bill Called 'Hitler Way,'" AFL *Weekly News Service*, May 5, 1941; "Labor Rallies Against May Bill as Vinson Measure is Sidetracked," AFL *Weekly News Service*, July 1, 1941; Green to Congressmen and Senators, July 28, 1941, file 32, box 4, Taft Papers.

30. "Attack on Democracy," *CIO News*, June 16, 1941, p. 4; "Looking Ahead," *CIO News*, June 23, 1941, p. 4; "Anti-Labor May Bill Killed by CIO Drive," *CIO News*, July 14, 1941, p. 1; "No Need for Labor Controls, CIO Declares," *CIO News*, July 28, 1941, p. 8; "Text of Statement on Anti-Labor Bills," *CIO News*, February 17, 1941, p. 3; "Looking Ahead," *CIO News*, February 17, 1941, p. 4; "Guard Labor's Rights," *CIO News*, February 24, 1941, p. 4; "Attempts to Tie Labor," *CIO News*, March 10, 1941, p. 4; "Stop the Vinson Bill," *CIO News*, May 12, 1941, p. 5; "Vinson Bill Called 'Hitler Way,'" AFL *Weekly News Service*, May 6, 1941; "Listen in Sunday to Vinson Bill Debate," AFL *Weekly News Service*, May 6, 1941; "Vinson Bill Denounced by Green; Imposes Serfdom on Labor, He Says," AFL *Weekly News Service*, April 22, 1941; "Labor Rallies Against May Bill as Vinson Measure is Sidetracked," AFL *Weekly News Service*, July 1, 1941; "Facing the Facts," AFL *Weekly News Service*, November 20, 1940; "Facing the Facts," AFL *Weekly News Service*, July 15, 1941; Meany Assails Forced Labor Laws," AFL *Weekly News Service*, January 28, 1941; "Green Attacks Anti-Strike Bills," AFL *Weekly News Service*, April 8, 1941; "Vinson Bill Would Cause Chaos, Meany Tells House Rules Committee," AFL *Weekly News Service*, April 29, 1941; Statements concerning special meeting, July 3, 1941 and July 7, 1941, CIO Press Releases; Report on ample labor supply, July 18, 1941, CIO Press Releases; Meeting Minutes, May 13-21, 1940, pp. 83-5, AFL Executive Council Minutes, vol. 86; "Tories Launch New Blitzkrieg Against Labor," *CIO News*, June 16, 1941, p. 8; Carey radio address, April 2, 1941, CIO Press Releases; Congress of Industrial Organizations, *Daily Proceedings of the Fourth Constitutional Convention* (Detroit: Congress of Industrial Organizations, 1941), p. 204; International Association of Machinists Press Release, May 23, 1940, folder 25, box 66, Sidney Hillman Papers, ACW Archives, Labor-Management Documentation Center, Cornell University, Ithaca, NY.

31. "Anti-Labor 'Nonsense' Ridiculed by Fleming," AFL *Weekly News Service*, September 17, 1940; "Facing the Facts," AFL *Weekly News Service*, March 11, 1941; "Fleming Hits Proposal to Relax 40-Hour Week," AFL *Weekly News Service*, Mary 6, 1941; "Smashes Canard That Labor Hinders Defense," AFL *Weekly News Service*, December 31, 1940; "Record Airplane Output Achieved in June," AFL *Weekly News Service*, July 15, 1941; "Liberal Labor Policy on Defense Announced by U.S. War Department," AFL *Weekly News Service*, November 12, 1940; "Labor Role in Training Plan Wins Praise," *CIO News*, January 20, 1941, p. 1; "Labor's Vast Service to Defense Ignored by Press," AFL *Weekly News Service*,

July 22, 1941; "Green Urges AFL Unions Ban Strikes During National Defense Emergency," AFL *Weekly News Service*, April 22, 1941; "Facing the Facts," AFL *Weekly News Service*, March 11, 1941; "19 Building Unions Limit Defense Fees and Banish Strikes," AFL *Weekly News Service*, January 14, 1941; "CIO Offers Defense Cooperation, Demands Protection of Rights," *CIO News*, June 10, 1940, p. 3; "U.S. Army 'Grateful' to CIO," *CIO News*, September 1, 1941, p. 2; "Labor Must Fight for All-Out Production," *CIO News*, November 3, 1941, p. 2; "Knox Lauds Labor in Shipbuilding," AFL *Weekly News Service*, July 15, 1941; "Collective Bargaining Upheld by Stimson," AFL *Weekly News Service*, November 28, 1940; McNutt Hits Anti-Strike Bills as Definite Approach to Slavery," AFL *Weekly News Service*, April 22, 1941; CIO, *1941 Proceedings*, p. 204; Robert Patterson to Green, July 28, 1941, in Meeting Minutes, August 4-13, 1941, pp. 13-4, AFL Executive Council Minutes, vol. 87A; Nelson Lichtenstein, "Defending the No-Strike Pledge: CIO Politics During World War II," *Radical America*, 9 (July-August 1975): 52-3, 59; Nelson Lichtenstein, *Labor's War at Home: The CIO in World War II* (Cambridge: Cambridge University Press, 1982), pp. 44-5, 48-9, 184-5, 195, 201.

32. "Gov. Lehman and Other Notables Urge Greater Aid to British Labor," AFL *Weekly News Service*, March 18, 1941; "Facing the Facts," AFL *Weekly News Service*, April 8, 1941; "National Defense Must Go Forward on Democratic Basis, Green Insists," AFL *Weekly News Service*, April 29, 1941; "Green, Woll, Urge All Local Unions to Raise Funds to Aid British Labor," AFL *Weekly News Service*, April 29, 1941; "750,000 New York AFL Unionists Pledge Full Aid to British Labor," AFL *Weekly News Service*, May 6, 1941; "British Workers Speak to America," AFL *Weekly News Service*, May 13, 1941; "Green Denounces Anti-Strike Bill," AFL *Weekly News Service*, May 20, 1941; "Green Lauds Subscription Books to Aid Labor in Great Britain," AFL *Weekly News Service*, May 29, 1941; "Greenwood Tells American Workers Hitler Victory Would Enslave Them," AFL *Weekly News Service*, June 17, 1941; "Green and Meany Assail Vinson Bill," AFL *Weekly News Service*, June 24, 1941; "Meany Pledges Workers Will Make Great Arsenal of Democracy Here," AFL *Weekly News Service*, July 22, 1941; "Altmeyer Urges Eight-Point Program for Broadening Social Security Act," AFL *Weekly News Service*, July 29, 1941; "Preserve Peace and Democracy, Build Strong National Defense and Maintain Social Gains, Report Urges," AFL *Weekly News Service*, November 20, 1940; "Citrine Warns Nazism Seeks Destruction of Democracy," AFL *Weekly News Service*, November 28, 1940; "Arms and Money Are Urged by Bevin to Aid Britain's War for Democracy," AFL *Weekly News Service*, December 5, 1940; "Labor Representation on Defense Units Asked," AFL *Weekly News Service*, December 17, 1940; "Bevin Sends Aid Plea to American Workers," AFL *Weekly News Service*, January 7, 1941; "AFL Supports Total Defense Program But Will Fight for Labor's Rights," AFL *Weekly News Service*, January 14, 1941; "Unions Back Campaign to Aid British Labor," AFL *Weekly News Service*, February 11, 1941; "All Legislation Outlawing Strikes Attacked by AFL Executive Council," AFL *Weekly News Service*, February 18, 1941; "Bevin Declares British Workers Fight

Against Nazi Enslavement," AFL *Weekly News Service*, March 4, 1941; "Federationist Explodes False Myth that Labor Gains Must Be Scrapped," AFL *Weekly News Service*, July 30, 1940; "Labor Must Work and Stand Together for Defense of Democracy," AFL *Weekly News Service*, September 10, 1940.

33. "Brown and Birthright Named to Fill Two Vacancies on Executive Council," AFL *Weekly News Service*, October 15, 1940; "Citrine Warns Nazism Seeks Destruction of Democracy," AFL *Weekly News Service*, November 28, 1940; "AFL To Give Dinner in Honor of Citrine," AFL *Weekly News Service*, December 5, 1940; "Citrine Appeals for U.S. Help So Britain May End Hitler Menace," AFL *Weekly News Service*, December 17, 1940. Also see "A Visit to the U.S.A.," "Call To Aid Britain," and "Goodwill Grows," *The T.U.C. in Wartime*, May 1941, pp. 24-5.

34. "Facing the Facts," AFL *Weekly News Service*, July 2, 1940; "Facing the Facts," AFL *Weekly News Service*, February 4, 1941; "Liberal Labor Policy on Defense Announced by U.S. War Department," AFL *Weekly News Service*, November 12, 1940; "Collective Bargaining Upheld by Stimson," AFL *Weekly News Service*, November 28, 1940; "Anti-Labor 'Nonsense' Ridiculed by Fleming," AFL *Weekly News Service*, September 17, 1940; "Fleming Hits Proposal to Relax 40-Hour Week," AFL *Weekly News Service*, May 6, 1941; "National Defense Must Go Forward on Democratic Basis, Green Insists," AFL *Weekly News Service*, April 29, 1941; "Facing the Facts," AFL *Weekly News Service*, April 15, 1941; "AFL Supports President's Plan for Federal Mediation Board," AFL *Weekly News Service*, March 18, 1941; "Green Urges AFL Unions Ban Strikes during National Defense Emergency," AFL *Weekly News Service*, April 22, 1941; "Facing the Facts," AFL *Weekly News Service*, March 4, 1941.

35. "Boost Unionism As Aid to Industrial Peace," *CIO News*, January 27, 1941, p. 1; "The New Canadian Congress of Labor," *CIO News*, September 9, 1940, p. 7; "British Union Raps Use of Troops in U.S. Plane Strike," *CIO News*, July 21, 1941, p. 8; "Text of Pres. Murray's Statement to Senate on 'Lease-Lend' Proposal," *CIO News*, February 10, 1941, p. 6; "Looking Ahead," *CIO News*, June 17, 1940, p. 4; "Remove Trojan Horses in High Places is Plea," *CIO News*, July 8, 1940, p. 8; "The Ford Myth," *CIO News*, June 3, 1940, p. 6; "From Hitler to Ford," *CIO News*, June 3, 1940, p. 2; "Attempt Blitzkrieg on Workers," *CIO News*, May 27, 1940, p. 8; "Looking Ahead," *CIO News*, May 27, 1940, p. 3; "Marine Engineers Warn of New Anti-Labor 'Axis,'" *CIO News*, December 30, 1940, p. 2; "Defense Sabotage," *CIO News*, August 26, 1940, p. 4; "Texas Oil Company Pals With Nazis," *CIO News*, August 12, 1940, p. 8; "Charge 'Gestapo' in U.S. Agencies," *CIO News*, July 28, 1941, p. 3; "Looking Ahead," *CIO News*, June 23, 1941, p. 4; "Tories Launch New Blitzkrieg Against Labor," *CIO News*, June 16, 1941, p. 8; "See Danger in 'Labor Control' Proposals," *CIO News*, June 9, 1941; "Jones Raps Anti-Labor Putsch Try," *CIO News*, June 9, 1941, p. 5.

36. Walter Reuther radio address, October 30, 1940, folder 539-13, box 539, Walter Reuther Papers, Walter Reuther Library, Wayne State University, Detroit, Mich.; Sidney Hillman speech, New York City, November 9, 1941, file: "Sidney

Hillman," box 16, Boris Shishkin Papers, AFL Collection, Wisconsin State Historical Society, Madison, Wis.; Carey radio address, September 1, 1941, CIO Press Releases; "Labor Must Fight for All-Our Production," *CIO News*, November 3, 1941, p. 2; "City Hall Labor Rally a Success," *Baltimore Labor Herald*, November 14, 1941; Press release, n.d. (ca. July 17, 1941), file: "Labor," box 45, Fight for Freedom Archives, Princeton University Library, Princeton, N.J.; "Willkie Calls for National Unity at New York 'Beat Hitler' Labor Rally," AFL *Weekly News Service*, July 22, 1941.

37. See Chapter 10, above. Roosevelt reference cited in Timothy R. Dzierba, *Organized Labor and the Coming of World War II, 1937-1941*, doctoral dissertation, State University of New York at Buffalo, 1983 (Ann Arbor, Mich.: University Microfilms International, 1984), pp. 114-15.

38. Carey radio address, April 2, 1941, CIO Press Releases; "Placing the Blame," *CIO News*, April 7, 1941, p. 4; "Facing the Facts," AFL *Weekly News Service*, March 18, 1941; "Green Attacks Anti-Strike Bills," AFL *Weekly News Service*, April 8, 1941; "Bethlehem to Blame for Strike—Bittner," *CIO News*, March 31, 1941, p. 5.

39. "AFL Union Drive in Aircraft Plants Nets 30,000 Members, Higher Pay," AFL *Weekly News Service*, December 10, 1940; "Facing the Facts," AFL *Weekly News Service*, December 24, 1940; "Facing the Facts," AFL *Weekly News Service*, January 14, 1941; "Facing the Facts," AFL *Weekly News Service*, January 21, 1941; "Communists Dominate Defense Plants Through CIO Unions, Writer Charges," AFL *Weekly News Service*, February 4, 1941; "CIO Strikes In Defense Industries Draw Attack from President Green; Also Assails CIO Group Opposing Lend-Lease Bill," AFL *Weekly News Service*, February 11, 1941; "CIO Sabotages Labor Disputes Adjustment," AFL *Weekly News Service*, February 11, 1941; "Facing the Facts," AFL *Weekly News Service*, March 18, 1941; "Facing the Facts," AFL *Weekly News Service*, April 8, 1941; "Murray Balks at Expelling Reds from the CIO, Dies Declares," AFL *Weekly News Service*, April 15, 1941; "Dies Expert Charges Communists Promote Strikes Called by CIO," AFL *Weekly News Service*, April 22, 1941; "Facing the Facts," AFL *Weekly News Service*, April 22, 1941; "Facing the Facts," AFL *Weekly News Service*, April 29, 1941; "Green Repudiates Lewis Slur on Labor," AFL *Weekly News Service*, May 6, 1941; "Facing the Facts," AFL *Weekly News Service*, May 13, 1941; "Facing the Facts," Afl *Weekly News Service*, July 22, 1941; "AFL Maps Vast Organizing Drive," AFL *Weekly News Service*, July 29, 1941; "Facing the Facts," AFL *Weekly News Service*, August 5, 1941; "Facing the Facts," AFL *Weekly News Service*, March 2, 1940; "A Message to General Motors Workers!," AFL *Weekly News Service*, March 19, 1940; "A Message to General Motors Workers!," AFL *Weekly News Service*, March 26, 1940; "The Indictment Against Lewis," AFL *Weekly News Service*, April 16, 1940; "Facing the Facts," AFL *Weekly News Service*, May 7, 1940; "Facing the Facts," AFL *Weekly News Service*, May 14, 1940; "Pres. Green Demands U.S. Outlaw Nazi-Communist 'Fifth Columnists,;" AFL *Weekly News Service*, May 28, 1940.

40. "Probe AFL Thuggery in St. Louis; Attack Menaces Low-Rent Housing Program," *CIO News*, September 9, 1940, p. 8; "CIO Unions' Plans Help Unravel U.S. Defense Housing Snarl," *CIO News*, August 18, 1941, p. 7; "Memorandum Submitted by the Housing Committee of the Congress of Industrial Organizations to the Office for Emergency Preparedness," April 14, 1941, CIO Press Releases; "Brown Assails Reuther Plan," AFL *Weekly News Service*.

As early as 1939, in fact, the CIO realized that it stood to gain more from federal housing legislation than did the AFL. It estimated that for every 10 AFL construction workers employed on a building site, there were 15 CIO workers involved in the fabrication of building materials. On the strength of those figures, the CIO determined to support the U.S. Housing Act—providing it could keep the AFL building trades unions from benefitting too much. See "Report of CIO Committee on Housing," June 13, 1939, "Housing" file, box 4B, John Brophy Papers, Catholic University, Washington, DC.

41. Bruno Stein, "Labor's Role in Government Agencies During World War II," *Journal of Economic History* XVII (1957): 389-91, 394-403; Milton Derber, "Labor-Management in World War II," *Current History*, June 1965, pp. 340-42; Francis X. Gannon, *Joseph D. Keenan, Labor's Ambassador in War and Peace: A Portrait of a Man and his Times* (Lanham, Md.: University Press of America, 1984), pp. 35-45.

42. See, for example, Hugh Wilson to Florence Thorn, November 27, 1941, file: "Priorities Cases—OPM," box 27, series 8A, Florence Thorne Papers (Files of Director of Research), American Federation of Labor Collection, Wisconsin State Historical Society, Madison, Wis.; Wilson to Thorn, December 6, 1941, Ibid.; W.C. Hunneman to Green, September 9, 1941, Ibid.; W.H. Whetro to Orville Dudding, September 9, 1941, Ibid.; J. Douglas Brown to Green, September 3, 1941, Ibid.; Green to Dudding, July 17, 1941, Ibid.; J.L. Rhodes to Green, July 21, 1941, Ibid.; Green to Brown, August 25, 1941, Ibid.; Green to Matthew Burns, July 31, 1941, Ibid.; Burns to Green, August 7, 1941, Ibid.; Roy Duquette to Green, July 14, 1941, Ibid.; Green to Duquette, August 15, 1941; Joseph Kennan to Green, April 9, 1942, file: "OPM . . . Coop. With," Ibid.

43. Chester Bowles, *Promises to Keep: My Years in Public Life, 1941-1969* (New York: Harper and Row, 1971), pp. 60, 88; Derber, "Labor-Management," p. 343; "Ryan Aircraft Lifts Pay, Averts Strike," *CIO News*, January 27, 1941, p. 2; "Bethlehem Shipyards to Bargain!," *CIO News*, January 27, 1941, p. 3; "U.S. Heeds CIO Pleas, Bars Order to Ford," *CIO News*, February 3, 1941, p. 3; "Organizing," *CIO News*, February 3, 1941, p. 6; "War Dept. Credits Hillman for Action Against Ford," *CIO News*, February 10, 1941, p. 5; "CIO Wins Bethlehem Strike," *CIO News*, March 3, 1941, p. 1; "CIO Wins Largest California Election at North American," *CIO News*, March 17, 1941, p. 8; "CIO on the Job," *CIO News*, March 31, 1941, p. 4; "CIO Wins Ford Strike," *CIO News*, April 14, 1941, p. 1; "Bethlehem Signs First CIO Contract," *CIO News*, May 12, 1941, p. 1; "Most Reactionary Bills Defeated in the States," *CIO News*, May 12, 1941, p. 8; "Bethlehem Plant Votes CIO," *CIO News*, May 19, 1941, p. 1; "CIO Wins Ford Poll,"

CIO News, May 26, 1941, p. 1; "Ship Union Signs Up Consolidated," *CIO News*, May 26, 1941, p. 2; "Ford Signs Union Shop Agreement," *CIO News*, June 23, 1941, p. 1; "Steel Union Sweeps Five Polls at Bethlehem by Big Margins," *CIO News*, June 30, 1941, p. 1; "Republic Steel to Sign," *CIO News*, July 21, 1941, p. 1; Meeting Minutes, December 15, 18, 1941, pp. 2-3, AFL Executive Council Minutes, volume 87-A; Meeting Minutes, August 4-13, 1941, pp. 3, 6, AFL Executive Council Minutes, volume 87-A.

44. Lichtenstein, *Labor's War at Home*, pp. 53, 82-92, 238; Lichtenstein, "Defending to No-Strike Pledge: CIO Politics During World War II," *Radical America* 9 (July-August 1975): 49-50, 53-8; Meeting Minutes, August 4-14, 1941, p. 6, AFL Executive Council Minutes, vol. 87-A; Bowles, *Promises to Keep*, p. 162; Derber, "Labor-Management," pp. 342-3; Stein, "Labor's Role in Government Agencies," pp. 398, 401-2; Gannon, *Keenan*, pp. 45-7, 51-2, 61-2.

45. See Gannon, *Keenan*, pp. 61-2.

Conclusion

CHAPTER 14

On December 8, 1941, the day after the Japanese air attack on Pearl Harbor, the United States declared war on Japan. Three days later, the United States was at war with the other two Axis powers, Germany and Italy.

Organized labor immediately pledged its unqualified support for the war effort. Leaders of the Congress of Industrial Organizations (CIO) took to the airwaves to promote national unity, denounce the Axis countries, and promise uninterrupted production for defense. CIO members were "ready and eager to do their utmost to defend our country against the outrageous aggression of Japanese imperialism, and to secure the final defeat of the forces of Hitler," said CIO President Philip Murray in a national broadcast. The Executive Council of the American Federation of Labor (AFL) convened a special meeting in Washington on December 15. It issued a declaration that "no worker must ever shirk his duty or withhold from the Government a full measure of service" and calling upon AFL members to "reach new heights of production." The AFL and the CIO promptly joined in a promise not to strike for the duration of the war.[1]

The official policies of the national labor centers notwithstanding, unanimous labor support for the wartime policies of President Franklin D. Roosevelt did not exist. Some unions, such as John L. Lewis's United Mine Workers, defied the no-strike pledge. Wildcat strikes in other industries tested the ability of the AFL and especially the CIO to follow through on commitments to full mobilization for the war effort. Many began to suspect that union leaders had sacrificed too much and obtained too little, and that government and industrialists were dictating to labor.[2]

Nonetheless, most union members earnestly supported the war effort. They agreed with the CIO's characterization of World War II as a "people's war" that would save political and economic democracy worldwide. Further, organized labor strengthened itself in many ways during the war. Union membership achieved record-breaking heights, partly due to wartime exigencies. Nearly 15 million workers belonged to unions at war's end in 1945—a 50 percent increase from 1941 and quintuple the membership in 1933. The expansion continued in the postwar era.[3]

World War II thus enhanced the domestic position of organized labor in the United States. Similarly, it confirmed labor's drift towards internationalism that had begun during the pre-war era. As David Dubinsky put it in 1942, American labor "once suffered from too much isolationism," but that had "disappeared," along with labor's "provincialism," as it fought "a war for world stakes."[4] The war was a turning point for the entire country in that regard. The internationalist/isolationist debate continued, but within a vastly altered context. Strict neutrality and continentalism had become anachronistic concepts. During the war, the United States assumed global responsibilities that it would carry for the rest of the century.

The national labor centers reflected America's new global perspective in many ways. Throughout the war, the AFL and the CIO urged the United States to participate in the postwar reconstruction of devastated areas—including Germany. After the war, they energetically supported American foreign aid packages. They endorsed Secretary of State George C. Marshall's European Recovery Program, for example, as well as President Harry S Truman's "Point Four" plan to provide technical assistance to underdeveloped countries. Both national labor centers favored a postwar United Nations and an American commitment to collective security. Both rejected economic nationalism and called for international economic cooperation. The CIO in particular gave considerable support to the extension of reciprocal trade programs.[5]

United Auto Workers President R.J. Thomas captured the new internationalist mood in remarks to his fellow CIO Executive Board members at a November 1944 meeting. "It seems to me our country has got to be governed somewhat by what happens in the rest of the world . . . [T]he people of America I think are pretty much convinced by now we can never hope to remain isolated from the rest of the world again. We have to have more cooperation between our country and the rest of the world."[6]

During the postwar period, the national labor centers participated to an unprecedented degree in governmental and diplomatic activities. AFL and CIO officials served as labor attaches at United States embassies abroad. AFL and CIO representatives also served on the Joint Trade Union Advisory Committee on International Labor Affairs, which the Department of Labor established in 1946. And the United Nations accorded the AFL membership in the Economic and Social Council as a non-voting, non-governmental consultant. The opportunities for involvement were expanding at such a pace that in 1948 AFL Vice President Matthew Woll sent out a call to AFL union presidents for nominees from their respective unions to fill the many positions that were opening up in the international field.[7]

Further, the AFL worked hand-in-glove with the United States military, the State Department, and the Central Intelligence Agency to prevent communist trade unions from making inroads in Western Europe and elsewhere. In 1944 the Federation established the Free Trade Union Committee, with Jay Lovestone in charge, to assist workers in Europe, Asia, and Latin America to form anti-Communist labor organizations. Irving Brown, head of the AFL's European Office, advised the State Department on labor affairs in Europe. Joseph Keenan, of the Chicago Federation of Labor, was Labor Advisor to the military government in Germany's American zone. The AFL disbursed desperately-needed relief funds, subsidized anti-communist trade unions throughout Europe, carried out an extensive education and propaganda effort, and furnished the automobiles, printing equipment, and office supplies that the European unions required for organizing. At the same time, it worked to undermine labor groups associated with the Communists, such as the World Federation of Trade Unions.[8]

In the early 1930s, America was enduring the Great Depression. The world was at peace—albeit an shaky one, with totalitarian states amassing power. The American labor movement had scant visibility in government circles, numbered only about three million members, and was composed primarily of unions belonging to a single national labor center, the American Federation of Labor. The AFL at that time paid close attention to world affairs—especially the ominous, anti-union provocations of the European dictators—but seemed to favor an isolationist course. It had cut its ties with the international labor movement and it expressed disillusionment with World War I, supported neutrality legislation, and resisted economic internationalism. By 1945, the United States economy was the strongest on earth. A Cold War was being waged. And the labor movement had expanded five-fold, had split into competing national centers, and had become resolutely internationalist.

The transformation of labor's views on foreign policy issues occurred for many reasons. The dictators in Europe and East Asia were a terrifying specter, inimical to the interests of organized labor. After war finally came to Europe, labor recognized that the fighting on the other side of the Atlantic could threaten American security and prosperity. Interventionism was not only a scheme for self-preservation, it also seemed to offer a variety of political, social, and economic gains for labor. And the schism in the labor movement further diminished the value of isolationism, as the international labor movement offered new territory over which the AFL and the CIO could squabble. Labor's movement from an isolationist to an internationalist perspective, and the internal debate that had to occur before that could take place, mirrored a national transformation in foreign policy views.

Notes

1. Philip Murray radio address, December 8, 1941, CIO Press Releases, AFL-CIO Archives, George Meany Center, Silver Spring, Md.; Allan Haywood radio address, December 8, 1941, Ibid.; R.J. Thomas radio address, December 11, 1941, Ibid.; Meeting Minutes, December 15, 18, 1941, pp. 7-19, AFL Executive Council Minutes, AFL-CIO Archives, George Meany Center, Silver Spring, Md.; "We Pledge Our Lives to America," AFL *Weekly News Service*, December 17, 1941; "Meany Predicts Certain U.S. Victory," AFL *Weekly News Service*, December 17, 1941; "Buy Defense Bonds!," AFL *Weekly News Service*, December 17, 1941; "No Strikes for Duration of War!," AFL *Weekly News Service*, December 23, 1941.

2. Joshua Freeman, "Delivering the Goods: Industrial Unionism During World War II," in Daniel J. Leab, ed., *The Labor History Reader* (Urbana: University of Illinois Press, 1985), pp. 383-87, 394-98; Nelson Lichtenstein, "Defending the No-Strike Pledge: CIO Politics During World War II," *Radical America* 9 (July-August 1975): 54-7.

3. Freeman, "Delivering the Goods," pp. 387, 403-4; Ronald L. Filippelli, *Labor in the U.S.A.: A History* (New York: Alfred A. Knopf, 1984), p. 214; Irving Bernstein, "The Growth of American Unions, 1945-60," *Labor History* 2 (Spring 1961): 156.

4. "American Labor and the Post-War World," typescript of David Dubinsky speech, n.d. (ca. May 1942), file 2C, box 174, David Dubinsky Papers, ILGWU Archives, Labor-Management Documentation Center, Cornell University, Ithaca, NY.

5. "Postwar Program, American Federation of Labor," April 12, 1944, file: "Post-War Planning," box 23, series 5C, Boris Shishkin Papers (Files of the Economist), American Federation of Labor Collection, Wisconsin State Historical Society, Madison, Wis.; William Green address, June 12, 1943, file: "American Labor Conference on International Affairs," box 3, series 5C, Ibid.; Statement of William Green on European Recovery Program, February 17, 1948, file: "Economic Cooperation Administration," box 15, series 8A, Florence Thorne Papers (Files of Director of Research), American Federation of Labor Collection, Wisconsin State Historical Society, Madison, Wis.; Statement of the AFL on the International Trade Organization, n.d., file: "International Trade Organization," box 18, series 8E, Ibid.; William Green statement re. Economic Cooperation Act of 1948, n.d. (ca. February 1949), file: "Economic Cooperation Administration," box 15, series 8A, Ibid.; Green statement re. European Recovery Program, February 17, 1848, file 14, box 5, Philip Taft Papers, Labor-Management Documentation Center, Cornell University, Ithaca, NY.; Statement of Executive Council, February 1950, file: "Point Four," box 16, series 8A, Ibid.; United States, Congress, House of Representatives, *1945 Extension of Reciprocal Trade Agreements Act: Hearings Before the Committee on Ways and Means*, pp. 981-95; "Textile Workers Union of American—Position Respecting Reciprocal Trade," April 17, 1945, file: "International Labor Office, 1939-53," box 132, James B. Carey Papers (CIO Secretary-Treasurer's Office Collection), Reuther Library, Wayne State University, Detroit, Mich.; Gerald Swope

to James Carey, April 26, 1948, file: "Reciprocal World Trade," box 32, Ibid.; Carey statement on reciprocal trade to House Ways and Means Committee, May 8, 1947, file: "Reciprocal World Trade," box 32, Ibid.; "United States Labor Leaders Stress the Importance of Reconstruction of Germany's Trade Unions," August 3, 1944, folder 449-9, box 449, Walter P. Reuther Papers, Reuther Library, Wayne State University, Detroit, Mich.; Walter Reuther to Ben Cherrington, January 10, 1947, folder 565-10, box 565, Ibid.; Nathan Cowan to Union Presidents, July 16, 1946, folder 415-11, box 415, Ibid.; Meeting Minutes, November 1-2, 1945, pp. 231-34, 280-82, roll 3, Congress of Industrial Organizations Executive Board Minutes, Reuther Library, Wayne State University, Detroit, Mich.; Meeting Minutes, October 28-29, 1943, pp. 86-9, 408-16, roll 2, CIO Executive Board Minutes.

6. Meeting Minutes, November 16, 17, 19, 25, 1944, pp. 142-43, roll 3, CIO Executive Board Minutes.

7. Peter Weiler, "The United States, International Labor, and the Cold War: The Breakup of the World Federation of Trade Unions," *Diplomatic History* 5 (Winter 1981): 6; typescript, "Editorial," March 15, 1948, file: "Articles by T. Sender," box 5, Toni Sender Papers, American Federation of Labor Collection, Wisconsin State Historical Society, Madison, Wis.; Untitled manuscript, n.d., (ca. 1947), Ibid.; "A.F. of L. in the United Nations," *International Free Trade Union News*, March 1947, p. 3; Matthew Woll to Union Presidents, June 8, 1948, file: "Economic Cooperation Administration," box 15, series 8A, Thorne Papers.

8. Varian Fry to Members, December 7, 1944, file: "American Labor Conference on International Affairs," box 3, series 5C, Shishkin Papers; "Fight for Free Labor is Fight for World's Future," *International Free Trade Union News*, March 1947, p. 1; Untitled typescript, "In addition to over $200,000 . . . ," n.d., (ca. 1948), file: International Labor, General," box 18, series 5C, Shishkin Papers; "A.F. of L. Educational Activities Among Unions Abroad," August 1946, Ibid.; Weiler, "United States, International Labor, and the Cold War," pp. 6-7; Philip Taft, *The A.F. of L. From the Death of Gompers to the Merger* (New York: Harper and Row, 1959), pp. 342-4, 362-3; Ronald Radosh, *American Labor and United States Foreign Policy* (New York: Random House, 1969), pp. 303, 309-10, 323; Roy Godson, *American Labor and European Politics: The AFL as a Transitional Force* (New York: Crane, Russak, and Co., 1976), pp. 3-5.

The AFL had always been anti-Communist, and had a history of encouraging conservative labor movements in other countries. Its postwar involvement in Western Europe thus did not represent a radical departure for the Federation. Some historians have implied that the United States government manipulated the AFL in Cold War Europe, but, as Roy Godson points out, the AFL developed its foreign policy positions independently of the government. See Roy Godson, "The AFL Foreign Policy Making Process From the End of World War II to the Merger," *Labor History* 16 (Summer 1975): 325-37.

Selected Bibliography

Unpublished Documentary Sources

George Addes Papers, Reuther Library, Wayne State University, Detroit, Mich.

American Federation of Labor Executive Council Minutes, AFL-CIO Archives, George Meany Center, Silver Spring, Md.

American Federation of State, County, and Municipal Employees Records, Reuther Library, Wayne State University, Detroit, Mich.

American Federation of Teachers Records, Reuther Library, Wayne State University, Detroit, Mich.

America First Committee Papers, Hoover Institution Archives, Stanford University, Palo Alto, Calif.

John Brophy Papers, Mullen Library, Catholic University of America, Washington, D.C.

Anthony Capraro Papers, Immigration History Research Center, University of Minnesota, St. Paul, Minn.

James B. Carey Papers (CIO Secretary-Treasurer's Office Collection), Reuther Library, Wayne State University, Detroit, Mich.

Committee to Defend America by Aiding the Allies Archives, Princeton University Library, Princeton, N.J.

Congress of Industrial Organizations, Proceedings of International Executive Board, Reuther Library, Wayne State University, Detroit, Mich.

Congress of Industrial Organizations Press Releases, AFL-CIO Archives, George Meany Center, Silver Spring, Md.

Alberto Cupelli Papers, Immigration History Research Center, University of Minnesota, St. Paul, Minn.

David Dubinsky Papers, International Ladies' Garment Workers Union Archives, Labor-Management Documentation Center, Cornell University, Ithaca, N.Y.

Ralph M. Easley Papers, Herbert Hoover Presidential Library, West Branch, Iowa.

Fight For Freedom Archives, Princeton University Library, Princeton, N.J.

John Frey Papers, Manuscript Division, Library of Congress, Washington, D.C.

William Green Papers, American Federation of Labor Collection, Wisconsin State Historical Society, Madison, Wis.

Sidney Hillman Papers, Amalgamated Clothing Workers Archives, Labor-Management Documentation Center, Cornell University, Ithaca, N.Y.

Francis Perkins Subject Files, Records of the United States Department of Labor, Record Group 174, National Archives, Washington, D.C.

George L. Quilici Papers, Immigration History Research Center, University of Minnesota, St. Paul, Minn.

Walter P. Reuther Papers, Reuther Library, Wayne State University, Detroit, Mich.

Toni Sender Papers, American Federation of Labor Collection, Wisconsin State Historical Society, Madison, Wis.

Boris Shishkin Papers (Files of the Economist), American Federation of Labor Collection, Wisconsin State Historical Society, Madison, Wis.

Adlai E. Stevenson Papers, Princeton University Library, Princeton, N.J.

Philip Taft Papers, Labor-Management Documentation Center, Cornell University, Ithaca, N.Y.

Florence Thorne Papers (Files of the Director of Research), American Federation of Labor Collection, Wisconsin State Historical Society, Madison, Wis.

Published Documentary Sources

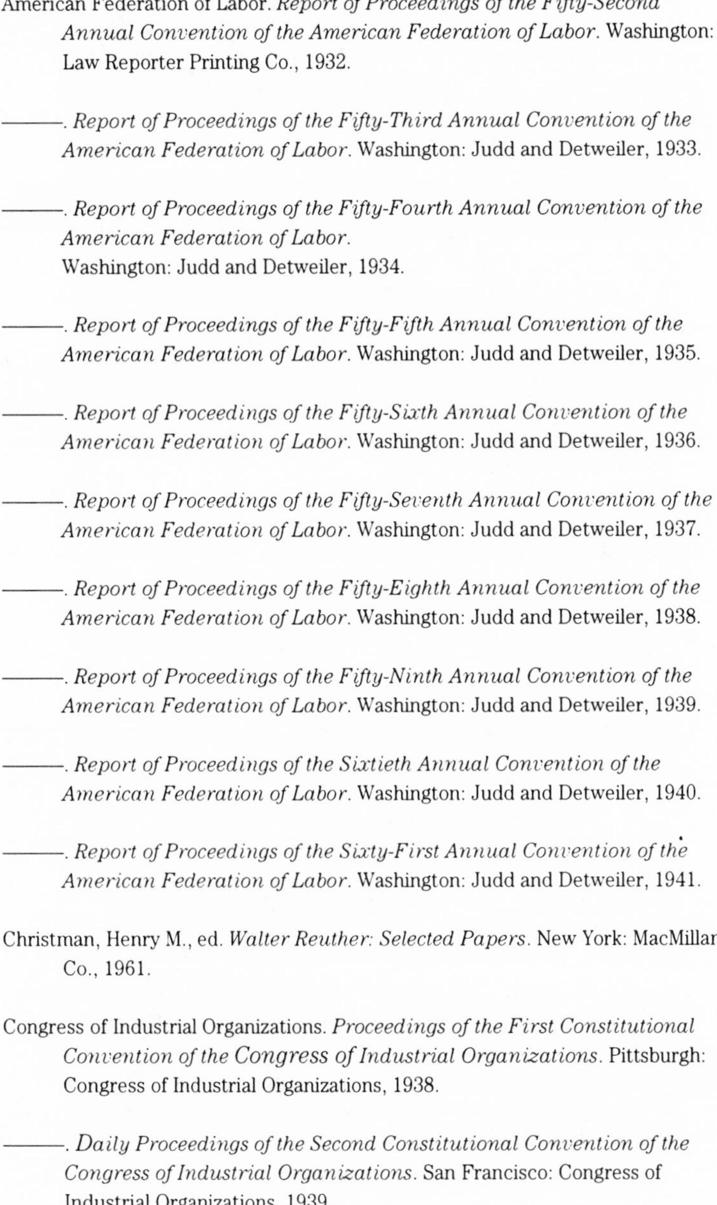

American Federation of Labor. *Report of Proceedings of the Fifty-Second Annual Convention of the American Federation of Labor*. Washington: Law Reporter Printing Co., 1932.

———. *Report of Proceedings of the Fifty-Third Annual Convention of the American Federation of Labor*. Washington: Judd and Detweiler, 1933.

———. *Report of Proceedings of the Fifty-Fourth Annual Convention of the American Federation of Labor*. Washington: Judd and Detweiler, 1934.

———. *Report of Proceedings of the Fifty-Fifth Annual Convention of the American Federation of Labor*. Washington: Judd and Detweiler, 1935.

———. *Report of Proceedings of the Fifty-Sixth Annual Convention of the American Federation of Labor*. Washington: Judd and Detweiler, 1936.

———. *Report of Proceedings of the Fifty-Seventh Annual Convention of the American Federation of Labor*. Washington: Judd and Detweiler, 1937.

———. *Report of Proceedings of the Fifty-Eighth Annual Convention of the American Federation of Labor*. Washington: Judd and Detweiler, 1938.

———. *Report of Proceedings of the Fifty-Ninth Annual Convention of the American Federation of Labor*. Washington: Judd and Detweiler, 1939.

———. *Report of Proceedings of the Sixtieth Annual Convention of the American Federation of Labor*. Washington: Judd and Detweiler, 1940.

———. *Report of Proceedings of the Sixty-First Annual Convention of the American Federation of Labor*. Washington: Judd and Detweiler, 1941.

Christman, Henry M., ed. *Walter Reuther: Selected Papers*. New York: MacMillan Co., 1961.

Congress of Industrial Organizations. *Proceedings of the First Constitutional Convention of the Congress of Industrial Organizations*. Pittsburgh: Congress of Industrial Organizations, 1938.

———. *Daily Proceedings of the Second Constitutional Convention of the Congress of Industrial Organizations*. San Francisco: Congress of Industrial Organizations, 1939.

———. *Daily Proceedings of the Fourth Constitutional Convention of the Congress of Industrial Organizations*. Detroit: Congress of Industrial Organizations, 1941.

Indiana State Federation of Labor. *Official Proceedings of the Fifty-First Annual Convention*. Muncie: Indiana State Federation of Labor, 1935.

———. *Official Proceedings of the Fifty-Seventh Annual Convention*. Evansville: Indiana State Federation of Labor, 1941.

International Labor Organization. *Provisional Record, 19th Session, Geneva, 7th Sitting, June 7, 1935, General Discussion of Hours of Work*. Geneva: International Labor Organization, 1935.

Johnson, Walter, ed. *The Papers of Adlai E. Stevenson*, vol. I. Boston: Little, Brown and Company, 1972.

Missouri State Federation of Labor. *Proceedings of the Forty-Third Annual and Third Biennial Convention of the Missouri State Federation of Labor*. Springfield: Missouri State Federation of Labor, 1939.

New Hampshire State Federation of Labor. *Journal of Proceedings*. Keene: New Hampshire State Federation of Labor, 1941.

New York State Federation of Labor. *1940 Official Proceedings, Seventy-Fourth Annual Convention*. n.p.: New York State Federation of Labor, 1940.

———. *1941 Official Proceedings, Seventy-Fifth Annual Convention*. n.p.: New York State Federation of Labor, 1941.

U.S. Department of Commerce. *Statistical Abstract of the United States, 1940*. Washington: U.S. Government Printing Office, 1941.

U.S. Congress. House. Ways and Means Committee. *Reciprocal Trade Agreements*. 73rd Congress, 2nd Session, March 1934.

———. *1945 Extension of Reciprocal Trade Agreements Act: Hearings Before the Committee on Ways and Means*. 79th Congress, 1st Session, 1945.

U.S. Congress. Senate. Special Committee on Investiga- tion of the Munitions Industry. *Munitions Industry: Naval Shipbuilding: Preliminary Report*. S. Report 944. 74th Congress, 1st Session, 1935.

Zieger, Robert H., ed. *The CIO Files of John L. Lewis*. Microfilm Collection. Frederick, Md.: University Publications of America, 1988.

Labor-Oriented Periodicals

American Federation of Labor Weekly News Service.

American Federationist.

American Pressman.

Atlanta *Journal of Labor*.

Baltimore Labor Herald.

Birmingham *Southern Labor Review*.

Boston *Wage Earner*.

Butte *Miner's Voice*.

Butte *Montana Labor News*.

Carpenter.

Catering Industry Employee.

Cheyenne *Wyoming Labor Journal*.

Chicago *Federation News*.

Cincinnati *Chronicle*.

CIO News (National Edition).

Council Bluffs *Farmer-Labor Press*.

Denver Labor Bulletin.

Des Moines *Iowa Unionist*.

Duluth *Labor World*.

Hannibal Labor Press.

International Free Trade Union News.

Jamestown *Tri-County Herald.*

Jersey City/New York *Giustizia.*

Kalispell *Flathead Labor Journal.*

Kalispell *Treasure State Labor Journal.*

Lansing Industrial News.

Los Angeles Citizen.

Madison *Union Label News.*

Michigan Labor Leader.

Omaha *Unionist.*

Peoria *Labor Temple News.*

Phoenix Labor Press.

Portland *Oregon Labor Press.*

Sacramento Valley Union Labor Bulletin.

Pulp, Sulphite, and Paper Mill Workers Journal.

St. Louis Labor Tribune.

St. Louis Union Labor Advocate.

St. Paul *Minnesota Leader.*

Salt Lake City *Utah Labor News.*

Sioux Falls *Union News.*

South Bend/Fort Wayne *Labor News.*

Toledo *CIO News.*

Topeka *Kansas Labor Weekly.*

T.U.C. in War-Time.

United Mine Workers Journal.

Waco Farm and Labor Journal.

Worcester *Labor News.*

Wisconsin Labor.

General Circulation Periodicals

Chicago Daily News.

New York *Herald-Tribune.*

New York *Il Progresso Italo-Americano.*

New York *PM.*

New York Times.

New York *World-Telegram.*

Newsweek.

Philadelphia *Evening Bulletin.*

Washington Post.

Washington *Star.*

Women's Wear Daily.

Doctoral Dissertaions

Dzierba, Timothy R. *Organized Labor and the Coming of World War II.* State University of New York, Buffalo, 1983. Ann Arbor, Mich.: University Microfilms International, 1984.

Gordon, Gerald R. *The AFL, the CIO, and the Quest for a Peaceful World Order.* University of Maine, Orono, 1967. Ann Arbor, Mich.: University Microfilms, 1968.

Lenburg, LeRoy James. *The CIO and American Foreign Policy, 1935-1955.* Pennsylvania State University, 1973. Ann Arbor, Mich.: University Microfilms, 1974.

Sallach, David L. *Enlightened Self Interest: The Congress of Industrial Organizations' Foreign Policy, 1935-1955.* Rutgers University, 1983. Ann Arbor, Mich: University Microfilms International, 1983.

Articles and Chapters

Adler, Selig. "The War Guilt Question and American Disillusionment," in Lawrence E. Gelfand, ed., *Essays on the History of American Foreign Relations.* New York: Holt, Rinehart, and Winston, 1972.

Blum, Albert. "Roosevelt, the M-Day Plans, and the Military Industrial Complex," *Military Affairs* 36 (April 1872): 44-6.

Beard, Charles A. "The Devil Theory of War," in Jerald A. Combs, ed., *Nationalist, Realist, and Radical: Three Views of American Diplomacy.* New York: Harper and Row, 1972.

Bernstein, Irving. "The Growth of American Unions, 1945-1960," *Labor History* 2 (Spring 1961):

Derber, Milton. "Labor-Management in World War II," *Current History* (June 1965): 340-45.

Donovan, John C. "Congressional Isolationists and the Roosevelt Foreign Policy," in Lawrence E. Gelfand, ed., *Essays on the History of American Foreign Relations.* New York: Hold, Rinehart, and Winston, 1972.

Dubinsky, David. "Rift and Realignment in World Labor," *Foreign Affairs* 27 (January 1949): 232-45.

Freeman, Joshua. "Delivering the Goods: Industrial Unionism During World War II," in Daniel J. Leab, ed., *The Labor History Reader.* Urbana: University of Illinois Press, 1985.

Godson, Roy. "The AFL Foreign Policy Making Process from the End of World War II to the Merger," *Labor History* 16 (Summer 1975): 225-37.

Larson, Simeon. "The American Federation of Labor and the Preparedness Controversy," *Historian* XXXVII (November 1974): 77-81.

Leighton, George R., "Beard and Foreign Policy," in Howard K. Beale, ed., *Charles A. Beard: An Appraisal*. Lexington: University of Kentucky Press, 1954.

Lichtenstein, Nelson A. "Defending the No-Strike Pledge: CIO Politics During World War II," *Radical America* 9 (July-August 1975): 49-76.

Stein, Bruno. "Labor's Role in Government Agencies During World War II," *Journal of Economic History* XVII (1957): 387-408.

Lauderbaugh, Richard A. "Business, Labor, and Foreign Policy: U.S. Steel, the International Steel Cartel, and Recognition of the Steel Workers Organizing Committee," *Politics and Society* 6, no. 4 (1976): 433-57.

Ostrower, Gary B. "The American Decision to Join the International Labor Organization," *Labor History* 16 (Fall 1975): 495-504.

Weiler, Peter. "The United States, International Labor, and the Cold War: The Breakup of the World Federation of Trade Unions," *Diplomatic History* 5 (Winter 1981): 1-22.

Books

Adler, Selig. *The Isolationist Impulse: Its Twentieth Century Reaction*. New York: The Free Press, 1957.

______. *The Uncertain Giant, 1921-1941: American Foreign Policy Between the Wars*. New York: MacMillan Co., 1965.

Albrecht-Carrie, Rene. *A Diplomatic History of Europe Since the Congress of Vienna*. New York: Harper and Row,1973.

Alcock, Antony. *History of the International Labor Organization*. London: MacMillan, 1971.

Alinsky, Saul. *John L. Lewis: An Unauthorized Biography*. New York: G.P. Putnam's Sons, 1949.

Anderson, Evelyn. *Hammer or Anvil: The Story of the German Working Class Movement*. London: Victory Gollancz Ltd., 1945.

Beard, Charles A. *The Devil Theory of War: An Inquiry Into the Nature of History and the Possibility of Keeping Out of War*. Westport, Conn.: Greenwood Press, 1972.

______. *The Idea of National Interest: An Analytical Study in American Foreign Policy*. Chicago: Quadrangle Books, 1966.

Bernstein, Irving. *Turbulent Years: A History of the American Worker, 1933-1941*. Boston: Houghton-Mifflin, 1970.

Burns, James MacGregor. *Roosevelt: The Lion and the Fox*. New York: Harcourt Brace and World, 1956.

Black, Robert. *Fascism in Germany: How Hitler Destroyed the World's Most Powerful Labour Movement*. London: Steyne Publications, 1975.

Bowles, Chester. *Promises to Keep: My Years in Public Life, 1941-1969*. New York: Harper and Row, 1971.

Brody, David. *Steelworkers in America: The Nonunion Era*. New York: Harper and Row, 1969.

Buell, Raymond Leslie. *The Hull Trade Program and the American System*. New York: National Peace Conference and Foreign Policy Association, 1938.

Chadwin, Mark Lincoln. *The Hawks of World War II*. Chapel Hill: University of North Carolina Press, 1968.

Cole, Wayne S. *America First: The Battle Against Intervention, 1940-1941*. Madison: University of Wisconsin Press, 1953.

______. *Senator Gerald P. Nye and American Foreign Relations*. Minneapolis: University of Minnesota Press, 1962.

______. *Charles A. Lindbergh and the Battle Against American Intervention in World War II*. New York: Harcourt Brace Jovanovich, 1974.

______. *Determinism and American Foreign Relations During the Franklin D. Roosevelt Era*. Lanham, Md.: University Press of America, 1995.

______. *An Interpretive History of American Foreign Relations*. Rev. ed. Homewood, Ill.: Dorsey Press, 1974.

______. *Roosevelt and the Isolationists, 1932-1945*. Lincoln: University of Nebraska Press, 1983.

Culbertson, William S. *Reciprocity: A National Policy for Foreign Trade*. New York: Whittlesey House, 1937.

DeBenedetti, Charles. *The Peace Reform in American History*. Bloomington: Indiana University Press, 1980.

DeConde, Alexander. *A History of American Foreign Policy*. 2nd edition. New York: Charles Scribner's Sons, 1971.

Diamond, Sander A. *The Nazi Movement in the United States, 1924-1941*. Ithaca, N.Y.: Cornell University Press, 1974.

Divine, Robert A. *The Reluctant Belligerent: American Entry into World War II*. New York: John Wiley and Sons, 1965.

Dozer, Donald Marquand. *Are We Good Neighbors? Three Decades of Inter-American Relations, 1930-1960*. Gainesville: University of Florida Press, 1959.

Dubinsky, David and A.H. Raskin. *David Dubinsky: A Life With Labor*. New York: Simon and Shuster, 1977.

Dubofsky, Melvin, and Warren Van Tine. *John L. Lewis: A Biography*. New York: Quadrangle, 1977.

Ekirch, Arthur A., Jr. *Ideas, Ideals, and American Diplomacy: A History of their Growth and Interaction*. New York: Appelton-Century-Crofts, 1966.

Ehrmann, Henry W. *French Labor: From Popular Front to Liberation*. New York: Oxford University Press, 1947.

Filippelli, Ronald L. *Labor in the U.S.A.: A History*. New York: Alfred A. Knopf, 1984.

Galenson, Walter. *The International Labor Organization: An American View*. Madison: University of Wisconsin Press, 1981.

Gallup, George H. *The Gallup Poll: Public Opinion, 1935-1971*. New York: Random House, 1972.

Gannon, Francis S. *Joseph D. Keenan, Labor's Ambassador in War and Peace: A Portrait of a Man and his Times*. Lanham, Md.: University Press of America.

Gardner, Lloyd C. *Economic Aspects of New Deal Diplomacy*. Madison: University of Wisconsin Press, 1964.

Godson, Roy. *American Labor and European Politics: The AFL as a Transitional Force*. New York: Crane, Russak, and Co., 1976.

Goldberg, Arthur J. *AFL-CIO Labor United*. New York: McGraw-Hill, 1956.

Gordon, Michael R. *Conflict and Consensus in Labour's Foreign Policy, 1914-1965*. Palo Alto, Calif.: Stanford University Press, 1969.

Green, William. *Labor and Democracy*. Princeton, N.J.: Princeton University Press, 1939.

______. *The Thirty-Hour Week*. Washington: American Federation of Labor, 1935.

Grob, Gerald N., and George Athan Billias, ed. *Interpretations of American History: Patterns and Perspectives*. New York: Free Press, 1982.

Harris, Herbert. *Labor's Civil War*. New York: Alfred A. Knopf, 1940.

Hero, Alfred O., Jr., and Emil Starr. *The Reuther-Meany Foreign Policy Dispute: Union Leaders and Members View World Affairs*. Dobbs Ferry, N.Y.: Oceana Publications, 1970.

Higham, John. *Strangers in the Land: Patterns of American Nativism, 1860-1925*. New York: Atheneum, 1973.

Howe, Irving, and B.J. Widick. *The UAW and Walter Reuther*. New York: Random House, 1949.

Johnson, Walter. *The Battle Against Isolation*. Chicago: University of Chicago Press, 1946.

Jordan, Mary V. *Survival: Labour's Trials and Tribulations in Canada*. Toronto: McDonald House, 1975.

Josephson, Matthew. *Sidney Hillman: Statesman of American Labor*. Garden City, N.Y.: Doubleday and Co., 1952.

Keeran, Roger. *The Communist Party and the Auto Workers Union.* Bloomington: Indiana University Press, 1980.

Kottman, Richard N. *Reciprocity and the North Atlantic Triangle, 1932-1938.* Ithaca, N.Y.: Cornell University Press, 1968.

Leuchtenburg, William E. *Franklin D. Roosevelt and the New Deal, 1932-1940.* New York: Harper and Row, 1963.

Levenstein, Harvey A. *Labor Organizations in the United States and Mexico: A History of Their Relations.* Westport, Conn.: Greenwood Publishing Co., 1971.

Lichtenstein, Nelson. *Labor's War at Home: The CIO in World War II.* Cambridge: Cambridge University Press, 1982.

Lorwin, Lewis L. *The International Labor Movement: History, Politics, Outlook.* New York: Harper and Brothers, 1953.

Lorwin, Val P. *The French Labor Movement.* Cambridge, Mass.: Harvard University Press, 1954.

Miller, James Edward. *The United States and Italy, 1940-1950: The Politics and Diplomacy of Stabilization.* Chapel Hill: University of North Carolina Press, 1986.

Pelling, Henry. *A History of British Trade Unionism.* London: MacMillan, 1972.

Peterson, Florence. *American Labor Unions: What They Are and How They Work.* New York: Harper and Brothers, 1945.

Raddock, Maxwell C. *Portrait of an American Labor Leader: William L. Hutcheson.* New York: American Institute of Social Science, 1955.

Radosh, Ronald. *American Labor and United States Foreign Policy.* New York: Random House, 1969.

Rayback, Joseph G. *A History of American Labor.* New York: Free Press, 1966.

Reuther, Victor. *The Brothers Reuther and the Story of the UAW.* Boston: Houghton-Mifflin Co., 1976.

Saposs, David J. *Communism in American Unions.* New York: McGraw-Hill, 1959.

Saxton, Alexander. *The Indispensable Enemy: Labor and the Anti-Chinese Movement in California*. Berkeley: University of California Press, 1971.

Sayre, Francis B. *The Way Forward: The American Trade Agreements Program*. New York: MacMillan, 1939.

Snow, Sinclair. *The Pan-American Federation of Labor*. Durham, N.C.: Duke University Press, 1964.

Taft, Philip. *The A. F. of L. From the Death of Gompers to the Merger*. New York: Octagon Books, 1970.

Tasca, Henry J. *The Reciprocal Trade Policy of the United States: A Study in Trade Philosophy*. Philadelphia: University of Pennsylvania Press, 1938.

Tipton, John Bruce. *Participation of the United States in the International Labor Organization*. Urbana: University of Illinois Institute of Labor and Industrial Relations, 1959.

Tucker, William Radburn. *The Attitude of the British Labour Party Towards European and Collective Security Problems, 1920-1939*. Geneva: Imprimerie du Journal de Geneve, 1950.

Weinstein, James. *The Corporate Ideal in the Liberal State, 1900-1918*. Boston: Beacon Press, 1968.

Weibe, Robert H. *The Search for Order, 1877-1920*. New York: Hill and Wang, 1967.

Welles, Orson, and Herman J. Mankiewicz, "The Shooting Script," in *The Citizen Kane Book*. Boston: Little Brown, 1971.

Williams, Jack. *The Story of Unions in Canada*. n.p. [Canada]: J.M. Dent and Sons, 1975.

Wiltz, John E. *In Search of Peace: The Senate Munitions Inquiry, 1934-36*. Baton Rouge: Louisiana State University Press, 1963.

Windmuller, John E. *American Labor and the International Labor Movement, 1940 to 1953*. Ithaca, N.Y.: Cornell University Institute of International Industrial and Labor Relations, 1954.

Zieger, Robert H. *John L. Lewis, Labor Leader*. Boston: Twayne Publishers, 1988.

Index

About the Author

John W. Roberts is Chief of Communications and Archives for the Federal Bureau of Prisons in Washington, DC. He has a Ph.D. in History from the University of Maryland, and his previous publications include *Escaping Prison Myths: Selected Topics in the History of Federal Corrections* (1994).

The opinions expressed in this volume are those of the author, and do not necessarily reflect the positions of the Federal Bureau of Prisons or the U.S. Department of Justice.